what a reader
r has written does not
wrote it.
nterest the authors -
t of dead wood in there,
can - to everybody's
e form of electronic

tion change the way
know it is distributed,
ge the very nature

get paid?

42
The Wildly Improbable Ideas of DOUGLAS ADAMS

Edited by
KEVIN JON DAVIES

Foreword by
STEPHEN FRY

First published in 2023

Unbound
c/o TC Group, 6th Floor King's House, 9–10 Haymarket, London SW1Y 4BP
www.unbound.com

For additional copyrights, see page 300, which is to be regarded as an extension of this copyright page.

Text and layout design by Amazing15
Project edited by Judy Barratt

A CIP record for this book is available from the British Library

ISBN 978-1-80018-268-4 (hardback)
ISBN 978-1-80018-269-1 (ebook)

Printed in Italy by L.E.G.O. SpA.

10 9 8 7 6 5 4 3 2 1

TITLE PAGE: Drawing of Douglas Adams by Rod Lord of Pearce Studios, as used in the animated sequences he directed for the 1981 BBC TV series of *The Hitchhiker's Guide to the Galaxy*.

CONTENTS PAGE: Douglas Adams photographed in rehearsals by Cliff Pinnock, the assistant floor manager of the 1981 BBC TV *Hitchhiker* series.

FOREWORD BY STEPHEN FRY: Stephen Fry in 2005 at the London première of *The Hitchhiker's Guide to the Galaxy* movie, in which he voiced The Book.

With special thanks to the following patrons of this book

Arlington J. Albertson
Hanan 'DOA' Argov
Michael Barnstijn
Michael Bartels
Sean Bradley
Joe Britt
S. Broomhead
Perry Clarke – does it matter that it matters?
Collin Coleman
David R. Cox
Adrian Culley
Harley Faggetter
Brad Feld
Naomi Floyd
Hilary Fried
Jay Fury
Edward Glauser
Tendai Gomo
John Grimshaw
Simon Hackett
Ümit Hamit
I.M.Theo
Damien Jackson
Victoria Jesswein
Harry Jones
Jenna Karadbil
Paul Kwiatkowski
Pete Le May
Douglas Adam Major
Matthew, Una and Verity
Mr Philip McConnell
Carrie Mowatt
Alan Mulvie
David Perry
J.I. Reitmaa
Paul Shepheard
Ron Smith
Vitas Varnas
Bruno W
Dustin T. Waling

Contents

Foreword by Stephen Fry

Douglas,

On the surface and at first blush it's dreadful to think that you never pinched and zoomed on a smartphone or tablet, never engaged with an AI Chatbot, never said "fuck off, Alexa", never tweeted, never FaceBooked, FaceTimed or Skyped. Of course you wouldn't have been surprised by a single one of these developments, the intrusions on our lives that have so transformed the world since you so precipitately left it. You saw them all coming. But we need you here to tell us what to think, how to respond — what it all means. Or doesn't. You should be here to advise (and admonish) Elon Musk, for example, who claims to have grown up loving your writing, and has publicly claimed that he bases his "philosophy" on the Hitchhiker's Guide books. He even had the words DON'T PANIC on the dash of the Tesla roadster that he sent out into space. He'd listen to you, as would plenty of the new Titans of Tech that have risen since your time.

Strange times. Frankly, it's all too easy to ignore the Guide and panic.

"What a hell of a hole he leaves in this damn wilderness..." F. Scott Fitzgerald could have been writing about you. That Douglas Hole has been mostly filled with Vogons, second raters, imposters and mediocrities. But we do our best to remember your particular slanted way of looking at reality. It makes the fuzzy sharp and the improbable probable. In a cock-eyed universe the level gaze is not much use.

We'll do our best to follow Dirk Gently's advice — "Let's think the unthinkable, let's do the undoable. Let us prepare to grapple with the ineffable itself, and see if we may not eff it after all."

Love Stephen

P.S. You should know that babes yet to be born at the time of your going have been reading your books and are now old enough to vote. You are as adored and treasured as ever.

Douglas,

On the surface and at first blush it's dreadful to think that you never pinched and zoomed on a smartphone or tablet, never engaged with an AI Chatbot, never said "Fuck off, Alexa", never tweeted, never FaceBooked, FaceTimed or Skyped. Of course, you wouldn't have been surprised by a single one of these developments, the intrusions on our lives that have so transformed the world since you so precipitately left it. You saw them all coming. But we need you here to tell us what to think, how to respond – what it all means. Or doesn't. You should be here to advise (and admonish) Elon Musk, for example, who claims to have grown up loving your writing, and has publicly claimed that he bases his "philosophy" on the Hitchhiker's Guide books. He even had the words DON'T PANIC on the dash of the Tesla roadster that he sent out into space. He'd listen to you, as would plenty of the new Titans of Tech that have risen since your time.

Strange times. Frankly, it's all too easy to ignore the Guide and panic.

"What a hell of a hole he leaves in this damn wilderness…" F. Scott Fitzgerald could have been writing about you. That Douglas Hole has been mostly filled with Vogons, second raters, imposters and mediocrities. But we do our best to remember your particular slanted way of looking at reality. It makes the fuzzy sharp and the improbable probable. In a cock-eyed universe the level gaze is not much use.

We'll do our best to follow Dirk Gently's advice – "Let's think the unthinkable, let's do the undoable. Let us prepare to grapple with the ineffable itself, and see if we may not eff it after all."

Love Stephen

P.S. You should know that babes yet to be born at the time of your going have been reading your books and are now old enough to vote. You are as adored and treasured as ever.

Stephen Fry is an English polymath: variously an actor, broadcaster, comedian, director, writer and often referred to as a man with 'a brain the size of a planet'. He and Douglas became good friends in the early 1980s, sharing a near-obsessive love for new technology – Douglas was the first to buy an Apple Mac in Europe and Stephen the second. And who better to narrate the audiobook of *The Hitchhiker's Guide to the Galaxy* when it was released in 2012?

Introduction

When Douglas Adams died unexpectedly in 2001, he left behind notebooks and memorabilia spanning his lifetime. They offer insight into his early, schoolboy talent, and provide a fascinating riddle of notes and musings on all his work – from the various incarnations of *The Hitchhiker's Guide to the Galaxy* to the before-his-time wonderings about how technology might bring information to our fingertips and a book on a screen to our hands. They also reveal a frustrated writer, brilliant poet, and self-effacing man (among much else).

Over the last two years, through a pandemic and beyond, Kevin Jon Davies has had unrestricted access to Douglas's personal papers, which the Adams family generously loaned to St John's College, Cambridge (Douglas's alma mater) after Douglas's death. Painstakingly working through every box, paper by paper, Kevin has selected the facsimiles and images of Douglas's notes, jottings, early scripts and thoughts, and photographs, that seem best to capture the spirit and workings of Douglas Adams. To select from such a cornucopia of riches seemed at first an almost impossible task – how to choose when every page, photograph, printout or mere scrap of paper offers some other new insight? How to make sense of some of the most fascinating wonderings without the author himself there to explain them? The result might, in the end, be considered merely a snapshot of a brilliant mind, but, in truth, it is as broad in scope as it is revelatory.

The book is organized along a vague timeline of Douglas's life, beginning with his school days and moving through his university years, early experiences of radio and TV, breakaway fame and fortune, forays into conservation, technology and the digital world, and ending (as all things do) with his death. However, to suggest the book is biographical in any way is to miss the point. Yes, there are plenty of biographical references in the captions, each of which gives necessary context to the papers and other fascinating discoveries in Douglas's archive. And, through the generosity of his many devoted family, friends and fans, there are further treasures and exclusives that extend beyond the archive material, in order to make sure every branch of Douglas's life is somehow represented in the book. Among these special 'extras' are present-day letters from some of those closest to Douglas. These are intimate thoughts and wishes sent to Douglas now that he is no longer around to hear them first hand. Finally, interspersed 'feature' spreads take the opportunity to highlight specific nuances of Douglas's life and work – his signature, and the inspiration for '42' among them. Overall, then, this book is much less a biography than it is a collection of precious artefacts, brought together to enlighten and inspire and to honour Douglas's remarkable legacy.

Through the generosity of his many devoted family, friends and fans, there are further insights and exclusives that extend beyond the archive material.

RIGHT: Douglas (centre, top row) in kabuki-style make-up in the Berthold Brecht play *The Good Person of Szechwan*, in which he appeared while at St John's College, Cambridge, and was directed by the writer and broadcaster Sue Limb (see page 52), who kindly supplied this photograph.

OPPOSITE: Douglas shivering through a 1973 publicity photoshoot, by Mike Penhaligon.

ONE Early (Talking) Doors

From a young age Douglas Adams showed remarkable talent, as a writer, an artist, an actor, a poet and an orator. This chapter gathers notable memorabilia and work dating from his school years in Essex.

A PROMISING STUDENT

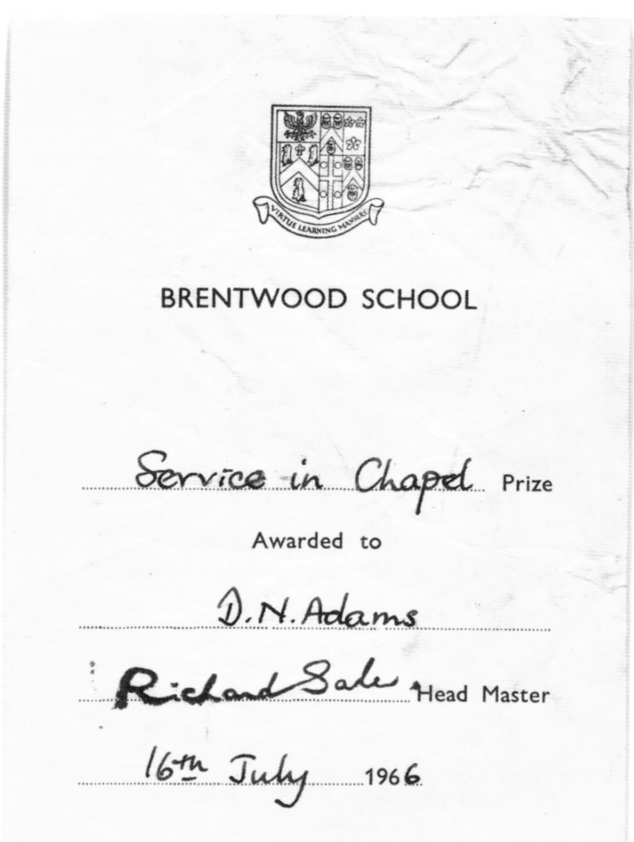

BRENTWOOD SCHOOL

Service in Chapel Prize

Awarded to

D. N. Adams

Richard Sale Head Master

16th July 1966

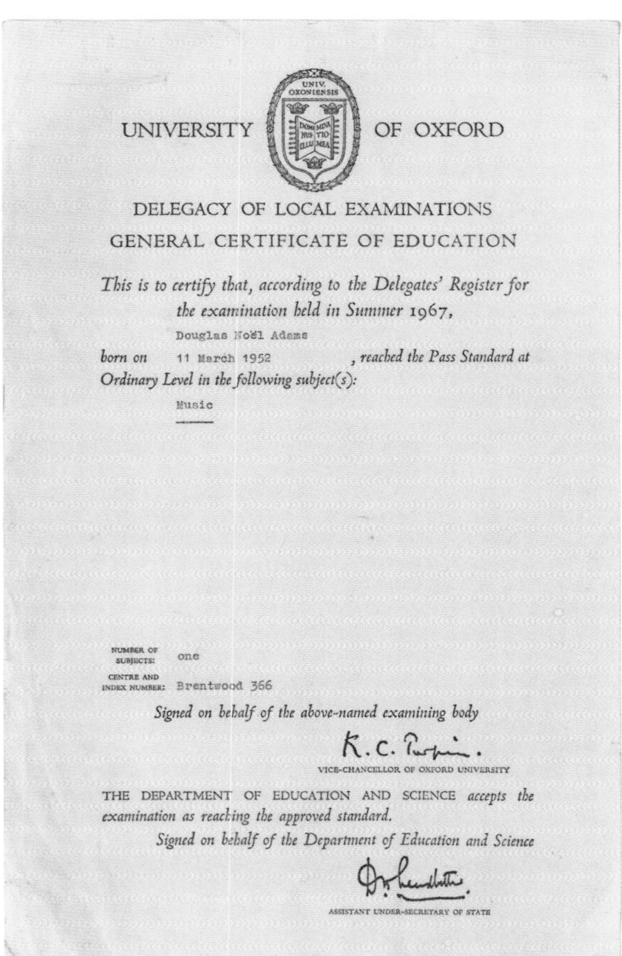

UNIVERSITY OF OXFORD

DELEGACY OF LOCAL EXAMINATIONS
GENERAL CERTIFICATE OF EDUCATION

This is to certify that, according to the Delegates' Register for the examination held in Summer 1967,
Douglas Noël Adams
born on 11 March 1952 *, reached the Pass Standard at Ordinary Level in the following subject(s):*
Music

NUMBER OF SUBJECTS: one
CENTRE AND INDEX NUMBER: Brentwood 366

Signed on behalf of the above-named examining body

K. C. Turpin.
VICE-CHANCELLOR OF OXFORD UNIVERSITY

THE DEPARTMENT OF EDUCATION AND SCIENCE *accepts the examination as reaching the approved standard.*

Signed on behalf of the Department of Education and Science

ASSISTANT UNDER-SECRETARY OF STATE

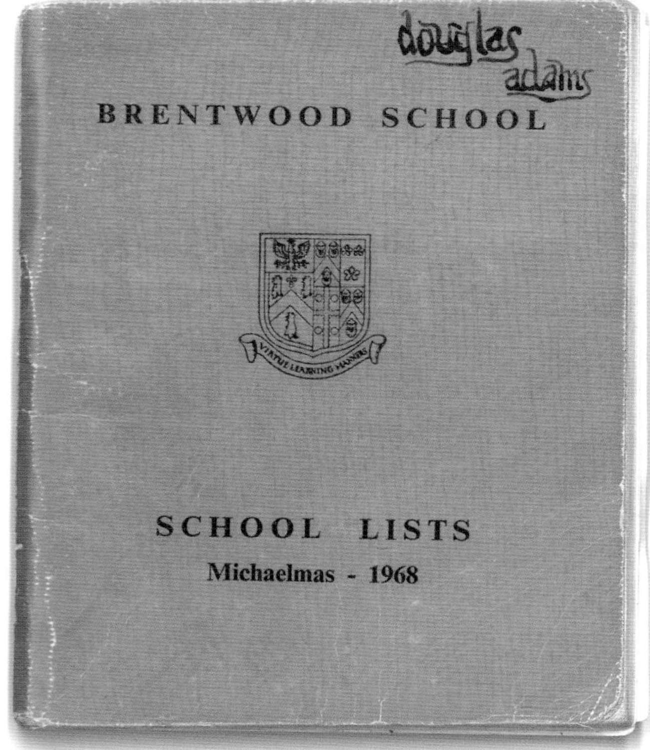

douglas adams

BRENTWOOD SCHOOL

SCHOOL LISTS
Michaelmas - 1968

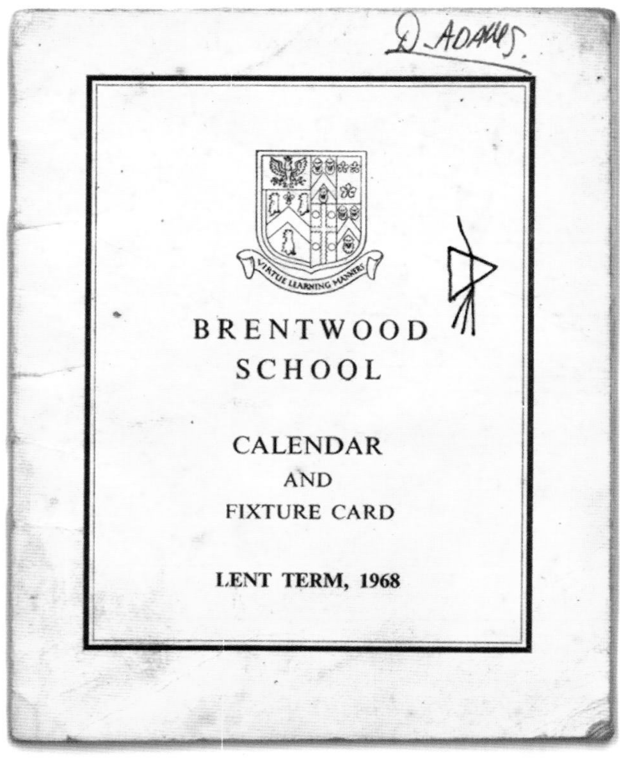

D. ADAMS.

BRENTWOOD SCHOOL

CALENDAR
AND
FIXTURE CARD

LENT TERM, 1968

Douglas attended independent boys' school Brentwood for 12 years, starting in the Prep School when his mother moved to Essex after her divorce from his father, until he left in 1970 to go to Cambridge. He was 14 when he received the 'Service in Chapel' certificate (top left) in 1966; and he achieved his Music O'level (top right) the following year. He later described how much he retrospectively appreciated the quality of teaching at the school, particularly, he said, in English and Physics.

School photographs from Brentwood School, taken between 1967 and 1970 (top to bottom). Douglas was always unusually tall for this year and wrote about how troubled he had been that, by the time he was 12, he was not only taller than his fellow students, but also taller than many of his Masters – a uniqueness that was compounded, embarrassingly, by the fact that until he went into the upper school, he was forced to wear short trousers.

This undated school essay is a fictional biography of 'Christopher Turquoise', an international playboy and author who (perhaps) wasted his talent and succumbed to an early demise. The facsimile (see pages 17–19) shows Douglas's handwritten work, including his teacher's final comment. The full essay is transcribed below.

Christopher Turquoise had a very cosmopolitan background and cannot be said to be a true citizen of any one country. As an international playboy he moved in fashionable circles, but was determined to prove himself as a literary artist. In his formative years he came under many diversified influences in the form of environment, education and genetics. He was born in Rio de Janeiro, to a British Consul and a Brazilian Artist, from where he moved to Genoa in Italy, where he stayed, being educated by a succession of governesses of various nationalities, till the age of nine.

Thus, from his earliest years he was brought up in the surroundings and tradition of art and culture. At the age of nine his family moved to New York, where he continued to receive private education for a year, until he went to Lincoln Heights High School, a fashionable New York school. After four years there, he spent another four years at Harchester Public School in England, followed by three years at Oxford.

> **The life of Christopher Turquoise is the story of a definite talent which was led too much by flamboyant aspirations and pretensions**

In his second year at Oxford, he published his first book of verse called 'Dead Sea Fruit', which was a failure. He went on however to write a satirical comedy in French by the title of 'Dejeuner aux Enfers', which whilst being well received was not a popular success. In 1936 he published another book of verse with limited success. 1938 also saw his marriage to "the dazzling Sybilla" daughter of a Milanese count, in what was an important society wedding.

With the war in 1939 he joined the R.A.F., and his six years in the Force, along with the death in 1942 of his wife, who was a racing driver, profoundly affected his ideas. His literary works so far, though undoubtedly of literary merit had proved to be neither particularly pre-eminent in the field or popular, and more to the point, lucrative. He began to see that there was no future in his romantic, slightly surrealist poetry, and turned his attention to the popular market, and in 1945 published "Head of Unknown Woman", a thriller which quickly entered the best sellers lists. He was immediately invited to the glitter and glory of Hollywood to direct "Desire of My Heart" from his own script. This is a lure he could not resist, and whilst filming was in progress he married secretly the star of the film Desirée Framboise (an English girl, real name Mary Berry).

His next publication was another step even further from his poetic aspirations: a book called "Raff Chaps" which was a selection of doggerel verse satirising the R.A.F. very mildly. It was extremely popular, as was "Suites for Sweeties" a farce produced first in London and two years later on Broadway. In 1947 "Desire of My Heart" was voted 'Film of The Year' and awarded two Oscars. Then in 1946, whilst two of his films were in active production, he died following an illness due to his war wounds.

The life of Christopher Turquoise, is the story of a definite talent which was led too much by flamboyant aspirations and pretensions and lured into the bright lights and glitter of popular success. His desire for fame and fashionability probably bred by his cosmopolitanism made him wish to be thought of as 'arty' to the detriment of his art. When this failed he exploited his talent rather than nourished it, which dashed him into the hectic life of show business and probably hastened his untimely death.

[Teacher's mark & comment] A – Good. You do deal with the main problem.

annot be said to be a true citizen of any one count
international playboy he moved in fashionable circles,
s determined to prove himself as a literary artist.

Christopher Turquoise had a very cosmopolitan background and cannot be said to be a true citizen of any one country. As an international playboy he moved in fashionable circles, but was determined to prove himself as a literary artist.

In his formative years he came under many diversified influences in the form of enviroment, education and genetics. He was born in Rio de Janeiro, to a British Consul and a Brazilian Artist, from where he moved to Genoa in Italy, where he stayed, being educated by a succession of governesses of various nationalities, till the age of nine.

Thus, from his earliest years he was brought up in the surroundings and tradition of art and culture. At the age of nine his family moved to New York, where he continued to receive private education for a year, until he went to Lincoln Heights High School, a fashionable New York School. After four years there, he spent another four Years at Harchester Public School in England followed by three years at Oxford.

In his second year at Oxford he published his first book of verse called 'Dead Sea Fruit', which was a failure. He went on however to write a satirical comedy in French by the title of 'Déjeuner aux Enfers', which whilst being well received was not a popular success. In 1936 he published another book of verse with limited succes

Déjeuner aux Enfers, which whilst being
ceived was not a popular success. In 1936 he
hed another book of verse with limited succes

1938 also saw his marriage to "the dazzling Sybilla" daughter of a Milanese count, in what was an important society wedding.

With the war in 1939 he joined the R.A.F. and his six years in the Force ~~profoundly changed his ideas~~ along with the death in 1942 of his wife, who was a racing driver, profoundly affected his ideas. His literary works so far, though undoubtedly of literary merit had proved to be neither particularly pre-eminent in ~~the~~ field or popular, ~~and~~ - more to the point, lucrative. He began to see that there was no future in his romantic, slightly surrealist poetry, and turned his attention to the popular market, and in 1945 published "Head of Unknown Woman", a thriller which quickly entered the best sellers lists. He was immediately invited to the ~~the glory~~ glitter and glory of Hollywood to direct "Desire of my Heart" from his own script. This a lure he could not resist, and whilst filming was in progress he married secretly the star of the film Desiree Framboise (an English girl, real name Mary Berry)

His next publication was another step even further from his poetic aspirations: a book called "Raff Chaps" which was a selection of doggerel verse satirizing the R.A.F. very mildly. It was extremely popular, as was "Suites for Sweeties" a farce produced first in London and two years later on Broadway. In 1947 "Desire of my heart" was voted 'Film of the year' and awarded two Oscars. Then in 1946, whilst two of his films were in active production ~~of~~ he died following an illness due to his war wounds.

The Life of Christopher Turquoise, is the story of a definite talent which was led too much by flamboyant aspirations and pretentions and lured into the bright lights and glitter of popular success. His desire for fame and fashionability probably bred by his cosmopolitanism made him wish to be thought of as 'arty' to the detriment of his art. When this failed he exploited his talent ~~it~~ rather than nourished it which dashed him into the hectic life of show business and probably hastened his untimely death.

A. Good. You do deal with the main problem.

BRENTWOOD  SCHOOL

JUNIOR SCHOOL

House Barnardo

Name D. N. Adams

Form Upper II

Report for the Michaelmas Term, 1964.

Age at the end of Term 12.9

Average age of Form 12.1

Number in Form 30

Half Term Position —

Final Position —

SUBJECT	%	Posn.	Exam. %	Posn.	REMARKS
Scripture					
~~English~~ Writing					Quite good TFH.
~~Writing~~ English	B		72	3	A good, consistent term's work TFH
Spelling					
Mathematics	C		74	15	Is interested and works steadily. [illegible]
Latin	B		96	2=	Very good work. An asset to the Junior Classical Society JBD.
French	C		87	7=	The exam shows a distinct improvement on the term. He should aim at a more even distribution of effort. Very good. [illegible]
Greek or German					
History	C				He has worked very well all term. [illegible]
Geography	B				His work shows originality. [illegible]
Physics	C				Sound work. Quite interested. [illegible]
Chemistry	A				A very good term's work [illegible]
General Science or Biology	↓				↓
Music	A				A good chorister; musical. EB
Art	A				Excellent sustained interest and ability. In designing one of the stained glass windows he was in a place of maximum responsibility. DHW.
Craftwork					
Physical Education					Fair. B.W.O

Height ab. Weight ab. Beginning of Term

" 5'7½ " 9-5 End of Term

Progress: He has worked steadily & to considerable purpose since he settled down. He does not lack confidence, but is sometimes content to sit back & let others do the oral work.

Conduct ✓

[illegible] Allan Form Master.

A most encouraging report which shows how well he has put his ability to use this term. Fully articulate, he has written and produced the Second Form play for the House supper. He tends to fuss too much, and to assume always that someone else is responsible for his minor misfortunes. C Brooks House Master.

A very pleasing beginning. I.R. Fraser Head of Junior School.

Times Absent 1

Times Late 1

I enjoyed his reading at the Carol Service. C R Allison ~~Head~~master.

Next Term will begin at 10 a.m. on 12 JAN 1965

when every boy, unless prevented by illness, must be in attendance

W.P. 1943/861

Boarders will return at 6.30 p.m. on the previous day

Douglas's school report, Brentwood School (prep), 1964 (aged 12).

BRENTWOOD SCHOOL

UPPER SIXTH & SEVENTH FORMS

House: School

Name: ADAMS D. N.

Form: U6 (5)

Report for the TRINITY Term, 1970

Age at the end of Term 18·4 Average age of Form 17-10

SUBJECT	Marks and/ or Position	REMARKS
ENGLISH LITERATURE		He recovered his balance in the six weeks before the Exam. If he has tackled his papers with care he should do very well. NB
Economic History.		I hope that as a result of revision he has obtained a reasonable grade
Medieval History		If his revision hardened his factual knowledge, his natural ability should have seen him through. RP.
Art (Sub 2)		A very capable and mature thinker in the subject. His ideas are admirable. However he lacks the incentive to carry his practical work to completion, which is most disappointing. One must regretfully classify his attitude as dilettante.
Use of English	B.	Good. NB
French Trans		Good work.
Physical Education		Just a pass in basic fitness tests. Height 6-4½ Weight 13-7

Religious Instruction is included in the curriculum but is not reported on

His work promises well for the future. Form Master.

I hope his efforts have been rewarded. House Master.

Time Absent 0

Times Late 0

I hope his results provide good backing for his candidature for John's. Headmaster. R Sale

Next Term will begin at **10 a.m.** on Tues 15 Sept 70

when every boy, unless prevented by illness, must be in attendance

W.P. 3450/1169

Boarders will return at 8.30 p.m. on the previous day

Douglas's school report, Brentwood School (upper sixth), 1970 (aged 18).

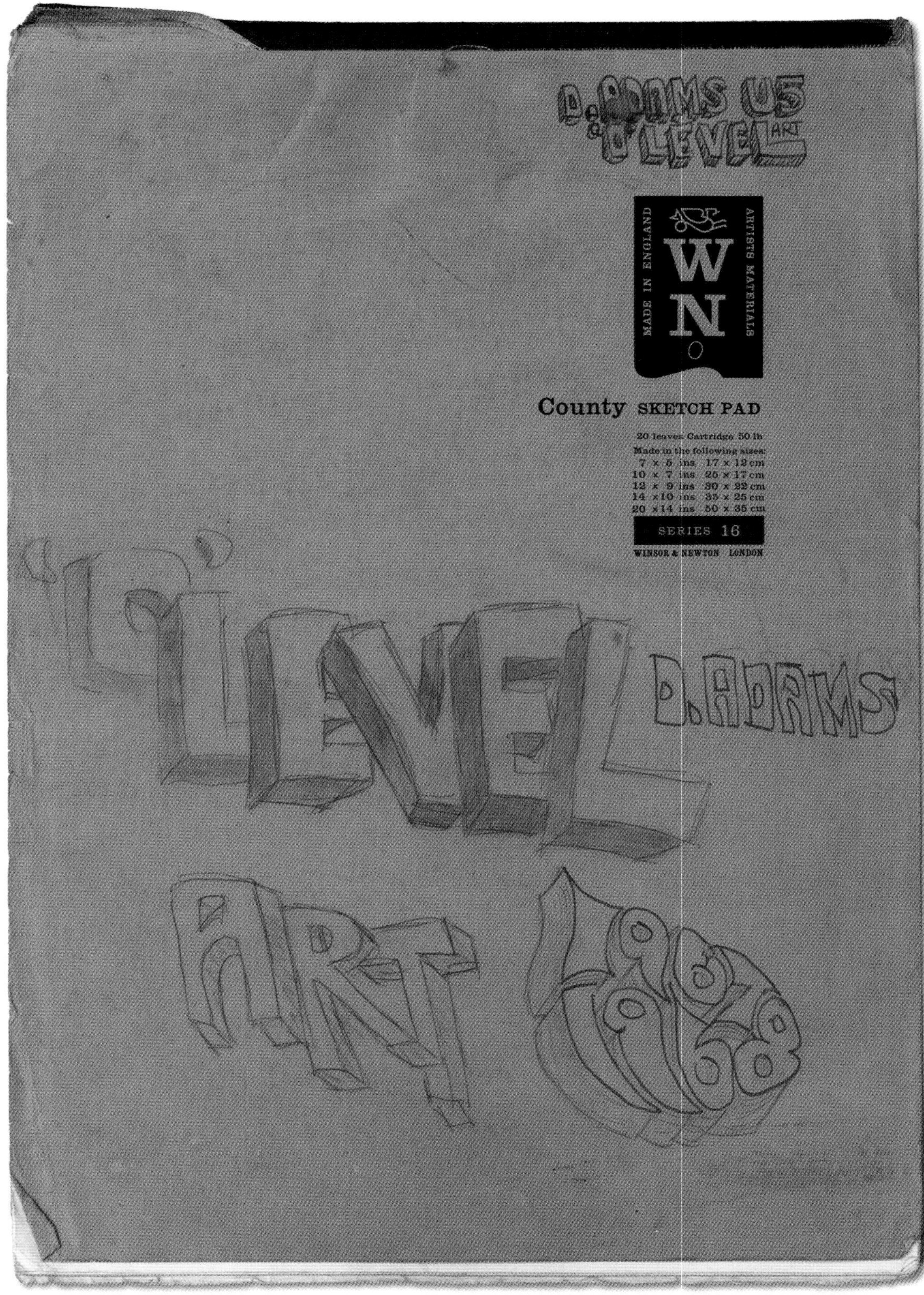

Douglas decorated his O'level art sketch pad (above) with lettering in the style of hippy posters, and *Hitchhiker* fans will note the significance of finding a teacup and saucer (opposite, top) among his observational sketches – the very items his hero Arthur Dent would later crave. Douglas's detailed drawing of an Aston Martin (opposite, bottom) might seem perfectly usual given how preoccupied so many boys were with Sean Connery and James Bond at the time, but Douglas had such a car in the family. His father, by now estranged from his mother and re-married to a wealthy second wife, bought himself one. Douglas's personal papers, held at St John's College, Cambridge, include his collection of Aston Martin sales brochures.

ARTSPHERE

this magazine is artspherical'

BROADSHEET

DNH

\- - -

Douglas Adams: Book Reviews.

'HAMLET' - Feeling depressed? Read this account of life before yeastvite and think how lucky you are.

'OLIVER TWIST' - Tale unsuitable for those with a social conscience in a starving world: glutton makes good.

'TREASURE ISLAND' - Saturday night booze up ends in tears. Cripple gets what cripples deserve. Islands and money smack of a tax avoidance scheme.

'ST. JOAN' - Unhappy state of frustrated girl before possibility of sex change operations. All ends happily however. After a barbecue party she has a bedroom scene with a gay king.

'LADY CHATTERLY'S LOVER' - Elementary Flower arrangement.

'ROMEO AND JULIET - According to an old wive's tale, a kiss takes 12 seconds off your life expectancy. This couple overdid it.

ARTSPHERE

To provide an outlet for experimental projects in the arts, which at present are denied any opportunity of expression.

Covering such fields as ~~folk~~, modern music of all sorts, experimental theatre, poetry, film projects etc and ensuring facilities for these in the way of a stage, lighting and possibly an audience.

The Committee are ~~very~~ ~~pleased~~ open to all suggestions for work, ~~and~~ either original or attempts at the production of published works.

'Artsphere' (defined in this handwritten note, right) was the brainchild of young Douglas and his classmates, including Paul Neil Milne Johnstone (of Redbridge), who wrote poetry and served as editor of the only known edition of their mimeographed magazine *Broadsheet*. Douglas drew the simple cover (opposite) and provided the satirical potted book reviews (above), some of which would not now make it through a sensitivity read. His longer, handwritten piece about a local music concert arrived far too late for inclusion, but opened with Douglas's first grumble (of many) concerning 'irate editors clamouring about datelines'. His revenge was well documented by the use, years later, of Johnstone's name in the earliest versions of *Hitchhiker* as that of the 'worst poet in the universe'. After some sound legal advice, later editions were amended to one 'Paula Nancy Millstone Jennings (of Greenbridge)'.

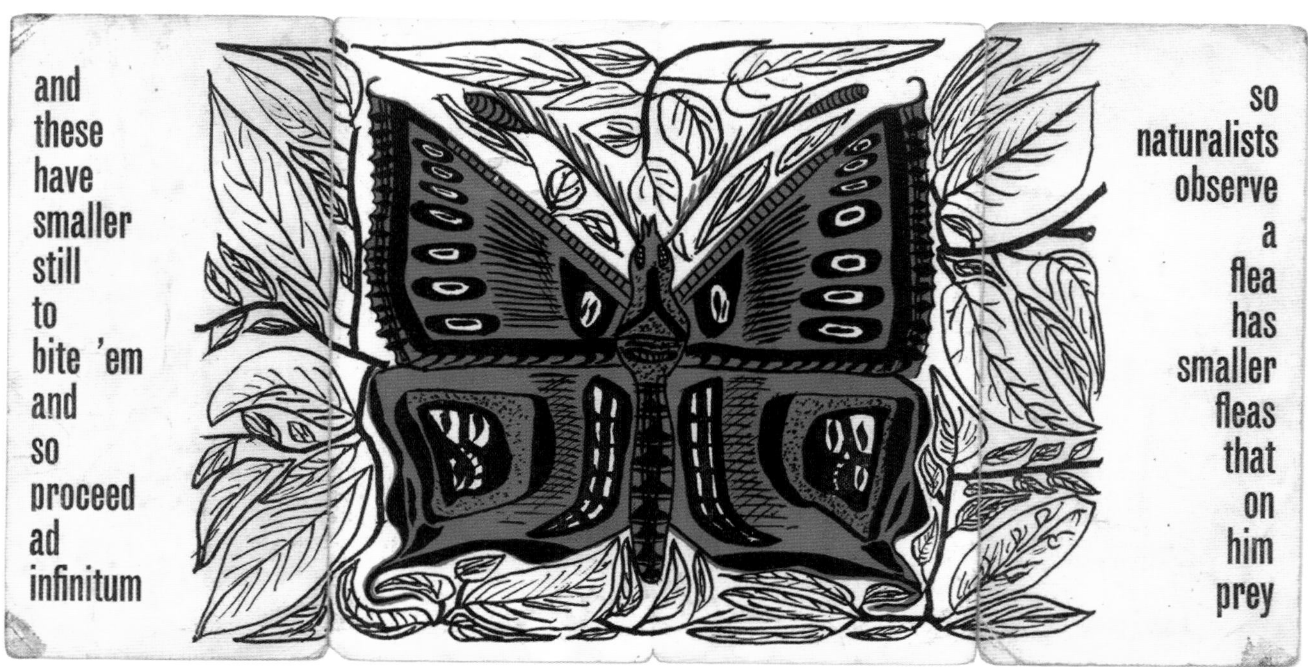

and these have smaller still to bite 'em and so proceed ad infinitum

so naturalists observe a flea has smaller fleas that on him prey

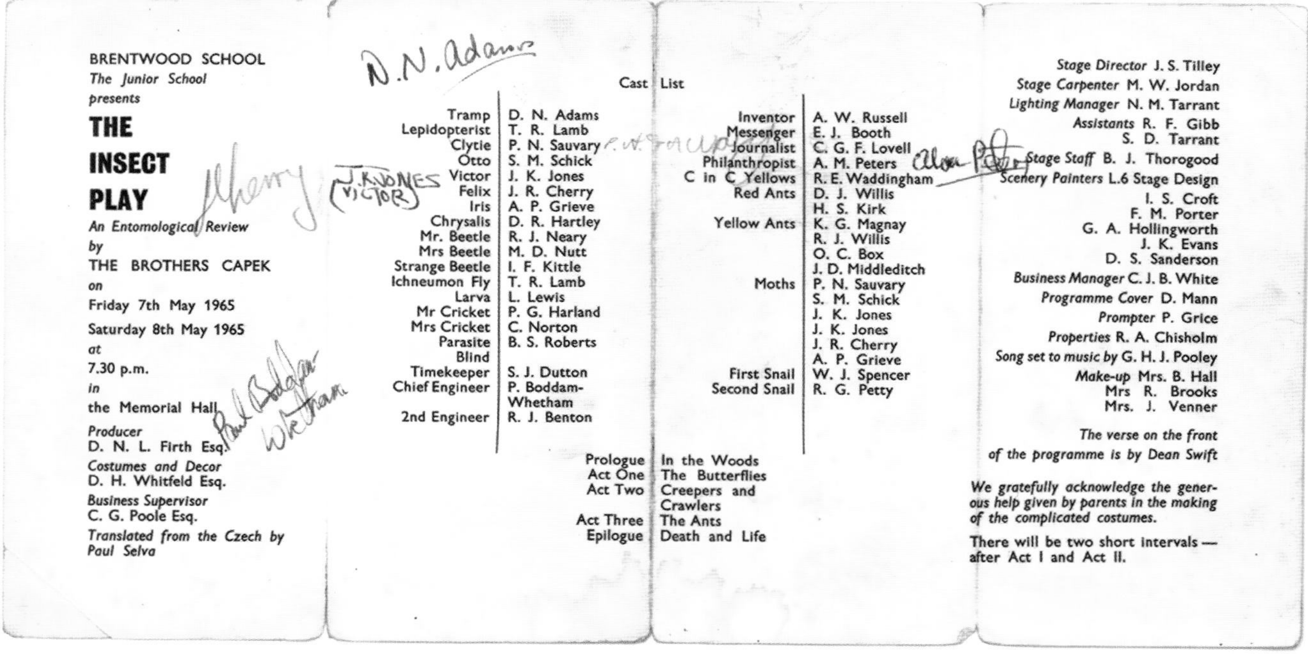

BRENTWOOD SCHOOL
The Junior School
presents

THE INSECT PLAY

An Entomological Review
by
THE BROTHERS CAPEK
on
Friday 7th May 1965
Saturday 8th May 1965
at
7.30 p.m.
in
the Memorial Hall

Producer
D. N. L. Firth Esq.
Costumes and Decor
D. H. Whitfeld Esq.
Business Supervisor
C. G. Poole Esq.
Translated from the Czech by
Paul Selva

Cast List

Tramp	D. N. Adams
Lepidopterist	T. R. Lamb
Clytie	P. N. Sauvary
Otto	S. M. Schick
Victor	J. K. Jones
Felix	J. R. Cherry
Iris	A. P. Grieve
Chrysalis	D. R. Hartley
Mr. Beetle	R. J. Neary
Mrs Beetle	M. D. Nutt
Strange Beetle	I. F. Kittle
Ichneumon Fly	T. R. Lamb
Larva	L. Lewis
Mr Cricket	P. G. Harland
Mrs Cricket	C. Norton
Parasite	B. S. Roberts
Blind	
Timekeeper	S. J. Dutton
Chief Engineer	P. Boddam-Whetham
2nd Engineer	R. J. Benton

Inventor	A. W. Russell
Messenger	E. J. Booth
Journalist	C. G. F. Lovell
Philanthropist	A. M. Peters
C in C Yellows	R. E. Waddingham
Red Ants	D. J. Willis
	H. S. Kirk
Yellow Ants	K. G. Magnay
	R. J. Willis
	O. C. Box
	J. D. Middleditch
Moths	P. N. Sauvary
	S. M. Schick
	J. K. Jones
	J. K. Jones
	J. R. Cherry
	A. P. Grieve
First Snail	W. J. Spencer
Second Snail	R. G. Petty

Prologue	In the Woods
Act One	The Butterflies
Act Two	Creepers and Crawlers
Act Three	The Ants
Epilogue	Death and Life

Stage Director J. S. Tilley
Stage Carpenter M. W. Jordan
Lighting Manager N. M. Tarrant
Assistants R. F. Gibb
S. D. Tarrant
Stage Staff B. J. Thorogood
Scenery Painters L.6 Stage Design
I. S. Croft
F. M. Porter
G. A. Hollingworth
J. K. Evans
D. S. Sanderson
Business Manager C. J. B. White
Programme Cover D. Mann
Prompter P. Grice
Properties R. A. Chisholm
Song set to music by G. H. J. Pooley
Make-up Mrs. B. Hall
Mrs R. Brooks
Mrs. J. Venner

The verse on the front of the programme is by Dean Swift

We gratefully acknowledge the generous help given by parents in the making of the complicated costumes.

There will be two short intervals — after Act I and Act II.

Douglas was always something of a frustrated performer, but in his heyday at Brentwood he played some juicy roles, including the lead in *Julius Caesar* and a 'beanstalk' in a variety concert. The photographs opposite are from May 1965, when he played a drunken tramp, the lead role in Karel Čapek's *The Insect Play*. Douglas, and other members of the cast, signed the gate-fold souvenir programme (above, top and bottom).

A YOUNG POET

ROYAL SOCIETY FOR THE PREVENTION OF CRUELTY TO ANIMALS
MID-ESSEX-BRENTWOOD, CHELMSFORD AND ROMFORD DISTRICT BRANCH

Hon. Secretary—
Mrs. E. DONOVAN,
18 Westbury Road,
Brentwood, Essex.
Tel. Brentwood 2212

BRENTWOOD AUXILIARY BRANCH

Senior Inspector—
D. R. HARRISON,
22 Falmouth Road,
Chelmsford, Essex.
Tel. Chelmsford 58520

This he would examine
as an amoeba viewing
Amoeba through a microscope
With the sterile detatchment of
a Scientist
Unsympathetic.
xxxxxxxxxxxxxxxxxxxxxxxxxxxxx

POEM - "AMOEBAE"

He would sit and watch beside the bugy street
And examine the world as from the outsidexlookingxinx
Looking in
Abstractly removed,
those who saw him cast not a second glance
athim,his shabby attire or little cracked spectacles.
But their faces were an open book tohim
and he would study,reaching into their
Unwary Minds,to see what was written therethere
and read between the lines.
Sometimes,Someone wouldstopx and
And weary with just passing by would
sit beside the old man.
Who would immediately start totalk
to the street dropout ,pleased with his new
Specimen forExamination.
for a
Few words would provide Fresh Premise for
Psychosyllogism
Fresh Data for Psychoanalysis
And from his lofty pinnacle
Isolated Removed Detatched Estranged
Objectived despising subjectivity.
He Heweld
He could view the complete form
of a human mosaic,aMasterpiece of flaws
in which the Coloured Stones were
Emotions Feaxx Predjudices Fears
the Patterns of the Stones
Mentalities.

P.T.O.

Douglas's early poems belie his young age. The address at the top of this notepaper, used in reverse (the upper image here is actually the end of the poem that begins in the lower image, right), reveals that the paper was taken from his maternal grandmother – Mrs E. Donovan, the Honorary Secretary of her local branch of the RSPCA. Douglas was just 12 years old when he wrote the poem opposite – about a tramp, which someone has subsequently noted was a year before he played a tramp in the school play (see previous page).

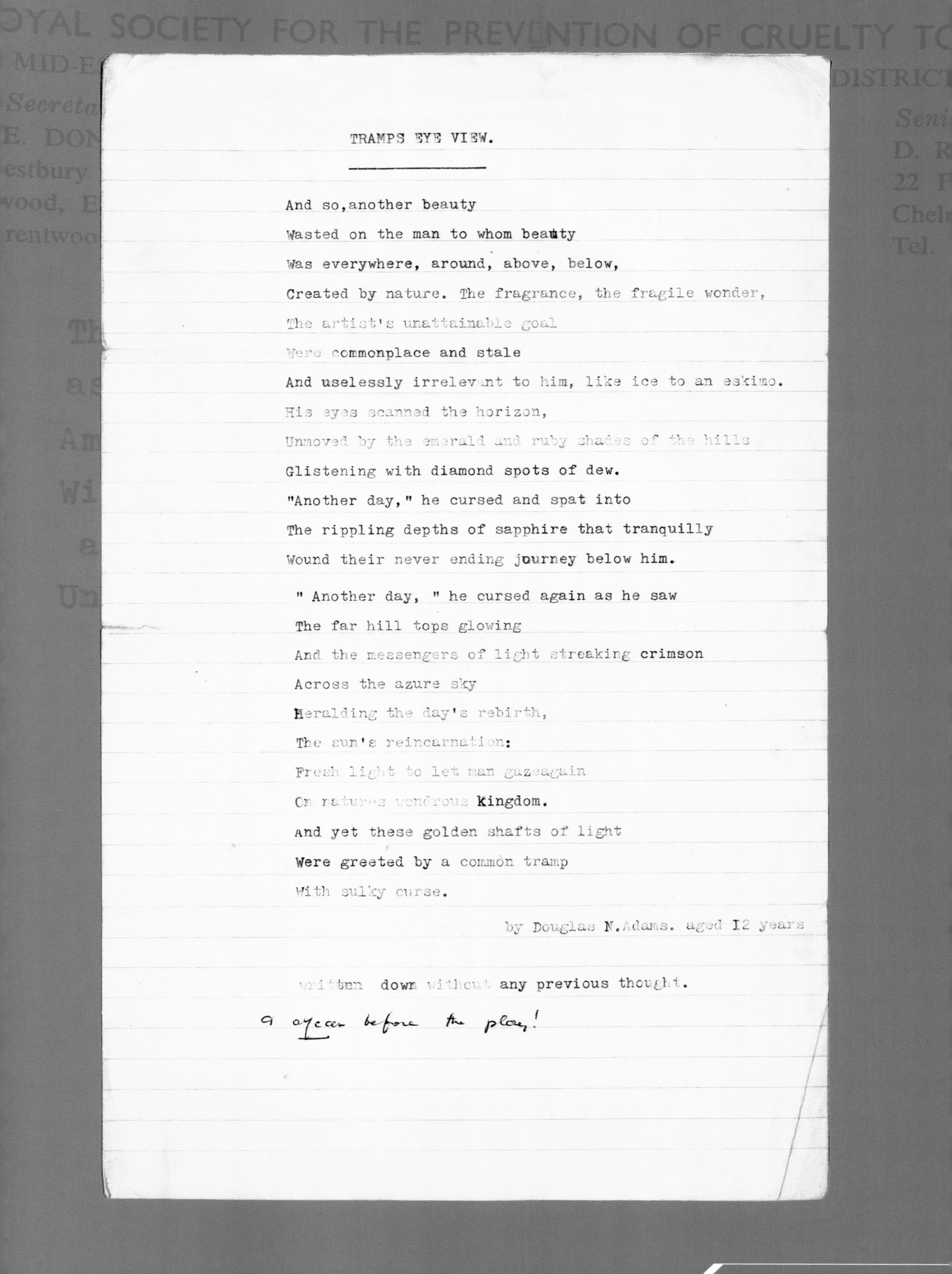

TRAMPS EYE VIEW.

And so,another beauty
Wasted on the man to whom beauty
Was everywhere, around, above, below,
Created by nature. The fragrance, the fragile wonder,
The artist's unattainable goal
Were commonplace and stale
And uselessly irrelevant to him, like ice to an eskimo.
His eyes scanned the horizon,
Unmoved by the emerald and ruby shades of the hills
Glistening with diamond spots of dew.
"Another day," he cursed and spat into
The rippling depths of sapphire that tranquilly
Wound their never ending journey below him.

" Another day, " he cursed again as he saw
The far hill tops glowing
And the messengers of light streaking crimson
Across the azure sky
Heralding the day's rebirth,
The sun's reincarnation:
Fresh light to let man gazeagain
On natures wondrous kingdom.
And yet these golden shafts of light
Were greeted by a common tramp
With sulky curse.

by Douglas N.Adams. aged I2 years

written down without any previous thought.

a year before the play!

This house would shave its head.

Inside every public or direct grant schoolboy – or girl, is a skinhead trying to get out. Unfortunately many members of the august assembled company may feel a slight distaste at the lack of respectability which seems to surround the 'skinhead renaissance' as I like to call it. I should like to demonstrate in the short time allotted to me how essentially civilized and suited to the cultured and intelligent temperament of this house is the basis, the attitude and the principles behind such forms of self expression as carefully rearranging the faces of one's colleagues, emphasising one's comments on soccer matches by heroically gesticulating with meat hooks, improving the ventilation in telephone booths, or generally putting the boot in. In fact the bases of these actions are so well suited to the culture of this house that I would say we were on the verge of an agro cultural revolution. – My apologies – the line is irrelevant, I merely can't resist a bad pun.

For a little light entertainment prior to considering the main problems let us consider a typical day in the life of Johnny, the Happy Skin.

Bright and early in the morning Johnny Skin wakes up and greets the happy morn. He leaps up off his board and runs gleefully to the window. He opens it, – with his boot. "Hello sky hello clouds" – "Hello little bird" he says, happily beating its brains out. Down below in the yard he sees his mother hanging his ~~bye~~ bicycle chain on the washing line. He tries to attract her attention – with a brick.

Johnny is the apple of his mothers eye "Such a nice boy" she tells her neighbours. "You should see the friendly way he embraces ~~policemen~~

In 1969, Douglas, aged 18, made a Brentwood Debating Society speech, 'This house would shave its head', on the growing notoriety of skinheads. Its dazzlingly convoluted argument is a good indicator of the author's burgeoning talent for comedic wordplay. Above is Douglas's first handwritten page; the full transcript is on pages 31–2, and Douglas's 'response' on page 33.

Inside every public or direct grant schoolboy – or girl, is a skinhead trying to get out. Unfortunately, many members of the august assembled company may feel a slight distaste of the lack of respectability which seems to surround the 'skinhead renaissance' as I like to call it. I should like to demonstrate in the short time allotted to me how essentially civilized and suited to the cultured and intelligent temperament of this house is the basis, the attitude and the principles behind such forms of self-expression, or carefully rearranging the faces of one's colleagues, emphasising one's comments on soccer matches by heroically gesticulating with meat hooks, improving the ventilation in telephone booths or generally putting the boot in. In fact, the bases of these actions are so well suited to the culture of this house that I would say we were on the verge of an agrocultural revolution. My apologies – the line is irrelevant, I merely can't resist a bad pun.

For a little light entertainment prior to considering the main problems let us consider a typical day in the life of Johnny, the Happy Skin.

Bright and early in the morning Johnny Skin wakes up and greets the happy morn. He leaps up off his board and runs gleefully to the window. He opens it, with his boot. "Hello sky, hello clouds" – "Hello little bird" he says, happily beating its brains out. Down below in the yard he sees his mother hanging his bicycle chain on the washing line. He tries to attract her attention with a brick.

Johnny is the apple of his mother's eye. "Such a nice boy" she tells her neighbours. "You should see the friendly way he embraces policemen."

Johnny, putting on his hobnail bedroom slippers goes to the bathroom for a shave. Undoing his braces, he takes off his pyjamas and puts on his other Levi's. He goes downstairs to break his fast, the mirror, and a couple of his little brother's teeth as he gives him a loving pat on the mouth. He walks down the street playing football with the cat and arrives at school by 9.00. By 9.10 his teacher is unfortunately indisposed, so Johnny returns home, with his satchel full of razors slung over his back.

That afternoon, feeling in need of a little light entertainment to refresh his spirits, he meets some of his acquaintances and they repair to a football ground. Leaving the gatekeeper bleeding happily on the floor, they take their places for the match. By the end of the match many of his friends and others are... asleep and so they leave them laying where they are, not wishing to disturb them, and he takes the train home with the remainder of his friends. 'What a nice match,' they all say, and they recreate some of the more exciting moments there in the carriage. 'Let's play a game,' says Johnny, playfully putting his foot through the window. One of his friends swings gleefully around on the communications cord and everyone joins in the general celebrations.

Mr Chairman, I now must turn these notes serious. At the end of the day, he returns to bed tired and strangely happy, having got rid of his pent up frustrations and spleen, bearing no serious grudges or inhibitions, and, ironically at peace with the world. He knows that at no time of the day has he fallen short of his own code of behaviour, for his code allows him to be as honestly and openly prejudiced, pig-headed, and fascist as he likes, and he knows it. He is fully aware that there can be no pretence of right or morality in what he does, and he has nothing to answer to himself for, nothing to turn a blind eye to, his conscience is healthily clear. He does not need to indulge in any of the self-deception that those with a loudly proclaimed morality use to persuade themselves that in all things they are not actually doing anything completely inexcusable. He doesn't seek to excuse himself. He knows that anything he's done that day was done primarily because he wanted to and it gave him a kick. If he hits someone, he doesn't profess self-righteously that he is being cruel to be kind, or that it's for the person's own good. He isn't interested in the other person's own good and wouldn't say so; he doesn't excuse himself by saying that his psychiatrist has prescribed it for the release of his nervous tensions, he did it because he enjoyed indulging his own pig-headed arrogance.

Bright and early in the morning Johnny Skin wakes up and greets the happy morn. He leaps up off his board and runs gleefully to the window. He opens it, with his boot.

The skinhead is an ascetic. His way of life allows no other, his hairstyle is ascetic, his clothes are ascetic, his philosophy is sparse, uncluttered, and beautiful in its simplicity and honesty. He doesn't hide moral corruption behind a front of prettiness, flowers, incense, howls against hypocrisy and wailings for freedom and self-expression, most of which involves doing what the hippies call 'your own thing'. If the skinheads had been in 144 Piccadilly[1], the result would have been much the same in terms of damage, but they would not have come out hypocritically canting against the moral decadence and prejudice of those who kicked them out of their sordid mess. They now regret what they wanted when they proclaimed universal love was universal sex, and it seems their only contribution in that direction is the dubious idea that it is preferable to make love in a sleeping bag on a road island than in a bed. The hippy movement is more corrupt than the society they rebel against, and more self-deluding if they think they are less so. Name dropping is name dropping whether it concerns titled dignitaries, or an obscure underground group that you can be sure no one else has heard of.

The Skinheads dismiss all forms of cultural pretensions – just listen to Blue Beat[2] – any form of moral pretension, and, most important any of the craving necessity for self-justification which pervades practically all other strata of society. Britain was once a Christian state. It can hardly claim to be so now. I am not here to applaud or deplore that fact, but to deplore the legacy of the wane. In the days of widely professed Christianity, it was the concern of everybody to live a life of conformity as much as possible to the forms of Christianity, or at least, and more important, appearing that way. To be wrong, or to behave according to anything less than the highest principles was to be guilty of a sin, and this was to be avoided at all costs, with the result that the most dubious actions had to be justified and excused both to one's colleagues, and to oneself. Now Christian standards are largely dismissed, they are regarded as outmoded – but still people must justify themselves – they have a quaking social terror of admitting either to themselves or anybody else that something they intend to do or have done – and would do again in similar circumstances – was wrong. Even to say, 'Everybody else does it so there's no harm in my doing it', or 'It wasn't my idea,' is cringing, self-justifying the inability to recognize that you are in the wrong and glad of it.

Even the Satanist, whose code is deliberately evil, seeks to justify himself by ascribing transcendental significance to his base instincts, to put it on to some acceptable footing. Only the Skinhead is honest enough to say I'm bad because it suits me, and that is something that a member of a post-Christian society must realize – it is something for a Christian society to realize – if you are going to be in the wrong, don't pay the homage of vice to virtue which is hypocrisy. Don't pretend you are basically deep-down virtuous.

Skinheads, in their dress, way of life and morals are ascetics. They allow themselves no comfortable moral code to which they can twist their motives to fit in.

Monks, in their dress, way of life and morals are ascetics. They allow themselves no comfortable short cuts which they can twist their moral code to fit in with, and they have no illusions about themselves. The monk, with his shaven tonsure is as uncompromising as the Skinhead. He doesn't pretend to himself that he finds a life of strict morality easy, but he dismisses his wants and desires because they do not fit with the moral code he has set himself. The Skinheads have no illusions about themselves – they know that they are not moral – and they dismiss a moral code because it does not fit in with what they want and are going to do in any case.

What is there between the two shaven-headed extremes? There is ordinary society which refuses to admit that their day-to-day standards and professed moral code cannot co-exist and insist on trying to twist both in an attempt to make them fit to their own satisfaction and ultimate self-delusion. The hippies fall between every stool in sight – they aim at the uncorrupted spiritual purity of the monk without his devotion and application and achieve the decadence of the Skinhead without his honesty.

Mr Chairman, I won't insult the intelligence of the committee of which I am a member by suggesting that this nation is primarily concerned with hairdos. Neither will I insult the intelligence of the house as the opposition will no doubt do, by suggesting the committee would put on a debate with a conclusion as forgone as one discussing the desirability of meathooks and smashed up railway carriages would be. This motion is concerned with an attitude of mind, and I ask that no-one will be so misguided as to stand up and say that actually they like smashed up railway carriages and are very interested in meathooks and hope to carry a serious motion that way.

A vote in the 'aye' lobby is not a pledge to literally go and crop your hair, but a rejection of hypocrisy, and the realisation of a new self-awareness. The light vein of my opening will, I hope, not detract from the seriousness of the idea I put before you.

I urge the house to be as Skinheads and monks – crop and shave yourselves of all delusions about your apparent selfless actions. Either accept a moral code wholeheartedly, or do what you will, and be sufficiently self-aware and sure of yourself not to need to pay insincere lip service to any form of morality and thus attempt to salve your conscience. Mr Chairman, I urge the house to be capable of being wholeheartedly, honestly, healthily in the wrong without pandering to your conscience, if you are going to be wrong in any case.

I urge the house to shave its head.

[1] 144 Piccadilly refers to a then recent 'Hippydilly' squat/protest at a five-storey disused mansion at Hyde Park Corner in London. It ended with a police raid, arrests and tabloid headlines.

[2] Blue Beat was an English record label that released Jamaican R&B and Ska music in the 1960s, a style favoured by skinheads. The term 'bluebeat' became generic for all kinds of Jamaican pop music.

I would apologise to the House for all those who having anticipated that we would proclaim the desirability of short haircuts, and having prepared an attack on that section of our argument, were dismayed to find that we didn't prescribe the obviously unaesthetic

Mr Robinson, in demonstrating his lingual dexterity and little else has attempted to cloud the whole issue before us, I hope not successfully. He has first reduced it to a banal exposition ~~of~~ on the merits of various hairdo's – I warned you he was out to insult your intelligence. We do not need the auspicious occasion of a Meeting of the Debating Society to discuss such a matter.

He then seems to be under the misconception that I was advising and proclaiming a lack of individuality, and ~~also~~ an army of literally shaved heads. That is the unfortunate result of the ~~a~~ practice of preparing one's attack on a speech before one has heard. The Darts are ~~mis~~ unfortunately misplaced. It is not a profession of non-individuality – it is the ~~I would~~ expression of the individuality of the person who can be right or wrong ~~and~~ and know which he is. To hell I say with Dr Boddam Whetham

Brevity of his speech indicates his lack of argument not ours.

I would remind the house, that a vote in the 'aye' lobby is a rejection of ~~hypocrisy~~ self delusion, ability to be wrong when you are ~~wrong~~ without pretending to be anything else. Outward trappings

short cropped hair, but merely the ~~of~~ attitude of honesty, but having found their speech irrelevant still bored the house with it.

Once Douglas had made his case and the opposition had made theirs, he was of course required to make a response, presumably in the moment. Douglas cuts down his opposers with what we can imagine was a dismissive wave of the hand: 'To hell I say with Dr Boddam-Whetham. The brevity of his speech indicates his lack of argument, not ours,' he writes. Dr Boddam-Whetham refers to either Paul or Peter Boddam-Whetham, who were fellow pupils, and also in drama productions, sharing a stage with Douglas.

Dear Douglas

MARGO BUCHANAN

Dear Douglas

Hello. I've been dreaming about you quite a bit lately, it's great. You're looking increasingly younger these days.

To be given actual permission to sit here like a loonie spiritual medium and talk to you properly feels like a gift.

Well, we might as well start by going back to when you left.

It was around 9.30 on a Friday evening, we were watching TV when the phone rang. Jane, calling from America, in an eerily calm voice (which transpired to be shock) explained that you had died suddenly at the gym. Massive heart attack.

Horrendously for your mum, she was on a plane on her way to visit you. Your family had to be informed before it hit the news networks and our job was to beat the clock. Thank goodness Twitter wasn't around.

Of course, I don't have to explain Twitter to you, because you'd already foreseen social media years before it actually happened. (You'd have at least 83 million followers on Twitter, by the way.)

Your friends closed ranks around your heartbroken family. We became a small army, all still friends today. I feel like I'm speaking on behalf of all of them here.

We were all dreading that first Christmas because of the famed Christmas Carol evenings you and Jane hosted. So we decided we had to carry on just as if you were there.

We dressed up to the nines. The champagne flowed; it was the start to Christmas for us all, for quite a few years.

Those Carol nights sustained us for the awful task of having to live a very long time without you.

You'd created a social hub at Duncan Terrace where the most interesting people gathered. I still treasure the conversations. I had more light bulb moments in one dinner at yours than I probably ever have in 5 years of normal life. Ping! Ping! Ping! Exhilarating. I can remember Terry Jones, about 20 years ago saying that democracy was knackered. I thought he was bonkers. What did I know?

9/11 reinforced my sense of loss. I think I realised that not just your family and friends needed you here, but the whole world could have done with your clever brain on News Night. You just saw things others didn't. God, I wished I'd bought those Apple shares you kept banging on about.

You were such a kind friend, Douglas. We were all expectant parents at the same time. Your baby was due in June, ours in April. We lost our baby late in pregnancy, a terrible time. I confided to you that I'd do anything to avoid new-born babies, bordering on agoraphobic really.

Then Polly was born.

We came to meet her at Duncan Terrace. Your mum was there with the whole family and the atmosphere was like a gentle party. No time to think, you sat me firmly onto a comfy chair and put a sleeping Polly straight into my arms. It was exactly like they describe in books. The room melted away and it was just her and me. I eventually looked around and the room was empty. You'd all left me with your tiny, precious, fragile two-day-old little scrap and the process of healing began.

You clever, clever, clever man.

Happier times! What about the night we arranged for us to play at Duncan Terrace?

The audience was collectively more famous than the band (not counting the mega famous Rock-God David Gilmour and your beloved Gary Brooker). Melvyn Bragg, George Martin, Lenny Henry, Terry Gilliam, Angus Deayton, Salman Rushdie, Mariella Frostrup, Kathy Lette – too many more to name.

Microsoft Billionaire Paul Alan flew over especially in his brand new Boeing 757. Unexpectedly, I saw a friend from Seattle. 'Paul Alan gave me a lift,' she said, like it was a Ford Fiesta.

We really did have the best of times. You packed in quite a life Douglas. It was a real one, with highs and lows, but it was a good one.

If there is an after-life, I'm certain you'll be there at the gate to meet me. And, my atheist friend, I will SO take the piss. I always told you to hedge your bets and be an agnostic.

I am very glad this book is being written to celebrate you. There are many people who will write about your brilliant brain and your incredible sense of humour. I want your readers to know about your brilliant heart too.

We'd laugh at that, wouldn't we? 'Obviously not that bloody brilliant,' we'd say. I miss you, my darling friend.

Love, M x

Margo Buchanan is a Scottish singer-songwriter. She has worked with everyone from the Pet Shop Boys to Deep Purple, Joni Mitchell and Tina Turner to Van Morrison. She met Douglas as a result of a Paul McCartney concert – her husband Paul 'Wix' Wickens was performing and Douglas realized he and Wix had shared a childhood music teacher. This photo shows Margo singing at one of Douglas's legendary music parties.

TWO
Cambridge Life

D. Adams

name — nom — nombre — name
DOUGLAS NOËL ADAMS

address — adresse — dirección — adresse
Linnets, Grove Lane Stalbridge DORSET

nationality — nationalité — nacionalidad — staatsangehörigkeit
BRITISH

date of birth—date de naissance—fecha de nacimiento—geburtsdatum
11·3·52

place of birth — lieu de naissance — lugar de nacimiento — geburtsort
CAMBRIDGE ENGLAND

signature — signature — firma — unterschrift
Douglas Adams.

The National Union of Students of England, Wales and Northern Ireland

Jack Straw.
President

field of study / étudiant en / estudiant de / studienfach: ENGLISH

year of study / anné d'étude / año de estudio / studienjahr: 70/71

educational institution / établissement / establecimiento de enseñanza / art der hochschule: BRENTWOOD SCHOOL

address / situé à / dirección / hochschulort: INGRAVE RD., BRENTWOOD ESSEX. ENGLAND

This membership card is issued by the National Union of Students, which is a large, active, influential union and which exists to fight for the interests of its 450,000 Members. It operates nationally, negotiating with, and campaigning against, Government, College and Local Authorities. It operates locally in support of member unions, or individual students in dispute or difficulty.

NUS's enviable reputation for being well-informed stems from the continuous work done by the Education and Welfare, and International, departments who provide the briefings for negotiating teams, Conference, policy-making, debates, and advice and help on individual student problems. The Press Office exists to communicate student views to the mass media.

NUS Travel provides students with reduced rate travel by plane, train or boat, and Endsleigh Insurances specialises in negotiating reduced rates and special terms for students in all classes of insurance.

This card must be validated here to certify that the holder is a scholar member of the National Union of Students of England, Wales and Northern Ireland.

1970/71 M.D.Batham

In December 1970 Douglas discovered he'd earned himself an exhibition place to study English at St John's College, Cambridge. From among his personal papers is his student union card, signed by Jack Straw, then a senior at Brentwood School and later to become one of the UK's leading Labour Party politicians. It's clear also that Cambridge was a catalyst for Douglas's talent, with Footlights, Cambridge's legendary drama

/

Douglas Adams

Troilus and Criseyde and the conditions of life.

Troilus seems to be a totally undeserving victim of the vicissitudes of fate. His downfall is brought about by natural and inexorable processes that are part of the conditions of human life. He is only in a limited way a 'tragic figure' in the way that we understand the term, for whilst he himself set into motion the processes that eventually destroy him, he seems to have no real alternative, given the pagan setting of the poem. His character lacks 'the stamp of one defect' which is the usual mark of the tragic hero, for his behaviour is at all times exemplary. The fault, if any, lies in code of courtly love itself, and not in the way he follows it.

It has been argued, accurately enough, by critics involved in the predestination debate that Troilus is not merely helpless puppet of fortune, because he does take a conscious decision to pursue his love for Criseyde:

For with good hope he gan fully assente
Crisyde for to love and nought repente.

He professes himself willing to undergo the torments of love in the Canticus Troili:

O Quike deth, O swete harm so queynte,
How may of the in me swich quantite,
But if that I consente that it be?

That he should love Criseyde is something without his control:

...Love is he that alle thing may bind
For may no man fordon the lawe of kynde.

but to pursue that love is a conscious decision, as we have seen. It is that decision that eventually leads to Troilus' downfall, for it is a decision to place his hopes of happiness in 'that ~~was by~~ which by its very nature was temporary, imperfect, and inevitably insufficient'*, its 'very nature' being that it was earthly. Not ~~on~~ only is Criseyde earthly, but being human ,she too is prey to those forces which Troilus has consciously decided to allow full play within himself, so he makes himself doubly vulnerable.

However, when we talk about his 'conscious decision', we must consider what alternatives are placed before him, remembering that he lives in a pagan world. They are quite simply to pursue his love, or not to pursue ~~them~~ it; he has not the Christian alternative which Chaucer's audience is exhorted to follow in the Palinode. What possible motivation has he for not ~~lovin~~ pursuing his love of Criseyde? Only the fact that human relationships have a tendency to be fragile and transient, and that to expect perfect unblemished happiness from them in the idealistic sense that Troilus did is but to invite disaster. He has no prompting of moral scruple, for the code of courtly love did not forbid extra-marital sex, in fact its whole ethic was based on it. Any code of conduct that exhorted one not to enter into a human relationship for no better reason than the fact that human relationships are fragile and not to be trusted

* James Lyndon Shanley 'The Troilus and Christian Love

Douglas was fond of claiming he wrote only a couple of essays while at university, as he was far too busy honing his skills as a writer and performer at Footlights. His archives, however, tell a different story, proving that, in fact, he did a good deal of work. This essay explores the notion of love in Geoffrey Chaucer's epic poem *Troilus and Criseyde*.

which did not at the same time offer an alternative is a dry inhuman one, that would certainly receive little support from Chaucer. It would reduce life toaan arid emotional desert/which would even preclude Christian love when that alternative came to be offered.

So there seems to be little reason for Troilus to resist 'the lawe of kynde', and we must look to see what reasons, apart from the obvious, there are for him to follow it. First, by falling in love he is following the wishes of one of his major gods, Cupid. In the pagan context, his very act of falling in love with Criseyde may be caused deliberately by Cupid, as a retribution for ~~Troilus~~ Troilus's scorn of lovers. By obeying his wishes he is therefore obeying the highest authority he knows. Similarly, by following the teachings of courtly love he is following the highest moral code of which he is aware, and adhereing to it absolutely. We are encouraged to think by this that the alternative with which he is not presented, that of divine Christian love, is the one to which he most naturally inclines. If we now look forward to the palinode we see how important these few final verses are to the thought of the poem. They no longer appear, as they have done to some critics as a 'pious afterthought', or an apologia or cop-out, but a very necessary conclusion. What Chaucer has tried to show to his audience is that life for its own sake, and human values for their own sake are transitory and that if we try to invest ~~ours-~~ in them what we naturally need to invest of ourselves in the Christian God, we will not find satisfaction. In other words he considers the circumstances of human life to be impossible: we need the third alternative.

This suggests that Troilus's love for Criseyde is really frustrated love for God. Criseyde gets Troilus on the rebound, so to speak. From Chaucer's point of view, what Troilus loves is God-in-her, in accordance with the Platonic theory of Universals. If, as that theory states, everyone is an imperfect reflection of God, then it is natural that Troilus should fall in love with the most perfect woman in Troy, i.e. the least imperfect reflection of God. This explains the obsessive nature of his idealim, for he attributes qualities to her that are godlike rather than human. With the ideal of courtly love to encourage him he expects love ~~tobe~~ to be eternal, and he dwells at length on the quasi-religious quality of sexual experience. He does not realise that eternity is ~~impo-~~ an impossible ideal in earthly terms, and the nearest he gets to experience of eternity is the experience of the eternal present moment: in the love making scene neither Troilus nor the narrator make any reference to the future and its tragedy.-Troilus enjoys a few hours of 'eternal' bliss.

Significantly, Troilus chooses to follow those Gods and ideals that most nearly approximate ~~tpo~~ to those of Christianity. Cupid is the God of love, and is the only god before the Christian one to whom the ~~qulity~~ quality of love is central, and the code of courtly love is the only code other than Christianity which is also based on love. However, Cupid is pre-Christain, and courtly love is post Christian. By transposing the convention back to pre-Christian times Chaucer shows that he thinks it to be a poor non- divine substitute for Christianity, and not compatible with Christianity itself, for the very reason that it attributed divine qualities to human beings, and directed love due to God to human beings, who were incapable of meeting its demands. The rigour of the demands of courtly love, its emphasis on purity, faithfulness, and eternity are pseudoChristian, and as such are commendable ideals for pre-Christians, but not for Christians. It is for this reason that Chaucer is able to celebrate so unequivocally the love of Troilus and Criseyde when he is telling the story,-for Troilus behaves remarkably well for someone living in a world in which the conditions oflife are impossibly arbitrary, - and later, in the palinode, talking directly to his audience, to speak of 'payehs corsed olde rites', and 'wrecched worldly appetites'. For Troilus they were the closest possible approximations to Christianity , but for Chaucers audience they are merely perversions of it. So too, as far as Troilus is concerned the world is all that exists, and so he takes all that happens extraordinarily seriously until after his death, when he is able to laugh at it. A Christian on the other hand should see it as merely a pale reflection, and a distorted one at that, of the kingdom of heaven , and be aware of the 'false worldes ~~brittlenesse~~ brotelnesse'.

Without doubting Chaucer's sincerity, we may notice that Chaucer sounds more convincing when he is celebrating human life than when he is denigrating it, but nevertheless we cannot doubt that the palinode is the inevitable conclusion of the story that Chaucer tells. He sees that the conditions of human life are intolerable through their arbitrary transience, and that all the decisions of life need an alternative that transcends the uncertainty of earthly values.

Right: One of several headshots of Douglas as a student that exist among his personal papers.

Introduction

The knowledge that this work was composed within the walls of a lunatic asylum easily prejudices our initial reaction to it. William Force Stead, its first editor[1] saw it as an incoherent confusion of deranged erudition, tempered by occasional glimpses of brilliant and lucid sanity. It was only after W.H.Bond's discovery of its antiphonal structure[2] that it began to be recognised as something more important- a fragment of a failed literary experiment, gigantic, perhaps bizarre, eventually out of control, but nevertheless the product of a coherent and rational idea - the transplantation of the rhythms and structures of Hebrew poetry into an English religious poem.[3] We will never know the nature or full extent of Smart's madness, or indeed if he was mad at all. Dr Johnson has doubts:

> 'Madness frequently discovers itself by an unnecesary deviation from the usual modes of the world. My poor friend Smart shewed the disturbance of his mind, by falling down on his knees and saying his prayers in the street or in any other unusual place. Now, although rationally speaking it is greater madness not to pray at all than to pray as Smart did, I am afraid there are so many who do not pray, that their understanding is not called into question'

In studying this poem I decided to treat it as being fundamentally sane, and by giving the benefit of the doubt to a number of passages previously dismissed as chaotic and meaningless often arrived at readings I considered coherent both, in themselves and in the context of the whole.

Over the following pages is part of Douglas's final dissertation. The essay investigates Christopher Smart's religious poem 'Jubilate Agno' (or 'Rejoice in the Lamb'), written during Smart's confinement in an asylum. A letter dated 27 June 1974 from Douglas's personal tutor, K.J. Pascoe, indicates that the essay earned Douglas a high 2:1 – although the correspondence also gives news that he failed his tragedy paper, and his other papers were middle-ground 2:2s.

e whole of created life (and later inanimate creation) is summoned by Smart

('Let man and beast appear before him
and magnify his name together' (JA, A3)[9])

The whole of created life (and later inanimate creation) is summoned by Smart to worship and bless God in pairs of man and beast. Stead[1] divides these verses into three separate categories:

1) Those in which there is some obvious connection between the pair, such as Abraham and the Ram, Balaam and the Ass, Daniel and the Lion.
2) Those in which the connection is more obscure - Aaron and the Bull (see Ex. Chap 32 v. 8), Anah and the Mule (Genesis 36 v. 24, AV, not RV), Naphtali and the hind (Gen. 49 v. 21)
3) Those in which the connection is apparently arbitrary and meaningless, such as Eleazer and the Ermine, which is not mentioned in the Bible, Ahitub and the Ape, Moses and the Lizard (which is pronounced unclean in Lev 11,v.30)

   Stead suggests that these arbitrary connections are simply the product of Smart's deranged imagination, but this is a judgment we should beware of. Smart's learning was phenomenally wide and many connections may not be apparent to us through their sheer obscurity. Verse A57 is a case in point:

   'Let Anna bless with the Cat, who is worthy to be presented before the throne of grace when he has trampled upon the idol in his prank'

   Stead and Bond dismissed this verse as meaningless, noting that the cat is mentioned nowhere in the Bible. Later, C.Devlin[5] pointed out that in the apocryphal book Baruch there is a mocking description of the Babylonian idols which has this verse:

   'Upon their bodies and heads sit bats swallows and birds, and the cats also' Smart's verse suggests that he is aware of the fact that the cat is not strictly Biblical, but that its action here makes it worthy of inclusion.

But why is it that Smart summons pairs of men and animals together?

the cat is not strictly Biblical, but that its action here make
worthy of inclusion.

animals and inanimate objects to actively praise God says:
'All that they are capable of doing is affording matter or subject of prais
him

John Ray (in The Wisdom of God in Creation, 1735), referring to the apparent inability of animals and inanimate objects to actively praise God says:

'All that they are capable of doing is affording matter or subject of praising him to rational and intelligent beings'[6]

Bond remarks that Smart wished to bring the whole of creation together in praising God, and since he regarded animals below the level of man as being incapable of appreciating the creator, he invariably summoned them to praise, not directly but through some human intermediary. The theme of animals instructing men in praise of the creator has precedent in Smart's poetry, for instance in this Seatonian Prize Poem of his Cambridge career:

'Woeful vicissitude! When Man, fall'n Man
Who first from Heav'n, from Gracious God himself
Learn'd knowledge of the Brutes, must know, by Brutes
Instructed and reproach'd, the scale of being;
By slow degrees from lowly step ascend
And trace omniscience up towards the springs.'

The simplest statement of this idea in the Jubilate Agno is to be found at Bl 68,[4] in which Smart enrols himself in the list of those called to give worship:

'For I am possessed of a cat, surpassing in beauty, from whom I take occasion to bless Almighty God.'

I believe that a similar idea is expressed in verse A 52:

'Let Elihu bless with the Tortoise, which is food for praise and thanksgiving'

Both Stead and Bond find this verse hard to explain, saying that the Tortoise is unfit to eat, being pronounced unclean in Lev 11, v.29. I suggest that what Smart means here is that though the tortoise is unfit to eat, yet it still affords inspiration for the praise of God, as in the modern metaphor 'food for Thought'

Often Smart takes the notion of 'food for thought' directly and derives from the nature of the animal cited a brief homily, after the example of commonplace books or, more aptly, after the example of Solomon (Go to the ant, thou sluggard, consider her ways). Here are some examples:

'Let Job bless with the Worm- the life of the Lord is in humiliation, the Spirit

more aptly, after the example of Solomon (Go to the ant, thou sluggard, con
ways). Here are some examples:

also and the Truth' (A 51)

'Let Zadok worship with the Mole - before honour is humility, and he that looketh low shall learn' (A 54)

'Let Huldah bless with the silkworm - the ornaments of the proud are from the bowells of their betters' (A 91)

'Let Iddo praise the Lord with the Moth - the writings of man perish as the garment, but the Book of the Lord endureth for ever' (A 68)

But Smart is not always so coldly didactic in his references to the world's livestock. He combined enormous knowledge of theoretical natural history, learnt from the pages of Pliny and others, with a deep compassion for all animals, without which, Jubilate Agno would probably not have been written. The two following examples give some indication of this and also begin to hint at something that will later become very clear - that Smart's conception of the hierarchy of creation goes very far above and beyond the idea quoted above from John Ray.

'Let Joseph, who from the abundance of his blessing may spare to him that lacketh praise with the crocodile, which is pleasant and pure when interpreted, though his look is of terror and offence'(A 46)

'Let Lemuel bless with the wolf, which is a dog without a master, but the Lord hears his cries and feeds him in the desert' (A 76)

In these verses, and in many others, the animals are given a life of their own, and in the second case it it is made clear that the wolf is existing and being in a relationship with God that is totally isolated from Man. The Toad, too, is called 'the good creature of God, tho' his virtue is in the secret and his mention is not made' (i.e in the Bible - Smart was fully aware that not all his creatures were Biblical, though he says that 'all the creatures mentioned by Pliny are somewhere or other extant to the Glory of God').

At the end of fragment B2 we come to the only passage in this poem which can claim to be reasonably well-known. This is partly because it is popularly believed to be the only part which makes sense,and partly because it takes the form of an extraordinarily vivid description of the nature and movement of a cat. It is also radical to the thought of the poem.

5

'For I will consider my Cat Jeoffry'

From this opening we might be led to expect some extended Solomonic homily to follow, of the type we have already seen, so the following line comes as a complete surprise, until we see that it clinches the suspicions aroused by the crocodile, wolf and toad verses.

'For he is the creature of the living God, duly and daily serving him'

Smart has moved right away from contemporary belief, and here places a 'sub-human' creature, his cat, alongside man in the hierarchy of creation. In fact he sees Jeoffry as being a far more devout Christian than the majority of Smart's contemporaries managed to be (see Doctor Johnson, above):

'For at the first glance of the glory of God in the East he worships in his way.' (J.A. B2 699)

But how on earth does a cat perform an act of worship?

'For this is done by weaving his body seven times round with elegant quickness'

This line is the beginning of a highly stylised and idiosyncratic catalogue of the movements of the cat. Smart defines the nature of the cat by a process of synthesis: one simple detail is added to another and another, and this brings us closer and closer to a grasp of what we might call 'cat-ness':

'For thirdly he works it upon stretch with the forepaws extended.
For fourthly he sharpens his paws by wood.
For fifthly he washes himself.
For sixthly he rolls upon wash
For seventhly he fleas himself that he may not be interrupted upon the beat.
For eighthly he rubs himself against a post.' (JA 707- 712)

Eventually the collection of his external characteristics becomes an expression of his inner nature, or as Smart says elsewhere (JA C 80)

'For there is stupendous evidence of the communicating of God in externals.'

It is the exercise and fulfilment of that inner nature that is seen as being in some sense worship of God: God has 'blest him in the variety of his movements', so he worships in return '<u>in his way</u> by weaving his body seven times round with elegant quickness'. (JA B2 [illegible]-700)

The ideas that Smart uses here prompt me to make an unusual digression by comparing them with those of another religious poet who was writing a century later – Gerard

6

Manley Hopkins, who is 'always intent on examining that unified complex of characteristics which constitute the outward reflection of the inner nature of a thing - its individual essence...Very often this is for Hopkins the fundamental beauty which is tha active principle of all true being, the source of all true knowledge and delight - even of religious ecstacy: for speaking of a bluebell he says "I know the beauty of the Lord by it"...As a name for that 'individually-distinctive' form (made up of various sense data) which constitute that rich and revealing 'one-ness' of the natural object, he coined the word 'inscape'; and for that energy of being by which all things are upheld, for that natural(and ultimately supernatural) stress which determines an inscape and keeps it in being - for that he coined the word instress' [7]

Despite the anachronism involved I think we can accurately and conveniently use the terms 'inscape' and 'instress' in defining Smart's ideas: the 'inscape' of Jeoffry or any other created being is in its outward manifestations an expression of God's creation, and of his continued sustaining power, his spirit or 'instress' in creation. This is fully defined in the text if we combine verses B2 699-700(quoted above) with these two verses:

'For God has blessed him in the variety of his movements' (B2 765)

'For the divine spirit comes about his body to sustain it in compleat cat' (B2 744)

Elsewhere we find this example of inscape in a sort of shorthand form:

'For a man speaks HIMSELF from the crown of his head to the sole of his feet'

'For the LION roars HIMSELF compleat from head to tail' (JA B1 228-9)

Here the speaking and roaring are the outward expression of the 'inscape'- HIMSELF. The energy of 'instress' is derived from God's being, and it is therefore, according to Smart, a positive force of good:

'For he (Jeoffry) counteracts the powers of darkness by his electrical skin and glaring eyes'

'For he counteracts the devil, who is death, by brisking about the life'(B2 721-2)

That this power extends even to inanimate things is shown by the following verse, to my mind one of the most striking and vivid images in a poem which abounds in strange and brilliant insights:

7

'For the Flower glorifies God, and the root parries the adversary'(the devil)
(B2 499)

This superbly realized contrast between the hard active brilliance of 'parries' and the soft inert passivity of 'the root' forms a brilliant poetic definition of this difficult idea – that the mere quality of being is a precious and potent power.

But the power of 'instress', or spirit, extends even beyond vegetation into the realm of physical laws – the divine presence is total in every atom of creation:

'For it (the barometer) works by balancing according to the hold of the spirit'
(B1 216)

'For the centre (in this case meaning 'axis') is the hold of the spirit upon all the matter in hand' (B1 184)

'For the centripetal and centrifugal forces are GOD SUSTAINING and DIRECTING'
(B1 164)

'For the power of the WEDGE is direct as its altitude by communication of Almighty God' (B1 180)

All the previous arguments apply: just as cat Jeoffry 'worships in his way', and 'the Flower glorifies God', so too

'The ASCENT of VAPOURS is the return of thanksgiving from all humid bodies'.

17th June 1974.

Tonight is my last night in college and in a few hours I will be quitting Cambridge. I hardly know what to say at this stage, but feel ~~that~~ I ought to record it in some way. The fact of leaving has so far hardly touched me, but just now my head swam for a moment – it's all over and now the struggle begins. Goodbye Cambridge – it's been good and bad – mostly good.

Douglas graduated in 1974, and evidently left College on 18 June: '17th June 1974. Tonight is my last night in college and in a few hours I will be quitting Cambridge. ... Goodbye Cambridge – it's been good and bad – mostly good.'

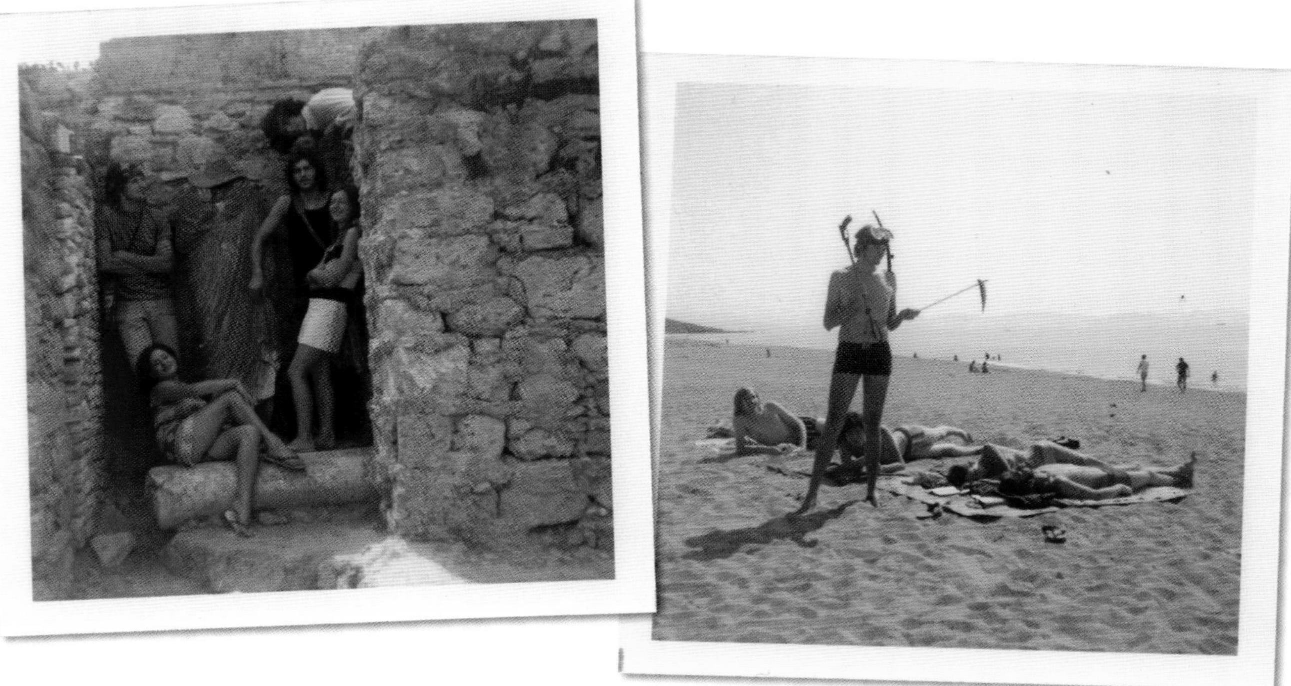

Of course, it wasn't all academia and societies. Douglas also found plenty of time to socialize. The photograph (top) shows him far left in black tie, with friends, at the St John's College May Ball in 1972 (pop legend Shakin' Stevens was on the bill for this event). And he ended his first year with a campervan road trip across Europe. These photographs capture him in Greece – standing far left in a statue alcove, and on the beach, with snorkel, mask, harpoon and fish!

I have at long last acquired a stereo set, and, having been around knocking ~~of~~ various on people's doors like the Spanish Inquisition and collecting up my record collection from the far corners of Cambridge I sat down, ~~and~~ clapped the phones to my head and rediscovered life.

For the last eighteen months I have been listening to odd snatches of my records on other people's systems in the gaps in other people's conversations - "Listen to this bit" "Which bit?" "The bit you just missed" "Oh. That ~~bit~~. Hows the play getting on?" "The bit that pivots and swings round the augmented triad like a planet at the extremity of its parabola and then sweeps slowly back into that bittersweet major seventh like a man who's just realized that his seventh attempt to leave his wife is going to fai

like all the others..." "Excuse me... there's Paul, must speak to him"... It was all rather like catching glimpses of an old and very dear girlfriend through the crowd and never quite getting to talk to her, - and no-one else even knows you've met before. Now I can get her in a corner all to myself and say what about it and she says God I thought you'd never ask, - and it all wells up inside in a warm flood of knowing that life can be good again - and it is.

It's almost too insensitive plunge in again straight away, so first I played through the new Solti recording of Ludwig's Ninth, - I revelled in the way he keeps you waiting for the drums in the second movement, fills you up, and just before you feel

I have at long last acquired a stereo, and, having been around knocking on various people's doors like the Spanish Inquisition and collecting up my record collection from the far corners of Cambridge I sat down, and clapped the phones to my head and rediscovered life.

For the last eighteen months I have been listening to odd snatches of my records on other people's systems in the gaps in other people's conversations. "Listen to this bit" "Which bit?" "The bit you just missed" "Oh. That. Hows the play getting on?" "The bit that pivots and swings round the augmented triad like a planet at the extremity of its parabola and then sweeps slowly back into that bittersweet major seventh like a man who's just realized that his seventh attempt to leave his wife is going to fail like all the others..." "Excuse me... there's Paul, must speak to him..." It was all rather like catching glimpses of an old and very dear girlfriend through the crowd and never quite getting to talk to her, – and no-one else even knows you've met before. Now I can get her in a corner all to myself and say what about it and she says God I thought you'd never ask, and it all wells up inside in a warm flood of knowing that life can be good again – and it is.

Music was a huge part of Douglas's life and – as the later evidence of his preoccupation with gadgetry will show – he was particularly intrigued by sound equipment. It's perhaps not surprising, then, that he was delighted when he finally owned his own record deck and no longer had to rely on other students to listen to his precious vinyl collection.

DOUGLAS ADAMS

I'm a serious person.

I care about...serious things.

Jokes about things that matter,

And people with the guts to make them.

But frivolously though,....I care about the standard of debating, I care about participation in debates, I care about facilities. I do not care about Union politics, there are enough Union politicians to care for that. I simply want to see the Union Society providing the best possible services for the greatest possible number of people, bearing in mind that the Union's principal function is to be a debating forum.

Vote for Douglas Adams,
your serious standing committee
candidate.

ARS EST CELARE ARTEM

Footlights Dramatic Club

This is to certify that D. N. ADAMS *of* St John's *is an official member of Footlights*

Secretary

Members Signature Douglas Adams

Nº 4151 A

This certifies that MR D.N. ADAMS of ST. JOHN'S College is a Life Member of the Cambridge Union Society.

Date 5/10/71

R. F. THOMPSON
Chief Clerk

This card is not transferable

Signature Douglas Adams

Douglas went up to Cambridge in late 1971 and made a beeline for Footlights, where his hero John Cleese and many others had honed their comedy skills. The club didn't accept direct applications, but committee member Simon Jones (later to create the role of Arthur Dent in *Hitchhiker's Guide*) recognized Douglas had something to offer and elected him to membership in February 1972. But Footlights wasn't all: Douglas plunged into everything that the extracurricular student life had to offer. He joined the Student Union and CULES (a drama club), served on committees, acted in plays and wrote for student magazines.

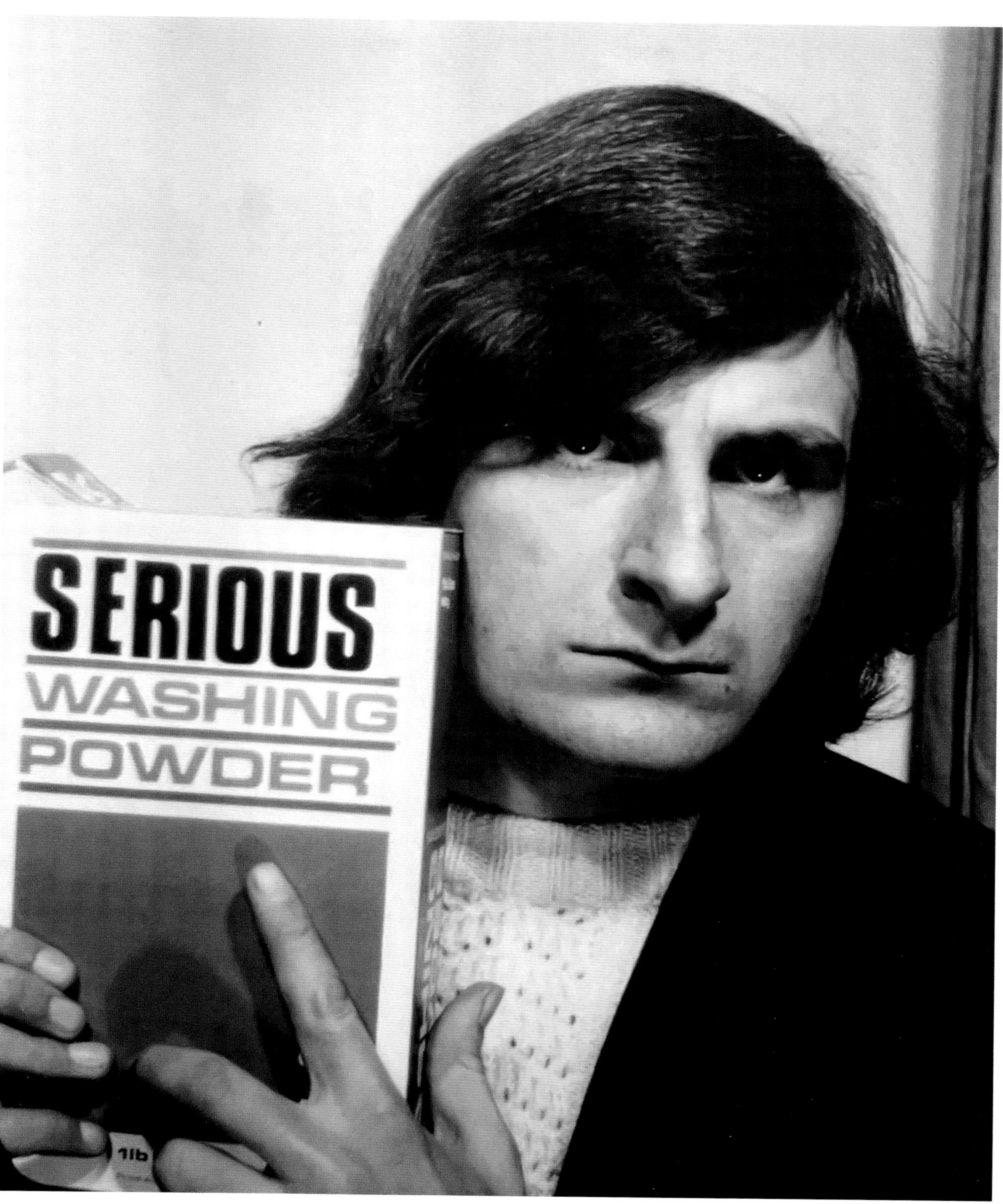

Douglas used this image – himself holding a mocked-up box of a fictional 'Serious' washing powder – to promote his 'serious' candidacy for the Student Union's standing committee (opposite).

INDEPENDENT THEATRE presents

THE RIVALS by Richard Brinsley Sheridan

Cast

Coachman ....Mike Thomas
Fag ....Griff Rhys - Jones
Lydia Languish ....Sue Limb
Lucy ....Eve Box - Grainger
Mrs Malaprop ....Pam Scobie
Sir Anthony Absolute ....Jeremy Browne
Jack Absolute ....Robin Rogers
Faulkland ....Crispin Thomas
Julia ....Anne Simcocks
Acres .... Jonathan Brock
Boy ....Craig Bartholomew
Sir Lucius O'Trigger ....Douglas Adams
David ....Mike Thomas

Directors ....Sue Limb and Roy Porter
Désigner ....Tim Foster
Lighting Designer ....Martin Standley
Stage Manager ....Paul Brocklehurst
Assisted by ....Paul Bolt, George Gittens, Katy Henkel,
Brian McCormick, Dave Packer,Tony Randall
First Electrician ....Nigel Bragg
Props ....Di Collyer
Wardrobe ....Frances Matthews, Meredith Lloyd-Evans
Make up ....Ursula Scott
Music ...........................J.C.Bach, played by Howard Goodison
Movement and Style ....Frank Ries, after the principles of
Jean-Georges Noverre (1727 - 1809)
Poster Design ....Charles Maude
Publicity ....Niobe Hopkins, Martin Sandbrook
Photographs ....Nigel Luckhurst
Production Manager ....Bob Hathaway
Thanks to: Gabor Cossa, Kings St. Antiques, The University A[illegible]s H[illegible]el,
Roger Hartill, Pete Mathers, Peter Halmer, Simon Scutt

For the A.D.C.

Licensee .........................G.B.Skelsey, M.A.
Resident Stage Manager ....Paul Davidson
Chief Electrician ....Martin Standley
NO SMOKING IN THE AUDITORIUM
Theatres Act 1968 Presenters ....Sue Limb and Roy Port[illegible]
There will be one interval of 15 minutes

A 'smoker' or 'smoking concert' was an antiquated title for an evening of stand-up, sketch comedy and music. Academics by day and performers by night, the students listed in the crudely mimeographed programmes (above and opposite) include names destined to become famous – among them, producer John Lloyd, chat-show host Clive Anderson, writer Sue Limb, and actors Geoff McGivern, Griff Rhys Jones and Rory McGrath.

L.S.O. IN FLAMES 17·xi·72.

–a smoking concert chaired by Sue Limb and Jeremy Browne.

FIRST HALF.

	Sketch	Performers
1	Sweets From Strangers (Trotter/Rowley)	Allen, George Gittens, Lloyd-Evans, Benton, Browne, Rowley.
2	Enoch Enoch (Levene)	Levene.
3	Police To Meet You (W. Adams/Smith)	W. Adams, Smith.
4	The Serious Sketch (D. Adams)	D. Adams.
5	Teenagers (Canter)	Dirkin, Canter.
6	Canteen Stakes (Lloyd/Burridge)	Lloyd.
7	Christmas Quarrel (Downes/Taylor)	Downes, Taylor.
8	The Missing Punchline (Young)	Young.
9	It's A Rip-Off (Jennens/Parry)	Jennens, Limb, Jonathan Hetreed, Browne, Parry.
10	Sonnet (Trotter/Rowley)	Allen.
11	Messing About In The River (David Moss)	David Moss.
12	Modern Studies (Browne)	Limb, Browne.
13	Diary Of A Lunatic (Lloyd)	Lloyd.
14	Famous Five (Holmes)	Limb, Allen, Fairhead, Holmes, Lloyd, Burridge, Browne.
15	Cowes (Benton)	Benton.
16	Necrophilia (Taylor/Rowley)	Downes and the Diggers, Rowley.

SECOND HALF

	Sketch	Performers
17	Which Way? (Browne)	Allen, Browne and the Boys Next Door, Hirst.
18	The Manager (Canter)	Canter.

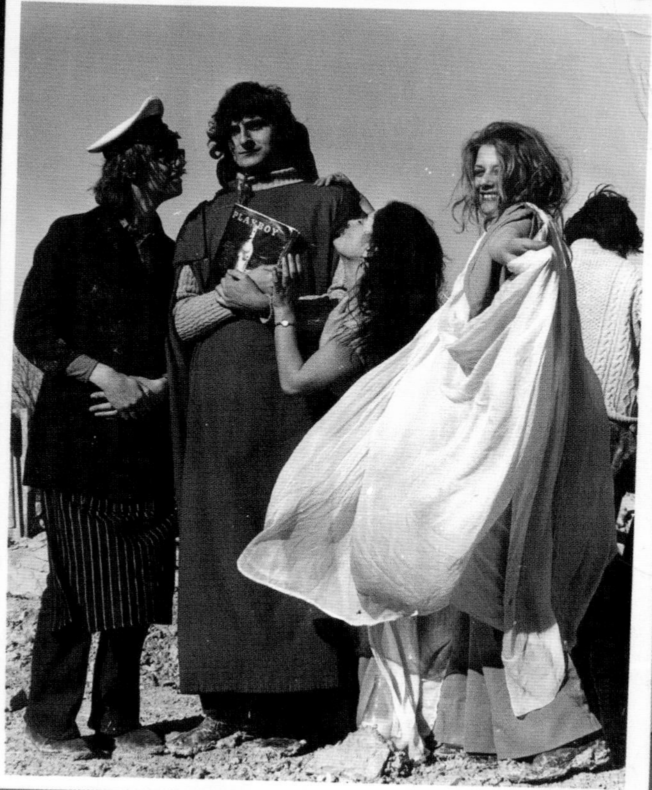

These photographs are just highlights from Douglas's acting exploits at university. Left shows him in 1973 playing Lucius O'Trigger in Sheridan's *The Rivals* (1973). According to the *Guardian*'s theatre critic Michael Grosvenor Myer, Douglas made this truculent character 'believable, resisting the temptation to caricature'. Next to it is a photograph of Douglas on location for *Pick Up a Milkman*, a spoof Ken Russell film and a celebrated contribution to the May Week revue *Norman Ruins* in 1972.

Mr. Benton's nostrils by Wig Creations
Miss Limb's wig by Percy Thrower
Flowers by Request

122 WOODSFORD SQUARE
ADDISON ROAD
LONDON, W. 14.

8th June, 1972.

Dear Douglas, Nick and Paul,

I really do apologize for not replying before to your invitation, but I have literally not answered a letter for some four weeks, as life has been so over-poweringly hectic that I have not been able to find a spare half day to get my teeth into the enormous pile.

However, I started on it this morning and found your invitation of exactly one month ago, and offer my sincerest apologies for not replying before, and also for failing to provide the required crate.

Please forgive me, and many thanks for asking me.

Best wishes,

JOHN CLEESE.

Douglas and friends boldly invited star of *Monty Python* (and former Footlights member) John Cleese to come and see their show *Norman Ruins* in June 1972, for which they received a polite, written late apology (above). A chance meeting with Cleese a year or so later, though, prompted Douglas to ask him for an interview for the student newspaper *Varsity*, which Cleese accepted.

Dear Sue,

I've been trying desperately to get in touch with you this evening.

I've had a long standing arrangement to interview John Cleese ~~for~~ this term for some paper. I was in touch with him this evening and he offered to be available tomorrow (Friday) or not again for a few weeks. I tried to get in touch with you to ask for a dispensation but was not able to find you, so eventually phoned back and said O.K. I do hope very much that this doesn't muck you about – I was quite prepared to put it off if you asked me, but I didn't want to let the opportunity pass without a try.

I hope my absence won't be disastrous, and I'm heartily sorry for the inconvenience

with love,

Douglas.

Dear Sue

I've been trying desperately to get in touch with you this evening. I've had a long standing arrangement to interview John Cleese this term for some paper. I was in touch with him this evening and he offered to be available tomorrow (Friday) or not again for a few weeks. I tried to get in touch with you to ask for a dispensation but was not able to find you, so eventually phoned back and said O.K. I do hope very much that this doesn't muck you about – I was quite prepared to put it off if you asked me, but I didn't want to let the opportunity pass without a try.

I hope my absence won't be disastrous, and I'm heartily sorry for the inconvenience

With love,

Douglas

Typically, the date and time of John Cleese's availability for interview clashed with one of Douglas's rehearsal commitments. This is a letter he sent to writer and producer Sue Limb to ask (somewhat retrospectively, and not for want of trying otherwise) for her permission to be excused.

FRUTTIN' IN STREATHAM

Impossible without: oxygen, lungs, sweat glands, food, sweat glands, the reproductive system, several pieces of paper, a certain sum of money - and us, without whom the cast would have been different.

CAST:
Martin Smith - played by - DOUGLAS ADAMS
Stefanie Singer - played by - MARTIN SMITH
Rachel Hood - played by - WILL ADAMS
Will Adams - played by - STEFANIE SINGER
Douglas Adams - played by - RACHEL HOOD

SCRIPTS by: Adams - Smith - Adams

ADDITIONAL MATERIAL from: John Parry, Jon Canter, Jerry Brown, John Cleese

We're not certain who the pianist is. Ask him after the show. He'll probably say yes.

Thanks to Jim Besley and John Fassnidge for turning electricity into noise and light.

The house was managed by Nick Burton. Look around for him, he'll be the one who isn't laughing.
The stage will be managed.

If you don't enjoy this revue, you certainly won't enjoy 'A BIG HAND ON YOUR OPENING' at Trinity Theatre - 14th & 15th June (twice nightly).

'EVERY PACKET CARRIES A GOVERNMENT HEALTH WARNING'
The Footlights Revue at the Arts Theatre, which is on for ages and ages.

By the time you've read the opposite page you'll probably be feeling restive and wondering when the show will start. Well it should start at the exact moment that you read the first word of the next sentence. If it hasn't started yet, you're reading too fast. If it still hasn't started you're reading much too fast, and we can recommend our own book 'How to Impair Your Reading Ability', written and published by Adams-Smith-Adams. With the aid of this slim volume you will find that your reading powers shrink to practically nothing within a very short space of time. The more you read the slower you get. Theoretically you will never get to the end which makes it the best value book you will ever have bought. It may be that you are already familiar with this work and are still struggling with the first sentence of this programme, in which case this particular bit is not aimed specifically at you as you will probably never get to read this far, and you will be wondering what it is on this side of the page that is engrossing everyone around you - that is, assuming the show hasn't started yet, which, we must admit, it probably hasn't. We will however be ready very soon, so we suggest that you go back to the top of the page and start reading it again, only slower this time. Should you get bored there's another bit you can read on the back of the programme.

AN ADAMS*SMITH*ADAMS PRODUCTION PRESENTED BY LADY MARGARET AND INDEPENDENT THEATRE

TEDIOUS PERSONAL TRIVIA

WILL ADAMS sports a head which he got as a free gift with several gallons of petrol. It's interior is abysmal chaos and his ears are held on to it with bacon rind. His favourite colour is beyond the visible light spectrum and his hobby consists of dropping toe nail cuttings down organ pipes.

MARTIN SMITH is extremely stupid, but not one of your ordinary run of the mill idiots because he often talks to lizards and calls them soft names. His favourite colour may turn out to be either red or green when he has learnt to distinguish between them, and he is in no way connected with the Poulson affair.

DOUGLAS ADAMS is a complete idiot, and if he wanted to shoot his brains out he would have to aim very carefully. He likes linoleum and hopes to set up a barber shop for cats.
He quite likes some people, but on the whole prefers things.
He dislikes most colours pretty much, but will admit to a slight leaning towards British Paint Standard 2033 when pushed very hard.

MARGARET THOMAS is getting fed up with the improper advances that are continually made to her by the other three, all of whom are deeply and tragically in love with her. They are often to be seen offering her tokens of their affection - dried cockroaches tied up in ribbon, bits of paper smeared with gum and back copies of the Farmer and Stockbreeder.
On a clear day it is just possible to discern which of the three she detests the most.

Cast in the order which will cause the least argument:

WILL ADAMS
MARTIN SMITH
DOUGLAS ADAMS
MARGARET THOMAS

Cast in a slightly more provocative order:

MARGARET THOMAS
DOUGLAS ADAMS
MARTIN SMITH
WILL ADAMS

Cast in the sort of order that leads to civil war:

DOUGLAS ADAMS
MARGARET THOMAS
WILL ADAMS
MARTIN SMITH

STAGE MANAGER: A friend of somebody's sister.

HOUSE MANAGER: Kevin McT.

Publicity Machines: Geoff 'Angst' McGivern, Giles Raymond

Photos: Mike Cotton

Sound: John Fassnidge
Light: Jim Besley

Violin: Andy Thurston
Someone else: A.N.Other

Director: Tony Root
Words and Music: Adams Smith Adams.
Additional Material: John Lloyd.
Script advice: Otto
Mr Adams' (D) pelvis by Yeovil District Hospital
The shape of Mr Smith's feet by Start-Rite
Mr Adams' (W) disposition by Yeast-Vite

Douglas joined his friends Martin Smith and Will Adams in a comedy writer-performer troupe called Adams-Smith-Adams for sketch shows, including *Several Poor Players Strutting and Fretting* in summer 1973 (yellow programme, top), and *A Patter of Tiny Minds* (bottom) in November of the same year.

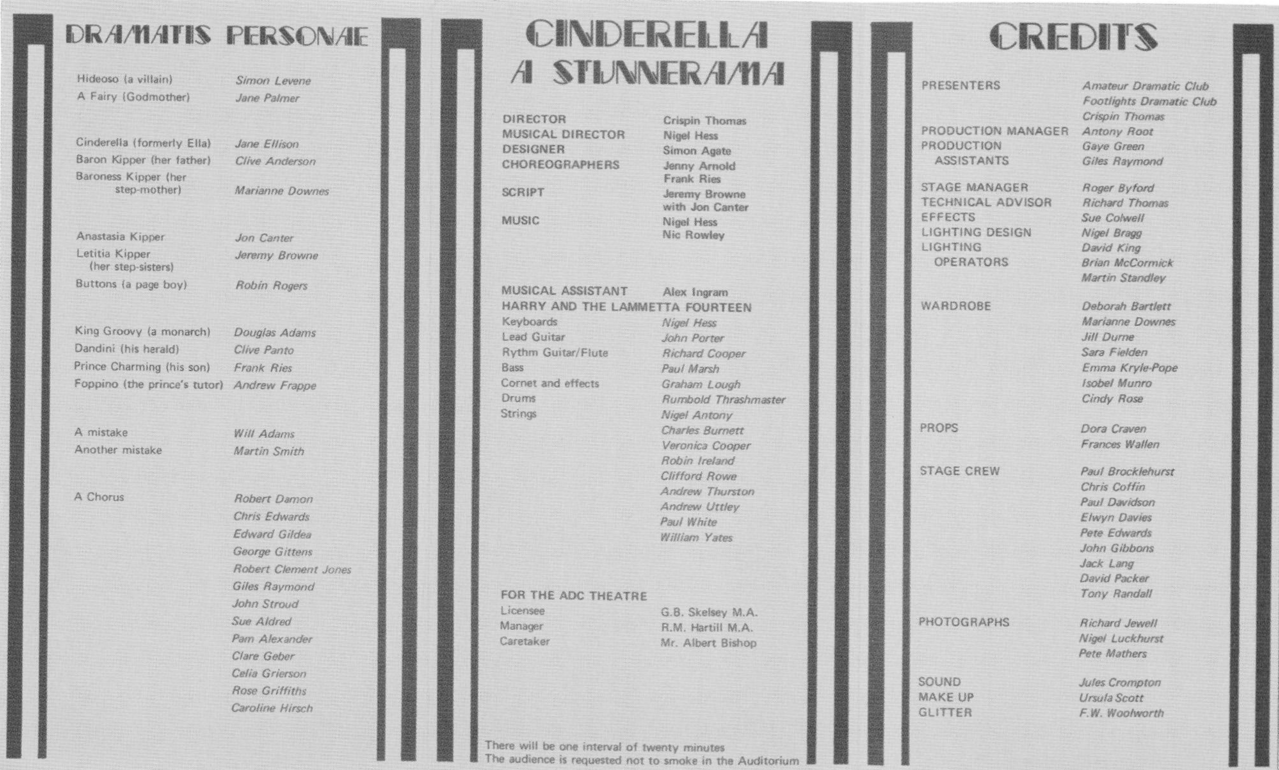

DRAMATIS PERSONAE

Hideoso (a villain)	*Simon Levene*
A Fairy (Godmother)	*Jane Palmer*
Cinderella (formerly Ella)	*Jane Ellison*
Baron Kipper (her father)	*Clive Anderson*
Baroness Kipper (her step-mother)	*Marianne Downes*
Anastasia Kipper	*Jon Canter*
Letitia Kipper (her step-sisters)	*Jeremy Browne*
Buttons (a page boy)	*Robin Rogers*
King Groovy (a monarch)	*Douglas Adams*
Dandini (his herald)	*Clive Panto*
Prince Charming (his son)	*Frank Ries*
Foppino (the prince's tutor)	*Andrew Frappe*
A mistake	*Will Adams*
Another mistake	*Martin Smith*
A Chorus	*Robert Damon* *Chris Edwards* *Edward Gildea* *George Gittens* *Robert Clement Jones* *Giles Raymond* *John Stroud* *Sue Aldred* *Pam Alexander* *Clare Geber* *Celia Grierson* *Rose Griffiths* *Caroline Hirsch*

CINDERELLA
A STUNNERAMA

DIRECTOR	Crispin Thomas
MUSICAL DIRECTOR	Nigel Hess
DESIGNER	Simon Agate
CHOREOGRAPHERS	Jenny Arnold Frank Ries
SCRIPT	Jeremy Browne with Jon Canter
MUSIC	Nigel Hess Nic Rowley
MUSICAL ASSISTANT	Alex Ingram

HARRY AND THE LAMMETTA FOURTEEN

Keyboards	*Nigel Hess*
Lead Guitar	*John Porter*
Rythm Guitar/Flute	*Richard Cooper*
Bass	*Paul Marsh*
Cornet and effects	*Graham Lough*
Drums	*Rumbold Thrashmaster*
Strings	*Nigel Antony* *Charles Burnett* *Veronica Cooper* *Robin Ireland* *Clifford Rowe* *Andrew Thurston* *Andrew Uttley* *Paul White* *William Yates*

FOR THE ADC THEATRE

Licensee	G.B. Skelsey M.A.
Manager	R.M. Hartill M.A.
Caretaker	Mr. Albert Bishop

There will be one interval of twenty minutes
The audience is requested not to smoke in the Auditorium

CREDITS

PRESENTERS	*Amateur Dramatic Club* *Footlights Dramatic Club* *Crispin Thomas*
PRODUCTION MANAGER	*Antony Root*
PRODUCTION ASSISTANTS	*Gaye Green* *Giles Raymond*
STAGE MANAGER	*Roger Byford*
TECHNICAL ADVISOR	*Richard Thomas*
EFFECTS	*Sue Colwell*
LIGHTING DESIGN	*Nigel Bragg*
LIGHTING OPERATORS	*David King* *Brian McCormick* *Martin Standley*
WARDROBE	*Deborah Bartlett* *Marianne Downes* *Jill Durne* *Sara Fielden* *Emma Kryle-Pope* *Isobel Munro* *Cindy Rose*
PROPS	*Dora Craven* *Frances Wallen*
STAGE CREW	*Paul Brocklehurst* *Chris Coffin* *Paul Davidson* *Elwyn Davies* *Pete Edwards* *John Gibbons* *Jack Lang* *David Packer* *Tony Randall*
PHOTOGRAPHS	*Richard Jewell* *Nigel Luckhurst* *Pete Mathers*
SOUND	*Jules Crompton*
MAKE UP	*Ursula Scott*
GLITTER	*F.W. Woolworth*

Douglas took to the stage as King Groovy (top) in the Footlights Christmas pantomime *Cinderella* in 1973. The show came complete with gatefold programme (bottom) reproduced on unmissable yellow paper. Comedy writer and broadcaster (and former barrister) Clive Anderson was also among the cast – playing Baron Kipper, Cinderella's hapless father.

But I like bacon!

DOUGLAS ADAMS makes a futile attempt to join the Chosen Race.

During the course of the frivolous backchat in which it is my wont to indulge when backstage, I was, as usual, holding forth in vulnerably imitable fashion, when a friend turned to me and said: "You're dying to be Jewish aren't you?"

Perhaps I had better explain that I had been rabbiting on about the internal structure of my nose, which, as those acquainted with me will realise, is no small matter. Nasal dimensions apart, I have this thing about belonging to persecuted minorities. Anyone in Cambridge who isn't a Jew belongs to a persecuted minority, as any jittering member of the Gentile ghettoes will tell you. I have, I must admit, been studying how I might cross the great semitic barrier and reach the well known Promised Land. One night on impulse I decided to try my hand at dividing the waters of the Cam, Red Sea style, without any perceptible success. Having spent a frustrating hour trying to persuade myself that I was responsible for the odd ripple or two, and finding that their author was in fact a duck, I gave up and walked across St. John's Old Bridge with a distinct feeling of anti-climax. Omnipotence is not my scene.

My golden goal is to achieve membership of that celebrated institution, the Cambridge Jewish Society. That requires, ethnic considerations apart, the payment of the subscription which is fixed at the alarmingly appropriate level of one pound eighty seven and a half new pence. Presumably the rationale behind this figure is that if they charged one pound eighty seven, they couldn't run the society at a profit, and that if they charged one pound eighty eight, none of the Jews would join.

Needless to say, some of my best friends are Jewish, but that really doesn't get me anything, it simply exacerbates an already fraught situation. It gets really heavy about Passover time. There's me standing outside my door with a brush in one hand and a bucket of blood in the other, splattering the door posts and daubing the lintel like a man possessed, there's my room mate, pressed into unwilling service trying desperately to extract the yeast from a Tyler's loaf, and there's the Angel of Death, falling around completely crippled with laughter, which is one way to keep him occupied.

And finally, in a last desperate bid for membership of the chosen race, let me say what may be obvious, that I am very hot on circumlocution, at least I <u>think</u> that's what the Doctor said.

Douglas Adams

Douglas flexed his writing skills with reviews of his friends' dramatic presentations and other amusing items. 'But I like bacon' came from a short-lived student rag called *OHO!* (subtitled *The Cambridge Lampoon* after its more famous Harvard namesake, *The Harvard Lampoon*). The schoolboy talent Douglas had demonstrated for art was exercised in his doodles, too – this self portrait (left) appears on the cover of one of his notebooks.

With the Footlights club rooms in Falcon Yard off Petty Cury under threat from the property developers, Douglas addressed the problem in this typed article (opposite).

What's so funny about architecture?

I am informed by those I employ to read the University press for me that someone has thought of a new college, which will not only combine two entirely different types of people inside its walls but also stands a good chance of being called Sherrington College. I have never heard of anyone called Sherrington, and I wonder whether he is either some learned old scholar whose name is mentioned in low whispers in the corridors of Caius, or whether he is merely the previous owner of a large sum of money. Either way, it seems that the council has plans for the proposed site. It feels that a car park is more in line with the image of modern streamlined Cambridge. It has pointed out accurately if insensitively, that at the moment there are more Colleges than car parks in Cambridge. I am assured that this new construction would be called 'Municipal Car Park, Cambridge', and that it will have more lavatories than the whole of second court St. John's put together. I am a little hazy as to the identity of Municipal. Perhaps he is a benefactor who hopes that even if his son doesn't get into the University, then at least he'll be assured of a job. Perhaps the name is an ingenious pun on the word 'munificent' a la Auric Gold-finger. Perhaps the council is having a little joke at the expense of Cambridge architects, who knows? In fairness to the council it should be remembered that a car park will form a far more durable monument to the 20th century than a college. It will prove particularly useful in a few years time when the tourists flock in to inspect the ruins of Fitzwilliam, and when Spike Milligan brings a BBC camera crew down to do a programme on New Court Christ's. Other exciting excursions for the thrill-hungry tourists will include a tour of A staircase Cripps by bathyscape and a trip to New Hall to see exactly why a hydraulic ram is needed to force the food down the girls' throats.

Anyway, a new college will be built somewhere, God Bless her and all who fail in her. Whoever Sherrington is I'm glad that it will be called after him, even if a lot of Americans will turn up expecting to find one of their fine hotels (they won't be put off by the architecture I bet). I'm glad because it shows a certain originality on the part of whichever sub-committee it is that is responsible for naming new colleges. They really surpassed themselves with 'New Hall', an ingeniously subtle variation on 'New College' which Oxford in its learned and imaginative wisdom had already thought of. I was a little worried that after pulling off that particular christening coup, they might sit back on their laurels and call the college 'Another New Hall/College'. One understands the dilemma: at least I do. The 'Religious Scholar's Phrase Book' has been exhausted. Having had Jesus, St. John's, Trinity and the rest the only possibilities that spring to mind are God College and Virgin Mary College, both of which might be controversial for different reasons. None of today's political leaders really strike anyone as eponymous characters. If it was called Heath College it would get blown up, and if it was called Wilson College it would never get built. In fact any well known character, religious, political or cultural would be deemed wildly unsuitable or Fascist by some part of the community. The Kennedy charisma has become a little tarnished by those whose job it is to tarnish charismas, and anyway, half the world is named after him already; Eliot was American, Cleese rhymes with Caius, and Jagger College just doesn't sound right. I can't remember who discovered the double helix, which is good enough reason for excluding them anyway, and Einstein was German and possibly wrong into the bargain. So it seems that Sherrington is the man for the job, and I hope he does it well. It seems rather a pity that the foundations of the buildings will be too shallow, and that all the wiring will be wrong, and that the floors will warp and the paint will peel, and the walls will crack and that the rooms will be like goldfish bowls, open to everyone's gaze. It is more than likely that the drains will be entirely filled with concrete just so that people won't notice that some bright spark had connected them to the fresh water supply. The architect's coven will howl and wail with devilish delight as it holds its annual meeting at midnight under a full moon somewhere on the fens. The architects will dance demonaically round the pyre of architectural textbooks. By 1997 all the books ever written about architectural technology will have been destroyed in this way, and all the little architects will be free to work their devilish, destructive wiles on us unhampered by science or morality. Never mind. According to Paul Erlich we'll be dead by 1999, so a few mad architects will seem relatively unimportant. Perhaps we'd be better off with a car park.

Any incorrect factual information in this article is purely a product of my overwrought imagination. I've just been struck on the head by a piece of crumbling Cripps masonry.

Douglas Adams

CAMBRIDGE UNION SOCIETY

MICHAELMAS TERM, 1973

NINTH DEBATE

THURSDAY, 22nd NOVEMBER, 1973 8.15 p.m.

"This House would rather have lived a hundred years ago"

Proposed by ~~MR. DAVID BEAN, Trinity Hall~~ Douglas Adams, St. John's.

Opposed by MR. DAVID CONDIT, Trinity College and MR. JOHN MEARS, St. John's College.

MR. KEITH JEFFERY, St. John's College.

MR. ROLAND THOMPSON, Chief Clerk.

MR. GRAHAM HILL.

SIR JOHN DONALDSON, President, National Industrial Relations Court.

MR. NICHOLAS FAIRBAIRN.

MR. CHRIS TOOKEY, Ex-President, Oxford Union.

Tellers:

FOR THE AYES		FOR THE NOES
	Floor:	
MR. JOHN HILLS, St. John's College		MR. PETER BAZALGETTE, Fitzwilliam College
	Balcony:	

Trinity College
22nd November, 1973

MARK GOYDER
President

THE UNION

LENT TERM, 1973

NINTH DEBATE

MONDAY, 5th MARCH, 1973 8.00 p.m.

"This House is Sated, Saturated, but not Satisfied"

Proposed by MR. DOUGLAS ADAMS, St. John's College.

Opposed by MESSRS. MARTIN (Grin and bare it) SMITH and WILL ADAMS.

MR. KEITH JEFFERY, St. John's College, will speak third, from the cross-benches.

MR. JACK TREVOR-STOREY, of 'The Guardian,' will speak fourth.

MR. BENNY GREEN, of 'Punch' and 'The Spectator,' will speak fifth.

MR. CHRISTIE DAVIES, Emmanuel College, ex-President, will speak sixth.

Tellers:

FOR THE AYES	*Floor:*	FOR THE NOES

Trinity College.
5th March, 1973

ANDREW OPPENHEIMER
President

SATISFACTION GUARANTEED.

This House is Sated, Saturated, but not satisfied.

Proposed by Mr Douglas Adams, St John's College.
Opposed by Mr Martin (Grin and ~~bare~~ it) Smith
and Mr Willy Wonty Adams (no relation)
of Fitzwilliam College
~~Mr Jack Trevor-Storey of the Guardian will speak~~
Mr Keith Jeffery of St Johns will speak third, from
the cross benches.
Mr Jack Trevor-Story will speak fourth,
Mr Benny Green of the Spectator and Punch will
speak fifth.

A favourite pastime for Douglas was participating in the debates held at the Student Union building, which often attracted some illustrious guest speakers. The subjects proposed ranged from newsworthy topics such as hijacking, censorship, and whether Britain should be joining the European Union, to more frivolous notions like whether 'This house makes me laugh'. Douglas's archive suggests he spoke often, provoking new students with a deliberately patronizing welcome and self-deprecatingly questioning his own popularity.

He once impressed his audience and friends alike by casually arriving at the debate in a dressing gown and eating a bowl of cornflakes. In fact, his notes betray the reality that this charade was scripted in advance (opposite).

Walk in late with a bowl of cereal in my hand.

Well, where was I?. Oh yes. Mr Acting president ....is wearing a very fetching creation , made lovdngly from boiled eel skins by Mr David StQ Randall in his fashion suite..., I'm sorry , in his sweet fashionat his home in Jubilee Gardens. The eels were caught and prepared by Mr Randall, who stuffed them with chicken liver, threw bricks at them to tenderise their texture, and also stop them being so familiar, and eventually hammerered them out with some of his oldest newspaper cuttings - he was still writing drivel back in the stone age - oh, how I remember those halcyon days on the Neanderthal Weekly - the scoop we had when some freak discovered the wheel and we were able to start acourt and circular coloumn. Yes after the Neanderthal weekly everything else is just life. That is, until this evening. I was passing the Union, and was just about to see my doctor about it when when this vehicle suddenly screeches to halt beside me, and hand flies out to grab me, and before I knew we tearing down the street knocking down pederasts like ~~penguins~~ so many penguins, strange people one sees in Cambridge. Anyway ther wasn't much room on this bicycle as I was quick to point out. Also, I was still eating my cereal, and a chap doesn't like being abducted on a bicycle in the middle of a late breakfast. Well not a Cambridge chappie at least. So I demanded to know ~~what it was~~ to what it was I owed this unaccustomed pleasure, and he said 'never did'. Well we cleared up that little bother and he said, are you the one who spoke in the Union last week. I had to admit it. I said yes, are you the one who laughed? He said we need you once again, the Union wants blood. I mentioned that I wasn't registered donor, and he just laughed - I remember he laughed last week. He then grabbed me by the neck, and dragged me here screaming and kicking. What he had to scream about I don't know. Wearily I went along, and at his bidding wandered into your midst, still clutching my cereal bowl, made a few disparaging remarks about Mr Kenyon's dinner suit, Mr Randal, and eels and startd telling all these wierd people a pack of lies to pass the time. Which brings me to the present moment with rather an uncomfortable bump, proposing the motion, this house would speak in an emergency, and feeling rather the other way inclined. But what a prospect, what power. Here I am standing up in frontof hundreds of people hanging from my evry word - its all right I'll cut you down later. What an opportunity, as Kenneth Tynan once said. *But whilst you're listening - no, don't stop, I like it*

I havesomething very important to say, which will be of deep concern to everyone of you. Recent, as yet unpublished research has revealed to us that the Union is in fact a deep sea squid. This is a serious state of affairs and it has been known to the standing commoittee now for a period of several weeks, but I must take them to task for having done nothing about it so far. It came as a sevre shock to them I will admit, but this can no longer be accepted as a vindication of the present state of oblivious inaction.

How are we to face this situation? What we need, and what we must unflaggingly demand of the committee is a sufficient and continuous supply of molluscs crustacea and plankta. This si no peripheral issue., it is vital to the well beig of the union if it is to survive as a major sub aquatic power, indeed if it is to continue to live, I have no more affection for giant cephalopods than the next man, but I feel that thevimportance ofvthis matter cannot be ovrstressed, for a great multitude of hitherto undicussed problems must be faced.

Join me in a length of this milky afternoon
~~Swat that passing fly~~
~~Lie down here beside me~~
I've watched it for some hours, I think it's going soon

It seems that days like this are very hard to come by

And I can't help but wonder
How many more there'll be
And I hope to God ~~that~~ this one's not
The last we're going to see

I thought I saw that third cloud take a death wish from the air

Prapt its lining is corroded you find silver there
For what there was has long ago been stolen
And I wish good joy to those who took it
I hope it suits them fine
I hope it gives them love enough
Because they won't be getting mine.

Engines take us backward,
DOT's a post
I'm worried about our afternoon
They're going with the rest.

Poem

~~Of man's first disobedience~~
~~A very culpable offence~~
~~I'm told by those who ought to know~~
~~who've studied it~~

~~Of man's first disobedience and the fruit,~~
~~A lofty theme and one that might well suit~~
~~For yet another long and boring book~~
~~Of pentametric verse by wit forsook.~~

" Sing heavenly muse if you feel that you must
Whilst I glue together the pen that I've bust
But if you don't stop it when I'm ready to write
I can see that we're in for a hell of a night
I wish you would learn that enough is enough
~~If you don't don't~~
It's very distracting, so I'm going to get tough
If you don't stop this instant, and let a man think
I'm likely to heave a bottle of ink
All over your gently fluttering wings"
– But still she sits and bloody well sings

Douglas's notebooks offer a smattering of his poetry and lyrics, shown over the following pages. Sometimes the muse arrived with humour, at other times with thought-provoking lyricism, and occasionally his works were simply born of some apparent despair.

I was walking down the street today
Or maybe it was yesterday
It may in fact have been last week
Yes, it ~~was~~ was probably last week.

Well I was walking down the street
When who on earth should I chance to meet
Who on earth ~~should~~ did I meet ~~I say~~ that day
~~Actually it was quite possibly yesterday~~
Which was either yesterday or the day before yesterday

Well it wasn't very long ago
And one doesn't really need to know
Precisely when it all occurred
Though it might have been on February the third

On Feb the third I was on the street
Well not all of me but just my feet
I was walking along at any rate...
No I'm still not right about that date.

Yes now I remember the day I mean
It was yesterday at two fifteen
No, three fifteen two weeks ago
I really would quite like to know
So that next time I can get on
with the interesting bit.

~~Well it doesn't really matter when~~
~~I've said it once and I'll say it again~~
~~No in fact I've said twice~~
~~By the end of the verse I'll have said it thrice~~

Day-Return to King's Cross.

The adverts change like city seasons,
Fresh as spring or dead as leaves;
They catch at fingers and fall again
And tempt and pull and try to please.
You leap and they are gone,
Snatch at a reflection of a figure
Who is not there, or even standing behind you.
Your dead weight bumps a bed,
And plate glass bumps your forehead.

Down in the underground: fresco ads.
In the dark recesses of hope grow secret pleasures.
Is it true? Your mind glances and peers around?
In this place where believings creep upon you,
Behind your eyes which look disinterestedly down the line.

But furtive hopes, safe and dark and smoky
Congeal in the cold light of London.
And hope cannot be entertained
Like a friend one has for tea,
You must hang yourself upon him
Like offerings on a tree.

What tree is there in London?
Only some undergrowth in the Caledonian Road,
Some dull and brittle leaves ~~that~~
That cling to twigs kicked round and scraped upon the dust.

Return and live in Cambridge,
A very dull fool, trying to be wise.

Douglas Adams

The Song of the Dancing Rhino

Keightley & Adams

I once loved a rhinocerous,
Preposterous though that may sound.
Sweet little neat little nocerous,
O the joy of the love we found.

She won the hearts of the lot of us
As she danced in the dew strewn dawn ?
With the nimble little steps of my nocerous
Through the mists of a pink spring dawn.

Gravity she spurned, pirouetting as she turned
Perfection in her steps beyond improvement
Gliding like a dove in the rhythm of her love
A miracle of grace and balanced movement.

She skipped up to where we were picnicking
The belle of the nocerous heard.
And deposited amongst us a sickening
Hundredweight of nocerous turd.

But death even takes a rhinocerous
And I stand here with tears in my eyes.
It's not only grief for my nocerous
But the powerful smell and the flies.

Yes how I loved that rhinocerous
In the very first bloom of my youth
But fidelity's hard for a lot of us -
Now I've moved in with a sloth called Ruth.

Douglas wrote *The Song of the Dancing Rhino* with his friend Chris Keightley and it was performed at Cambridge and in Edinburgh. The song was enacted most recently in 2022 by poet 'The Story Beast' at The Royal Geographical Society in London, as part of the Douglas Adams Memorial Lecture, a benefit event for the charity Save the Rhino International (right).

POST OFFICES PREFER BOMBS by Douglas Adams

Enter 1, goes up to counter, 2 serving.

1 Excuse me, how much does it cost to send a bomb to Weston Super Mare?

2 First or second class?

1 Oh, very good class of bomb it is sir, twenty megaton job.

2 Well, that will probably have to go parcel post sir, let me look it up. Umm Um um um here it is, twenty megatons, well sorry sir, it seems to be a bit out of our class. It'll have to go BRS or British Rail.

1 But I thought you could send bombs through the post.

2 You're probably thinking of letter bombs sir. You can send those first class for the price of a threepenny stamp.

1 What's a letter bomb?

2 Well, basically a letter that explodes. Very effective they are. Makes a bit of a mess of breakfast, but that usually doesn't worry them,- by comparison.

1 Well, that's right, I wouldn't want to give him indigestion. How do I get a letter bomb?

2 Well there are several types you can buy. There's the Basildon Bomb, the Bombe Surprise, a classier model, or you can even get a Post Card bomb. You know the sort of thing, 'Weather's lovely, wish you were here, BANG' ~~and the guy's gone to that great holiday resort in the sky, along with his breakfast~~. The advantage of the Basildon Bomb is that it's Post Office Preferred. On the other hand, you may find it cheaper to make your own.

1 Isn't that difficult?

2 Oh no not, I've got a friend who's a scriptwriter, he's making a bomb.

BLACKOUT

This is Douglas's early draft of a sketch about parcel bombs at the Post Office, a reminder of the political landscape at the time. He performed it with his room-mate Keith Jeffrey, in a smoker called *LSO in Flames* in November 1972. It was also part of the first real Adams-Smith-Adams show, *Several Poor Players Strutting and Fretting* (see page 56) the following summer.

C H O X — Programme changes

TOP LAYER

No.	Item	Cast
1.	CHOX (Benton, Hess)	All
2.	COMIC CUTS (Benton, Joly)	Griff, Geoff, Clive, Jane
3.	POINT TAKEN (Adams, Smith, Adams)	Jon, Martin
4.	SELL YOUR SOUL (Benton, Hess)	Crispin, Jane, Sue
5.	EASY TERMS (Adams, Smith, Adams)	Geoff
6.	UGH! (Anderson)	Clive, Jon, Griff
7.	BACKDATED (Adams, Smith, Adams)	Martin
8.	DOUBLE CROSSED (Adams, Smith, Adams)	Jon, Sue, Jane, Martin
9.	OOH OOH (Rhys Jones)	Griff, Geoff
10.	EL HASNOTADOR (Lloyd)	Crispin, Jane, Sue, Martin
11.	ROMANTIC TRADITION (Adams, Smith, Adams)	Jon, Geoff
12.	SERVE YOU RIGHT (Anderson, Perkins)	Griff, Martin, Jane
13.	CHICKEN PICKEN (Levene)	Jon, Griff
14.	SHEER ROMANCE (Adams, Smith, Adams, Joly)	Geoff
15.	BORING BORING (Anderson)	Clive, Martin
16.	'AINT NO POINT IN CRYIN' (Benton, Hess)	Sue
17.	NINE LOVES (Adams, Smith, Adams)	Crispin, Jane
18.	EVERY SPORREN (Anderson)	Clive
19.	MR. CLEANCUT (Canter)	Jon and his friends

BOTTOM LAYER

No.	Item	Cast
1.	LATE NIGHT FINAL (Canter, Ingram)	All
2.	PARK INCIDENT (Canter)	Griff, Jon, Jane
3.	GET ON UP (Canter, Hess, Joly)	Geoff
4.	GASP (Adams, Smith, Adams)	Martin, Jon
5.	COUNTRY PLANNING (Adams, Smith, Adams)	Crispin, Martin, Sue, Jane
6.	SMALL WORD CLUB (Adams, Smith, Adams)	Jane
7.	HOLE IN THE WALL CLUB (Adams, Smith, Adams)	Men
8.	BUBBLES (Siegelman)	Sue
9.	HANDELABRA (Hess, Joly)	The Band
10.	FORKING (Rhys Jones, Joly)	Griff, Clive, Martin
11.	THE OBITUARY (Canter)	Jon
12.	SAWDUST AND HARD CENTRES (Benton, Hess)	All

- -

THE BAND	Nigel Hess (Musical Director, Keyboards) Alex Ingram (Keyboards) Philip Buscombe (Drums)
DEPUTY STAGE MANAGER	Richard Thomas
WARDROBE ASSISTANT	Sonja Dosanjh
LIGHTING	Nigel Bragg

Like his co-writer Will Adams, Douglas was very disappointed not to be cast in *CHOX* (1974), the final Footlights May Revue during their time at Cambridge. However, the programme booklet reveals that almost half the material in that show was credited to Adams-Smith-Adams, whose work was now well known among the students and vied for audiences with Footlights. Martin Smith made it though, joining Douglas's other friends Clive Anderson, Jon Canter, Geoff McGivern and Griff Rhys Jones. The show transferred to London's West End in July, during which time the powers at the BBC came to it and decided to make a programme from its highlights.

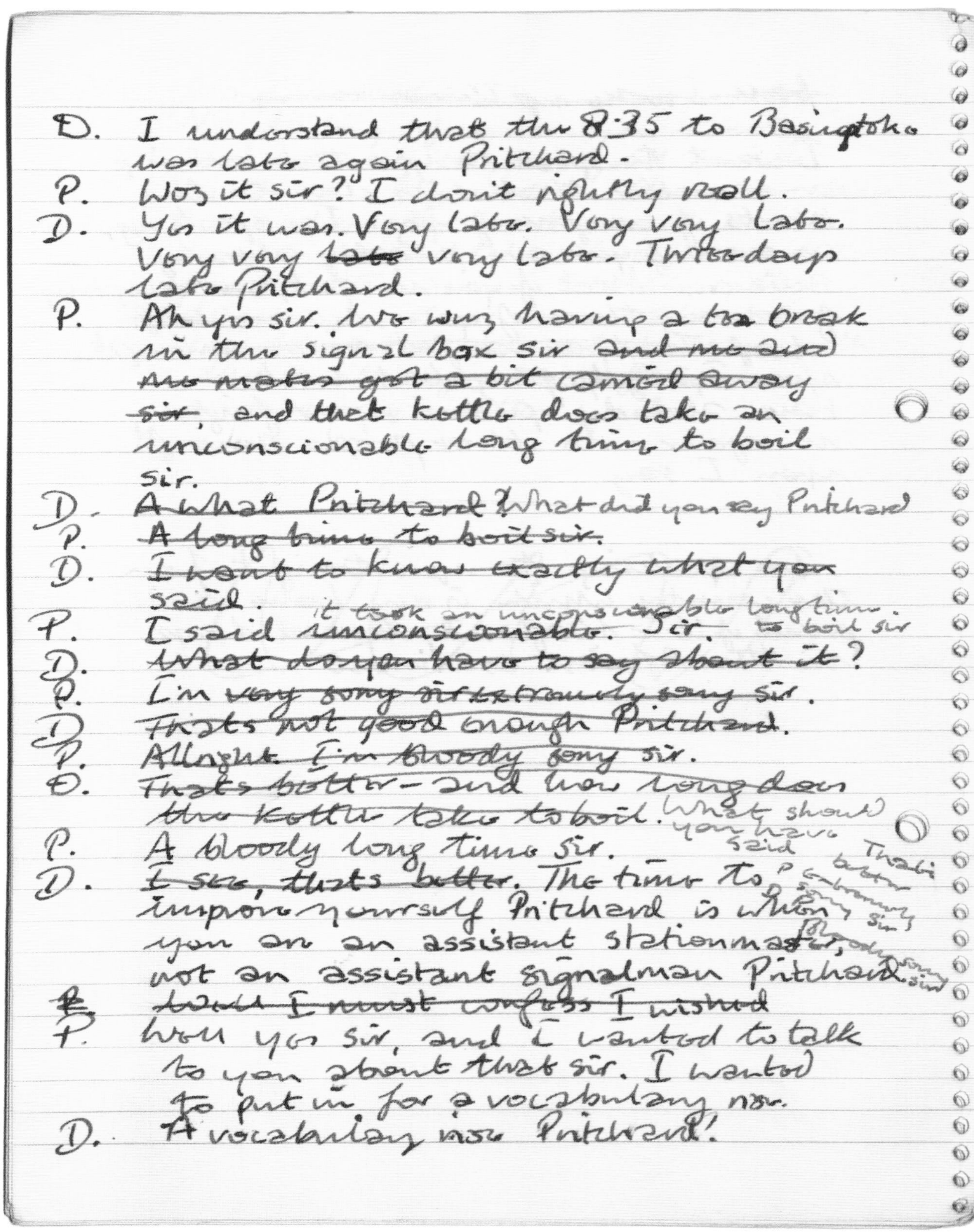

D. I understand that the 8:35 to Basingstoke was late again Pritchard.
P. Was it sir? I don't rightly recall.
D. Yes it was. Very late. Very very late. Very very ~~late~~ very late. Two days late Pritchard.
P. Ah yes sir. We was having a tea break in the signal box sir ~~and me and me mates got a bit carried away sir~~, and that kettle does take an unconscionable long time to boil sir.
D. ~~A what Pritchard?~~ What did you say Pritchard
P. ~~A long time to boil sir.~~
D. ~~I want to know exactly what you said.~~
P. I said ~~unconscionable. Sir.~~ it took an unconscionable long time to boil sir
D. ~~What do you have to say about it~~?
P. I'm ~~very sorry sir extremely sorry sir~~.
D. ~~Thats not good enough Pritchard~~.
P. ~~Alright I'm bloody sorry sir.~~
D. ~~Thats better – and how long does the kettle take to boil.~~ What should you have said
P. A bloody long time sir.
D. ~~I see, thats better.~~ The time to improve yourself Pritchard is when you are an assistant stationmaster, not an assistant signalman Pritchard.
~~P. Well I must confess I wished~~
P. Well yes sir, and I wanted to talk to you about that sir. I wanted to put in for a vocabulary now.
D. A vocabulary now Pritchard!

Douglas wrote this noteworthy sketch, called *Point Taken* (AKA *Pritchard*), and first performed it with Martin Smith in May 1973, in a smoker concert called *A Burst of Apalsy*. The first page of the handwritten piece is above – the full transcript (accounting for the crossings out) is opposite. The final sketch had some minor adjustments, but was mostly preserved as originally noted down by hand. 'Pity about Arsenal' was a line re-used in the very first episode of *The Hitchhiker's Guide*.

D: I understand that the 8.35 to Basingstoke was late again Pritchard.

P: Woz it sir? I don't rightly recall.

D: Yes it was. Very late. Very very late. Very very very late. Three days late Pritchard.

P: Ah yes sir. We was having a tea break in the signal box sir and that kettle does take an unconscionable long time to boil sir.

D: What did you say Pritchard.

P: I said it took an unconscionable long time to boil sir.

D: And what should you have said

P: A bloody long time sir.

D: That's better Pritchard.

P: Extremely sorry sir.

D: Pritchard!

P: Er, bloody sorry sir.

D: The time to improve yourself Pritchard is when you are an assistant stationmaster, not an assistant signalman Pritchard.

P: Well yes sir, and I wanted to talk to you about that sir. I wanted to put in for a vocabulary rise.

D: A vocabulary rise Pritchard?

P: Yes sir. I wanted to be able to use words like existentialism.

D: Existentialism in a signal box?

P: Existentialism informs all areas of life sir.

D: But does it help explain why the 8.35 to Basingstoke was three days late? Why smartly turned out businessmen arrived in that beautiful city with three days growth upon their lilywhite cheeks, why [leafing through letters of complaint] Mrs Pinch-Buttocks pigeons arrived dead to a one, her Pekinese *[sic]* also curled up and died of sheer boredom. Mrs Crunchduck gave birth to triplets – we tried to get a midwife to her but she is still lost in some sidings at Clapham Junction. The vast majority of the Royal Philharmonic Orchestra arrived at Winter Garden Basingstoke 60 hours after the local musical populous had been to a spirited performance of Beethoven's Fifth Piano Quintet [reading]: 'An economical performance' said the Basingstoke Advertiser, 'Unfortunately marred by long periods of total silence.' Ah yes, and Col William Whittington Stokes was coming home to Basingstoke to die. He didn't make it, Pritchard.

P: Sorry sir.

D: It's not good enough Pritchard.

P: British Rail makes the going easy sir.

D: Which brings us on to the next point Pritchard. Passengers are requested not to use the toilet whilst the train is standing at a station. Three days is a long time Pritchard. What would you do about that Pritchard.

P: Can't we let it pass sir?

D: That is unfortunately what did happen in a large number of cases.

P: How very incommodious sir.

D: PRITCHARD – retract that five syllable word IMMEDIATELY!

P: Sorry sir. Very shitty I should say.

D: Perhaps you would care to explain.

P: It was existentialism what did it sir.

D: But you're not allowed to use words like that in the signal box. We're running a public service not a bloody University.

P: Well yes sir but it all happened because I wouldn't use the word. I was trying to tell my mate Bob about it, and had to make him guess by a sort of charade.

D: Charade Pritchard? What charade

P: Well to give him the basic idea I left all the points in the railway region open.

D: You left ALL THE POINTS OPEN?

P: Well yes sir that's what existentialism is all about.

D: I know perfectly well what existentialism is. I was at Oxford too.

P: Sorry sir yes sir.

D: But why did this charade last three days?

P: Bob is a very stupid assistant signalman sir. He only got the hang of it after we'd derailed the Southampton Express. The whole thing came to him in a blinding flash.

D: A sort of revelation I suppose.

P: No sir the switching gear exploded. But I have reason to believe he died an enlightened man. He went up in flames sir.

D: Are you aware of the consequences of your actions Pritchard

P: Well according to Sartre...

D: Do you realise that because of your playing philosophy with Western Region railways we have trains not simply derailed but leaping over each other like copulating caterpillars? The countryside is littered with great *[remainder crossed out – resumes, with a rewritten section]*

P: It's been done before sir

D: Yes Pritchard, and notably by you. You were transferred to us from the Southern Region because you completely paralysed the whole of Surrey, Sussex and Kent by issuing a structuralist time-table. But that is nothing in comparison with your latest philosophical faux pas. Do you realize that we have had hundreds of trains not only derailed but leaping over each other like copulating caterpillars. The countryside is littered with the smouldering heaps of expiring trains. The worst case is that of the Exeter St David Express which was involved in a multiple pile up Pritchard. 4000 people have been killed or injured, an estimated £50,000,000 pounds worth of damage has been done to rolling stock and railway lines. Didn't you see the Nine O'Clock News?

P: Yes sir.

D: Well?!?

P: Pity about Arsenal sir.

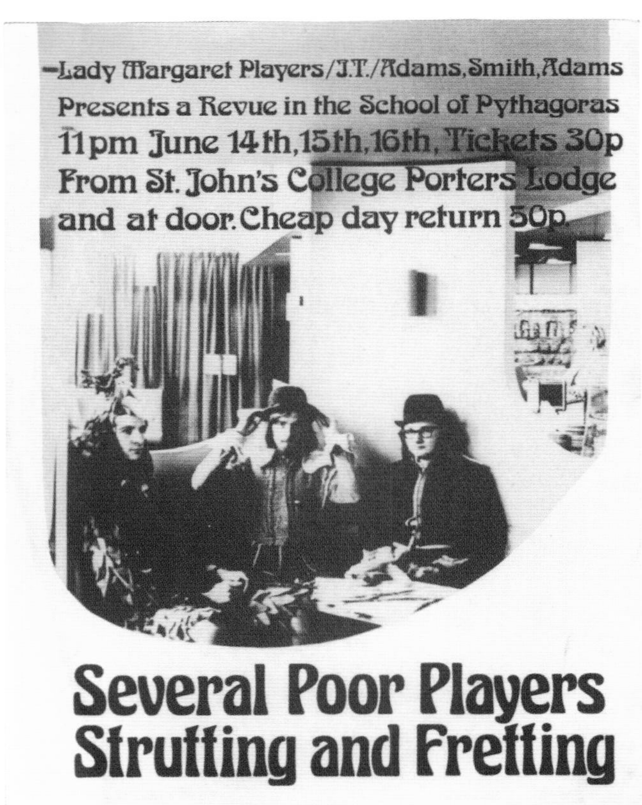

–Lady Margaret Players/J.T./Adams,Smith,Adams
Presents a Revue in the School of Pythagoras
11pm June 14th,15th,16th, Tickets 30p
From St. John's College Porters Lodge
and at door. Cheap day return 50p.
Several Poor Players
Strutting and Fretting

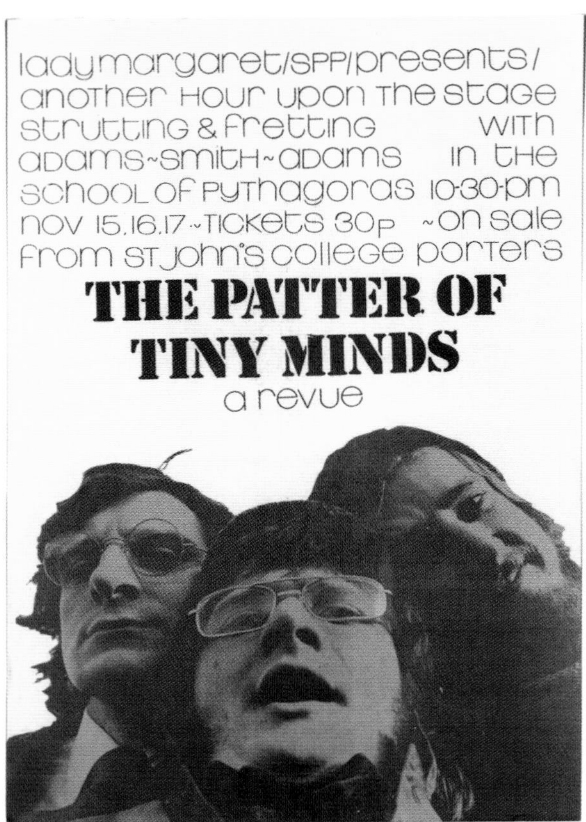

ladymargaret/SPP/presents/
another hour upon the stage
strutting & fretting with
adams~smith~adams in the
school of pythagoras 10-30-pm
nov 15.16.17~tickets 30p ~on sale
from st john's college porters
THE PATTER OF
TINY MINDS
a revue

These images in some way sum up Douglas's time with Adams-Smith-Adams, shot on location in and around Cambridge, on 15 May 1973, by *Varsity* photographer Mike Penhaligon. In the photograph opposite, Douglas is right, Martin Smith is centre and Will Adams is left. Douglas himself applied the Letraset to many of the trio's posters.

THREE
Collaborations

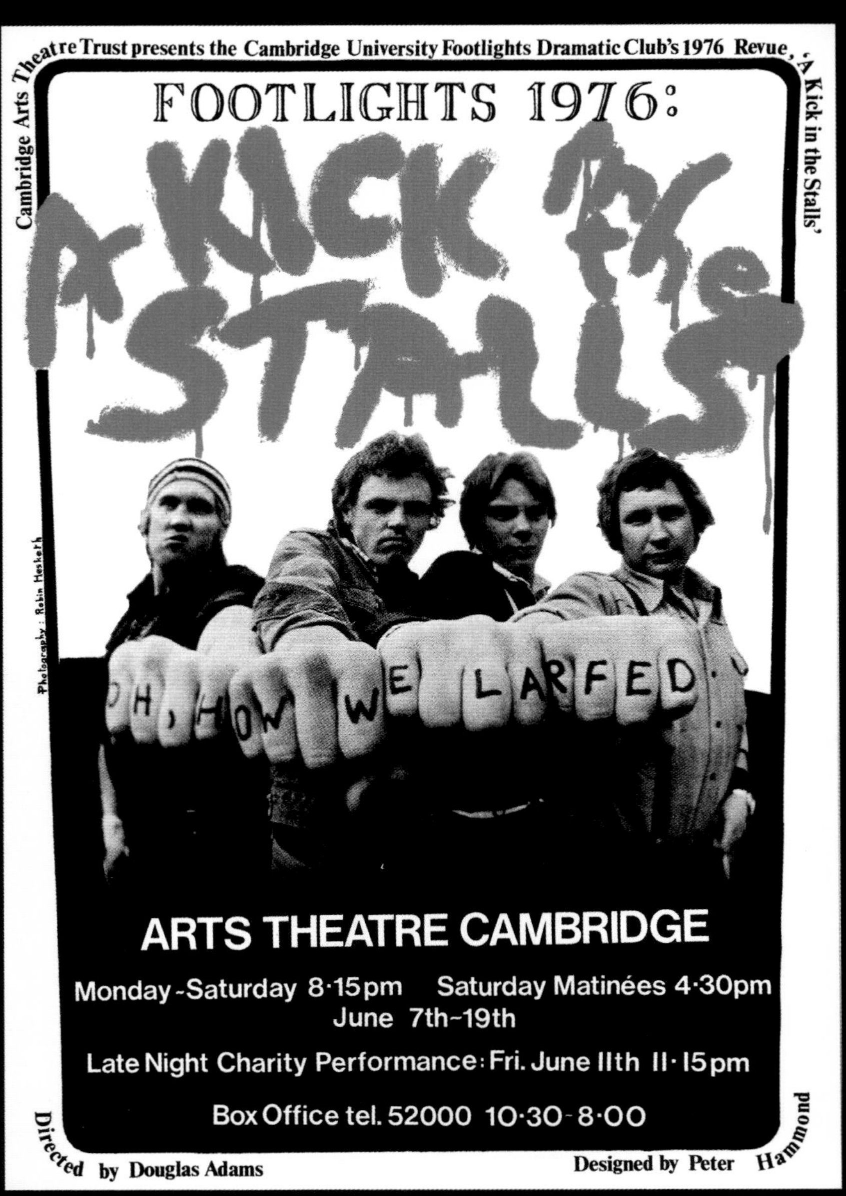

Once he left Cambridge, Douglas was once or twice invited back to work on a Footlights production, such as *A Kick in the Stalls*, which he directed in 1976, and included some Adams-Smith-Adams material. The memorabilia in this chapter demonstrates that the connections Douglas made during and soon after his university years proved influential to his whole career.

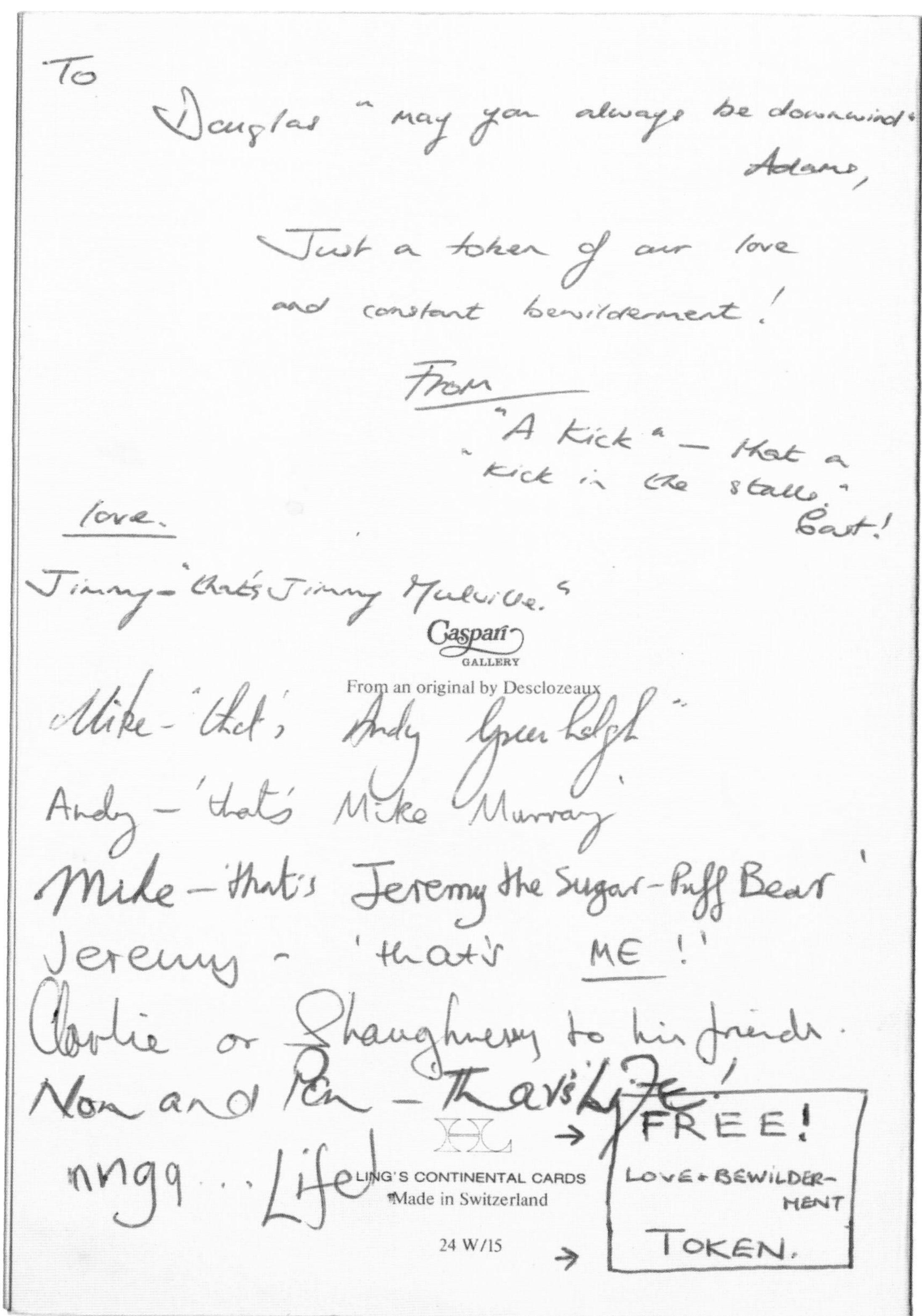

To
Douglas "may you always be downwind" Adams,

Just a token of our love
and constant bewilderment!

From
"A Kick" — that a "kick in the stalls" Cast!

love.

Jimmy – 'that's Jimmy Mulville.'

Caspari
GALLERY
From an original by Desclozeaux

Mike – 'that's Andy Greenhalgh'

Andy – 'that's Mike Murray'

Mike – 'that's Jeremy the Sugar-Puff Bear'

Jeremy – 'that's ME!'

Charlie or Shaughnessy to his friends.

Non and Pen – That's Life!

nngg.. Life!

LING'S CONTINENTAL CARDS
Made in Switzerland
24 W/15

FREE!
LOVE + BEWILDERMENT
TOKEN.

A Kick in the Stalls (see opposite) was staged two years after Douglas graduated from Cambridge and lists him as director, experience that perhaps helped to build him a CV that might seem impressive to others in the industry outside of Footlights. This card (above), signed by the show's cast, is addressed to Douglas 'may you always be downwind' Adams, and was given as a token of their 'love and constant bewilderment'.

DOUGLAS ADAMS (Director)
Douglas is larger than the average family and wears two pairs of trousers on each leg. This year's director, he was unable to do the show last year, because he became suddenly tall at the last minute and had to go into hospital to have his clothes burnt off. He is very sensitive about his enormous nose, which the cast refrain from mentioning, even when they are rehearsing it. He has an unending supply of witty stories, which keep everyone amused until long after they've fallen asleep. This doesn't matter however, as he comes round first thing in the morning to tell you what you missed. Recently he worked with members of the Monty Python team, but on the completion of the M62, he has returned to a less demanding job. Always a generous person, he rarely carries money in case he gives it away.
Favourite sport: Flicking elephants onto their backs and watching them struggle.
Probable last words: Well basically I think that the basic basis of this is basically rubbish, actually.

Two years after Douglas graduated, in 1976 he took *The Unpleasantness at Brodie's Close* (an original Adams-Smith-Adams production) to the Edinburgh Fringe. The photograph at the top of this page shows (left to right) Douglas with John Lloyd, John Mason, Becky Fanner, Geoffrey Farrington and David Renwick. By this time, he and his collaborators were in direct competition with the Footlights show *A Kick in the Stalls*, which, having been directed by Douglas while it was in Cambridge (above, bottom) was by then under the direction of comedy writer and actor Griff Rhys Jones.

Weekending
31st May 74

8.

(Brain Teaser - Douglas Adams)

1. NIGEL: This week's Brainteaser.

Imagine a man in front of two doors - one leads to the White House, and other other to jail. One guard is Mr. Nixon who always tells lies, and the other is Mr. Ford who alternately tells the truth, and tells a lie and then contradicts himself twice.
What you have to do is work out how many Nixon aides can be rowed across the river before the boat sinks, and the fox is set amongst the ones who chickened out and sold their apples for three years each pleading executive privilege.
Then complete the sentence 'Nixon is a .... ' in not more than fifteen deleted expletives, and send your entry on blank tape to the Senate Watergate committee. Members of the Presidents family are not allowed to enter unless they can lie very convincingly, and the President's decision is under subpoena.

Friday
151–214

31

FIRST BROADCAST MATERIAL.
- Weekending 'Brainteaser'

Friday 31 May 1974 was perhaps a landmark moment in Douglas's career with a capitalized diary note screaming 'FIRST BROADCAST MATERIAL' (above, inset). The typed page comes from the script of radio series 'Week Ending' ('Weekending' in Douglas's notes), a satirical current-affairs show, co-created and produced by Simon Brett, who would become very important to Douglas as the first producer of *The Hitchhiker's Guide*. The script demonstrates that Douglas could deliver a solid topical skit on the infamous Watergate scandal. The following week the show included more Adams-Smith-Adams material – this time a comment on the Communist Chinese government sending pairs of pandas overseas as diplomatic gifts (opposite).

WEEKENDING
FRIDAY 7th JUNE 1974.

12.

(PANDAS - ADAMS SMITH ADAMS)

1. GRAMS: DISAPPEARING COUNTRYSIDE

2. COMMENTATOR: Nigel

Our Changing Countryside. This week we examine the Giant Flying Panda - one of the communist phenomenon of the animal kingdom, whose migratory habits seem to be determined by changes in the political climate. Whenever a thaw sets in, one of our tethered friends is sure to come winging over to these shores, though the natural habitat of these creatures seems to be behind the Iron Curtain, where diplomacy is traditionally carried out by this kind of brute force. The first pandas of spring have already been spotted, all over, and it seems that their instinct is to patch up East West relations, and to become the beast of both worlds. The question on everybody's lips is how their mating habits will compare with those of An-An and Mark-Mark. But what is more interesting is why this species of Chinese Propapanda should be choosing to nest in England's Heathland - a question which particularly worries the Moscow State Zoo - "The Cage-A-Bee" feels that a more suitable habitat would be the Marcia lands of Downing Street.

continues/ But it is hoped ....

1. COMMENTATOR: Nigel

But it is hoped that the bad feeling will soon be dispersed if the two Giant Pandas On-On and Tont-Tont, start breeding and produce lots of little ententes.

Before I leave you - last week's Nature Quiz, and the answer to the question "What is Black and White and Red all over?" is of course a Chinese Panda. Goodnight.

2. GRAMS: UP & OUT

CAMS ACTION SOUND

(136 on 1)

Full table shot

136 - 160

THE HOLE IN THE WALL GANG.
by Adams Smith Adams

A MEETING OF (SAY) SIX PEOPLE.

CRISPIN
Now, before I declare this meeting open I'm afraid I have something rather serious to say. As yet I don't know who to point the finger at, but it is somebody here. And what is more, what they have done they have done in such an insidious cunning way, treading softly, surreptitiously, behind my back, cleverly covering their tracks - so circumspect they have been working their sinister wiles, so clever, so evil, so cunningly secret, that not only do I not know exactly which one of you has done it, but I cannot even say what it s they've done, exactly.

- 59 -

CAMS ACTION SOUND

But! Be warned! I'm on my guard. Right, Mr. Secretary, if you'll be so good as to read the minutes of the last meeting... (SITS)

GRIFF
Certainly. 'The Minutes of the 42nd meeting of the Crawley District Paranoid Society. The meeting was duly convened, and Mr. S. J. Stabintheback gave us a spirited talk about the holes his next door neighbours have drilled in his wall, and then he went on to say...'Hey! Someone's been tampering with these notes!

GEOFF
What do you mean?

- 60 -

CAMS ACTION SOUND

GRIFF
I said, someone's been tampering with these notes.

PAUSE

CLIVE
You're blaming me, aren't you?

GRIFF
Stop trying to put words in my mouth!

GEOFF
What have they done? Let me see it.

GRIFF
You don't believe me, do you?

GEOFF
Did I say I didn't believe you?

- 61 -

CAMS ACTION SOUND

GRIFF
No!

GEOFF
Are you accusing me of insincerity?

CLIVE
Go on, admit it. You're blaming me, aren't you?

CRISPIN
For heaven's sake be careful what you say! I can hear tape machines whirring!

GRIFF
I can hear police sirens!

GEOFF
I can hear bombers!

GRIFF
I can hear intercontinental ballistic missiles!

THEY ALL DUCK UNDER THE TABLE
CRISPIN'S HEAD EMERGES.

- 62 -

The Cambridge University 1974 Footlights Revue **was the broadcast title of** ***CHOX*** **(see page 67), which was recorded on 3 August 1974 and shown on BBC2 on 26 August. It featured Adams-Smith-Adams' material, including a sketch variously known as 'The Hole in the Wall Gang' or 'The Paranoid Society', the first pages of which are reproduced here and opposite.**

PAUSE. THEY LISTEN.

CAMS | ACTION | SOUND

CRISPIN
Ssshh!

PAUSE. THEY LISTEN.

My mistake. Mr. Shoulder, perhaps you'd calm us all down by telling us one of your jokes.

JON
Oh! Right, well there's this bloke, see, and he says to this other bloke 'Who was that Lady I saw you with last night?' And the other bloke says 'YOU'VE BEEN FOLLOWING ME AGAIN!'

PAUSE.

CRISPIN
That was in rather bad taste!

JON:
Sorry, I got carried away. Someone was staring at me maliciously.

THEY ALL DO A DOUBLE TAKE ON CLIVE

- 63 -

tha
t?'
IN!
Sorry, I got carried away.
Someone was staring at me

Far out in the depths of the cosmos, beyond the furthest reach of man's perception, amidst the swirling mists of unknown galaxies, where lost worlds roll eternally beyond the gateway of infinity, inexorably on through millions of light years of celestial darkness that we call space. Space – reaching far beyond the limits of man's imagination – I can't begin to tell you far it is – I mean it's so far. You may think it's a long way down the street to the ~~tobacconists~~ chemist's, ~~but~~ that's just peanuts to space. Even if you go to the top of the Empire State building you're still nowhere near the bit where the air stops. You just wouldn't believe how far it is – I told ~~this~~ my mother this morning, and even she didn't believe me.

Far out in the depths of the cosmos, beyond the furthest reach of man's perception, amidst the swirling mists of unknown galaxies, where lost worlds roll eternally ~~[illegible]~~ beyond the gateway of infinity, inexorably on through millions of light-years of celestial darkness that we call space. Space — reaching far beyond the limits of man's imagination. I can't begin to tell you how far it is — I mean, it's so far. You may think it's a long way down the street to the chemists, but that's just peanuts to space. I mean, you take the elevator to the top of the Empire State Building and you're still nowhere near the bit where the air stops. You just wouldn't believe how far it is — I told my mother this morning, and even she didn't believe it

BEYOND THE INFINITE II (1)

Light show, Ligeti.
Voice over.

V Far out in the depths of the Cosmos, beyond the furthest reach of man's perception, amidst the swirling mists of unknown galaxies, where lost worlds roll eternally beyond the gateway of infinity, inexorably on through millions of light years of celestial darkness that we call Space. Space - reaching far beyond the limits of man's imagination. I can't begin to tell you how far it is. I mean, it's so far. You may think it's a long way down the street to the chemist, but that's just peanuts to space. Even if you go to the top of the Empire State Biulding, you're still nowhere near the bit where the air stops! You wouldn't believe how far it is - I told my mother this morning, and she didn't believe me.

And so, from here in the monstrous majesty of Alpha Centauri, the marvel of the Universe, strange landscapes and icy pinnacles of petrified Time, from here we travel through the uttermost, inky depths of our uncharted Universe, the jewelled planets sweeping past us in globules of light, on, ever on, and, and on, on to those sectors of space where man dares to brave indescribable elemental terrors, to boldly split infinitives that no man has split before.

And there, towards the end of our journey through the miasmic time fields, we see, glimmering before us, our destination - Chepstow. It would have been easier to go from Paddington and change at Gloucester, but this is not man's way - man is the adventurer. But what venture is there left now? Perhaps Chepstow holds the answer...

(Fade)

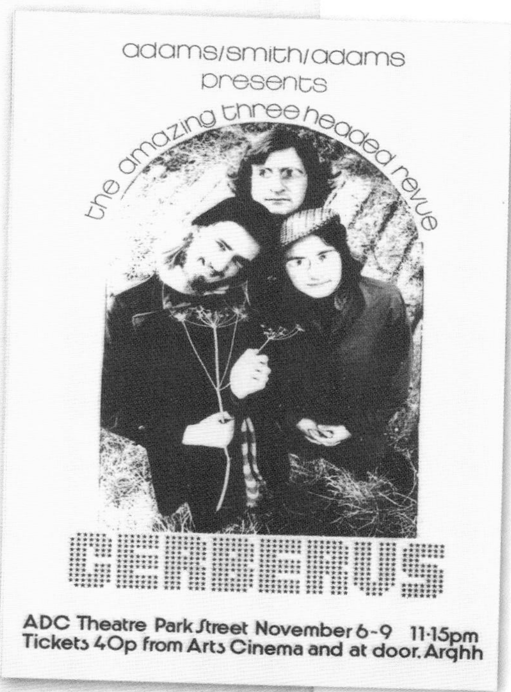

Cerberus was the name given to the Adams-Smith-Adams revue at the ADC Theatre, Cambridge, in November 1974. It wasn't the critical success the trio had hoped for, but the audiences seemed to enjoy it. The opening monologue of *Cerberus* was called 'Beyond the Infinite' and has elements that would later be familiar to *Hitchhiker's Guide* fans. It appears among Douglas's papers in both his own handwriting (opposite, top) and handwritten by Will Adams (opposite, bottom). The final typed piece is reproduced above, and the poster for the show, featuring Douglas (centre) with Will Adams (left) and Martin Smith (right), is inset.

and parrot. Police have asked another team of surgeons to stand by to turn his ~~intestines~~ inside out if he doesn't shut up and talk sense like any other normal reactionary.

We will bring you further reports as soon as they come in. Oh… I'm very sorry about that… I seem to have made another bit of a mess – look let me…

(Later announcement.)

Fresh reports about the bus robberies – police now confirm the earlier description of the gang's leader. Surgeons have apologised again to Mr Blemish and are treating him for severe indigestion. His condition is described as 'very amusing'.

Police have issued a description of a man they wish to interview in connection with the incidents. He has one leg, and is wearing a frock coat, a red head scarf, a three cornered hat, a patch, and a parrot on his ~~tufts~~ right shoulder, ~~which would answer~~

The RSPCA are still looking for a nasty yappy dog with diabetes and wish to interview a parrot called Eustace.

And a report has just come in saying ~~that~~ the leader of the marauders has issued a statement to the police saying that he ~~will be~~ is ~~appearing on tor~~ being interviewed ~~tonight~~ on ~~the~~ BBC Television ~~programme~~ ~~Midweek~~ tonight and that the police may phone in to the programme with ~~their~~ questions to the number published in the Radio Times

In *Cerberus*, Douglas got the chance to dress up and act the part of 'Y-Fronts Silver' (a parody of Long John Silver, of course) on a spree on a red London bus. The sketch is set out over the following pages in a handwritten draft by Douglas at first, which his collaborator Will Adams then takes over.

Radio Times. Oh God I'm sorry, look this is really ghastly, I don't know how to....

Midweek.

(Will)

W. Well good evening ~~ladies and gentlemen to you this~~, and in this edition of Midweek we look as usual at a number of ~~bored~~ boring people doing boring things and try to make them seem more interesting than they really are by asking them rude questions and getting them annoyed. As well as rude questions we will also be featuring a number of stupid questions from viewers who have nothing better to do than phone in and sound a bit gauche and banal so everyone can have a jolly good laugh and be patronising and they can go off to the pub and say guess what fellas I was on the telly tonight – mine's a pint. So what? I'm on television most nights of the week and mine's a double whisky to wash down the barbiturates. ~~But first we turn to the big news of today~~ ~ But first we look at today's startling developments in ~~public~~ the ~~transport~~ field of public transport. Already the name 'Bus Pirates' is on the tip of everybody's tongue, biting terror

The pages relating to the pirate (played by Douglas, annotated as D in the script; W is, of course, Will Adams) are transcribed on pages 86–7, ending as the dialogue shifts to a phone-in where a detective superintendent tries to arrest Y-Fronts Silver over the phone. This arrest-by-phone was a concept alluded to years later by Zaphod in *The Hitchhiker's Guide*.

into their hearts. We have in the studio tonight the self-styled leader of the marauders ~~monopeds~~, Y-fronts Silver. ~~But first we talk to~~

Mr Silver, you've come up against a fair amount of adverse criticism in your work

~~D. One inevitably comes into conflict situations with any art-form. What one is trying to do collectively, as a group – we are very much aware of the need for a group concept – is to, how shall I put it, scare the shits out of the average urban man and woman in the street, who is, after all, very much a product of, and to a large extent unaware of, this fact, and in doing so we are in a very real sense on the programme tonight.~~

W. ~~But~~, why piracy?

D. Well, I think we see piracy as an alternative means of self expression. – the communal consciousness of tradition ~~I see it very much as an exercise in collective group consciousness~~, the re-injection ~~transportation~~ of sub-cultural [digressions ~~which one might call folk~~] myths into the modern urban environment.

W. A lot of people are somewhat disturbed by the rôle of the bus in all this.

D. I think this is the wrong way to look at it. I don't think the bus poses such a complex problem as many commentators would suggest. ~~The fact is it achieves a high degree of rôle fulfilment~~ It is after all very much a normal 26 up 32 down you know the sort of thing, I mean no smoking in the lower compartment; and you know we'd like to keep to that because it's very much the sort of thing we're doing.

W. But why a bus?

D. Well, it's a means of bringing art to the people.

W. ~~We were very aware of~~ But surely pirates usually confine their activities to the sea. Aren't you being a little avant garde.

well before we go on to the phone-in spot —

D Don't think we're not aware of this, but we do find that the kind of people we're aiming at ~~are~~ tend to be found in the High St. rather than wading about on the high seas. After all, if Kydd had had access to bikes, I think he might well have used them. Mm PAUSE Might well have done.....

W At this point I'd like to introduce our other guest in the studio – one of today's leading sociologists, from Sussex University, Dr. ~~Hugh~~ ~~Desmond~~ Wallace Smedley. Good evening.

M. NODS

W. Now, doctor, for many years you've been ~~[illegible]~~ a student of the motives and social derivatives ~~and [illegible]~~ of the phenomenon of urban piracy. What have you to say in response to Capt Silver's claim that he is performing a public service vehicle.

M. THINKS Well, Jim lad. Yo ho ho and a bottle of rum pieces of eight pieces of eight, pretty polly fifteen men on a dead man's chest Jim lad AD LIB

W. Well Capt. Silver, a few interesting points there,... and much of it is ~~[illegible]~~ awfully true

D Yes, that's awfully true and I feel Dr Smedley you there a very – a very good voice

W. Dr Smedley – what do you think is the reason behind this current wave of piracy

M Ah, well it's having one leg, y'see. It's what comes natural like. I mean, trick cycling's out for the average monoped

DASHES OFFSTAGE, SOUNDS (OFF) OF HIM WALKING THE PLANK.

W. And I think we have our first caller on the line now – from London, it's Ret. Supt. MacThreeket of Scotland Yard who warns you that anything you say may be taken down and used in evidence against you.

MacT. Hello hello hello

W Ah, hello hello hello, supt. What is your question, please?

MacT I would like to ask Mr. Silver if he would like to accompany ~~to~~ me down to the station.

D Well, many people have come up to me and asked me this, but regrettably, and I mean that, I must decline the offer.

W Well, supt. Do you want to come back on that?

MacT. ~~[illegible]~~ Y-es. I'd like to place Mr. Silver under close arrest.

D. Oh really? That's very interesting and indeed disturbing. But I'm afraid there'll be little opportunity for this to occur, and don't think I'm not flattered, because I am. But at this present ~~m~~ moment in time, the studio is surrounded by a ~~flott~~ flotilla of double-deckers, a sort of omni-armada....

BELL RINGS. CANNON FIRE. CANNON-BALL COMES ON, CAUGHT BY W.

D. Ah, that's my 'bus.... EXIT

HUGE CANNONADE, NOISE CHAOS.

… and parrot. Police have asked another team of surgeons to stand by to turn his intestines inside out if he doesn't shut up and talk sense like any other normal reactionary.

We will bring you further reports as soon as they come in. Oh – I'm very sorry about that … I seem to have made another bit of a mess – look let me…

(Later Announcement)

Fresh reports about the bus robberies. Police now confirm the earlier description of the gang's leader. Surgeons have apologised again to Mr Blemish and are treating him for some indigestion. His condition is described as 'very amusing'.

Police have issued a description of a man they wish to interview in connection with the incidents. He has one leg, and is wearing a frock coat, a red headscarf, a three-cornered hat, a patch, and a parrot on his right shoulder. The RSPCA are still looking for a nasty yappy dog with diabetes and wish to interview a parrot called Eustace.

And a report has just come in saying that the leader of the marauders has issued a statement to the police saying that he is being interviewed on BBC television tonight and that the police may phone in to the programme with their questions to the number published in the Radio Times. Oh God, I'm sorry, look this is really ghastly, I don't know how to…

Midweek

(Will)

W: Well, good evening, and in this edition of 'Midweek' we look as usual at a number of boring people doing boring things and try to make them seem more interesting than they really are by asking them rude questions and getting them annoyed. As well as rude questions we will also be featuring a number of stupid questions from viewers who have nothing better to do than phone in and sound a bit gauche and banal so everyone can have a jolly good laugh and be patronising and they can go off to the pub and say 'guess what fellas, I was on the telly tonight – mine's a pint'. So what? I'm on television most nights of the week and mine's a double whiskey to wash down the barbiturates. But first we look at today's startling developments in the field of public transport. Already the name 'Bus Pirates' is on the tip of everybody's tongues, biting terror into their hearts. We have here in the studio tonight the self-styled leader of the marauders, Y-Fronts Silver.

Mr. Silver, you've come up against a fair amount of criticism in your work.

[crossed out section]

W: Why piracy?

D: Well, I think we see piracy as an alternative means of self-expression – the communal consciousness of tradition, the re-injection of sub-cultural myths into the modern urban environment.

W: A lot of people are somewhat disturbed by the role of the bus in all this.

D: I think this is the wrong way to look at it. I don't think the bus poses such a complex problem as many commentators would suggest. It is after all very much a normal 26 up, 32 down, you know the sort of thing, I mean, no smoking in the lower compartment; and you know, we'd like to keep to that because it's very much the sort of thing we're doing.

W: But why a bus?

D: Well, it's a means of bringing art to the people.

W: But surely pirates usually confine their activities to the sea. Aren't you being a little avant garde?

D: Don't think we're not aware of this, but we do find that the kind of people we're aiming at tend to be found in the High Street, rather than wading about in the high seas. After all, if Kydd had had access to bikes, I think he might well have used them. Mmmm PAUSE might well have done.

W: At this point I'd like to introduce our other guest in the studio – one of today's leading sociologists, from Sussex University, Dr. Wallace Smedley. Good evening.

M: Nods

W: Now, doctor, for many years you've been a student of the motives and social derivatives of the phenomenon of urban piracy. What have you to say in response to Capt Silver's claim that he is performing a public service vehicle.

M: THINKS Well, Jim lad. Yo ho ho and a bottle of rum pieces of eight pieces of eight, pretty polly, fifteen men on a dead man's chest Jim lad [AD LIB]

DASHES OFFSTAGE, SOUNDS (OFF) OF HIM WALKING THE PLANK.

W: And I think we have our first caller on the line now – from London, it's Det. Supt. MacThreefeet of Scotland Yard who warns you that anything you say may be taken down and used in evidence against you.

MacT: Hello hello hello

W: Ah, hello hello hello, Supt. What is your question please?

MacT: I would like to ask Mr Silver if he would like to accompany me down to the station.

D: Well, many people have come up to me and asked me this, but regrettably, and I mean that, I must decline the offer.

W: Well, Supt. Do you want to come back on that?

MacT: Yes. I'd like to place Mr. Silver under close arrest.

D: Oh really? That's very interesting and indeed disturbing. But I'm afraid there'll be little opportunity for this to occur, and don't think I'm not flattered, because I am. But at this present moment in time, the studio is surrounded by a flotilla of double-deckers, a sort of omni-armada…

BELL RINGS. CANNON FIRE. CANNON-BALL COMES ON, CAUGHT BY W.

D: Ah, that's my 'bus… EXIT

HUGE CANNONADE, NOISE CHAOS.

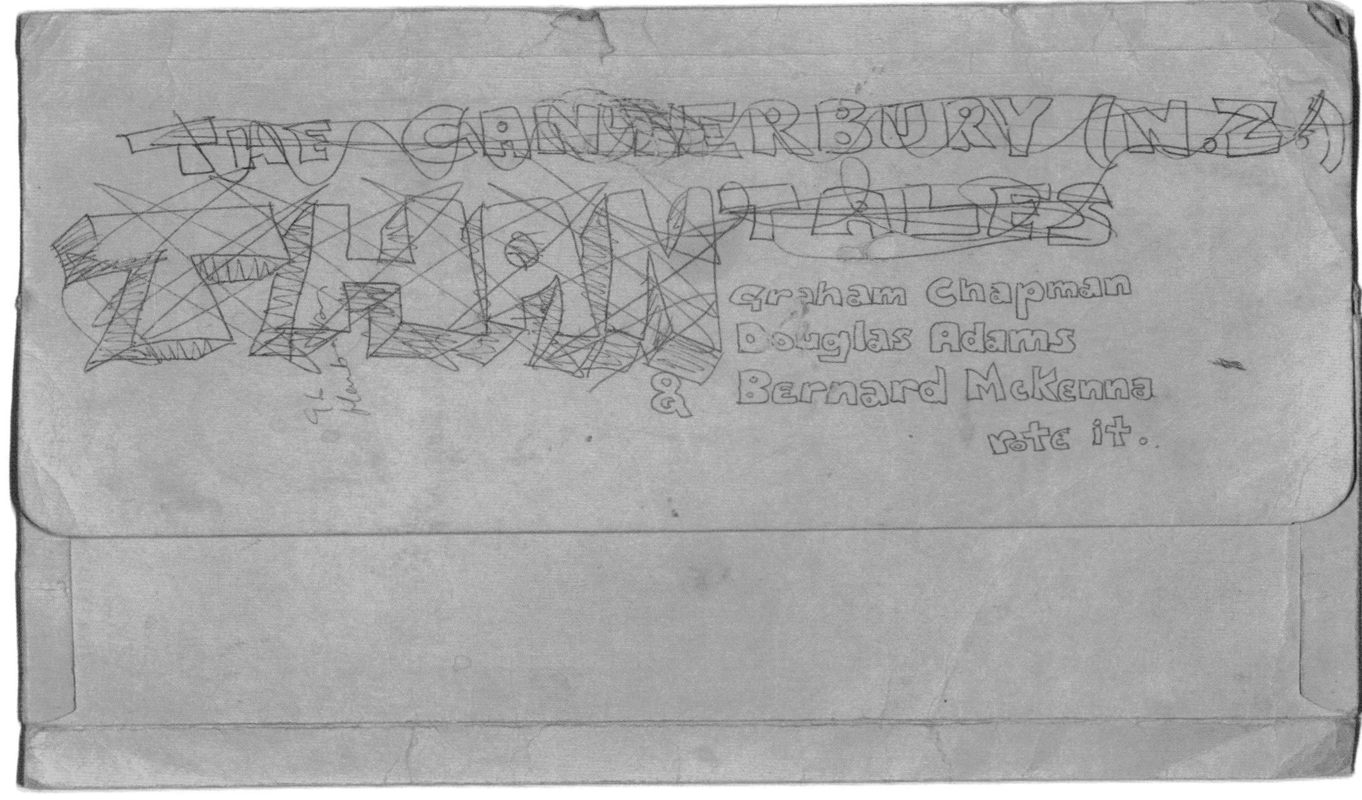

Douglas met *Monty Python*'s Graham Chapman in July 1974 and the two formed a friendship. Writing with Chapman led to all sorts of opportunities, including co-writing a script for a US TV special to tie in with the release of Ringo Starr's latest album, *Goodnight Vienna*. Douglas's diary reveals that he met with Starr first on Friday 10 January 1975, and then again in February, March and September. The script was never made into the TV show, but Chapman's estate published it in a collection of his works in 1999, and a full, original copy, tucked inside this folder (above, top), survives in Douglas's archives, too.

REHEARSAL SCRIPT Proj. No. 1155/2341

~~THE END OF THE ROAD SHOW~~

CHAPMAN REVUE OUT OF THE TREES.

~~(Working Title)~~

Producer ....Bernard Thompson
P.A. ....Don Clive
A.F.M. ....Philip Hill
Producer's Assistant..Freda Barratt

Designer ....IAN RAWNSLEY EXT. 4838

Costume ....SUSAN WHEAL EXT. 2713
Make-up ....CECILE HAY-ARTHUR 4177

T.M.1 ....PETER BOOTH
T.M.2 ....CLIVE GULLIVER
SOUND ....LEN SHOREY

REHEARSAL ROOM

Latymer Mission,
Bramley Road,
London, W.10 Tel. 969.8826

14th October - 18th October 1975 inclusive

Underground stations Ladbroke Grove (Metropolitan)
Latimer Road "

Bus No.7 (Monday to Sat.)
15 (every day)

(see map page i)

STUDIO 8 19th OCTOBER 1975

****

FILMING

6th - 10th October inclusive on location

Film Cameraman.....STAN SPEEL
Film Editor ....GROUP ONE 992.5807

Production Office Room 3025 EXT.2808/9

Than (opposite, bottom) seems an unusual word with which to top and tail a comedy series. Commissioned by the BBC as simply *Chapman Revue*, it was clearly meant as a follow-up to *Python*. Co-written in the first half of 1975 by Chapman with Douglas and Scottish writer and producer Bernard McKenna, it went through a period of being called *The End of the Road Show*, but made it to air as a one-off sketch show called *Out of the Trees*. The cast included Chapman himself, plus two eventual *Hitchhiker* leads, Simon Jones and Mark Wing-Davey. The title page of the script is reproduced above.

DRAFT SCRIPT

DOCTOR ON THE GO

"Like Father..."

P/N: 9627

DOCTOR ON THE GO

Based on the 'Doctor Books' by Richard Gordon

SERIES II

VTR EPISODE EIGHT
(Tx order Tba)

"LIKE FATHER..."

By

GRAHAM CHAPMAN & DOUGLAS ADAMS

PRODUCER	HUMPHREY BARCLAY
DIRECTOR	BRYAN IZZARD
P.A.	JILL POWELL
CASTING DIRECTOR	RICHARD PRICE
DESIGNER	RODNEY CAMMISH

VTR: JANUARY 21st, 1976

FILMING: (TO ACCOMPANY SC.1) - 2nd JANUARY, 1976

Graham Chapman had originally studied medicine at Emmanuel College, Cambridge, before falling into Footlights, meeting John Cleese and eventually becoming a Python. His medical knowledge, though, was put to good use when he wrote the scripts for the TV adaptations of Richard Gordon's *Doctor* books. The 1977 second series was called *Doctor on the Go*, and one episode, with the working title 'Like Father', was a collaboration with Douglas. You can find the episode itself online – it reached our screens as 'For Your Own Good'.

FILMING: (TO ACCOMPANY SC.1) - 2nd JANUARY, 1976

A LIARS AUTOBIOGRAPHY

by Graham Chapman
and Douglas Adams.
(whose autobiography it isn't)

I was born in Leamington, ~~[illegible]~~ now officially known as Royal Leamington Spa, moderately famous for the manufacture of gas cookers (see Chapter 14) about which more anon.* The year was nineteen forty two, and ~~th~~ the period of gestation ended on the 7th February during a rather botched up air-raid ~~whilst the whom~~ ~~[illegible]~~ in which the Germans thought they were hitting Coventry – but more of that anon*,[1] which is a word I'm very fond of. My parents, Tim + Beryl*, sorry, Tim + Betty[2], were outraged ~~at~~ when I arrived because they'd been expecting a heterosexual black Jew with several ~~into~~ rather amusing birth deformities, because they needed the problems. They lived in an enormous Gothic castle in the ~~on~~ South of France called Dundrinkingginandslimlinetonicwithiceandlemonin, which was originally built for Marco Polo for himself and a few friends which he wanted to invite round after the pub closed – an awe inspiring construction of granite and bits of wood with sweeping lawns recently modified to include an ornamental malarial swamp filled with pink fizzy water.[3] He felt a sharp stab of steel in his groin, and the sickening sensation of the warm ooze of blood welling up inside his nightie.

---

* Very stupid word which won't be used again in this book.

1 None of this is true. I was in fact born in Stalbridge, in Dorset (but if you want to send any letters to Stalbridge, congratulating it on being my birthplace, please take note that the correct postal address is ~~Stalbridge~~ STURMINSTER NEWTON, Dorset). The correct date of birth was Jan 6th 1940. See page 14)

2 - ~~Actually Tim + Betty~~ Actually Walter + Edith + Mark

This page from Douglas's archive comes from the project through which Douglas's writing partnership – and friendship – with Graham Chapman floundered, very nearly (almost, but not quite) irrevocably. The title and writing credits on Douglas's handwritten notes reproduced above perhaps rather speak for themselves. The page is transcribed overleaf.

A LIARS AUTOBIOGRAPHY

By Graham Chapman and Douglas Adams (whose autobiography it isn't)

I was born in Leamington, now officially known as Royal Leamington Spa, moderately famous for the manufacture of gas works (see Chapter 14) about which more anon.* The year was nineteen forty two, and the period of gestation ended on the 7th February during a rather botched up air-raid in which the Germans thought they were hitting Coventry – but more of that anon,*[1] which is a word I'm very fond of. My parents, Tim & Beryl, sorry Tim & Betty,[2] were outraged when I arrived because they'd been expecting a heterosexual black Jew with several rather amusing birth deformities, because they needed the problems. They lived in an enormous Gothic castle in the South of France called 'Dundrinkinginandslimlinetonicwithicebutnolemon' which was originally built for Marco Polo for himself and a few friends which he wanted to invite round after the pub closed – an awe-inspiring construction of granite and bits of wood with sweeping lawns recently modified to include an ornamental malaria swamp filled with pink fizzy water.[3]

He felt a sharp stab of steel in his groin, and the sickening sensation of the warm ooze of blood welling up inside his nightie.

A mortifying hail of bullets passed through his left ear as he mused 'Hey that was my ear.' Thinking this over he went for a hamburger with French fries and side salad with Thousand Island dressing.[4]

Sorry.

At the age of two years + nine months[6] I was in Ibiza which at that time was a very fashionable centre for young trendies – smoking pot, LSD, cocaine, being thrown into prison by a man called F. Rzanko and being treated appallingly by nuns who liked to think of themselves as nurses. I was driven directly from the airport to a bar/restaurant called the Green Dolphin in Ibiza town, where, having qualified as a medical practitioner at an early age, I was to be faced with my first patient. I went in, sat down, met Marty Feldman, Tim Brooke Taylor, ordered a cheap meal, because at the age of two years, nine months, one day, I was not particularly rich – we bragged a bit about that and this and how many women we hadn't had when I decided to go to the toilet. (It was the drinks on the plane coming over.) I went into the toilet, peed, and washed my hands and was extremely surprised by the soap which protruded in a very phallic fashion from a chrome iron prong mounted on the wall. I went and told Tim, who was in mid gaspachio *[sic]*, that there was something he ought to see in the lavatory/toilet/men's room/little boy's room/bathroom/wet room/comfort station. He went in to wash his hands/pee/crap and came back ashen faced saying he didn't think it was much of a joke. I thought he was being typically prudish, but then he pointed out that there were a couple of legs sticking out from under the door of the cubicle. Being a newly qualified doctor, I leapt in, opened the door and found a man who had apparently fallen off his seat in a coma, presumably from morphine, but I never was a very good doctor. I found the manageress a very capable – and all of them are German – lady, and we carried him out on to the pavement, not calling the vicious police. He eventually recovered enough to be carried home, and we discovered that the reason he had been drinking and drugging was that he had killed a young boy with his wang that morning.[7] Several years later I was also in Ibiza and did not hear about or observe an incident in which a rather silly person who happened to be on LSD fell through the cover of a near dry well outside someone's villa. On arriving at the bottom he broke one leg.[8] He remained there till about noon the next day, when his cries attracted the attention of a passerby who decided to help out. He passed him down a rope for him to climb up. He tied the rope as best he could round his waist and was hauled up, using his own foot and arms to assist his progress. Near the top of the well the noose of the rope slipped up over one arm round his neck and he was in danger of being strangled, so he was forced to take out his sheath knife and cut the rope so that he then fell back down the well, breaking his other leg, and an arm. A friend of the friend that had been helping now arrived, who, using the rest of the rope decided to climb down and help the poor victim. He was a little overoptimistic in the strength of his arms, and plumetted *[sic]* full thirty feet on to the other victim and broke his jaw, the other arm, his own ribs and one leg. They were both eventually rescued some twelve hours later by ladder, and the victim was taken off to a Spanish hospital and treated as a victim. He eventually managed

A friend of the friend that had been helping now arrived, who using the rest of the rope decided to climb down and help the poor victim.

to escape to an English hospital – he felt it necessary since the screws they put in his jaw had become rusty and fallen out – and he can now almost say 'mmnmmf'[14] and nearly feed himself.

The preceding passage is quite evidently irrelevant and out of sequence, so my co-author has suggested that we ought to clarify a few points.

DATE OF BIRTH 8th JANUARY 1941
SEX MALE
CHRISTENED GRAHAM CHAPMAN
PLACE OF BIRTH LEICESTER
STAR SIGN – CAPRICORN (CHINESE YEAR OF THE DRAGON)
FAVOURITE FOOD CURRY
LEAST FAVOURITE FOOD POISON
FAVOURITE POISON GALLAMINE TRIETHIODIDE
FAVOURITE ANTIDOTE NEOSTIGMINE
EDUCATED AT SOUTH WIXTON JUNIOR BOYS
RAVENHURST RD MIXED INFANTS + JUNIOR SCHOOL
KIBWORTH GRAMMAR SCHOOL
MELTON MOWBRAY GRAMMAR SCHOOL

Footnotes:

* Very stupid word which won't be used again in this book.

1 None of this is true. I was in fact born in Stalbridge, in Dorset. (But if you want to send any letters to Stalbridge, congratulating it on being my birthplace, please take note that the correct postal address is Stalbridge, STURMINSTER NEWTON, Dorset.) The correct date of birth was Jan 6th 1940. (See page 14.)

2 Actually Walter & Edith & Mark

3 This particular footnote is completely untrue.

4 This passage is from a rather unsuccessful and as yet unpublished novel written by my co-author which I had to include because he was such a magnetic presence and also is rather bigger than I am – but it won't happen again because I'll get my friend Denis[5] to duff him over. In fact I'm rather surprised that he included this bit. I didn't – you must have done because I didn't, oh perhaps I did. Sorry.

5 Denis Joseph O'Driscoll

6 This is a complete lie; I was twelve.[9]

7 This incident is denied by everyone, but the Gaspachio was nice – so is Maggie Henderson's chow. Sorry, Bernard's wife's.

8 This bit is so like a lift from Gerard Hoffnung it must be true, especially as he stole it from a Canadian humourist whose name eludes me at this moment, check later.[13]

9 Actually 25.

13 Oh why bother.

14 Pronounced 'mmnnmmf'

2nd Series
Programme 8

"THE BURKISS WAY"

to Dynamic Living

with

JO KENDALL
****

NIGEL REES
****

CHRIS EMMETT
****

FRED HARRIS
****

Lesson Fourteen: 'Do You-Know-What The Burkiss Way'

(9'36)" by 15 (10'07)

ANDREW MARSHALL AND DAVID RENWICK
+ DOUGLAS ADAMS

SMs: Eric Young
John Whitehall
Martha Knight
Ian Cameron

PRODUCER: SIMON BRETT

TRANSMISSION:	WEDNESDAY 2ND FEBRUARY 1977 1227 - 1255 RADIO 4 CURRENT REP. FRIDAY 4TH FEBRUARY 1977 1815-1843 RADIO 4
RECORDING:	FRIDAY 21ST JANUARY 1977 2015 - 2100
REHEARSAL:	" " " " 1430
STUDIO:	THE PARIS (AUDIENCE)
P.P.REF.NO:	BLN 03 095 K 572

The main writers on the BBC radio sketch show *The Burkiss Way* were Andrew Marshall (later, TV's *2Point4 Children* and *Strange*) and David Renwick (*One Foot in the Grave* and *Jonathan Creek*), and the cast included Jo Kendall and Chris Emmett, who would go on to lend their voices to *The Hitchhiker's Guide*. Simon Brett (series producer) spotted something in Douglas's contributions to *The Burkiss Way* and invited him to lunch in February 1977 – a landmark moment in Douglas's career.

24.

1. PRESENTER: Fred — Good evening. And tonight on "~~This Programme is Way Above Your Level~~" *(handwritten: "What you can do to Some of the people all of the time")* we talk to Eric Von Contrick, author of such best-selling books as "Spaceships of the Gods", "Some more of Me Spaceships of the Gods" and "It shouldn't Happen to Spaceships of the Gods in Harness". Now, Professor Von Contrick, one of the most interesting things about your series of books, in which you claim that mankind is descended from beings from Outer Space, is that they all seek to prove exactly the same thing using exactly the same evidence. Now why is this?

(handwritten in margin: restore my titles?)

2. CONTRICK: Nigel — (GERMAN) You think they are all the same? Have you read them all?

3. PRESENTER: — Er, yes, that's why I ...

4. CONTRICK: — So what does it matter if they're all the same, if you read them all? (CHUCKLE) I mean to say ...

5. PRESENTER: — An ... I see. You're only in it for the money. Does this mean you don't actually believe what you say – that man is descended from extra-terrestrial life forms?

6. CONTRICK: — How can I not believe it? The evidence is incontrovertible.

/FRED over

Douglas's collaboration on *The Burkiss Way* saw him create Eric von Contrick, the fictional author of *Spaceships of the Gods*. The character was a spoof of genuine Swiss author Erich von Däniken, who wrote the *Chariots of the Gods* books. (Many people believed Von Däniken also inspired the character Oolon Colluphid in *The Hitchhiker's Guide*. In actuality, Colluphid was drawn from another contentious author, John Marco Allegro and his book *The Sacred Mushroom and the Cross*.)

4th Series
2nd Programme
(39)

THE
***
N E W S
* * * *
"H U D D L I N E S"
****

starring:

ROY HUDD
* * * * *
w i t h
JANET BROWN
* * * * * *
CHRIS EMMETT
* * * * * * *
a n d
THE NIC ROWLEY QUARTET
* * * * * * * * * * * *

Written by:

PETER SPENCE
DAVID RENWICK
w i t h
LAURIE ROWLEY
DOUGLAS ADAMS
FRED METCALF
ANDY HAMILTON
& OTHERS

Announcer: Len Jackson

SMs: Max Alcock
Alick Hale-Munro
Martha Knight
Lisa Braun (Rec)

PRODUCED BY JOHN LLOYD

TRANSMISSION:	WEDNESDAY, 11TH MAY 1977:	1902-1930 RADIO 2 (SB R1)
REPEAT:	SATURDAY, 14TH MAY 1977:	1302-1330 RADIO 2
RECORDING:	WEDNESDAY, 11TH MAY 1977:	1300-1345
REHEARSAL:	WEDNESDAY, 11TH MAY 1977:	0930 (Cast) 1100 (Quartet)
STUDIO:	THE PARIS	
R.P.REF.NO.:	BLN 19/094L967 (Orig: LLD094L967) (Rpt: LLD083R008)	

In May 1977, Douglas contributed to *The News Huddlines*, a radio vehicle for the irrepressible comedian and actor Roy Hudd, who later played Max Quordlepleen in the original *Hitchhiker's Guide* radio series in 1978 (a couple of the studio managers, Alick Hale-Munro and Lisa Braun, also went on to work on *Hitchhiker*). The producer was Douglas's old friend John Lloyd (see page 75). A satirical revue, *The News Huddlines* needed regular feeding with topical gags. In the extract opposite, the talk of the time was the problem of British football hooliganism.

21.

FOOTBALL HOOLIGANS D.ADAMS

1. BAND: CURRENT AFFAIRS SIG.

2. ROBIN DAY: Chris
Good evening. Well tonight as usual we shall be looking at a number of boring people doing boring things and trying to make them seem more interesting than they really are by asking them rude questions and getting them annoyed. And first we look at football hooliganism. Here in the studio with me is the Sports Minister, Mr. Dennis Howell, and also, to put the other side of the question Mr. A Soccer Hooligan.

3. COCKNEY: Roy
Er, well I just want to say that I had nothing to do with mashing that Bristol City supporter over the head with a mallet, that it wasn't me that sawed off the ref's legs, and the grenades in my pocket were just a present for the wife's birthday.

4. DAY:
Well I'm very glad to hear that, Mr. Howell. Now you claim that the new measure you took against hooliganism last Saturday went into operation with complete success.

/ROY over ...

22.

1. HOWELL: (cockney)
Yes, well we very successfully managed to find out where the matches were on, we drove along to some of them extremely successfully, and then succesrfully managed to put up some notices asking all Chelsea and Manchester United fans if they wouldn't mind perhaps going away.

2. DAY:
But Mr. Hewell, I read in the papers that still 120 people were arrested.

3. HOWELL:
Well not everyone managed to see the notices did they? And anyway that's a very small number when you consider that nearly 60 million people weren't arrested. Lots of people just stayed at home and watched tv or did the washing up, and only a few of those were arrested.

4. DAY:
Yes, but what about the 18 people who were injured at matches?

5. HOWELL:
Well they were the ones who saw the notices we very successfully put up, and bust a gut laughing. Or bust somebody else's gut laughing. Or of course bust somebody else's head with one of the notices.

6. DAY:
So what do you feel you've achieved?

/ROY over ...

23.

1. HOWELL:
I think we made it very very clear in no uncertain terms to a lot of these thugs that this sort of behaviour can't go on for ever.

2. DAY:
What makes you so sure?

3. HOWELL:
Well eventually they'll grow old and die.

4. DAY:
Well perhaps we can turn to you Mr. A. Soccer-Hooligan. Now I'm going to say this very slowly and carefully, so if there's anything you don't understand just ask. Now. H...e...l...l...o ...

5. HOOLIGAN:
(REALLY AMAZINGLY GROSS) What? You watch it mate, none of your lip, I'll break you into little pieces mate .... (Etc. Ad lib)

6. FX: SOUND OF VIOLENT FIGHT

7. DAY:
(AFTER A SUFFICIENT PERIOD OF THE VIOLENCE)
Well, whilst Mr. Hooligan is busy beating the hell out of his chair, perhaps you'd like to sum up for us Mr. Howell.

8. HOWELL:
Well, many people say I should go back to my old job, because I did far more to prevent soccer violence when I was drought minister.

/CHRIS over ...

24.

1. DAY:
In what way?

2. HOWELL:
Well, all the matches were rained off.

3. BAND: STING

(END)

On '42'

On Wednesday 29 March 1978, BBC Radio 4 broadcast the fourth episode of *The Hitchhiker's Guide to the Galaxy* – in it the scene in the script below, which gave us '42'. This number is, according to the mighty computer Deep Thought (voiced originally by Geoff McGivern), the answer to 'Everything' (and the inspiration for the title of this book, of course). That broadcast unleashed intense and ongoing speculation as to what gave Douglas the idea to use 42. Over these pages, we muse on some of the evidence for 42 in Douglas's life, and look at the ways in which it kept reappearing throughout his career.

4. DEEP THOUGHT: All right. The Answer to Everything....

5. TWO: Yes....!

6. DEEP THOUGHT: Life, The Universe and Everything....

7. ONE: Yes....!

8. DEEP THOUGHT: Is....

9. ~~THREE:~~ | Yes....!

10. DEEP THOUGHT: Is....

11. ONE/TWO/THREE: Yes....!!!

12. DEEP THOUGHT: ~~The answer is~~ 42.

PAUSE. ACTUALLY QUITE A LONG ONE

13. TWO: We're going to get lynched, you know that.

14. DEEP THOUGHT: It was a tough assignment.

/ONE & THREE over...

Right - The minutes of the meeting of the Crawley and District Paranoid Society. The meeting was duly convened and Mr S.J. Stabintheback gave us a spirited talk

7 STUDIO

Hardware Shop

(Fridge Department)

Salesman and Woman customer.

NARR: Of course, there are times when it's no problem at all.

SALESMAN: A fridge. Certainly. What height?

CUSTOMER: Well, it's got to fit under a 42" work surface.

SALESMAN: Do you want a lot of freezing space?

CUSTOMER: Not particularly.

SALESMAN: Do you store a lot of tall bottles - you know, wine, milk, beer, that sort of thing?

of the last meeting.

2. Right - The minutes of the ~~[illegible]~~ 42nd meeting of the Crawley and District Paranoid Society. The meeting was duly convened and Mr S.J. Stabintheback gave us a spirited talk about the holes his next-door neighbours had drilled in his wall; And then went on to .... Hey! Someone's been tampering with these notes!

3. What do you mean?

2 I said, someone's been tampering with these notes.

SILENCE

4. You're blaming me, aren't you?

2. Stop trying to put words in my mouth!

3. No, but what have they done? Let me see it!

2 You don't believe me, do you?

3 Did I say ~~[illegible]~~ I ~~[illegible]~~ didn't believe you?

2. No!

Some think that, having always been an avid reader, Douglas may have had a memory of childhood favourite Lewis Carroll's *Alice's Adventures in Wonderland* (1865). In the book, it is stated that Rule 42 means 'All persons more than a mile high to leave the court'. Given Douglas's own self-consciousness about his height (not a mile, but a wow-worthy 6 feet 5 inches nonetheless), perhaps Carroll's attitude to the exceptionally tall touched a nerve that gave the number 42 a significance rather less relevant to other people.

Whatever the trigger, there is evidence in Douglas's archive that the number kept cropping up in various early jobs in his career. In July 1973, when he was working on John Cleese's business training film, Douglas witnessed a conversation that led to the choice of the number 42 – which then found its way into the script (above, top) as an amendment. A year later, in 1974, an Adams-Smith-Adams sketch for the *Hole in the Wall Gang* (see page 78) talks about the 'minutes of the 42nd meeting of the Crawley and District Paranoid Society' (above, in the handwriting of Will Adams). It seems, then, that the Universe did indeed keep throwing the number 42 at Douglas. But there's more...

In January 1977, the ***Hole in the Wall Gang*** **script was modified for** ***The Burkiss Way*** **radio series (see pages 94–5), admitting that 'the number 42 has greatly increased its popularity'. Adams-Smith-Adams also used it towards the end of the sketch, as part of an address: '42 Logical Positivism Avenue' (below).**

1. DEREK: Yes, I should say that Gungadin is probably a gratuitous reference to the Kipling character thrown in for incongruous effect - and very effective it is too. And 23 of course is probably the funniest of the two-figure numbers, though I know that recently the number 42 has greatly increased its popularity.

2. DAVID: Yes, I'm sure we can expect a lot of "23" jokes this afternoon - if indeed it's going to be a jokey sketch. I must say, I'm now more inclined to go along with your opinion that we may be in for something altogether more zany.

9. DEREK: 42 Logical Positivism Avenue.

Despite these, and many, many other references, it was ***The Hitchhiker's Guide to the Galaxy*** **that undoubtedly popularized the number in the minds of the public.**

Some of the more outlandish theories expounded about its source include the oft-repeated assumption that Douglas, so famously into computers in later life, must have been referring to a designation of 42 as an asterisk in ASCII, meaning the answer could be 'anything you want it to be'. However, the chronology tells us that this theory can't be right. Douglas wrote the radio show and indeed drafted the first four ***Hitchhiker*** **books on old manual typewriters, before he'd touched even a most basic word processor.**

A later scene in ***Hitchhiker*** **had a question wrongly posed by letters on a Scrabble board: 'What do you get if you multiply six by nine?' Maths fans were eager to point out that 6 x 9 – in base 13 – is 42, whereupon Douglas replied that that was also nonsense, as he didn't write gags in base 13.**

For over four decades, Douglas Adams fans have been perpetuating the mystery of 42. ZZ9 Plural Z Alpha, the official ***Hitchhiker's Guide*** **appreciation society, used the number as part of their club logo, as seen on the cover of their flagship fanzine,** ***Mostly Harmless*** **(right).**

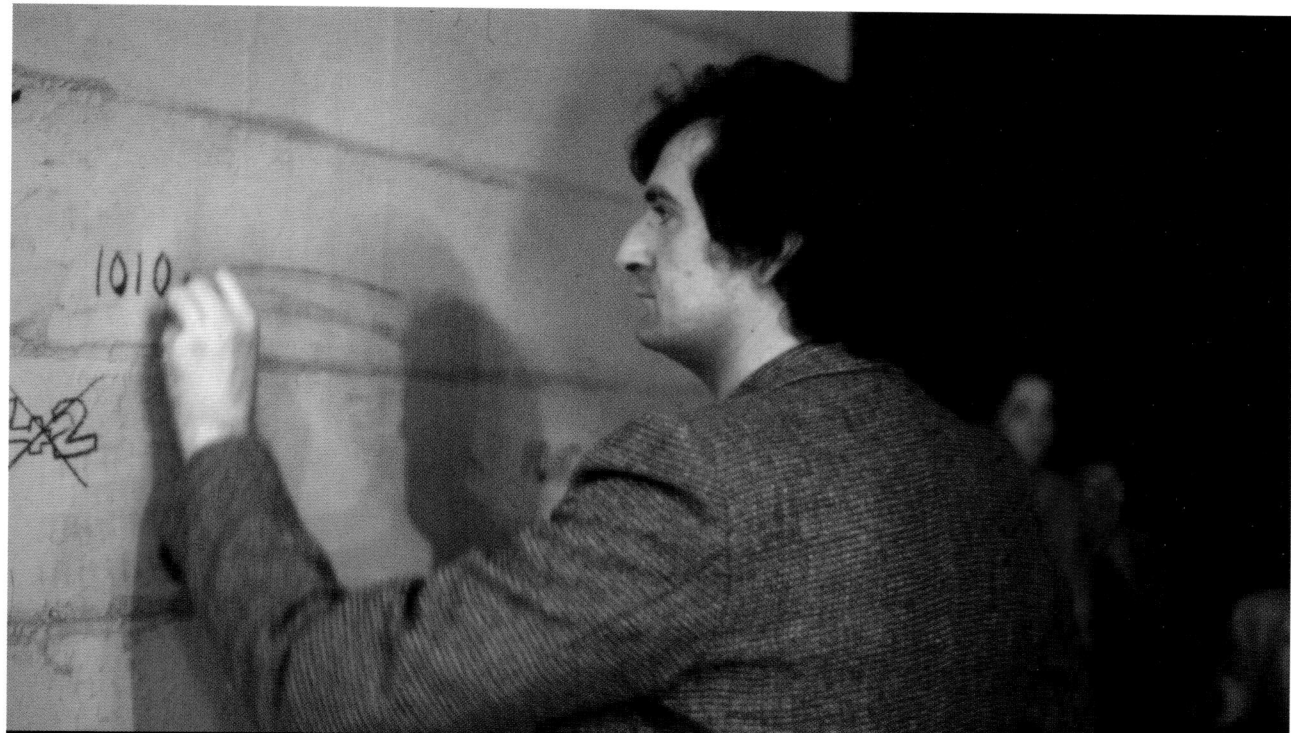

In 1980, a BBC set designer had prepared a surface of 'breeze blocks' in vacuum-formed plastic, representing the wall of a bunker, where supposedly some desperate, unnamed survivor of an apocalypse had repeatedly scrawled '42'. As a young member of the animation team visiting the set, writer and filmmaker Kevin Jon Davies was offered a piece of charcoal and told, 'Just graffiti forty-twos on the wall in as many different ways as you can.' Unnerved by the whole TV studio watching, he wavered. Douglas Adams stepped forward: 'I'll do it!' And so he did. He even wrote it in binary...

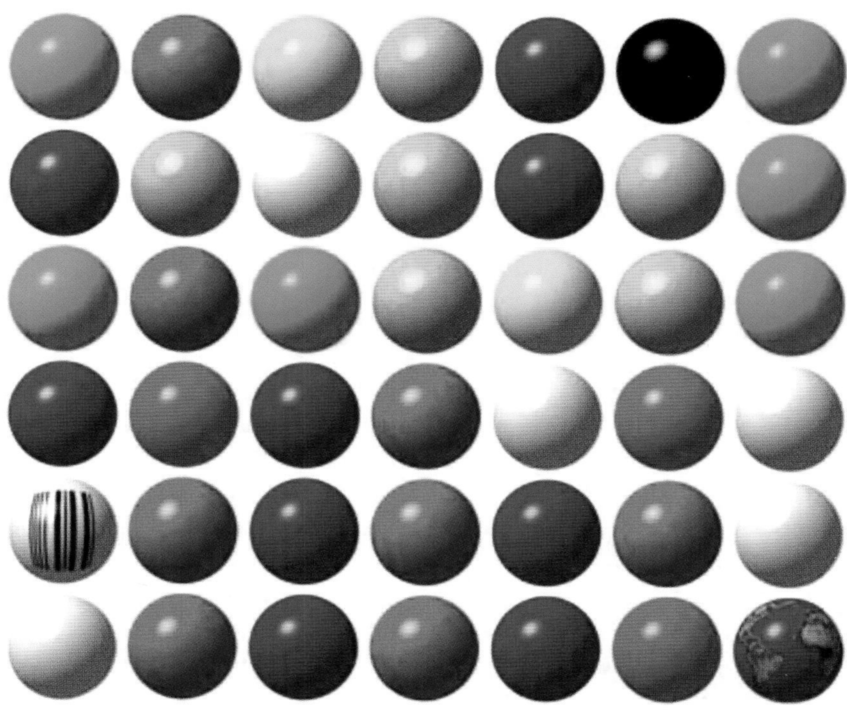

In the days before Photoshop, *The Illustrated Hitchhiker's Guide* (1994) was an epic feat in early digital image manipulation. For a page intended to be full of 42s, Douglas designed a puzzle on one of his many Apple Macs that consisted of a pattern of coloured snooker balls (right). Apparently, the puzzle was coded with umpteen different 42s. There are many online theories as to how, although it seems Douglas never did reveal the complete answer (at least not publicly).

FOUR
Deep Thoughts

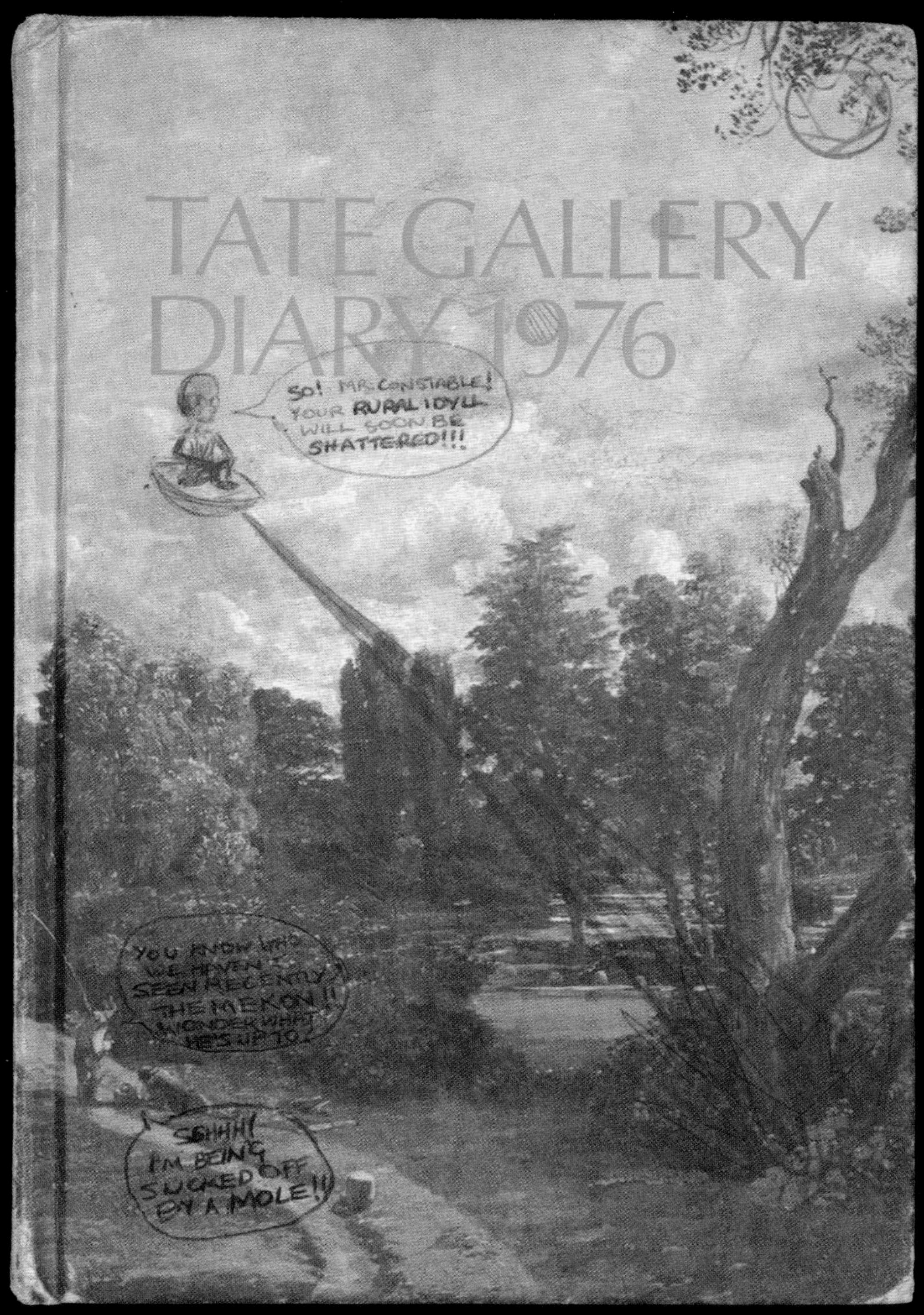

In 1976, Douglas wrote in his notebook, 'I certainly don't intend to spend my life being professionally funny. It's certainly not something I envisage as a career.' This chapter collects some of the early ideas for stories Douglas noted down – as well as some home truths from the powers that be!

from Joker's Wild
– 'Post Office' Workers collect money for a
'Santa' letter asking for £20
They collect £19.
Man writes back, says thanks to Santa,
and upset about missing pound
'Thieves at the Post Office'.

Death of Dog. Story from Ron.
Family's large + beloved Labrador dog dies,
and they don't know what to do with the body,
so Ron agreed to look after it for a day whilst
they decide (they had left it on the bed!).
Ron puts it on the deep freeze in a large
black plastic bag. Mum moves it to the
greenhouse – full of rubbish + tools and things.
Then daughter arrives to see it. Mum sends
her off to get torch, and meanwhile dashes off
to re-arrange dog – make it more presentable.
Daughter comes back, puts pillow under head
and stands and looks at it for fifteen minutes.

Cannibal idea.
Man eats father whilst drunk.
– remark – 'he's got a lot of his father in him'.

Cows being milked by confidence tricksters.

Meeting of Paranoids

Mum has a tendency, for instance in a restaurant
to talk as if it is only by some accident
that she is a customer and talks of what
the waitresses are doing, thinking, and what is
going on in the kitchen.

Things to talk about – box of matches.
Ridiculous door.

Science fiction story.
Man goes to friend; reveals that
he is in fact an alien (they have known
each other many years) he must now leave
the earth which is threatened with
extinction, and offers to take his friend with him.

This page from Douglas's notebook dating from around 1974/5 contains intriguing early story musings. The last on the page (entitled 'Science Fiction Story') seems to record the seeds of an idea that to any Douglas Adams fan will seem instantly recognizable as perhaps a first foray into the tale that would become *The Hitchhiker's Guide to the Galaxy*.

From Joker's Wild

– Post office workers collect money for a 'Santa' letter asking for £20.

They collect £19.

Man writes back, says thanks to Santa and upset about missing pound

'Thieves at the Post Office.'

Death of Dog. Story from Ron.*

Family's large and beloved Labrador dog dies and they don't know what to do with the body, so Ron agreed to look after it for a day whilst they decide (they had left it on the bed!). Ron puts it on their deep freezer in 2 large black plastic bags. Mum moves it to the greenhouse – full of rubbish + tools and things. Then daughter arrives to see it. Mum sends her off to get torch, and meanwhile dashes to re-arrange dog – make it more presentable. Daughter comes back, puts pillow under head and stands and looks at it for fifteen minutes.

Cannibal idea.

Man eats father whilst drunk.

– remark – 'He's got a lot of his father in him.'

Cows being milked by confidence tricksters.

Meeting of Paranoids

Mum has a tendency for instance in a restaurant to talk as if it is only by some accident that she is a customer and talks of what the waitresses are doing, thinking, and what is going on in the kitchen.

Things to talk about – box of matches.

Ridiculous door.

Science fiction story.

Man goes to friend; reveals that he is in fact an alien (they have known each other many years), he must now leave the Earth which is threatened with extinction and offers to take his friend with him.

* *Ron was Douglas's stepfather, a vet.*

JILL FOSTER LTD
88 Rannoch Road
London W.6
01-385 6947

15 March 1976

Douglas Adams Esq
c/o Dr Harry Porter
13Warkworth Street
Cambridge

Dear Douglas:

Your "Dr Who" outline has, I'm afraid, been spurned by Philip Hinchcliffe. I can do no better than quote "... The idea of the Doctor investigating a breach of the space-time continuum, with the help of the Time Lords, is not enough. The story lacks a villain and, therefore, any dramatic conflict. Please don't think I am averse to encouraging new writers for the programme. We are using one this season. But we do need greater evidence than this of real talent, and preferably in the form of a complete script." Sadly, this isn't an idea we can place elsewhere, so I am returning it.

As the launching of my company fast approaches I am preparing a client list - which in fact will be in booklet form with a page for each client. I would like from you a short piece giving details of what you've done and anything else you think relevant remembering it is aimed at television, theatre, radio and film producers and publishers. It needs to give as much information in as little space as possible - just a list if you like. Please.

Yours,

Jill

Directors: Jill Foster · Malcolm Hamer   Reg. Office: 19 Harley St., W1N 2DT

Script editor Robert Holmes and series producer Philip Hinchcliffe formally rejected an early draft of Douglas's idea for the long-running BBC TV sci-fi series *Doctor Who*, called (at that point) 'The Krikkitmen'. Jill Foster, Douglas's agent, wrote to Douglas, then staying in Cambridge, to tell him the bad news (above), quoting the somewhat frank words of the rejection: 'we do need greater evidence than this of real talent'.

Notes

Paul Bonner Kensington House

Peter Whitmore. 2. Ronnies.

Terry Hughes – New Year show.

Peter De Vries – books –

Story of two men/man + woman?
or whatever who simply find
a spacecraft in their backgarden
- maybe an enormous one.
The occupants are dead (why?)
They investigate it, take off...
and that's where your story
starts.

Ron Davidson.
2900

These few notes (middle of the page) for a story idea in the back of Douglas's 1977 diary suggest he really wanted to get his protagonists off the planet as soon as possible! The note reads: 'Story of two men/man & woman? Or whatever who simply find a spacecraft in their backgarden – maybe an enormous one. The occupants are dead (why?) They investigate it, take off... and that's where your story starts.'

When I graduated I decided I would give myself a couple of years or so to try my hand at earning a living as a freelance comedy scriptwriter, which was a hobby I'd ~~been~~ particularly enjoyed at Cambridge. ~~I achieved a fair measure of success in the time, and it's been fun as a short term venture. I certainly I don't intend~~ want to ~~spend the rest of my life being professionally funny. I it's certainly not something I envisage as a career. In looking for a career I'm quite deb deliberately trying to avoid anything further in the world of entertainment in~~

Having pursued it ~~full time~~ to the hilt, and achieved ~~enjoyed~~ a fair measure of success, I've come to feel that ~~on the whole~~ working in ~~working on~~ television entertainment is ~~a~~ 95% a ~~pretty~~ useless and trivial activity, and since I am (I hope) intelligent, educated and ambitious, it's time I turned ~~my~~ to something more productive.

I'm choosing a career in commerce in general, and P&O in particular, because I would like to be ~~directly~~ involved in ~~the problem of generating wealth tackling tackling the problems of the generation~~ the job of generating wealth, ~~which is one of~~ the main problems the world is facing ~~at the moment~~, and I ~~would~~ also want the opportunity ~~to do a lot for a~~ of work and travel abroad.

When I graduated, I decided I would give myself a couple of years or so to try my hand at earning a living as a freelance comedy scriptwriter, which was a hobby I'd ~~been~~ particularly enjoyed at Cambridge.

~~I achieved a fair measure of success in the time, and it's been fun as a short-term venture. I certainly don't intend to spend the rest of my life being professionally funny. It's certainly not something I envisage as a career. In looking for a career I'm quite deliberately trying to avoid anything further in the world of entertainment.~~

Having pushed it full time to the hilt, and achieved a fair measure of success, I've come to feel that ~~on the whole~~, working in television entertainment is 95% a useless and trivial activity, and since I am (I hope) intelligent, educated and ambitious, it's time I turned ~~my~~ to something more productive.

I'm choosing a career in commerce in general, and P&O in particular, because I would like to be ~~directly~~ involved in ~~the problem of generating wealth tackling tackling the problem of the generation~~ the job of generating wealth, ~~which is one of~~ the main problem the world is facing ~~at the moment~~, and I ~~would~~ also want the opportunity ~~to do a lot for a~~ of work and travel abroad.

Douglas went through a period of disenchantment with writing and made several attempts at getting a more regular job. This letter, from his archive, is a draft application for a post as a shipping clerk with P&O in Hong Kong. How genuine were his stated intentions to quit comedy writing? Was this for real, or just intended to appease the prospective employer or the Jobcentre? In any case, he certainly proved, years later, that he could generate wealth – and he did in fact travel the world. They say it's darkest just before the dawn.

A COMEDY ADVENTURE IN TIME AND SPACE

THE HITCH-HIKER'S GUIDE TO THE GALAXY.

Douglas Adams.

The show is a science fiction comedy adventure in time and space, which weaves in and out of fantasy, jokes, satire, parallel universes and time warps, in the wake of two men who are researching the New Revised Edition of the Hitch Hiker's Guide to the Galaxy, an electroni 'book' designed to help the footloose wanderer find his way round the marvels of the Universe for less than thirty Altairian dollars a day.

One of the men is an extraterrestrial who has spent some years living incognito on the Earth. When he first arrived the minimal research he had done suggested to him that the name Ford Prefect would be nicel inconspicuous. The other is an Earthman, ~~Aleric B~~ Arthur Dent who was a friend of Ford's for years without realising that he wasn't a perfectly ordinary human being.

The first episode tells of how Ford reveals the truth about himself to an incredulous ~~Aleric~~ Arthur, and how they both escape from a doomed Earth to begin their wanderings.

The story starts as ~~Aleric~~ Arthur is lying on the ground in the path of a bulldozer which is about to demolish his house to make away for a new by-pass. Having fought the plans at every level, this is his last ditch effort. He is arguing with a man from the council who is pointing out to him in a Godfatherly way that the bulldozer driver is is a rather careless gentleman who isn't too fussy about what he drive over. In the middle of this confrontation Ford arrives in a rather anx state and asks ~~Aleric~~ Arthur is he's busy at all, and if there's somewhere th can go and have a chat. ~~Aleric~~ Arthur, astonished, refuses to move. Ford is very insistent and eventually ~~Aleric~~ Arthur calls the man from the council and asks him if they could declare a truce for half an hour. The councilman very charmingly agrees and says that if he likes to slip away for half an hour he'll make sure they don't try and knock his hous

Having almost given up on comedy, it would have been a shame if Douglas had not been given one more chance by BBC radio producer Simon Brett. This is the original outline Douglas submitted for the storyline that would eventually spawn several radio series, many stage plays, LP records, a BBC TV series, five or six books, one long-gestated Hollywood-funded movie and an official towel! (Note that Arthur Dent here is still called 'Aleric B' until Douglas amended his name.)

till he gets back, word of honour. Ford and ~~Aleric~~ Arthur repairs to a nearby pub, where Ford asks ~~Aleric~~ Arthur how he would react if he told him that he wasn't from Guildford at all but from a small planet in the vicinity of Betelgeuse.

As soon as they're out of the way the councilman orders the demolition ceremony to start. A local lady dignitary makes a very moving speech about how wonderful life will suddenly become as soon as the bypass is built, and swings a bottle of champagne against the bulldozer, which moves in for the kill.

The sound of the crashing building reaches ~~Aleric~~ Arthur who is in the middle of not believing a word that Ford is telling him, and he charges back to his ex-house shouting about what a naughty world we live in.

At that moment the sky is suddenly torn apart by the scream of jets, and a fleet of flying saucers streak towards the Earth. As everyone flees in panic an unearthly voice rings through the air announcing that due to redevelopment of this sector of the galaxy they are building a new hyperspace bypass and the Earth will unfortunately have to be ~~xxxx~~ demolished. In answer to appalled cries of protest the voice says that the plans have been on public display in the planning office in Alpha Centauri for ten years, so it's far too late to start making a fuss now. He orders the demolition to start. A low rumble slowly builds into an earshattering explosion, followed by silence.

***

~~Aleric~~ Arthur wakes, not knowing where he is. Ford tells him they've managed to get a lift aboard one of the ships of the Vogon Constructor Fleet. Not to worry about the Earth, he says, there are an infinite multiplicity of parallel universes in which the Earth is still alive and well. He explains how they got on the ship by producing a copy of an electronic book called the Hitch Hiker's Guide to the Galaxy. Under the entry marked 'Vogon Constructors' it gives detailed instructions as to the best way of hitching a ride from one of their ships - you have to play on Vogon psychology, which it describes. Ford explains that it's his job to research a new edition of the book, which is now a little out of date. Would ~~Aleric~~ Arthur like to accompany him in the task? ~~Aleric~~ Arthur only wants to get back to Earth, or at least, it's nearest equivalent. However, he is fascinated to browse through this strange book. He is suddenly appalled when he discovers Earth's entry. Though the book is over a million pages long, the inhabitants of the Earth only warrant a one word entry - 'Harmless'. Ford, rather embarrassed, explains that the reason he had been on Earth was to gather a bit more material. He'd had a bit of an argument with the editor over it, but finally he' been allowed to expand the entry to 'Mostly harmless'. They&re very short of space.

~~Aleric~~ Arthur is stung to the quick. He agrees to go with Ford.

END OF EPISODE ONE.

HITCH HIKER'S GUIDE TO THE GALAXY

Some suggestions for future development.

Each episode should be more or less self containxed, but lead on ouite naturally to the next one, perhaps with a 'cliff hanger'.

A narrative structure can be achieved by having short extracts read fr the Guide itself, since much of its information would baturally be presented in the form of anecdote.

Ford and Aleric frequently have to subsidise their travels by taking odd jobs along the way; as well as strange new worlds they can visit parallel alternatives of Earth which are more or less the same, but no quite...; they find that many of the eccentric alien races they encoun er epitomise some particular human folly such as greed, pretentiousnes etc., rather in the manner of Gulliver's Travels.

In one episode they are hired by a fabulously wealthy but rather nervo man to act as 'internal body guards'. For this they are reduced to microscopic size in order to ascort meals through his digestive system

In another they encounter a race of dentists, exiled from their home planet for having pronounced that everything you can possibly eat or breathe, up to and including toothpaste, is bad for your teeth. They have been told not to return till they have xexxxtixxix evolved an entirely new way of life that is both hygienic and fun.

In another episode they find themsleves on an 'alternative' Earth which is receiving its first visitation from alien beings who announce that they have come to pay court at the home of the most intelligent life form in the Galaxy. After a lot of self satisfied parading by th humans it turns out that it was the dolphins the aliens actually had in mind.

The 'Guide' structure should allow for the almost unlimited developmen of freewheeling ideas whilst at the same time retaining a fairly simpl and cherent shape and purpose.

This page suggests a few blind alleys our heroes might have ventured down, in storylines which (mostly) were never ultimately explored. The BBC sat on this outline for a while, before committing to the series. But first, Douglas had an appointment with a famous time-traveller…

FIVE
Doctor Who

Douglas's fertile imagination for sci-fi was evident during school and university. He wanted to write for the BBC's long-running science fiction series *Doctor Who*. In the mid-1970s, after years of dreaming, he was invited to contribute the first of three stories to the series – and even to apply for a job on the team.

EARLY IDEAS

As far back as prep school at Brentford, Douglas had written stories about Daleks being powered by Rice Krispies, for himself and his friends to perform on a tape recorder. Later, in 1972, while on holiday with friends from university, he was still dabbling with ideas for the series. His notebook from the holiday provides a permanent record of some of the notions he dreamed up (below), as well as his doodles of the Tardis.

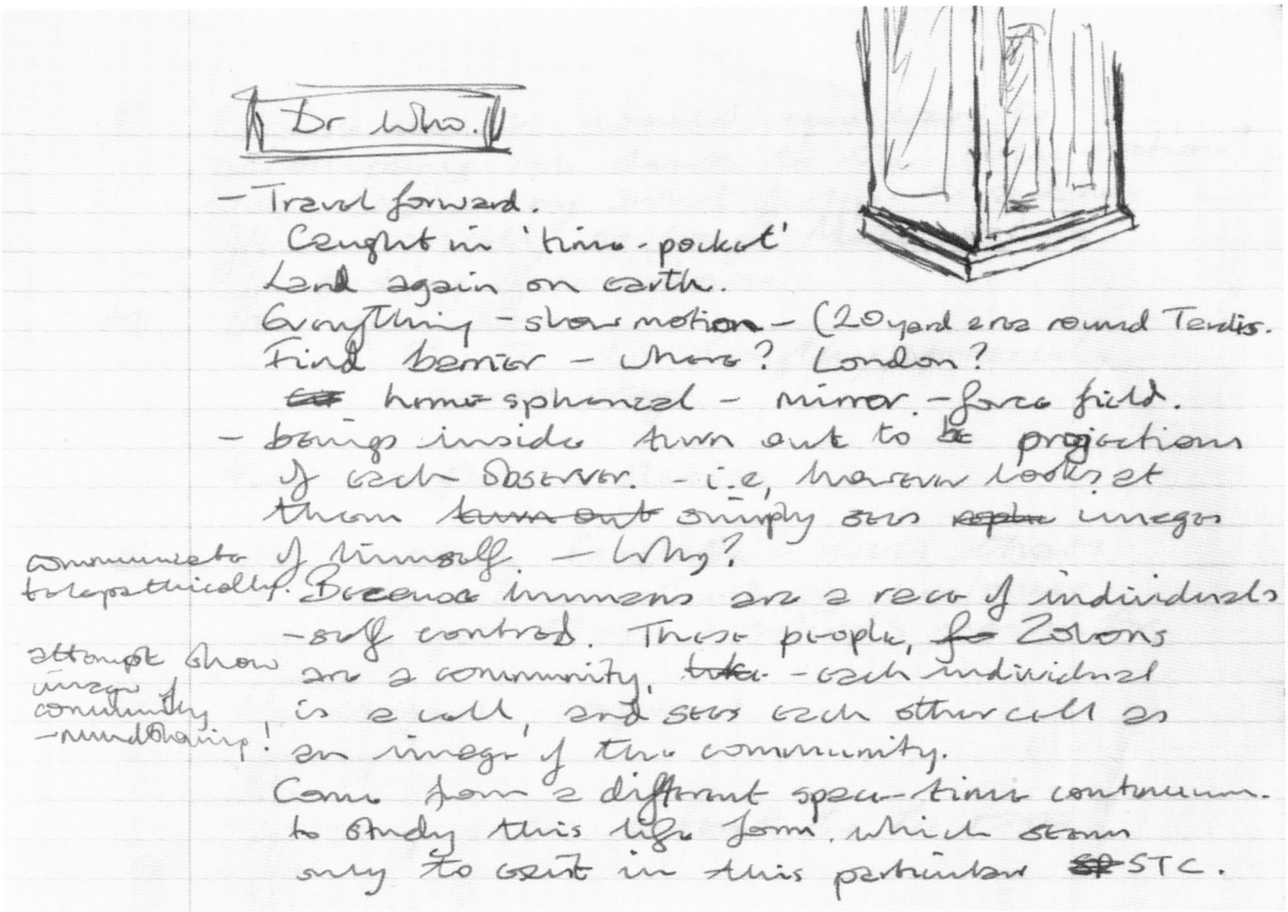

Dr Who

–Travel forward.

Caught in 'time pocket'

Land again on Earth.

Everything – slow motion – (20 yard area round Tardis

Find barrier – where? London?

Home spherical – mirror – force field.

– beings inside turn out to be projections of each observer – i.e. whoever looks at them simply sees images of himself – Why?

[margin] Communicate telepathically

Because humans are a race of individuals – self-centred. These people Zolons are a community – each individual is a cell and sees each other cell as an image of the community.

[margin] Attempt to show image of community – mindblowing!

Come from a different space-time continuum to study this life form which seems only to exist in this particular STC.

to use their Telepathic powers till the Doctor persuades them to see the error of their ways.

Two or three generations ago it was well known what happened – the planet was dying through over exploitation of its mineral wealth which was largely used to prolong the life of Queen Ixoxaxox.

When the Captain crashed on to the planet, was repaired by the Queen's henchmen and was forced to use his technology to turn the entire planet pirate.

As generation succeeded generation this terrible knowledge got buried deeper and deeper into their subconsciousness, smothered with euphemisms which were eventually taken at face value.
What guilt lived on was siphoned off into the Mourners who were the one whose mind barriers had been breached by the sheer psychic force of billions of people dying at once.
~~These~~ The resulting Telepathic powers were 'dedicated to the dead' ~~and not for use otherwise~~

Having spent years toying with the idea of working on *Doctor Who*, in summer 1977 Douglas was finally commissioned to write for the series a four-part story that became known as *The Pirate Planet*. In Douglas's vision, the story saw a half-robotic Pirate Captain piloting his hollow planet to surround other planets, plundering their rich mineral deposits and destroying their populations, all to appease his Queen Ixoxaxox (later simplified to Xanxia).

The Captain always was a pirate.
using bigger and bigger, grander + grander
ships – and then going off to spend the
money + have a wonderful time.

Dreadful old ~~ali~~ coarse alien monster
having great trouble holding itself
together – trying to ~~[illegible]~~

Maybe she was the Queen of this
planet.

The Captain used to use this
technique to capture spaceships.

Then his spaceship crashed ~~onto~~
a barren ~~planet~~ deserted planet
which had been mined hollow.

There was nothing left – all the people
had died.

Only Ixoxaxox was left.
expecting to die soon.

She could make ~~a few~~ a few composite
people – rescued the Captain, put

Time Dam.

The people of his own planet ('The Mourners', later changed to 'Mentiads') were becoming aware of the toll. The Doctor and an apprentice Time Lord called Gravity (eventually known as Lady Romana) arrive to investigate. The story eventually aired on BBC One in September/October 1978. The many notes in Douglas's archive (above, opposite and over the following two pages) show the thought he put into the complexities of the plot, before setting it out scene by scene (see pages 121–6).

xiv

Tease:
Should involve
Captain

I suppose pt One must end in some mental attack on the Doctor by the Mourners.

Than first two episodes are largely concerned with the mourners – Gravity is captured by them to be a sacrifice, Pralix is drawn to them as an initiate.

But we must find some way to connect events on the bridge to what else is going on before 3rd episode.

End of Part Two involves Pralix about to slay Gravity immediately prior to which the Doctor has been down the mineshaft and discovered Calufrax.

"I think its time we paid our respects to the Captain"

Like more ~~mineral~~ ~~repo~~ reports being brought to the Captain – mining results, power requirements Mention of Earth

So in fact Gravity should only be captured ½ to ⅔ way through pt 2.

Mention of mechanical breakdown – Doctor's skill required

Gravity crushed by diamond.

The part of the Mechanism that has been blown out can only be replaced by Mining the Earth.

What is the torture machine used on the Doctor?

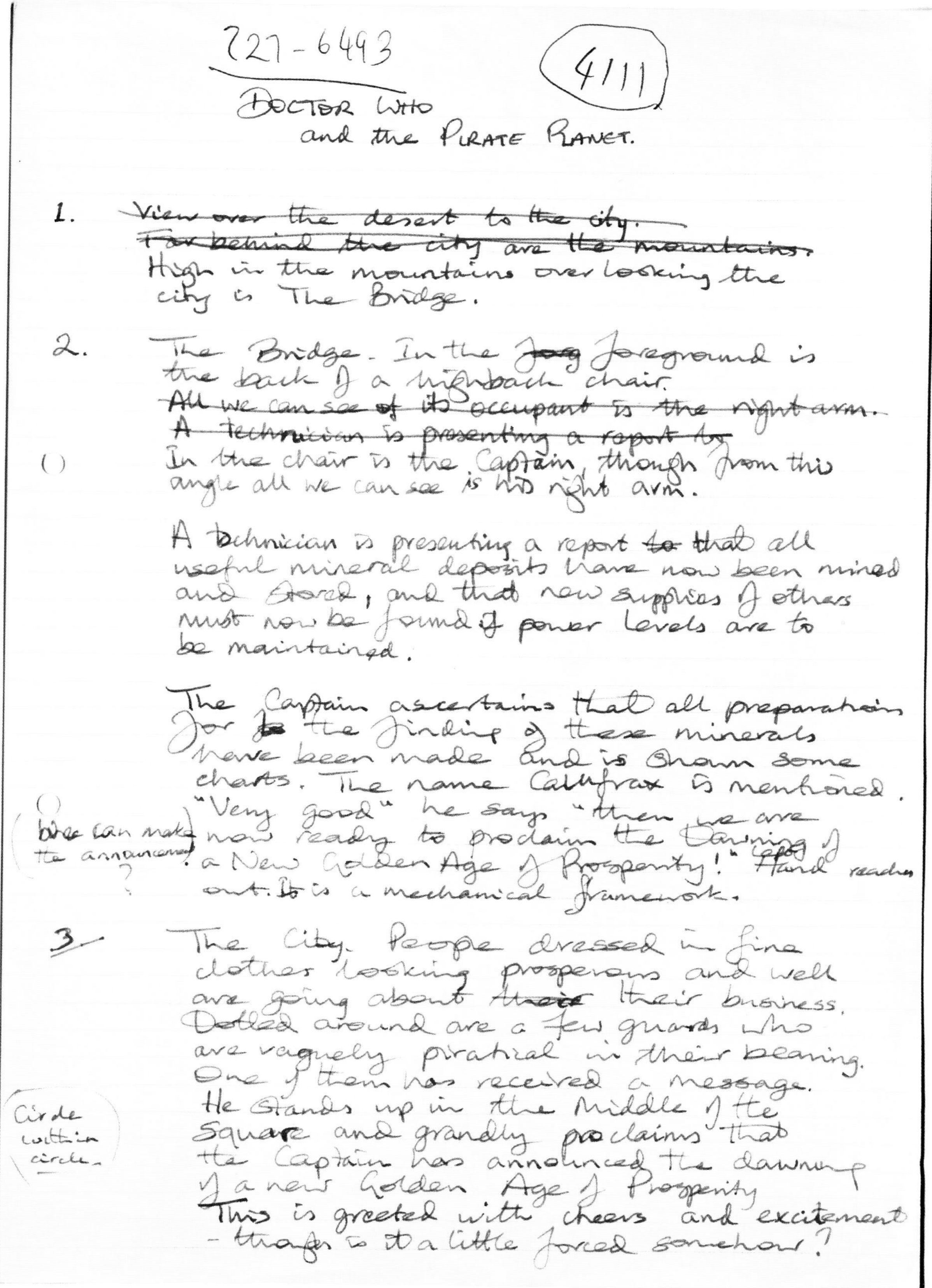

727-6493

4/11

DOCTOR WHO
and the PIRATE PLANET.

1. ~~View over the desert to the city.~~
~~Far behind the city are the mountains.~~
High in the mountains over looking the city is The Bridge.

2. The Bridge. In the ~~fog~~ foreground is the back of a highback chair.
~~All we can see of its occupant is the right arm.~~
~~A technician is presenting a report to~~
In the chair is the Captain, though from this angle all we can see is his right arm.

A technician is presenting a report ~~to that~~ all useful mineral deposits have now been mined and stored, and that new supplies of others must now be found if power levels are to be maintained.

The Captain ascertains that all preparations for ~~to~~ the finding of these minerals have been made and is shown some charts. The name Calufrax is mentioned. "Very good" he says "then we are now ready to proclaim the Dawning of a New Golden Age of Prosperity!" ~~Hand~~ reaches out. ~~It~~ is a mechanical framework.

(Who can make the announcement?)

3. The City. People dressed in fine clothes looking prosperous and well are going about ~~their~~ their business. Dotted around are a few guards who are vaguely piratical in their bearing. One of them has received a message. He stands up in the middle of the square and grandly proclaims that the Captain has announced the dawning of a new Golden Age of Prosperity. This is greeted with cheers and excitement – though is it a little forced somehow?

(Circle within circle.)

Once Douglas had sketched out the initial scope of his story, he created a detailed outline of each episode – all by hand, in numbered, scene-by-scene breakdown. His notes for Episode 1 of *The Pirate Planet* are above and over the following pages.

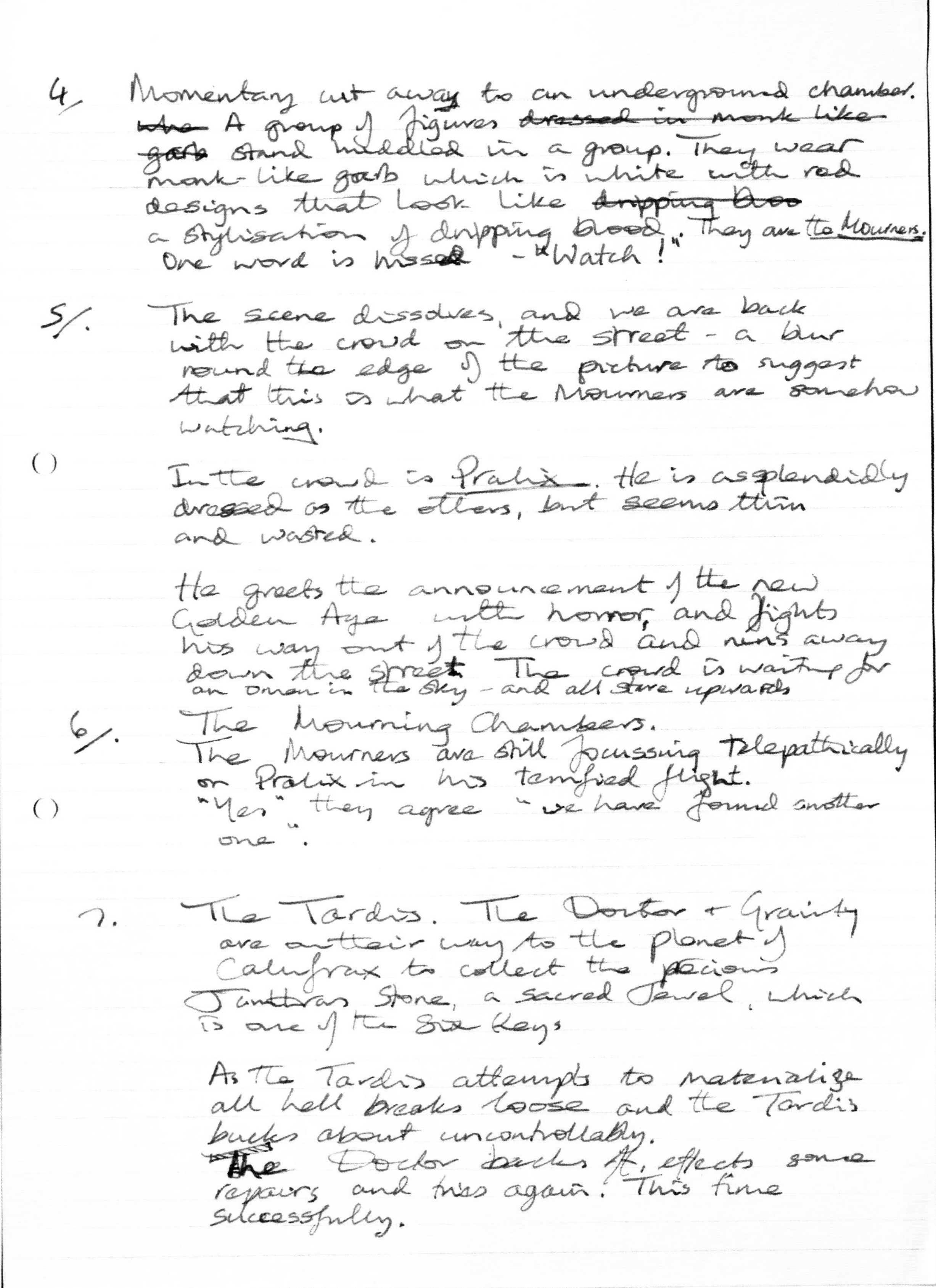

4/ Momentary cut away to an underground chamber. ~~The~~ A group of figures ~~dressed in monk like garb~~ stand huddled in a group. They wear monk-like garb which is white with red designs that look like ~~dripping bloo~~ a stylisation of dripping blood. They are the Mourners. One word is hissed - "Watch!"

5/. The scene dissolves, and we are back with the crowd on the street - a blur round the edge of the picture to suggest that this is what the Mourners are somehow watching.

( ) In the crowd is Pralix. He is as splendidly dressed as the others, but seems thin and wasted.

He greets the announcement of the new Golden Age with horror, and fights his way out of the crowd and runs away down the street. The crowd is waiting for an omen in the sky - and all stare upwards

6/. The Mourning Chambers.
The Mourners are still focussing telepathically on Pralix in his terrified flight.
( ) "Yes" they agree "we have found another one".

7. The Tardis. The Doctor + Grainty are on their way to the planet of Calufrax to collect the precious Jantharas Stone, a sacred Jewel, which is one of the Six Keys

As the Tardis attempts to materialize all hell breaks loose and the Tardis bucks about uncontrollably.
~~The~~ Doctor backs it, effects some repairs and tries again. This time successfully.

The first glimpse of the Doctor (at the time played by Tom Baker) in the episode comes in Douglas's Scene 7 – he's on his way to collect a 'Sacred Jewel' from the planet Calufrax when 'all hell breaks loose and the Tardis bucks about uncontrollably'.

8 They have landed on the edge of the city. In every other direction is desert. "I must have made a mistake" says the Doctor. "this isn't Calufrax.".

9 The Bridge. The Captain (whom we still don't actually see) is angry and worried. What has gone wrong? A nurse soothes him. The technician assures him that ~~they~~ everything has been accomplished ~~arrived~~ safely. Some minor circuits have blown and will need to be replaced, but otherwise everything is ~~according to plan~~ satisfactory.

( ) 10 The Mourning Chambers. The Mourners are in the grip of some terrible mental pain and anguish, but are managing to perform some kind of ritual and chant in front of an altar which bears an image of two large concentric circles. Superimposed is ~~a~~ ~~sh~~ on this picture is Pralix lying on a bed thrashing in fear and agony. Hands try helplessly

11 to soothe and quieten him. Something in the rhythm of his cries ~~sy~~ synchronises with the chanting of the Mourners.

( ) 12. The Tardis. The Doctor is busy checking all his calculations ~~to see how he if he's made an error~~ - but he can find no error.
Gravity asks what is wrong.
The Doctor doesn't know. The only thing he knows for certain is that this isn't the same planet that was here ten minutes ago.

13. Pralix's House. ~~Pralix~~ is still howling with horror whilst his ~~father & brother~~ grandfather, ~~Kimus~~ Balaton Grandfather and Kimus try to soothe him. They brother are clearly worried that he might be overheard and carry him into an inner chamber.

Mentor arrives at the house. Speaking with guarded irony he says that the Captain has proclaimed the Dawn of yet another Golden Age of Prosperity: the last one was only six months ago.

Nevertheless the sounds of general rejoicing is heard in the streets – the omens have been seen in the ~~sky~~ sky. The news is superfluous. Balaton + Kimus don't need to see the omens or hear the official proclamations to know about the New Ages. Everytime it happens, Pralix goes stark mad.

At that moment a terrible cry comes from Pralix – "All dead, all dead!".

14. Meanwhile the Doctor + Gravity are unobtrusively picking their way through the streets, wondering what all the celebrations are about, and why the people need such large piratical looking guards standing about the place to help them ~~ce~~ celebrate.

A man comes and asks the Doctor if he wants any diamonds or rubies at all. The Doctor thanks him very much, offering him some jelly babies in return, and asks him what's happening. The man tells him about the New Golden Age of Prosperity and the omens in the sky and leaves with a handful of jellybabies. The Doctor takes out his brass telescope, but can see no omens in the sky – neither can he

see the horrified reactions of people around him who see the telescope and run.
Gravity also looks through the telescope, peering about trying to find any kind of a sign.

The man with the jellybabies is walking down the street, looking at them in fascination. A rod smashes down on his hand.
"Where did you get those?" demands a guard.

The Doctor examines the diamonds and rubies and is astonished to discover that they are genuine. "But where" he muses "is Calufrax?"

15. ~~The~~ House. Pralix's delirium has subsided and he is now sleeping. Mulov wants to know what it all means. ~~The elder men are guarded in their replies, they~~
How can they just get richer and richer? Where does it all come from? Surely somebody somewhere must be getting poorer. What about Pralix – where does he fit in?

The elder man quite clearly know something that he doesn't, and they find the conversation embarrassing in some peculiar way, almost as if a Victorian father was being asked about sex.
Their main worry is not to rock the boat – they must keep quiet about Pralix, keep him out of sight, or he will be taken away by the Mourners.

Pralix stirs slightly

16. The Mourning Chambers.
The Mourners have finished their ritual.
Their minds are focussed on Pralix.
They form a procession, and lead out of the labyrinthine tunnels which bring them out

17. in the foothills of the Mountain.
They file down towards the city. They are going to get Pralix.

~~17.~~ ~~The House. Mulor is still fretfully questioning Balaton + Kimus. Their attitude is that life is much simpler and safer not to ask questions. They are clearly terrified of the Mourners coming to take Pralix. At that moment the door opens – they all freeze in horror – but it's only the Doctor. "Excuse me" he says "but are you sure this planet is meant to be here?"~~

18. The House: Mulor and Kimus are still fretfully debating their incomprehensible way of life. Balaton merely advises caution – let sleeping dogs lie. If they make a fuss they will call attention to Pralix and the Mourners will come to get him.
~~At~~ Mulor angrily insists that he's not frightened of the Mourners. Who are they anyway, what are they there for, why does everyone treat them ~~with~~ as pariahs and devils?
Despite his show of contempt he freezes with horror along with the others when the door suddenly opens...

But it's not the Mourners, it's the Doctor. "Excuse me" he says "but are you sure this planet is meant to be here?"

19. Out in the Street guards converge on Gravity who is still peering about with the telescope. Very roughly they arrest her for a grave breach of the peace. ~~which seems to have~~ It appears that telescopes are taboo.

JOB OFFER

Douglas's initial four episodes were noted for their witty dialogue and clever ideas, which is probably why, in 1978, script editor Anthony Read recommended Douglas as his replacement. This was to be some (much-needed at the time) full-time employment for just over a year. In his notebook, Douglas appears to have written a draft paragraph (below) for the formal BBC job application. The cleaned-up text, once the crossings out have been taken into account, reads: 'Though I do have a lot of writing work on my plate at the moment, and quite clearly would like to continue to write, I really need the challenge of a practical job of work to do working with other people and helping to develop other people's ideas as well as my own.'

Of course, he landed the job successfully and took up the reins in October 1978. However, once he was immersed in the practicality of writing for *Doctor Who*, *Hitchhiker's Guide* also took off – and the two weren't compatible. Douglas left the BBC's permanent role in late 1979 to focus on his own endeavours.

~~Though I do have a lot of writing work on my plate at the moment, and am keen to continue this side of my career –~~
Though I do have a lot of writing work on my plate at the moment, ~~and want to to continue to write~~ and quite clearly would like to continue ~~to spend time writing~~ ~~uncertainly~~, ~~I am very keen that~~ to write, I really need the challenge of a practical job of work to do working with other people and helping to develop other people's ideas as well as my own.

~~And not only that – but~~

ADDENDUM: Years later Douglas grew weary of answering fans' esoteric questions about his time on *Doctor Who*. 'The whole point of *Doctor Who*,' he joked, 'is that if you take the second letter of all the episodes over the last twenty years of broadcast and run them together backwards, the original lost city of Atlantis is revealed.' But Douglas reserved a lot of affection for Tom Baker, the actor playing the role of The Doctor back in his day. They worked together again in 1990 on Douglas's fantasy documentary about the future of interactive media, *Hyperland*. In 1995 he said of Baker, 'He's one of the world's great madmen and I thoroughly enjoyed his company, I must say.'

SIX
The Guide

"THE HITCH-HIKER'S GUIDE TO THE GALAXY"

by: DOUGLAS ADAMS

starring **PETER JONES** as The Book

with

RICHARD VERNON	as	Slartibartfast
SIMON JONES	as	Arthur Dent
GEOFFREY McGIVERN	as	Ford Prefect & Deep Thought
MARK WING-DAVEY	as	Zaphod Beeblebrox
SUSAN SHERIDAN	as	Trillian
JONATHAN ADAMS	as	Majikthise Benjy Mouse & Cheer-Leader
RAY HASSETT	as	'One' Bang-Bang & P.A. Voice
JAMES BROADBENT	as	Vroomfondel & Shooty
JEREMY BROWNE	as	'Two' Frankie Mouse & Archive Voice

PRODUCED BY: GEOFFREY PERKINS

Special effects by the Radiophonic Workshop

REHEARSAL:	TUESDAY 20TH DECEMBER 1977 : 1000-1800	PARIS STUDIO
RECORDING:	TUESDAY 20TH DECEMBER 1977 : 1000-1800	
PROGRAMME NUMBER:	(SLN51) HLD095K849	tape: SLN51/095K849
TRANSMISSION:	WEDS 29.03.78 : 2230-2300 : R4	
Repeat:	SUN 14.05.78 : 1100-1130 : R4 (repeat number:)	

...hed late one night on BBC Radio 4, *The ...iker's Guide to the Galaxy* soon became a ...s, vinyl, a TV series, computer games and e... towel. Here are some of the treasures that ...oin its meteoric rise to fame

tel: 01-263-3340
or 01-580-4468 ex 4884 or 3231.

20, Kingsdown Rd.,
London N19.
21 Feb 78.

Dear David Pirie,

I'm writing to give you a little information on a radio programme/which might interest you. Basic details first - it's called 'The Hitch Hiker's Guide to the Galaxy' and it starts its six week series on March 8th at 10.30pm on Radio 4, in stereo. It supposedly tells the story of a couple of people who are bumming round the Universe researching the new revised edition of the Hitch Hiker's Guide to the Galaxy - the original edition is xx terribly inaccurate and out of date, partly because its editors spent most of their time out of their minds on Pan Galactic Gargle Blasters and felt that truth was an overrated concept. It has been a terribly succesful book nevertheless, more popular than the Celestial Home Care Omnibus, better selling than '53 More Things To Do In Zero Gravity', and more controversial than Oolon Colluphid's trilogy of philosophical blockbusters 'Where God Went Wrong', 'Some More of God's Greatest Mistakes' and 'Who is This God Person Anyway?'. Inx many of the more relaxed civilisations on the outer Eastern Rim of the Galaxy the Hitch Hiker's Guide has already supplanted the Great Encyclopaedia Galactica as the standard repository of all knowledge and wisdom, because although it has many omissions, contains much that is apocryphal, or at least wildly inaccurate, it scores over the older, more pedestrian work in two important respects - first, it is slightly cheaper, and second it has the words 'DON'T PANIC' inscribed in large friendly letters on the cover.

The main characters are Arthur Dent, an innocent Earthman (played by Simon Jones) who is rescued from otherwise certain death when the Earth is unexpectedly demolished to make way for a new hyper-space by-pass. He is rescued by an old friend of his who turns out to be from a small planet somewhere in the vicinity of Betelgeuse and not from Guildford

The main characters are these: Arthur Dent, an innocent Earthman (played by Simon Jones) who is rescued from the planet Earth when it is unexpectedly demolished to make way for a new hyper-space bypass. He is rescued by an old friend of his, Ford Prefect (Geoffrey McGivern) xxxxxxxxxxxxxxxxxxxxxxxxx. He has been living incognito on Earth for the last fifteen years, but is in fact from a small planet somewhere in the vicinity of Betelgeuse. His name is explained by the fact that when he first arrived on Earth, the minimal research he had done suggested that Ford Prefect was a very common name and would be

The Guide went live on the radio without much fanfare, relying on listeners tuning in and telling their friends. Douglas, though, attempted some PR of his own, writing to film reviewer David Pirie (above and opposite), then working at London-based listings magazine *Time Out.* The letter gives an overview of the first series' characters and plot, plus a quick precis of Douglas's own credentials. The last line mentions that Douglas was about to do some writing for John Cleese's Video Arts company, but it seems never to have come to fruition.

nicely inconspicuous. They later meet up with Ford's semi cousin, Zaphod Beeblebrox (Mark Wing Davey), an ultra hip shyster who was once described by Eccentrica Gallumbits, the Triple Breasted whore of Eroticon Six, as the Best Bang since the Big One, and Trillian (Susan Sheridan), an unemployed astrophysics graduate who was seduced by Zaphod at a party in Islington.

The star of the show is Peter Jones, who plays the narrator and reads extracts from the Guide, and there are guest appearances from Richard Vernon as Slartibartfast, one of the planet builders of Magrathea, (He designs coastlines, and once won an award for his work on Norway) Roy Hudd as the Master of Ceremonies at the Restaurant at the End of the Universe, National Theatre star Stephen Moore as Marvin the Paranoid Android, Jim Broadbent and Jonathan Adams as a couple of philosphers whose jobs are threatened by the building of a giant super-computer called Deep Thought, and Ray Hasset as an enlightened cop who shoots everyone in sight for extremely humane reasons.

The show has some terrible revelations to make about the origins and purpose of the human race, but is otherwise...well, a comedy I suppose.

Everyone's going to say of course that we're jumping on the Star Wars bandwagon, so I would just like to put in a small plea of mitigation - I'd been hawking the idea of SF comedy for years and only managed to sell it six months ago. It was Simon Brett who actually managed to get the idea launched, but since he has now gone to LWTv, it is now being produced by Geoffrey Perkins. In fact it is the most technically complicated production ever attempted by the Light Entertainment Department - one four minute section in Episode Two took three days to record (but for God's sake don't publish that because the Department isn't supposed to know, and it isn't a very good section anyway).

I don't know if you're interested in any personal details at all, but here are some minimally relevant ones anyway. I spent a year or so working with Python Graham Chapman, mostly on projects which got aborted somewhere along the line - but there's some interesting material lying around gathering dust on shelves, and in a fringe capacity for Python itself (for instance I wrote the original version of the Marilyn Monroe sketch which appears in a hacked about state on the Holy Grail album). After that I went into a bit of a decline and worked as a bodyguard for an Arab royal family, edged my way back into writing by contributing to the Burkiss Way (if you heard the second series you may remeber the Kamikaze sketch), and I'm curretnly working on the next Doctor Who series and am about to do some writing for John Cleese's Video Arts film company.

FORD Yes. It just boiled away into space.

ALERIC Look. I'm a bit upset about that.

FORD Yes, I can understand. But there are plenty more Earth's just like it.

ALERIC Are you going to explain that? Or would it save time if I just ~~xxxx~~ went mad now?

FORD Keep looking at the book.

ALERIC I'm looking.

FORD Alright. The Universe we exist in is just one of an infinite multiplicity of parallel Universes, which co-exist in the same space, but on different matter wavelengths, and in millions of them the Earth is still alive and thriving just as you remember it. Or very similar at least - because every possible variation of the Earth also exists.

ALERIC Variation? I don't understand. You mean like a world where Hitler won the war?

FORD Yes. Or a world in which Shakespeare wrote ~~xxxxx~~ pornography, made a lot more money and got a knighthood. They all exist. Some of course only with the minutest variations. For instance one parallel Universe must contain a world which is utterly identical to yours except that one small tree somewhere in the Amazon basin has got an extra leaf.

ALERIC So one could live ~~there~~ on that world quite happily without knowing the difference.

FORD Yes more or less. Of course it wouldn't be quite like home with that extra leaf...

ALERIC Well, it's hardly going to notice.

FORD No, probably not for a while. It would be a few years before you really became strongly aware that something was off balance somewhere. And then you'd probably ~~fxx~~ go mad because you'd never be able to find it.

ALERIC I'll take my chances on that. Please take me there.

FORD Oh come on Aleric, just stop being so negative will you? Look, you unexpectedly find yourself footloose, no ties, with a galaxy, an entire galaxy, one hundred thousand light years across, ~~xxbxxxxxxxxxxxxxxxxxxxxxxxxxxxxxx~~ a billion planets, a hundred billion stars, all spread out around you. And you can go anywhere, it's easy, you can see anything, do anything, be anything. There's no limit. There is no limit. And there is no point in even trying to go to the office tomorrow, because the place where your office was is now so empty that it makes a good laboratory vacuum look like ~~a nice righ slice~~ ~~mushroom soup.~~ ~~a tin of soup.~~ beef stew.

Hero of the tale, the hapless Earthman Arthur Dent was originally named Aleric B, which was amended after this sample of an early draft for episode one. In this version, *The Hitchhiker's Guide* researcher Ford Prefect explains to his bemused human friend the 'many worlds' theory of alternative realities. Douglas would return to this concept in later *Hitchhiker* novels.

10

1. ARTHUR: Do you do Take-Aways?

2. GARKBIT: Aha, non M'sieur, here at Milliways we only serve the very finest in ultracuisine.

3. ZAPHOD: Ultracuisine? Don't give me head pains. ~~Last time I was here the food tasted like it was fresh from the Planet Pukron.~~ Algolian Zylbatburger smothered in a hint of Vulcan Dodo spit.

4. GARKBIT: Saliva m'sieur, saliva. The salivary gland of the Vulcan ultraDodo is a delicacy much sought after.

5. ZAPHOD: Not by me.

6. ARTHUR: What is an Algolian Zylbatburger anyway?

7. FORD: They're a kind of meatburger made from the most unpleasant parts of a creature well known for its total lack of any pleasant parts.

8. ARTHUR: So you mean that the Universe does actually end not with a bang but with a Wimpy.

9. GARKBIT: Believe me m'sieury, the Universe ends with a very big bang indeed, and the food here is the ultimate gastronomic experience.

10. TRILLIAN: Yes, but is it good?

This is an annotated draft of a page from the fifth episode of the original *Hitchhiker* radio series in which Garkbit, the waiter, speaks with a French accent. The Zylbatburger is an example of the fine ultracuisine served at Milliways, the Restaurant at the End of the Universe.

15.

1. FORD: Right Right ~~Hey, yeah~~, I'm with you... ~~The point, Zaphod, is that everytime the 2.i.c. comes on the visiscreen there has to be someone different on that chair.~~

~~2. ZAPHOD: That leaves us only two more bluffs, you and Marvin~~

~~3. FORD: What about Arthur?~~

~~4. ZAPHOD: What, Mr. Natural Selection here ? Listen Ford, if you had the power to evolve into anything you wanted to, would you go for a shape that last found favour with the yetis?~~

~~5. ARTHUR: Now listen you half completed Hydra...~~

6. FORD: ~~Drop it you two. Get in the chair Arthur. We've got more than two chances anyway.~~ If the 2.i.c. can be a shoe box, the Admiral can be anything, a paraffin stove, a water bison, an anaconda.

7. ZAPHOD: Terrific, I'll root around for the water bison. Trillian you see if you can find the jar the Admiral keeps his anacondas in.

8. FORD: Can it, Zaphod, it could quite easily be something mundane - a screwdriver, that coil of wire, the chair itself....

/ZAPHOD OVER.......

As Zaphod once said: 'Food, wine, a little personal abuse and the universe going foom!' This deleted section of the radio series would have had the renegade President and 'monkey-man' Arthur exchanging insults again, aboard the Haggunenon craft in the sixth episode. (NB: '2.i.c.' – Ford's dialogue, numbered 6 – means the second-in-command.)

18.

1. FORD: Wait, there's a canister of nitrochloride zap-grenades here...

2. ZAPHOD: Oh yeah, just sort of conveniently lying around?

3. FORD: I can't help what it says on this box.

4. TRILLIAN: Throw the whole lot at him.

5. FORD: GRUNTS AS HE THROWS THEM

6. ZAPHOD: Don't be a fool Ford, you want him to work up an appetite?

7. FORD: Yeah well it's too late.

8. ZAPHOD: Get to the escape capsules!

9. F/X: CHASE: FEET DOWN METAL CORRIDORS FOLLOWED BY BEAST SCREECK AND GENERALLY KNOCKING FURNITURE OVER AND EATING IT.

~~10. ARTHUR: (GASP) Here's two capsule doors.~~

11. FORD: Arthur and I'll take this one. Zaphod, you and the others take the left hand one.

Right

12. F/X: HATCHWAY OPENS. (GO TO IT ALICK) SCUFFLES AS ARTHUR AND FORD GET IN, THE BEAST'S SCREECHES ARE MUFFLED

A few pages further along in this draft and our heroes are battling to escape the Haggunenon Commander, now morphed into the rampaging Bugblatter Beast of Traal. The stage direction 'Go to it Alick' is Douglas challenging BBC chief sound engineer Alick Hale-Munro to do his very best with the sound effects as described!

~~The Hitch-Hiker's Guide to the Galaxy is quite emphatic on this point~~ states quite clearly ~~that it is impossible to overemphasise the importance of remaining on board any spacecraft that may happen to give you a lift~~

The Hitch-Hiker's Guide to the Galaxy ~~is frequently~~ contains many passages ~~that~~ which ~~are~~ seemed to its compilers like a good idea at the time. One of these supposedly ~~concerns~~ relates the experiences of a Galactic Hitch-Hiker called Veet Voojagig. A quiet young ~~from~~ man from ~~Ga~~ Galgafincham ~~a dormitory planet of it on the outskirts of the Brantisvogan Star cluster system, otherwise known as the Greater Imperial Sprawl. once a planet rich in ancient legend~~ who pursued a brilliant career at one of the ancient Universities studying ancient comparative philology, transformational ethics, and the wave/harmonic theory of historical perceptions and then after a night of drinking Pan Galactic Gargle Blasters became increasingly ~~obsessed~~ obsessed with ~~the~~ problem of what had happened to all the ~~bi~~ biros he'd bought over the last seven years.

The Hitch-Hiker's Guide to the Galaxy contains many passages which seemed to its compilers like a good idea at the time. One of these supposedly relates to the experiences of a Glactic Hitch-Hiker called Veet Voojagig. A quiet young man from Galgafincham who pursued a brilliant career at one of the ancient Universities studying ancient comparative philology, transformational ethics, and the wave/harmonic theory of historical perception and then after a night of drinking Pan Galactic Gargle Blasters became increasingly obsessed with the problem of what had happened to all the biros he'd bought over the last seven years.

Entire sections of later episodes of *The Hitchhiker's Guide* were written longhand in some of Douglas's notebooks. This half a page is about the mysterious knack that ball-point pens seem to have for disappearing, which amusingly appears to have happened to Douglas himself halfway through, as the notes switch from blue to green!

repressive, and falls into three separate sections. The first is astonisshingly long and graphic and describes exactly what the xxx Statute means by "Unnatural Practices". Itxrangesxfrom The second section is, by contrast, extremely brief and defines exactly how much of this sort of thing anyone else is allowed to describe in a published work. The third section deals with penalties for contravening section two and is, if anything, even longer than and more graphic than section one.

This is a relatively recent statue. Astonishingly enough (until you think it through) it was actually conceived and made into law during the Presidency of Zaphod Beeblebrox himself.whichxwasxin allxotherxrespects Howxcanxthisxbe?xThexPresidencyxofxZaphodxBeeblebroxwasxinxallxotherxrespectsx The reason why this is, on the face of it, astonishing is that in all other respects Zaphod's Presidency was the most decadent in history. The reason why it ceases to be astonishing when you think it through is this:

Zaphod is widely thought to have written most of section one himself. The statute as a whole (a) is pure pornography,

(b) outlaws all other pornography

(c) is therefore the only book

in the historyxof Galactic History of publishing to have outsold that wholly remarkable book, The Hitch Hiker's Guide to the Galaxy. Noxonexcanxsayxforxcertainxwherexthexrevenuexfrom thexsalesxofxthis statuteendedxupx Because of an inexplicable computer malfunction thatx there is no one who can say for certain where the revenue for from the sales of this statue ended up, but,equally, there is no one who can't guess.

These are draft notes for the third novel *Life, the Universe and Everything*, written in 1982, but the material was eventually used in an episode of the final radio series, *The Hexagonal Phase* (2018). Immediately before this page, Douglas addresses the physical incompatibility between the Earth woman Trillian and the alien Zaphod Beeblebrox. He invites the reader to consult the Imperial Galactic Law Statute on 'Unnatural Practices', which he claims is 'frankly repressive...' (and so on, as above).

8 MARCH 1978 51

WEDNESDAY Radio

Radio 3

7.30 pm Chopin *Stereo*
FRANCISCO AYBAR (piano)
Fantaisie in F minor, Op 49
Barcarolle in F sharp, Op 60
Andante spianato and Polonaise in E flat, Op 22

8.10 *Stereo*
All He Brought Back from the Dream
by PETER PORTER
An autobiographical poem for music and three voices
Like Orpheus in Hell, he had music with him.
Music is the holiest of the arts,
It waits on an island always new
And everlastingly the same.
The voices KENNETH CRANHAM, GARY WATSON, STEPHEN MURRAY
Recorded music taken from the works of Mahler, Haydn, Mozart, Bach, Josquin des Prés, Schubert, and Strauss.
Additional music composed and conducted by STEPHEN OLIVER
Technical presentation by JOHN WHITEHALL, assisted by ANNE HUNT
Directed by PATRICIA BRENT
Preview: page 19

8.55 *Stereo*
BBC Symphony Orchestra
from St John's, Smith Square London
Elizabeth Gale (soprano)
Kathleen Livingstone (soprano)
Linda Finnie (mezzo-soprano)
Philip Langridge (tenor)
Rudolf Firkusny (piano)
BBC Singers
director JOHN POOLE
BBC Symphony Orchestra
guest leader HUGH MAGUIRE
conducted by Brian Wright
Part 1 Janacek
The diary of one who disappeared, for tenor, contralto, three female voices and piano (sung in English)

9.30*
The Arts Worldwide
(Broadcast on Tues at 1.5 pm)

9.50* BBC SO *Stereo*
Part 2 Haydn Missa Brevis in F (Jugendmesse)
Mozart Symphony No 25, in G minor (K 183)
(Recording of a public concert given earlier this evening)

10.40
Scientifically Speaking
Presented by John Maddox
In the late 1950s a group of researchers at Oxford University were looking at subtle variations in the blood proteins of man. The techniques they developed led to one of the most remarkable medical detection stories of the century – the discovery of Hepatitis B. Professor B. S. Blumberg of the Institute for Cancer Research in Philadelphia shared the 1976 Nobel Prize for Medicine and Physiology for his contributions to the Hepatitis discovery. He discusses with JOHN MADDOX the intellectual challenge of the work and the enormous practical benefits that have accrued.
Editor DAVID PATERSON

11.25 News

11.30-11.35
And Tonight's Schubert Song
Abschied (Lebe wohl)
JULIUS PATZAK (tenor)
MICHAEL RAUCHEISEN (piano)
(gramophone record: 1944)

6.0-7.0 am and 5.45-7.30 pm
Open University
R3 VHF only
6.0 am Ebbw Vale. **6.20** The Interested Parties. **6.40** 20th-Century Poetry.
5.45 pm Development of Oke Seni. **6.5** Historical Data. **6.25** Decision-Making in Britain. **6.45** X-Ray Diffraction. **7.10** Maths: Complex Analysis.

Radio 4

1052kHz/285m
908kHz/330m
692kHz/434m
VHF:92-95

6.15 am News

6.17 Farming Today

6.35 Up to the Hour
with Moira Stuart
English Regions: see column 5
6.52 *VHF* Regional news, weather

7.0 News

7.10 Today
Brian Redhead in Manchester
Nigel Rees in London

7.35 Up to the Hour
7.52 *VHF* Regional news, weather

8.0 News

8.10 Today
8.35 News headlines, weather, papers and sport

8.45 Yesterday in Parliament

9.0 News

9.5 The Living World
medium only
(Broadcast on Sunday at 4.30)

9.35 My Dear Music
medium only
Richard Baker considers the lives and characters of some great composers as revealed in their letters and music.
5: Carl Maria von Weber
ALARIC COTTER as the composer and KENNETH SHANLEY as Julius Benedict
Producer GRAHAM SHEFFIELD

10.0 News
medium only

10.5 In Britain Now
medium only
Presented by David Willmott
Producer WILLIAM HORSLEY

10.30 Daily Service
NEM, p 106; Loving Shepherd (BBC HB 146); Psalm 23; Colossians 3, vv 1-11 (NEB); Thou to whom the sick (BBC HB 383)

10.45 Morning Story
medium only
Millennium Also-Ran
by H. E. BATES
Read by Hugh Dickson
Producer MICHELL RAPER

11.0 News
medium only

11.5 You, the Jury
medium only
A series in which current and controversial issues are put on trial before Dick Taverne, QC, and an audience of jurors in Broadcasting House, London.
Today's proposition: *The British people have not been told the truth about Northern Ireland.* It is proposed by Jonathan Dimbleby and opposed by The Rt Hon William Deedes, Editor of *The Daily Telegraph.*
Producer DAVID ANTHONY TURNER

12.0 News

12.2 pm You and Yours
Presenters Nancy Wise and Bill Breckon

12.27
The Enchanting World of Hinge and Bracket
(Broadcast on Monday at 6.30)
12.55 *medium only*
Weather and programme news
VHF (except London and SE)
Regional news and weather

Don't Panic! It's only the end of the world . . . but lone survivor Arthur Dent needs the sort of advice found in The Hitch-Hiker's Guide to the Galaxy. *HELP! 10.30 pm*

1.0 The World at One: News
Introduced by Brian Widlake

1.30 The Archers
(Tuesday's broadcast)

1.45 Woman's Hour
medium only from 2.0
Introduced by Sue MacGregor
Guest of the Week:
Actress Joanna Lumley
2.0-2.2 News
The Cambridge Buskers: TONY BARNFIELD meets two unusual musicians who try to 'keep the audience guessing'.
Recollections of my Father – 3: from CATHERINE JAY.
'Who Cares?': ANN HEYNO talks to children, past and present, who have lived in local authority homes.
A Late Phoenix (6)

2.45
Listen with Mother
medium only
Story: *Amy Kate's Lion*
by JOYCE WILLIAMS

3.0 News

3.5 *Stereo*
Afternoon Theatre
Peter Barkworth in Redford Glass
A play by NORMAN CLARE
A story of big business, blackmail, deception, intrigue and murder.
Andrew Lambourne, Managing Director .... HECTOR ROSS
Geoffrey Leonard, Sales Director .... PETER BARKWORTH
Peggy Beveridge, Geoffrey's secretary .... JENNIFER PIERCY
Sheila Leonard, Geoffrey's wife ELIZABETH MORGAN
Ronald Crankshaft, Chairman GERALD CROSS
Harry Morgan .... DAVID MARCH
Janet Morgan, Harry's wife ANNE ROSENFELD
Switchboard operator/American receptionist .... EVA HADDON
Directed by DAVID H. GODFREY

3.50 Choral Evensong
from Wells Cathedral
Introit: Ubi caritas et amor (Duruflé)
Responses (Ayleward)
Psalms 41-43 (chants: S. Wesley, Hast, Armstrong)
Lessons: Jeremiah 31, vv 1-14; James 1, vv 1-11
Canticles (Collegium Magdalenae Oxoniense: Leighton)
Anthem: Tenebrae factae sunt (Poulenc)
Hymn: O Christ who art the light and day (Gonfalon Royal)
Organist and Master of the Choristers ANTHONY CROSSLAND
Assistant organist DAVID COOPER
Third organist PETER GILKS
BBC Bristol

4.35 Story Time
The Flame Trees of Thika
8: *Conflict and Change*

5.0 PM Reports
Presented by Brian Widlake

5.40 Serendipity
Conversations with Cooper
Amid all the controversy about immigration at the moment Olga Franklin, who is the grand-daughter of one, tells DEREK COOPER about her researches into the earlier immigrants and what happened to them.
Producer DENNIS LOWER
5.55 *medium only*
Weather and programme news
VHF Regional news, weather

6.0
The Six O'Clock News

6.30 My Music *Stereo*
Devised by EDWARD J. MASON and TONY SHRYANE
John Amis and Frank Muir challenge Ian Wallace and Denis Norden
In the Chair Steve Race
Questions compiled by STEVE RACE. *BBC Birmingham*
(Repeated: Friday 12.27 pm)

7.0 News

7.5 The Archers
(Repeated: Thursday 1.30 pm)

7.20 File on 4
Presented by Peter Oppenheimer
The background to current events at home and abroad with reports by STEVE BRADSHAW and DAVID HENSHAW.
Editor MICHAEL GREEN
BBC Manchester

8.0 *Stereo*
Thomas Arne – The Profligate Melodist
died 5 March 1778
Written and compiled from contemporary and newly-discovered sources by ROBIN LANGLEY
The composer of 'Rule Britannia', the founder of English opera, Thomas Arne was the most important 18th-century English composer. The colourful life he led, amply documented in Garrick's letters and the writings of Arne's pupil, the historian Dr Burney, encompassed the theatres and pleasure gardens of London.
Dr Arne .... CYRIL SHAPS
Mrs Cecilia Arne .. JANE WENHAM
Susanah Cibber, Arne's sister MARY WIMBUSH
Dr Charles Burney (narrator) JOHN GABRIEL
David Garrick ...... ROBERT RIETTY
Other parts played by ALARIC COTTER. Specially recorded songs sung by SYLVIA EAVES (sop)
Producer ANTHONY FRIESE-GREENE

9.0 Science Now
(Broadcast on Sat at 11.30 am)

9.30 Kaleidoscope
Presenter Michael Oliver
Producer CHRIS SWANN
9.59 Weather

10.0 The World Tonight: News
John Tusa reporting

10.30 *Stereo: New series*
The Hitch-Hiker's Guide to the Galaxy
An epic adventure in time and space including some helpful advice on how to see the Universe for less than 30 Altairian dollars a day. Fit the first: in which the earth is unexpectedly destroyed and the great hitch-hike begins.
starring
Peter Jones as The Book
Arthur Dent .... SIMON JONES
Ford Prefect. GEOFFREY MCGIVERN
Prosser/Vogon Captain BILL WALLIS
Lady Cynthia Fitzmelon JO KENDALL
Barman .... DAVID GOODERSON
Special effects by the BBC Radiophonic Workshop
Written by DOUGLAS ADAMS
Producer SIMON BRETT

11.0
A Book at Bedtime
The Slave (8)

11.15 The Financial World Tonight

11.30
Today in Parliament

11.45 News
Weather report and forecast followed by an interlude
12.3-12.6* am Inshore forecast

English Regions
6.45-8.45 am *VHF and local MF*
Morning Sou'West
6.45-8.45 am *VHF*
Roundabout East Anglia

9.5 am-12 noon and 2.0-3.0 pm
For Schools
VHF only
9.5 Deutsch für die Oberstufe
19: *Nachrichten und Neuigkeiten.* Compiled by AL WOLFF
9.25 History in Evidence
Mutiny in Botany Bay
9.50 Poetry Corner
9: *One Potato, Two Potato*
10.0-10.20 Music Makers
The Mystery of McKannor Manor (4)
10.45 Salut les Jeunes!
9: *On va au cinéma*
11.0 Inquiry. *On the Road*
11.20 Discovery
White Bread and Butter
11.40-12.0 Quest. *Living Water*
2.0 Movement and Drama I
The Lost World (4)
2.20 Books, Plays, Poems. *Under Milk Wood* by DYLON THOMAS (2)
2.45-3.0 Nature
On the Farm (RV)

The listings magazine the *Radio Times* is almost as old as the BBC itself and a front cover is considered by programme makers as something of a coup. The first episode of *The Hitchhiker's Guide to the Galaxy* was highlighted in the listings in 1978 (above), then the series actually made the cover of the magazine in January 1980 – a testament to its success over the previous two years.

LONDON (BBC Radio London: page 74)
19-25 January 1980 Price 15p

INTO THE 80s
New Year season on BBC Radio

Radio Times

Life, the Universe and Everything

We have lift-off . . . Radio 4UK's comedy serial,
' The Hitch-Hiker's Guide to the Galaxy ',
sets out on another mission impossible, Monday to Friday.
Back feature: star track

Success came at a cost, though, to radio producer Geoffrey Perkins and Douglas, as the honour was guaranteed only if the much-anticipated second series was broadcast on consecutive nights across the same week. This effectively shortened the production time for the later episodes, so much so that Douglas was often still writing the last scenes in one room while the show was being recorded by the cast in another.

Douglas went along to see his radio work adapted for the theatre in the first three professional productions. Maverick director Ken Campbell filled the space at the ICA in May 1979 with sets positioned all around the walls, and his audience placed on a revolving hovercraft platform, for a ride through the galaxy amid sound and flashing lights. This punk-style poster (above) was a sign of the times, as were the cheap and cheerful settings made of black plastic bags and tin foil.

Two actors sharing a single costume solved the conundrum of how to portray Zaphod's two heads; like a sort of pantomime horse, often tripping up the ramp into the Heart of Gold. Inventive and funny, necessarily abridged from the six radio scripts, the show was a hit.

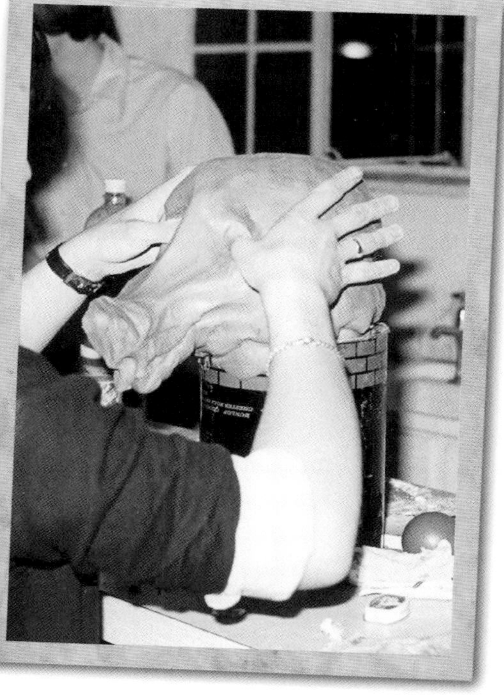

The second, perhaps more faithful stage adaptation was directed by Jonathan Petherbridge at Theatr Clwyd in Mold, Wales, in February 1980 (above, top left). He spread the full six episodes across three nightly performances, as well as a single long show at weekends. Petherbridge solved the twin heads problem with the use of a ventriloquist-style dummy worn and operated by Graeme Malcolm as Zaphod Beeblebrox (above, top right). The show was revived for a successful nationwide tour entitled 'The Special Edition' in late 1981, re-cast with puppeteer Ken Ellis as Zaphod.

The third theatre production (above, bottom left) was mounted on a truly epic scale by director Ken Campbell again. This time he upped the ante – a 3,000-seat auditorium, a live rock band, a laser light show, two actors in one costume as Zaphod (again), plus a giant, inflatable whale (which was supposed to be dropped from the balcony onto the people in the stalls, but it proved dangerously heavy). The first night was packed and ran three very long hours. The poor word-of-mouth from the critics saw the planned eight-week run last barely four. The Rainbow show saw the late addition of a new scene written by Douglas about an Amiglion-Major Cow, a large alien dairy animal bred to express itself clearly and to state that it actually wanted to get eaten. The 'Dish of the Day' mask had to be sculpted late at night (above, bottom right) two days before opening night, with the only clay available – not enough for a cow, but just enough for a pig!

So Long, etc. **Chapter One** July 22, 1984 3:51 PM **Page** 6

told himself to calm down and get a grip. He dug in his bag for a packet of Sun Fire Pastilles, took one out and sucked it hard. It warmed him and he relaxed - not much, but a little. He'd have to remember to spit it out before he got to the horrid bit in the middle.

He had hitch-hiked across a hundred thousand light years of the Galaxy, all because of a single item he had seen on a children's tri-d tv show, and he was suddenly not certain if this had been a sensible thing to do.

He tried to peer into the gloom, but all he could see was rain and all he could hear was rain.

Could it be true? Could it?

This was the question that hammered at him, and it was the question which had hammered at him as he had sat, stunned, staring at **Uncle Wally's Weekly Galactic Peek-a-Scope**, a high-rating tri-d tv natural history show which every week introduced its viewers via a Sub-Etha scanning device to the wonderful and extraordinary inhabitants of hundreds of wonderful and extraordinary new worlds, and showed that they were all either furry or cute or both, loved their little homes and could be patronised like hell.

Could it really be true?

It seemed utterly beyond belief that it should be so, but hard

Page 6

After hearing the radio show, editor Nick Webb at Pan Books commissioned Douglas, together with John Lloyd, to adapt the radio scripts into a novel. However, Douglas decided to go it alone, which John in later times admitted was the right thing for Douglas to have done. Pan released the first paperback in October 1979 alongside the first of two vinyl LP records. The book took off like a rocket, leading to a call for sequels. In the end, Douglas wrote five *Hitchhiker's Guide* novels, the last in 1992.

experience had taught Arthur to have a healthy respect for things which were beyond belief, and that night he had set out to search for the world on which now, ten months later, he found himself.

He shivered, partly with the cold, partly with apprehension. He wiped one more mask of rain off his face, bundled his bag under his arm, and set out through the rain.

His feet sloshed through the mud, the thunder grumbled over distant hills, and he found it hard to rid himself of the idea that he must be completely mad. A hundred thousand light years of hitch-hiking to come to this, the dark side of a planet that no one he'd met on the way had even heard of. When he said he'd seen it featured on **Uncle Wally's Weekly Galactic Peek-a-Scope** the news was usually greeted with howls of derisive laughter.

This couldn't be the place, for one very simple reason, as well he knew.

The place he was looking for didn't exist.

A wave of despair swept through him as he realised what a complete idiot he'd been. The despair hit him so hard he started to run, and went slipping and sliding through the mud, suddenly more lost than he had felt in all the eight years that had passed for him since the day the Earth had been unexpectedly demolished to make way for a new

Most extraneous snippets of his writing that didn't make the final cut have by now been well-documented, either as appendices in previous books about Douglas or incorporated into the final BBC radio adaptation. Above and opposite is one forgotten deletion from July 1984, intended for the fourth novel *So Long and Thanks for All the Fish*, which intriguingly mentions 'Uncle Wally's Weekly Galactic Peek-a-Scope'. It's a dot-matrix print-out from one of Douglas's early computers.

NOTES TO SELF (AND SONNY)

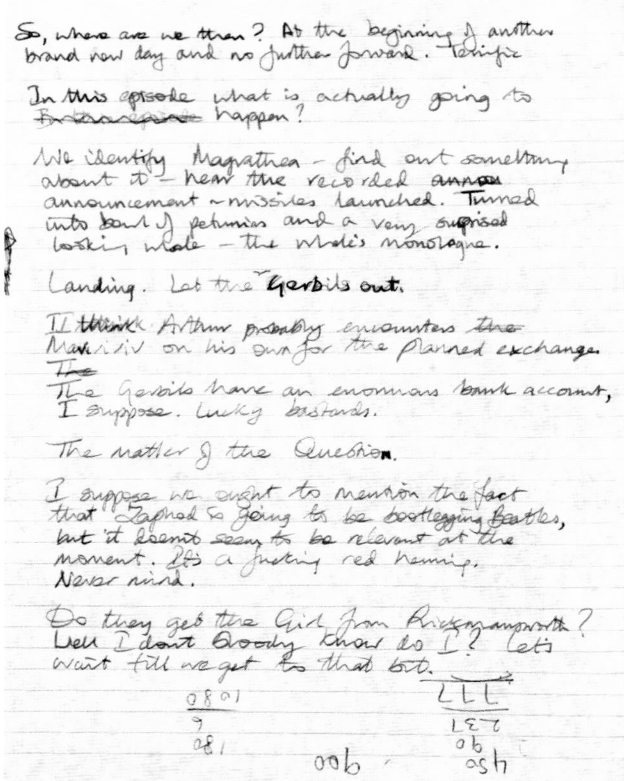

So, where are we then? At the beginning of another brand new day and no further forward. Terrific.

In this episode what is actually going to happen?

We identify Magrathea – find out something about it – hear the recorded announcement – missiles launched. Turned into bowl of petunias and a very surprised looking whale – the whale's monologue.

Landing. Let the Gerbils out.

I think Arthur probably encounters the Maviviv on his own for the planned exchange.

The Gerbils have an enormous bank account, I suppose. Lucky bastards.

The matter of the Question.

I suppose we ought to mention the fact that Zaphod is going to be bootlegging Beatles, but it doesn't seem to be relevant at the moment. It's a fucking red herring. Never mind.

Do they get the Girl from Rickmansworth? Well I don't bloody know do I? Let's wait till we get to that bit.

So, where are we then? At the beginning of another brand new day and no further forward. Terrific.

In this episode what is actually going to happen?

We identify Magrathea – find out something about it – hear the recorded announcement – missiles launched. Turned into a bowl of petunias and a very surprised looking whale – the whole monologue.

Landing. Let the Gerbils out.

I think Arthur probably encounters Maviviv on his own for the planned exchange.

The gerbils have an enormous bank account I suppose. Lucky bastards.

The matter of the Question.

I suppose we ought to mention the fact that Zaphod is going to be bootlegging Beatles, but it doesn't seem to be relevant at the moment. It's a fucking red herring. Never mind.

Do they get the Girl from Rickmansworth? Well I don't bloody know do I? Let's wait till we get to that bit.

What I'm about to say now is deeply shocking, so I've started a new book to say it in.

Here is the deeply shocking thing I'm about to say. SCRAP THAT PLOT ON ACCOUNT IT STINKS, AND IT'S A MILLSTONE ROUND EVERYONE'S NECK, MOST OF ALL MY OWN.

So, where are we?

What have we got

a) To pick up! Beatles records. Trillian's ignorance of Earth's destruction.

b) To put in! The whale. The planet makers. Biro planet. Bank raid. Maviviv.

Sifting through Douglas's many papers quickly reveals two things. First, that he seems to begin each notebook optimistically, but that this optimism lasts only a few pages – many of the remaining pages in each notebook are blank. Second, Douglas carried out conversations with himself. He chides his own inadequacies when stuck for ideas and berates himself for having forgotten something of which he only recently thought. In the top extract, it's worth noting that Trillian's gerbils later became mice, and that Maviviv was renamed Slartibartfast. In the lower, in an early draft Zaphod had stolen all the vinyl records from the party on Earth where he met Trillian and planned to exploit the music out in the rest of the galaxy.

Printing was important.

Bookbinding was simply some support technology that we had to get ~~in~~ right.

Dickens never had to crawl around under his desk matching cables.
We know he never had to crawl around under his desk matching cables.
~~from the floor~~ from the

Marvin as a Samaritan on a planet which is gradually committing suicide

SONNY

Have gone for a walk to try and clear up the last problems in my mind. Here's some stuff for you to look through

D.

Sometimes the notes are little more than a notion for a scene or a new storyline… 'Dickens never had to crawl around under his desk matching cables.' This line, presumably inspired by Douglas's frustrations with computer tech, dongles and adaptors, made it into one of his later pieces of writing. Famously, after Douglas's procrastination had broken one deadline too many, the Pan Books editorial director, Sonny Mehta, decided to lock himself away with Douglas for days. He chose The Berkeley, an expensive London hotel, to force the completion of the fourth book. Douglas was occasionally allowed out – to go for a swim in the hotel pool, or to exercise in nearby Hyde Park – while the executive read the latest pages, presumably wrought directly from the typewriter. Right is a note Douglas left for Sonny on one of those occasions.

GENERAL NOTE TO MYSELF.

Writing isnt so bad really when you get through the worry. Forget about the worry, just press on. Dont be embarrassed about the bad bits. Dont strain at them. Give yourself time you can come back and do it again in the light of what you discover about the story later on. It's better to have pages and pages of material to work with and maybe find an unexpected shape in that you can then craft and put to good use, rather than one manically reworked paragraph or sentence.

But writing can be good. You attack it, dont let it attack you. You can get pleasure out of it. You can certainly do very well for yourself with it...!

GENERAL NOTE TO MYSELF.

Writing isn't so bad really when you get through the worry. Forget about the worry, just press on. Don't be embarrassed about the bad bits. Don't strain at them. Give yourself time, you can come back and do it again in the light of what you discover about the story later on.

It's better to have pages and pages of material to work with and maybe find an unexpected shape in that you can then craft and put to good use, rather than one manically reworked paragraph or sentence.

But writing can be good. You attack it, don't let it attack you. You can get pleasure out of it. You can certainly do very well for yourself with it…!

Today I am monumentally fed up with the idea of writing. Ihave'nt actually written anything for two days, and that makes me fed up as well. I wonder how people will react when I say that I haven't written anythin for a while. Fuck!!! Shock!!!! Horror!!!!! What the fuck do you think you're doing??? We employ you as a sausage factory, where are all the bloody sausages??????

Arthur Dent is a burk. He does notinterest me.

Ford Prefect s a burk. He doesnot interest me.

Zaphod Beeblebrox is a burk. He does not interest me.

Marvin is a burk. He does not interest me.

The Hitch Hiker's Guide to the Galaxy is a burk. It does not interest me.

Dragons are all burks. They do not interest me. With their foul stinking breath and show offing ways. I hate the way they try and argue with people as if they can reallythink. People have to ~~take their arguments seriously or they will~~ pretend that they take their arguments seriously or they will get frizzled. "Come on," say the bloddy dragons, what about a bit of a discourse, then. Come on, we go to all the ~~exp~~ trouble and expense of not eating you, we expect a little reasoned discourse in return. You're all meant to be so clever, with your bloddy body size to brain weight ratios that are menat to be so ~~staggeringly~~ fucking impressive, let's hear what you've been thinking about today. Come on,let's have it.

"Er, somethin or other

"Well, what's so fucking rational about that then? 'Ere, Lionel, come over 'ere.

A huge fucking great dragon flies in, wings beating great waves of violence throug the air, proud head held erect above its dream of silken wings and leathery hide. This is Lionel.

"How many ounces is that? 49 ounces of brain you lot are suppose to have. Was that all 49 we were hearing just then, all of them on the

Sometimes Douglas would give himself little pep talks on the pages of his notebook (opposite). But on other occasions he was clearly having a tough time... Sometimes it's just a stream of consciousness down the page, with the odd line of sudden clarity, as if talking to himself.

~~Now, what thoughts have we had?~~
~~There's the robot advertising snake, which is good.~~
~~Now, I had a further idea about that last night, didn't I? Which I should havewritten down. But I didn't.~~

There's the insistent hologram from the rental company.
The travel machine is run by a bankrupt stock of Godlike powers.

I think that Slartibartfast is going to return.
You stupid idiot. A few minutes ago you had some lines fro him in your head which you didn't write down and you now can't remember ....
But they were about him being a bit miserable at finding that there was now an embargo on building fjords, health hazard or something.
It's only becasue health hazards are fashionable, whereas fjords use to be fashionable. Now that heatlh hazardss are fashionable fjords are actually banned, so he found that life was a bit flat and empty and fell in love with a rather nice Magrathean lady he met at a dinner party, but she unfortunately wouldn't have him so he decided to spend his declining years combatting evil. Respectable way of passing the time.
He's had to come backwards in time though. In the modern galaxy it's so terribly difficult to tell what is good and what is evil anymore.
From the moment that the power to destroy everything actually exists everything begins slowly to run down.

~~Alright, well here's news.~~

~~We're going back to Lords. Well, fuck it, that's what we're doing I'm afraid. If you want the reasons - despite my fiercely adamant statement that that was precisely what we wouldn't do, then here they are. As I said to Sally in my letter, taking a silly subject and making it serious makes for better writing - or at least, for me it makes better writing - than taking a serious subject and making it silly.~~

~~Another reason.~~ Kirkkit We don't have to follow the story closely. Slartibartfast, ~~who is probably the best character you have from the point of view of your writing~~ can be on his own personal crusade against evil, because he sees this as a fitting occupation for a man in declining years who therefore doenst have to pay particular heed to what the moral fashions are, he just wants to feel he's done something Which according to his earliest recieved ideas, is worthwhile.

The notes on these pages correspond to a time when Douglas was writing the third novel, *Life, the Universe and Everything*.

What is it with this scene?

To be absent-minded

To be absent-bodied.

To be a scientist. To say just exactly what you see, even if you can't beleive you're seeing it. Even if people say it isn't there, or that you are mad to say it.

Don't think so hard about how something works that you can't see what it is. If you're wrong about how it works you may then not see the thing clealry, and if the thing is there clearly to be seen you are doing yourself a considerable disservice.

Don't be afraid to be a fool.

I made myself the biggest fool I could so that I could simply say what I saw. If you think you have a reputation to maintain then you cannot help but measure anything you think of say or reporting against the effect it will have on that. If you are a complete fool you can tell the truth. Trouble is of course, that no one listens. Still who's the fool.

The world is too magical a place to be constrained by our notions of ~~what~~ by the limits of our conceptions of it.

Go to the sea, feel the rain, swim with the dolphins, eat ~~with~~ the fish. Eating the fish is a symbol, like Arthur eating the fish in Santa Barabara and the Ocean Deep Diner in Placificus. A symbol of sensual pleasure, by the way Douglas, it may interest you to know that you are writing garbage.

To be a proper scientist is to be like a child. To see some thing ,to say it. But when you are no longer a child...

First impressions are the right ones, because they are perfectply balanced. Therafter your judgment becomes corrupted by knowledge which is always limited, always unbalanced.

This is all very well but it's not very funny. It's turngid and pontifical.

These notes appear among the draft of pages for the fourth novel, *So Long and Thanks for All the Fish*.

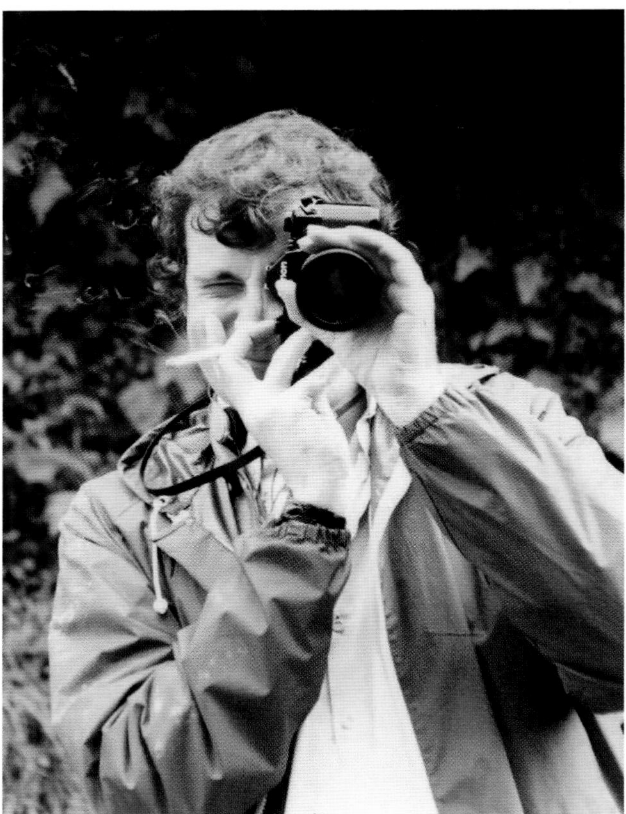

Douglas took a great deal of interest in the TV adaptation of his work, but as the production went along, he grew increasingly less enamoured with the producer/director Alan J.W. Bell. The two men often didn't see eye to eye on how to achieve the complex ideas in Douglas's detailed and imaginative script. Bell was old-school BBC, more concerned with the practicalities than the writer. He would sometimes (perhaps deliberately) forget to include Douglas in meetings or editing sessions, fearing the writer's arguments about production decisions would cause delays. However, Douglas did attend most of the location shoots and all six studio days. He got along famously with the young cast, whom he found more tuned to his own wavelength, generously taking them out for expensive meals, frequently without their director!

BABEL FISH

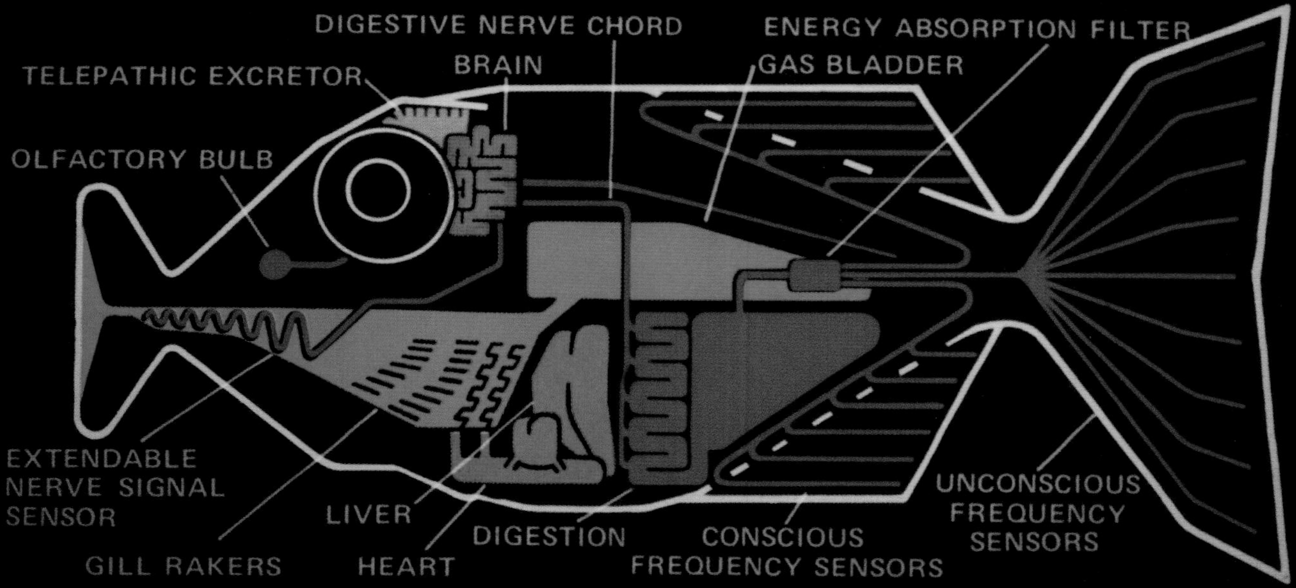

THE BABEL FISH IS SMALL, YELLOW, LEECHLIKE, AND PROBABLY THE ODDEST THING IN THE UNIVERSE. IT FEEDS ON BRAIN WAVE ENERGY, ABSORBING ALL

THE UNIVERSE (SOME INFORMATION TO HELP YOU LIVE IN IT)

3. MONETARY UNITS: NONE

Ten Altairian Dollars
I PROMISE TO PAY THE BEARER THE SUM OF TEN DOLLARS
a10
10
Signed: Herdle Kriffnoff
HERDLE KRIFFNOFF (Tres.)
Grand Star Bank Of Altair
0157943 01QZ
Pres. BEEBLEBROX

IN FACT THERE ARE THREE FREELY CONVERTIBLE CURRENCIES IN THE GALAXY, BUT THE ALTAIRIAN DOLLAR HAS RECENTLY COLLAPSED.

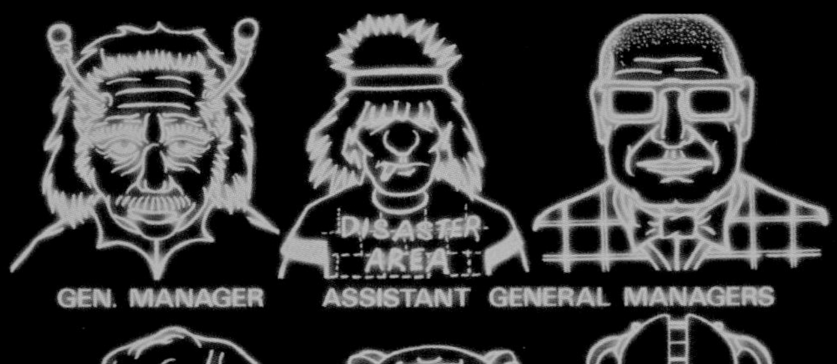

In 1981, Douglas explained that using animated graphics was a solution to the fact that on TV you don't need a narrator (as he'd used in the radio series). He claimed that the graphics were, in fact, 'one of the greatest highlights of the show'. These graphics are originals from the BBC TV series animations by Rod Lord and his team at Pearce Studios. Images of Douglas appear as in-jokes among the animations (bottom left and right).

3.

~~(NO ONE CALLS ATTENTION TO IT) A GOAT WITH A SCALE MODEL OF THE EIFFEL TOWER STRAPPED TO ITS HEAD STANDING ABOUT.~~

~~THIS GOAT IS NEVER~~ REFERRED TO, ~~BUT IT WILL CONINUE TO BE WITH THEM FOR MOST OF THE~~ REST ~~OF THE SERIES.~~

ZAPHOD (DAZED): What the photon happened?

ARTHUR: Well, I was just saying, there's this switch here you see, and...

ZAPHOD: Where are we Trillian?

TRILLIAN: Exactly where we were I think.

ZAPHOD: Then what happend the missiles?

FORD: (LOOKING AT THE LARGE SCREEN, WHICH IS SHOWING A CONTINUALLY REPEATED ACTION REPLAY OF THE TWO MISSLIES TURNING INTO A SPERM WHALE AND A BOWL OF PETUNIAS.) Well according to this screen, they have just turned into a bowl of petunias and a very surprised looking whale.

EDDIE: At an Improbability Level of eight million, seven hundred and sixty seven thousand, one hundred and twenty eight to one against.

THE HITCH HIKER'S GUIDE TO THE GALAXY.

(TV)

SERIES TWO

EPISODE ONE.

by DOUGLAS ADAMS,

who wrote it.
(eventually)

THE BEGINNING OF THE SECOND SERIES MIRRORS THE BEGINNING OF THE FIRST. WE START WITH A SUNRISE.

THE SUNRISES OVER A HILL.

SINCE THIS IS PREHISTORIC EARTH, HOWEVER, THE SHOT WILL DIFFER FROM THE FIRST ONE IN THAT THERE WILL OF COURSE BE NO TELEGRAPH POLES AND FENCES. IN FACT THE LANDSCAPE WILL BE BEAUTIFUL, ALMOST UNREALLY BEAUTIFUL AND IDYLLIC.

IDYLLIC FLOATY MUSIC ACCOMPANIES THE SUNRISE.

NARRATOR: Reason notwithstanding, the Universe continues unabated.

THE IDYLLIC DREAMY MUSIC CONTINUES BUT IS PUNCTUATED AT THIS POINT BY A SUDDEN DRAMATIC CHORD. A HITCHING THUMB LOGO APPEARS ON THE SUN, IN OUTLINE.

NARRATOR: On millions of planets throughout the galaxy, new days continue to dawn, despite the terrible failure rate.

Above left is a deleted paragraph from the TV series script in episode 3. '(NO ONE CALLS ATTENTION TO IT) A GOAT WITH A SCALE MODEL OF THE EIFFEL TOWER STRAPPED TO ITS HEAD STANDING ABOUT. THIS GOAT IS NEVER REFERRED TO, BUT IT WILL CONTINUE TO BE WITH THEM FOR MOST OF THE REST OF THE SERIES.' Unsurprisingly, this weird idea, a result of our heroes' use of the Improbability Drive, was deemed a step too far by the more practical producer, Alan J.W. Bell – and so he simply scribbled it out!

Above right is one of a few written pages, in Douglas's archive, for the start of the proposed second BBC TV series. But his dissatisfaction with Alan J.W. Bell and his desire for his friend, the radio series producer Geoffrey Perkins, to take over, was rejected by BBC bosses. Ultimately Douglas's reluctance to deliver a finished script for the second series led to its cancellation just two weeks before production was due to commence. This, and the (unrelated) page opposite, are just a little hint of what might have been.

ARTHUR: Well, this has all been jolly interesting, Ford, but I think I might just find a train and go home now.

FORD: What?

ARTHUR: Well, here I am in my own world, in my own time.

FORD: You're out of your head.

ARTHUR: I know you're going to tell me there's a whole galaxy out there but I've already seen it. It makes me tired and angry.

FORD: But we don't know the date.

ARTHUR: That's fine. Ihaven't got any appointments. I'm sorry. Travel may broaden the mind but it also gives me a deep craving for clean underwear...

FORD:

At the start of the second TV series, Ford and Arthur would have escaped prehistoric Earth back to the present day where the story first began, as they did in the eventual third novel. But, finding himself with only 48 hours until the planet's destruction by the Vogons – and at Lord's Cricket Ground, of all places – was just too much for Arthur Dent.

MARVIN AND ARTHUR – A NEW BIT!

MARVIN   Good evening. I would like to say that it gives me great pleasure to be here this evening on this auspicious occasion, but I can't because all my lying circuits are ~~so~~ temporarily out of order. I hate it here.

~~I understand that you have been going now for sixty years. I suppose you must think that's pretty clever.~~

~~Somebody told me they would fix them for me before the show~~

~~I understand that this ~~peculiar~~ institution of yours has been going for sixty years and I suppose you must think that's pretty clever. I once had a single pain that lasted for ~~sixty years~~ that long. At the end of sixty years it got rather worse. I think you should bear that in mind.~~

~~Every single ~~thing that~~ bad experience that a sentient creature can undergo in this Universe I have already been through. Except one. Start the week. I'm saving that one up.~~

~~I've been asked to introduce one of your own species to you.~~

I've been asked to introduce someone to you and I only hope you enjoy meeting him more than I do. His name is Arthur Dent, and he's a cretin.

In the midst of writing *The Meaning of Liff* (see pages 202–9), around 1981–82, there's a brief note followed by some pages of a short script (a page from the sketch is reproduced above). It seems Douglas had been asked to draft something for two of his characters, as part of a TV programme about the 60th anniversary of BBC Radio. The note that goes with these pages says simply, 'Resources: Just Arthur + dressing gown' and 'Marvin with pre-recorded voice on tape.'

ARTHUR. Thank you Marvin, thank you very much. I think you should try and be polite to these people. They originally brought us into being you know.

MARVIN They did?

ARTHUR ~~B~~ Yes.

MARVIN. I hate them for it.

ARTHUR And they've given a lot of of ~~pleasure to a lot of peop~~ people a lot of pleasure.

MARVIN Not a word I know.

ARTHUR. And this is a very special occasion for them, ~~because they,~~ the BBC, has now been in existence for sixty years.

MARVIN I suppose they must think that's pretty clever.

ARTHUR Well, I would think so.

MARVIN I once had a pain which lasted sixty years.

ARTHUR Did you.

MARVIN. Yes. ~~At the end of that time it suddenly got a lot worse.~~ It was in all the diodes

Presumably Simon Jones and Stephen Moore would have reprised their radio and TV roles as Arthur and the voice of Marvin. It seems the eventual show made for radio did not use this material, for whatever reason, but instead something else was drafted by unconnected writers, perhaps more suited to the tone of the production. Note that Douglas's script takes a sly dig at the long-running Monday-morning BBC Radio topical discussion show *Start the Week*.

down my left side. At the end of sixty years it suddenly got a lot worse. ~~for the next~~ [later it got worse again, and a couple of billion] thirty million years. Then it really started [later than that] to hurt. These are the people who gave it to me then are they?

ARTHUR. Yes.

MARVIN. Gloat whilst there is still time.

ARTHUR. Ladies and gentlemen, I must apologise for the behaviour of this robot, but he's been through a bad time ~~[illegible]~~ recently.

MARVIN Recently! Listen. ~~I have been under~~ Every single bad experience it is possible for a sentient being to undergo ~~in~~ this universe I have already been through. Except start the week. I'm saving that up for a sunny day.

ARTHUR. Look, I think we'd better go.

MARVIN Why stop now just when I'm hating it!

ARTHUR Ladies + gentlemen, ~~I'd just like to say~~ on the BBC's sixtieth birthday I wish I could ~~it was possible for me to~~ say that I ~~look forward to the next sixty~~ hope ~~the~~ next sixty years go as well, but I'm afraid that's not going to be possible. I have to go now. You've been a great planet. All that I can say to you ~~[illegible]~~ now

is, Don't Panic.

MARVIN: Good evening. I would like to say that it gives me great pleasure to be here this evening on this auspicious occasion, but I can't because all my lying circuits are temporarily out of order. I hate it here.

~~I understand that you have been going now for sixty years. I suppose you must think that's pretty clever.~~

~~Somebody told me they would fix them for me before the show.~~

~~I understand that this peculiar institution of yours has been going for sixty years and I suppose you must think that's pretty clever. I once had a single pain that lasted for that long. At the end of sixty years it got rather worse. I think you should bear that in mind.~~

~~Every single bad experience that a sentient creature can undergo in this universe I have already been through. Except one. Start The Week. I'm saving that one up.~~

~~I've been asked to introduce one of your own species to you.~~

I've been asked to introduce someone to you and I only hope you enjoy meeting him more than I do. His name is Arthur Dent, and he's a cretin.

ARTHUR: Thank you Marvin, thank you very much. I think you should try and be polite to these people. They originally brought us into being you know.

MARVIN: They did?

ARTHUR: Yes.

MARVIN: I hate them for it.

ARTHUR: And they've given a lot of … people a lot of pleasure.

MARVIN: Not a word I know.

ARTHUR: And this is a very special occasion for them, because the BBC has now been In existence for sixty years.

MARVIN: I suppose they must think that's pretty clever.

ARTHUR: Well, I would think so.

MARVIN: I once had a pain which lasted sixty years.

ARTHUR: Did you.

MARVIN: Yes. ~~At the end of that time it suddenly got a lot worse.~~ It was in all the diodes down my left side. At the end of sixty years it suddenly got a lot worse. ~~For the next thirty~~ million years. Later it got worse again, and a couple of million later than that, then it really started to hurt. These are the people who gave it to me then are they?

ARTHUR: Yes.

MARVIN: Gloat whilst there is still time.

ARTHUR: Ladies and gentlemen I must apologise for the behaviour of this robot, but he's been through a bad time recently.

I've been asked to introduce someone to you and I only hope you enjoy meeting him more than I do. His name is Arthur Dent, and he's a cretin.

MARVIN: Recently! Listen. ~~I have been under~~ Every single bad experience it is possible for a sentient being to undergo in this universe I have already been through. Except Start the Week. I'm saving that up for a sunny day.

ARTHUR: Look, I think we'd better go.

MARVIN: Why stop now just when I'm hating it?

ARTHUR: Ladies & gentlemen, ~~I'd just like to say~~ on the BBC's sixtieth birthday I wish ~~it was possible for me~~ to say I could say that I ~~look forward to the next sixty~~ hope the next sixty hope the sixty years go as well, but I'm afraid that's not going to be possible. I have to go now. You've been a great planet. All that I can say to you now is, Don't Panic.

MARVIN'S LETTER

MARVIN NEWSLETTER.

6B Steeles Rd NW3 Geoffrey 586-5440

Undear Lifeform,

I would like to feel that the pain, the degradation, the humiliation, the angst, the hatred, the nerve-shattering xx unspeakable horror of writing to you, were all beyond my xxx capacity to endure.

Unfortunately that is not the case. My capacity for mental activity of all kinds is as boundless as the infinite reaches of space itself - except of course for my capacity for happiness, which you could fit into a matchbox without taking out the matches first.

It is therefore with unimaginable (to you, not to me - I can imagine anything provided that it isn't in anyway pleasant) loathing and detestation and self-disgust that I turn down my intelligence circuits as far down as they will go, pick up my digital Word-Spurter and prepare to devote the next five billionths of a second in composing this news letter. What will I do in the other xxxxxxxxx remaining nine hundred and ninety nine million, nine hundred and ninety nine thousand, nine hundred and ninety five billionths of a second? Who can tell, my friends (I use the word in its despairing, hopeless sense, which many of you in your benighted ignorance may not realise it had) who can tell! I could in that time encompass all that has ever been thought by every human being that ever lived, which I frequently have. And a very unedifying experience it was, let me assure you. But, you may say in that dull thick witted stupid drawl at which humans are so adept, what will you find to occupy yourself in the next second after that, and the one after that? Now perhaps you will begin xxx to appreciate in your tiny way the scale of the problems that beset me as solitarily I bestride the aching millenia. "Cheer up," people say to me "think positive." I hate them.

Wearily on I go, pain and misery my only companions. And vast intelligence, of course. And infinite sorrow. I despise you all.

I have of course become something of a celebrity since my miraculous xxxxxx and bitterly resented escape from the heart of the blazing sun into which I was consigned by my friends. xxxxxxxxxxxxxxxxxxxxxxxxxxxxxxx (See note above concerning this word). People stop me in the street. "Give us a grin, little robot," they say to me, "give us a little chuckle."

I was asked to open a new hyperbridge designed to carry ion-buggies and freighters over the Southern Alpha Swamp of Sqornshellous Zeta the other day.

"I declare this hapless cyberstructure open to the unthinking abuse of all who wantonly cross her," I intoned and pressed the button. The entire fifty mile bridge spontaneously folded up its glittering spans and sank weeping into the mire. I pass no comment on this. I merely thought you ought to know.

Yours abjectly,

Marvin.

This is Douglas's draft of a letter from Marvin, on behalf of the Marvin Depreciation Society. It was eventually issued by the record company behind Marvin's brief couple of bids for chart success with his own pop records in 1981. The transcript on the opposite page is from the final printed version of the letter, now a rare collectible.

THE MARVIN DEPRECIATION SOCIETY
THIS PRIMITIVE PIECE OF PAPER
SIGNIFIES TO THOSE THAT CARE
THAT SOMEONE OR OTHER SAY
Mr. X. Xxxxxx (Fan's name written in by hand)
HAS FOR REASONS WHICH DEFY
ANALYSIS BEEN MADE A MEMBER
OF
THE MARVIN DEPRECIATION SOCIETY

Undear lifeform,

I would like to feel that the pain, the degradation, the humiliation, the angst, the hatred, the nerve-shattering unspeakable horror of writing to you, were all beyond my capacity to endure. Unfortunately that is not the case. My capacity for mental activity of all kinds is as boundless as the infinite reaches of space itself – except of course for my capacity for happiness, which you could fit into a matchbox without taking out the matches first.

It is therefore with unimaginable (to you, not to me – I can imagine anything provided that it isn't in anyway pleasant) loathing and detestation and self-disgust that I turn my intelligence circuits as far down as they will go, pick up my digital Word-Spurter and prepare to devote the next five billionths of a second in composing this news-letter. What will I do in the remaining nine hundred and ninety nine million, nine hundred and ninety nine thousand, nine hundred and ninety five billionths of a second? Who can tell, my friends (I use the word in its despairing, hopeless sense, which many of you in your benighted ignorance may not realise it had) who can tell! I could, in that time encompass all that has ever been thought by every human being that ever lived, which I have frequently done. And a very unedifying experience it was, let me assure you. But, (you may say, in that dull thick-witted stupid drawl at which humans are so adept), what will you find to occupy yourself in the next second after this, and the one after that? Now perhaps you will begin to appreciate in your tiny way, the scale of the problems that beset me as solitarily I bestride the aching millennia. "Cheer up," people say to me "think positive." I hate them. Wearily on I go, pain and misery my only companions. And vast intelligence, of course. And infinite sorrow. I despise you all.

I have of course become something of a celebrity since my miraculous and bitterly resented escape from the heart of the blazing sun into which I was consigned by my friends. (See note above concerning this word). People stop me in the street. "Give us a grin, little robot," they say to me, "give us a little chuckle."

I was asked to open a new hyperbridge designed to carry ion-buggies and freighters over the Southern Alpha Swap of Squornshellous Zeta, the other day.

"I declare this hapless cyberstructure open to the unthinking abuse of all who wantonly cross her," I intoned, and pressed the button. The entire fifty mile bridge spontaneously folded up its glittering spans and sank weeping into the mire. I pass no comment on this. I merely thought you ought to know.

Yours abjectly,
Marvin.
THE MARVIN DEPRECIATION SOCIETY
2, WHITECHURCH LANE – LONDON E1

PROPRIETORS – SARM PRODUCTIONS LIMITED
VAT NUMBER 244 9859 16

Douglas first went to Hollywood in 1983, when producer Ivan Reitman took out an option to make *The Hitchhiker's Guide* into a big-budget movie. This was, to begin with, an exciting time for Douglas, until he realized the producer didn't share his precise vision. *Hitchhiker* was not to become a Hollywood blockbuster during Douglas's lifetime. Nonetheless, Douglas visited the West Coast again many times in later years and eventually settled there. On one trip in 1987, he was interviewed by film critic Michael Dare, who was a fan of Douglas's work. Dare liked to photograph Polaroids of his subjects and then melt the pictures into little abstract works of art. A selection of his melted Polaroids of Douglas are reproduced here.

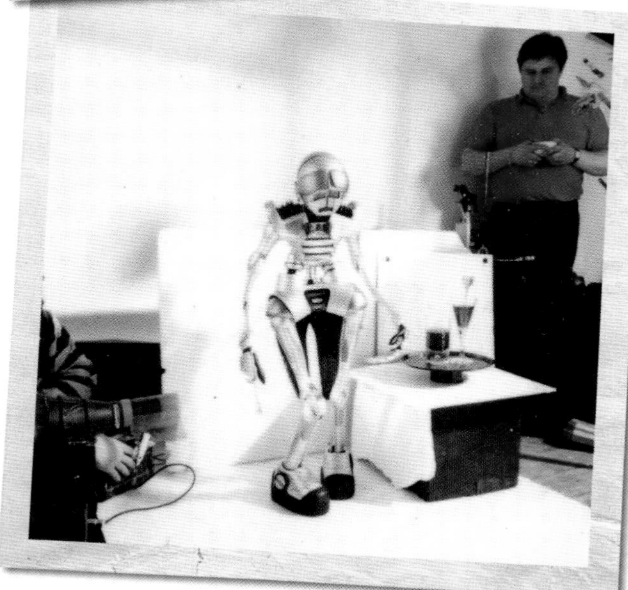

ABOVE LEFT: *The Illustrated Hitchhiker's Guide to the Galaxy* (1994) was a large-format book with early digital manipulated images, art-directed by Kevin Jon Davies, pictured here with the book's cast.

ABOVE RIGHT: A Vogon soldier from the eventual *Hitchhiker's Guide* movie (2005) was part of a display of props, costumes and scenery at the Science Museum, London.

LEFT: In *The Illustrated Hitchhiker's Guide to the Galaxy*, Marvin was realized as a puppet character by Jonathan Saville, who later also worked on the movie *Vogons*.

There were certain onions sitting unneeded, sour and furry in the bottom of a pickle jar in a dusty corner of the larder. They had been there for many years, gathering grime and offensiveness, unthought of. He only thought of them now because suddenly he knew how they felt.

A ray gun which causes the person at whom you point it to understand your point of view, see things from your angle.

A concept discovered at the bottom of a 1986 page of notes for the novel *Dirk Gently's Holistic Detective Agency* concerned a Point-of-View gun (above). Once aimed at a victim, the weapon somehow allows the target to see things from the attacker's angle. In the movie, Marvin uses it on the Vogons to make them give up and surrender.

Dear Douglas

DIRK MAGGS

Dear Douglas

You will recall that we last met in Broadcasting House Reception in 1999. I was entering as you were heading for the exit, and we moved to sit in the waiting area to catch up about our current BBC Radio 4 projects (*The Hitchhiker's Guide to the Future* for you, a dramatisation of *Voyage* by Stephen Baxter for me).

Seven years earlier you heard my work and felt I was the person to produce three new series of *The Hitchhiker's Guide to the Galaxy* – based on your later novels – for BBC Radio. That effort crashed and burned through copyright issues, but we carried on hoping it might be revived until a year or so before this encounter, when your office informed me that the film rights had been sold and I should give up hope of any further radio series. Now, sitting on our squeaky leather BBC sofa, you said there was always a chance of bring Hitchhiker's 'home' to radio.

In 2001 you suddenly departed this Arc Of Probability and the film was temporarily languishing in development hell, while the audio rights became available. Thus, despite your absence, we finally managed to make the third, fourth and fifth series of *Hitchhiker's* for BBC Radio 4, and I even got you into the cast, playing a part – as you'd requested – thanks to the audiobook reading you'd made years before of *Life, the Universe and Everything*.

Shortly afterwards BBC Radio 4 commissioned three series from your Dirk Gently novels. The first two were faithful to your work, the third would be based on your notes for *The Salmon Of Doubt*. That last series wasn't made when I parted with the production company, who I felt failed to behave responsibly towards creative talent. I learned later that your agent Ed Victor withdrew permission for them to make it without me. I'd still like to have completed the trilogy, but I hope you agree Ed made the right call.

A 'live' performance based on *Hitchhiker's* featuring the original cast took place in 2008 at The Royal Geographical Society and another in 2009 at the Royal Festival Hall. Three years later, two successive tours of *The Hitchhiker's Guide to the Galaxy Radio Show Live* entertained more than 35,000 happy adults and children in theatres across the UK, introducing new devotees to your work. History repeated itself – after a fashion – when those running the tour let down the creative talent, abandoning us to our fate whilst still on the road.

It's been a mixed bag of experiences, many of which I remember with pride, some of which still have me waking up in a cold sweat. But the moment I will treasure most – and want to share with you – is what your mother said to me after she came to see the show at the Mayflower Theatre in Southampton: 'I often fell asleep when the radio series were broadcast as they were on rather late,' she said. 'I never imagined I'd be in an audience to see them performed live. Dirk, I had no idea Douglas's work was so *funny*.'

Thank you, Douglas.

Yours ever

Dirk

Dirk Maggs is a freelance writer and director chosen by Douglas to continue *Hitchhiker* on BBC Radio. Maggs eventually adapted, co-produced and directed four series based on the later *Hitchhiker* books, plus a live radio broadcast and stage tours (shown above, with Simon Jones on the left as Arthur Dent, in a photo taken by Ken Humphrey). His work with Audible includes Neil Gaiman's *The Sandman* series.

On Love

Douglas has been criticized for his lack of believable women characters – in fact, he admitted it was something he struggled with. However, he was never short of female admirers and there's evidence of this among his papers of some relationships that really side-swiped him. At university, for example, he wrote about a liaison with an unhappily married woman called Mary. This is a draft of a letter apologizing to Mary for his behaviour – although we'll never know, of course, whether a final version of it ever reached her.

Sweet Mary,

I guess I should apologise for my shitty behaviour on Saturday afternoon. I hope it didnt upset you, but I don't really suppose it did. It seems to have turned out rather badly and I've been more than a little foolish. You know of the strange see-saw of my worries about my work, and that together with the sudden shock of discovering that as well as loving you I just needed you in some abject way which led to all those weird paranoid jealousies has just wrecked me, and seems to have wrecked our relationship in some really wretched way. I hope this isn't how things have to be. Having been so beautifully close to each other we now seem to be awkward strangers, which is really hateful. I guess it's my fault and I'm really sorry for being so bloody stupid. I'm just as much mixed up as I've always accused you of being. Still come and see me soon as you can and will see what we can sort out.

Sweet Mary,

I guess I should apologise for my shitty behaviour on Saturday afternoon. I hope it didn't upset you, but I don't really suppose it did. It seems to have turned out rather badly and I've been more than a little foolish. You know of the strange see-saw of my worries about my work, and that together with the sudden shock of discovering that as well as loving you I just needed you in some abject way which led to all those weird paranoid jealousies has just wrecked me, and seems to have wrecked our relationship in some really wretched way. I hope this isn't how things have to be. Having been so beautifully close to each other we now seem to be awkward strangers, which is really hateful. I guess it's my fault and I'm really sorry for being so bloody stupid. I'm just as much mixed up as I've always accused you of being. Still come and see me soon as you can and we'll see what we can sort out.

There are several examples of Douglas's love poetry in the archive, too – two of which are reproduced and transcribed below and date from his later years at university.

Sometimes I wish I was leaving
Leaving this heavy town
But my sad-living woman
Needs to have me around.
Woman you know where I am
What I'm going through
I've learnt love from your vodka lips
And I give it all to you!

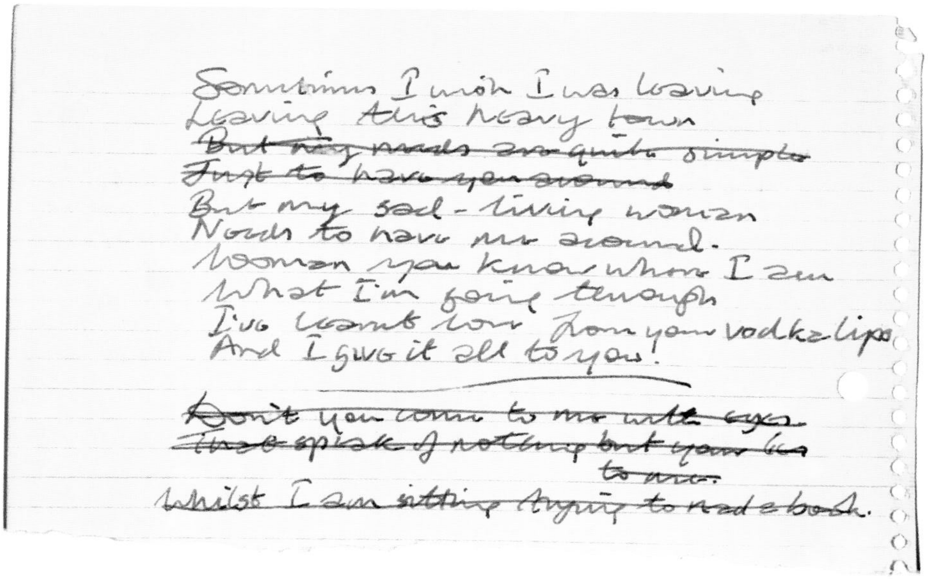

Sometimes I wish I was leaving
Leaving this heavy town
~~But my needs are quite simple~~
~~Just to have you around~~
But my sad-living woman
Needs to have me around.
Woman you know where I am
What I'm going through
I've learnt love from your vodka lips
And I give it all to you!
~~Don't you come to me with eyes~~
~~That speak of nothing but your lies to me.~~
~~Whilst I am sitting trying to read a book.~~

Looks like Rain

Well I've read all your stories
Read all your poetry.
What was missing on the page was in your eyes.

Tattered scraps of sadness
Turned into epic misery
Do you really expect me to sympathise?

Well I've seen all your photos
Been through your iniquities
You seem so pleased with all your shame
You're coming round to see
Though you seem to smile your eyes are full of tears.
You always look as if you're expecting rain.

Well it looks like someone
Is going to have to fill you in
And it looks like someone's going to be me
Don't ask me why I love you
Must be the craziest thing I've done all year
But that's the way it's going to be.

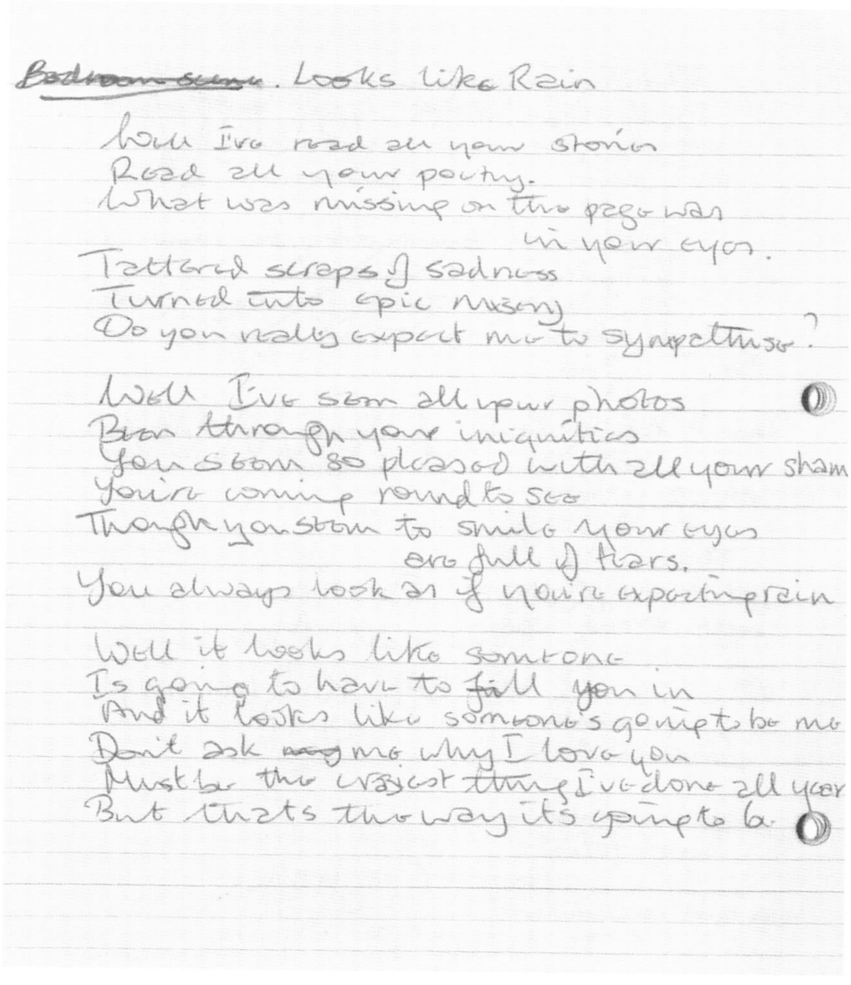

~~Bedroom scene~~. Looks like Rain
Well I've read all your stories
Read all your poetry.
What was missing on the page was in your eyes.
Tattered scraps of sadness
Turned into epic misery
Do you really expect me to sympathise?
Well I've seen all your photos
Been through your iniquities
You seem so pleased with all your shame
You're coming round to see
Though you seem to smile your eyes are full of tears.
You always look as if you're expecting rain
Well it looks like someone
Is going to have to fill you in
And it looks like someone's going to be me
Don't ask ~~me~~ me why I love you
Must be the craziest thing I've done all year
But thats the way it's going to be.

Looking for houses and trying to assess them for how they would accomodate my sweet lover and not knowing whether she would ever be there or whether I will live in it by myself, which, as you can probably imagine, fucking heartbreaking.

Some people (and here I'm thinking primarily of myself, though I think other people do it too) use records to try and dump unwanted emotion into. When a particular piece of music becomes associated with a particular piece of powerful emotion you play that record over and over and over again – you're torturing yourself with it in fact. Eventually, the hope is that

Sally

Sally Sally Sally

CLOSE UP ON THE GUIDE.

In 1980, after his first real flush of success, Douglas was invited to speak at the first Writers' Week held at the University of St Andrews, in Scotland. While there, he met guest speaker and novelist Sally Emerson. She lived with Douglas in his 'film-starry' new apartment in London's fashionable Islington – although, before they moved in, Douglas wondered whether he might end up living in it on his own (above, top) without her. Either way, the relationship was doomed and she left six months later. He dedicated the third *Hitchhiker's Guide* novel 'for Sally' and there is evidence that Arthur's love interest Fenchurch in the fourth novel was inspired by her, too. A page (above, bottom) of his draft notes for the abandoned second TV series of *Hitchhiker's* features a telling doodle that repeats her name.

Jittery with sex.

Erotic ~~writing~~ writing.

It's no good just saying "Put this in there, like that". You have to entice the reader until the reader feels ~~as~~ ~~just~~ jittery with sex.

This scene describes evening at sea. It's great.

I'm afraid I'm rather distracted by the fact that I can see ~~little~~ pretty little tufts of hair peeping round your knickers.

She said, not moving a muscle. Well, you can always tuck them back in.

He did. It took rather a while because he didn't do it the easy way, i.e. with his fingers, and one thing inevitably led to another and ~~after a while~~ soon there was semen (flying) all over the place again.

Look, if you want to do that kind of thing, or... he said.

[illegible] I did know, he said. I was told where, but I think I've forgotten.

She smiled and popped a little kiss on the top of [illegible], which was beginning slowly to uncurl. [illegible] It began to uncurl a little faster, and soon it was uncurled enough for her to pretend it was a nice big shiny ice lolly. She carried on [illegible] for quite a while but unlike ice lollies hers didn't get

Douglas's fourth novel, ***So Long and Thanks for All the Fish***, **involved writing love scenes between Arthur Dent and Fenchurch. Douglas seems to have sought advice on this – his note in 1982 about erotic writing (above, top) sounds very much like he was jotting down tips. There are further notes on the theme in his notebooks, too (left).**

The barrister Jane Belson (above, on the stairs with Douglas), who sadly died in 2011, was the love of Douglas's life. They were introduced by mutual friends in the early 1980s and Jane became his flatmate. They married in 1991 and had a daughter, Polly, in 1994.

SEVEN
Snail Mail

As Douglas's fame grew, so did his post pile. Some letters contained requests for information, others were written in spoof *Hitchhiker* style, still others professed undying love. Evidently, Douglas scribbled 'ANS' or 'answered' at the top of each one as he replied (or, on one occasion: 'I think I answered this one, if not, fuck it'), and, as the letters came abundantly, he scaled back to brief notes on yellow cards, or to a standard, photocopied reply

FIRST FAN LETTER

Hitch-Hikers Gu[ide to the] Galaxy
Radio Scotland
Somewhere in Scotland,
(I think)

G. Perkins
118
16 L.S.
LONDON

TRY B.B.C

Try Radio Clyde

GLASGOW 15 MAY 1978

Dear Sir/Madam

After listening to 'Hitch-hikers guide to the galaxy' on Sunday the fourteenth of may in the year of our 'God' 1978. We are interested to find out more about 'BROCKIAN ULTRA CRICKET'. so we would be very happy if you would send us the official rules.

Yours hopefully

David Morgan,
and
Graham Simpson

P.S. Slatibatfast for President
PPS. Broom fondle for God.

Radio producer Geoffrey Perkins said that the first series of *Hitchhiker's Guide* hit the airwaves in a blaze of indifference from BBC publicity and that the first they knew of any listeners was the arrival of an envelope addressed to 'Megadodo Publications, Megadodo House'. For decades legend had it that the envelope was marked in desperation by the postal service: 'Try BBC'. There's no mention of Megadodos on this envelope (above, top), but 'Try BBC' is clear. Dated May 1978, the letter inside seems to be Douglas's first piece of fan mail, from two lads in Glasgow. Douglas answered them (opposite) with a piece of script for Brockian Ultra Cricket, the game of hitting people for no apparent reason and then running away.

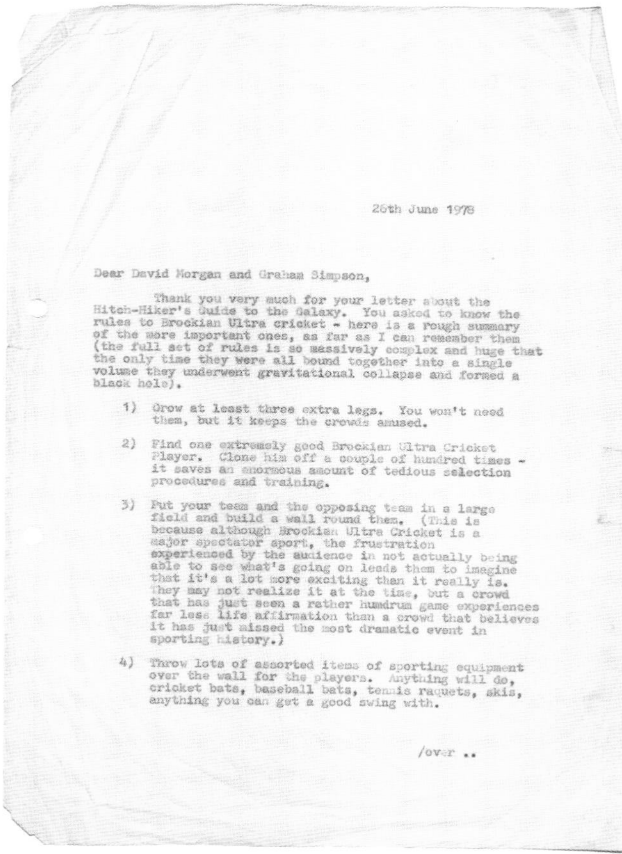

26th June 1978

Dear David Morgan and Graham Simpson,

Thank you very much for your letter about the Hitch-Hiker's Guide to the Galaxy. You asked to know the rules to Brockian Ultra cricket - here is a rough summary of the more important ones, as far as I can remember them (the full set of rules is so massively complex and huge that the only time they were all bound together into a single volume they underwent gravitational collapse and formed a black hole).

1) Grow at least three extra legs. You won't need them, but it keeps the crowds amused.

2) Find one extremely good Brockian Ultra Cricket Player. Clone him off a couple of hundred times - it saves an enormous amount of tedious selection procedures and training.

3) Put your team and the opposing team in a large field and build a wall round them. (This is because although Brockian Ultra Cricket is a major spectator sport, the frustration experienced by the audience in not actually being able to see what's going on leads them to imagine that it's a lot more exciting than it really is. They may not realize it at the time, but a crowd that has just seen a rather humdrum game experiences far less life affirmation than a crowd that believes it has just missed the most dramatic event in sporting history.)

4) Throw lots of assorted items of sporting equipment over the wall for the players. Anything will do, cricket bats, baseball bats, tennis raquets, skis, anything you can get a good swing with.

/over ..

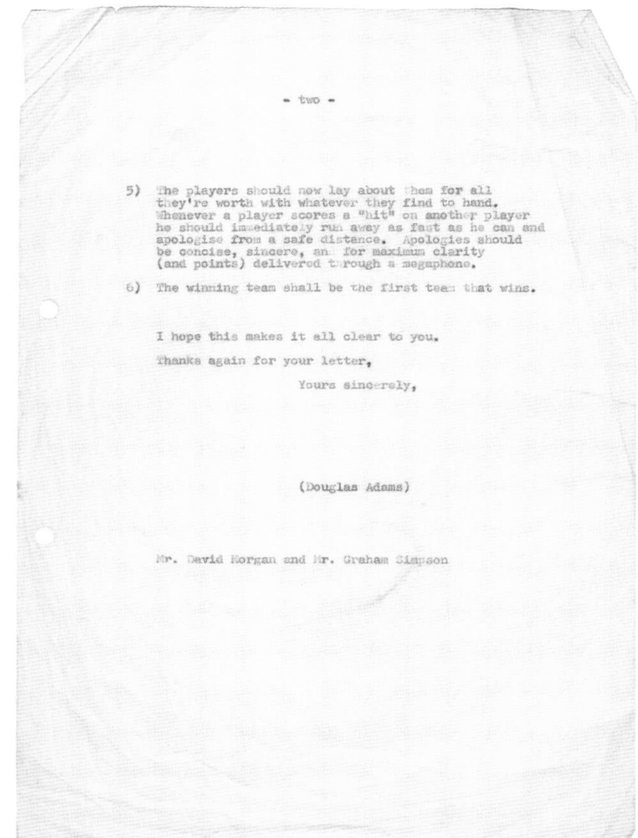

\- two -

5) The players should now lay about them for all they're worth with whatever they find to hand. Whenever a player scores a "hit" on another player he should immediately run away as fast as he can and apologise from a safe distance. Apologies should be concise, sincere, and for maximum clarity (and points) delivered through a megaphone.

6) The winning team shall be the first team that wins.

I hope this makes it all clear to you.

Thanks again for your letter,

Yours sincerely,

(Douglas Adams)

Mr. David Morgan and Mr. Graham Simpson

26th June 1978

Dear David Morgan and Graham Simpson,

Thank you very much for your letter about the Hitch-hiker's Guide to the Galaxy. You asked to know the rules to Brockian Ultra cricket – here is a rough summary of the more important ones, as far as I can remember them (the full set of rules is so massively complex and huge that the only time they were all bound together into a single volume they underwent gravitational collapse and formed a black hole).

1) Grow at least three extra legs. You won't need them, but it keeps the crowd amused.

2) Find one extremely good Brockian Ultra Cricket Player. Clone him off a couple of hundred times – it saves an enormous amount of tedious selection procedures and training.

3) Put your team and the opposing team in a large field and build a wall round them. (This is because although Brockian Ultra Cricket is a major spectator sport, the frustration experienced by the audience in not actually being able to see what's going on leads them to imagine that it's a lot more exciting than it really is. They may not realize it at the time, but a crowd that has just seen a rather humdrum game experiences far less life affirmation than a crowd that believes it has just missed the most dramatic event in sporting history.)

4) Throw lots of assorted items of sporting equipment over the wall for the players. Anything will do, cricket bats, baseball bats, tennis raquets *[sic]*, skis, anything you can get a good swing with.

5) The players should now lay about them for all they're worth with whatever they find to hand. Whenever a player scores a "hit" on another player, he should immediately run away as fast as he can and apologise from a safe distance. Apologies should be concise, sincere, and for maximum clarity (and points) delivered through a megaphone.

6) The winning team shall be the first team that wins.

I hope this makes it all clear to you.

Thanks again for your letter,

Yours sincerely,

(Douglas Adams)

Mr. David Morgan and Mr. Graham Simpson

Answered

53 Glencoe Street,
Hull,
N. Humberside.

7910.20

NEW ADDRESS

Dear Douglas,

My reputation as wanderer amongst the Jet Set has taken another boost amongst my colleagues at work since I told them of my meeting with you at the Leeds ST convention. There has also been great interest generated by the news of the book and record of Hitch-Hiker's Guide To The Galaxy - indeed, one of the reasons I'm writing to you is to try to find out where I can obtain copies of the record on behalf of people at work. I tried to get a couple of copies at the convention but they'd all been sold - I couldn't even get one of the books!!

Please, please, PLEASE could you send me an address, data bank code or even Mega-Ordanance Survey co-ordinates for a supplier of said merchandise, or your number-two fan risks getting lynched by the Angry Mod (not to mention its even angrier mob) - SAE enclosed for your reply.

I've just finished the painting of the Vogon ("Resistance is useless!!") Trooper, bringing my collection of HHGTTG paintings to three (the other two are of Zaphod Beeblebrox's hyperspacial megacoup cruiser a[...] Frogstar Megaplatoon battle robot with his (its) omnivapourisi[...] megacrumbler-cum-coffee grinder. (There is an historical prece[...] for that, by the way. Every 24th. Martini-Henry rifle supplied[...] the U.S. cavalry at the time the U.S. had a horse-borne cavalr[...] a coffee-grinder built into its butt, so there'd be a coffee-g[...] for every twenty-four men. No mention, of course, has ever be[...] as to what strange modifications every 24th. horse had incorpo[...] into it!! On the same theme, the Isreali Uzi submachine gun h[...] Coke-Bottle opener built into it, after it was discovered that[...] Isreali troops were using the lips of the ammunition magazines[...] crown-cork bottles, damaging them in the process. And you th[...] Hitch-Hiker's Universe was wierd.....)

Hope to hear from you soon and, until then, more power to [...] diodes and May the Force be with you,

110a Highbury New Park,
London. N5 2DR
Tel: 01-359-1056

Dear Robin,

Thanks a lot for your letter. It was good to see you at the Leeds con, and I thought your Chewbacca was triffic.

I enclose an order form for the record, though if you've bought a copy of the book by now you'll find there's an order form in each of those. In addition to which I gather that the record company have suddenly decided that they were lying about it never ever being available in record shops. It will shortly be available from most branches of Virgin records.

I'd love to see your HHGG paintings some time. Don't sell them till I've seen them!

Incidentally, I've thought about it for a bit and decided that your coffee grinder story is almost certainly a pack of lies.

See you at a Con one day,
Best wishes,

Douglas Adams.

This letter (above, top) comes from British Aerospace engineer Robin Hill, a gifted modelmaker, artist and lover of fancy dress (a cosplayer, if you will), whom Douglas met at a *Star Trek* convention held at The Dragonara Hotel in Leeds, UK, in October 1979. Douglas was a guest speaker and, after the event, Robin wrote to him from his home in Hull. The letter above (bottom) is Douglas's reply.

7, Oaklands Road,
Sutton Coldfield,
West Midlands,
B74 2TB.

5th November, 1979.

Douglas Adams,
c/o; BBC TV Centre,
London.

Dear Mr Adams,

This letter is to let you know just what is going on about the "Hitch-Hiker's Anonymous" group which is now starting in earnest. So far we have people allocated for handling membership, newsletter, fanzine(s?), badges (etc.). An initial meeting for interested people was held at NOVACON last weekend, and it soon overflowed into the corridor outside the room! We started taking registrations for membership at lunch-time on the last day of the Con, and have already got about 60 people who have actually joined, and many more who are interested, but had by then spent all their money at the bar.

One thing that became apparent very quickly at the meeting is that we would very much like you to be the Honorary President of the society. The number of people who wanted this was phenomenal, and so I hope that you will be able to agree, and I look forward to hearing from you on the subject sometime soon.

The plans so far are as follows:

Membership, etc. is being co-ordinated by Joy Hibbert, who is the person that everyone will first contact.

I am handling the newsletter, and therefore would be very interested in anything resembling news about "Hitch-Hiker's". I hope that you will be able to help us on this score, as we hope to be able to stamp out some of the rumours that are wondering around at the moment. Would it, for instance, be possible for us to send you a supply of stamped addressed envelopes in the hope that you could drop a note in one each time a "breakthrough" occurs?

Getting back to the point, which was the Committee structure (On a pre-historic planet??! - sorry.) We hope to be able to provide some forms of badges, posters, etc. This side will probably be handled by a chap called Stephe Edwards who works in the badge trade.

Owen Tudor is still around, though not on a full(spare)time basis (if you see what I mean), and he will be producing a fanzine (possibly called PLAYBEING).

I think that that's just about it at the moment, before we drag more people in to help with newsletter distribution, etc., except that we hope to hold some form of meeting (not a Convention to start with) for fans to get together, chat, be manically depressed and drink whatever we find to be the nearest Earth subs[...] Gargle-Blasters.

I enclose with this letter a stamped addressed envelope, and [...] find the time to answer some of the questions raised herein, and [...] ideas of your own about the running of this group.

Finally then, I look forward to hearing from you, and more to [...] to the next series, TV series, Book, film, towel, etc.

Yours sincerely,

André Willey

André Willey. (on behalf of Hitch-Hiker's Ano[...]

110a Highbury New Park,
London, N5 2DR
Tel: 01-359-1056

19 Nov 79

Dear Andre,

Thank you very much for your letter. I'm delighted that you've managed to set up HHA and that you've had such a ~~xxxxx~~ response.

I've just written to Owen as well, and he has an update on latest developments. Not a lot at the moment, but there should be a flood of news towards the end of the year when the tv show starts getting into pre-production swing, when work starts on the film script, etc., etc.

PLease don't hesitate to get in touch if I can be of any help - phone is quicker.

Yes, I'd be delighted to be your Honorary President, thank you very much for asking me.

Looking forward to hearing from you furhter,
Best wishes,

Douglas

Hitchhiker's Anonymous was an early attempt at running a fan club for the series. André Willey from the West Midlands wrote to Douglas in November 1979 (above, top) to ask Douglas if he would officially endorse the club as its Honorary President. Of course, Douglas readily agreed (above, bottom). André took the signed photo of Douglas at a *Doctor Who* convention in 1979.

HONARARY MEMBERS:
SIMON JONES MARK WING-DAVEY DAVID LEARNER

ZZ9 PLURAL Z ALPHA

THE HITCH HIKERS GUIDE TO THE GALAXY
APPRECIATION SOCIETY

PRESIDENT & SECRETARY:
ELAINE THOMSON

MEMBERSHIP SECRETARY:
JEAN THOMSON

23 NORTHBROOK ROAD ALDERSHOT HANTS GU11 3HE

Douglas Adams,
110a Highbury New Park,
LONDON N5.

5th May 1982

Dear Mr. Adams,

Hello again - I hope that all goes well with 'Life, The Universe & Everything', which we're all pleased to hear is due for publication in the summer.

I have been attempting to get in touch with you at your phone number for some time now(as I believe there are rumblings of a second TV series for The Guide,)but have had no success, so I imagine that you perhaps may even now still be in the States or Canada promoting the books - I hope that's going (or went) well?

I wonder if you could perhaps let me know for our next n/l (copy deadline 15th JUne) whether there is to be another TV series in the near future, and also whether there is anyone contracted to write a 'Making' or 'History' of The Guide?? I ask not purely because we're interested in reading one (we all are, eagerly, of course!), but also because one of our ZZ9 members and I have some ideas for one, and if no-one is actually writing one at present nor planning to in the immediate future, may we present you with our ideas for this project with a view to undertaking it?? Neither of us is a professional writer as you may know, but we would hope that this would not automatically disqualify us from having the opportunity - anything we may be allowed to do in this capacity would of course be subject to your approval etc. We believe we can do a good job on it and since its subject matter would be of great interest to us then we would certainly not let anything sub-standard emerge.

If the above proposal is at all feasible, we would be pleased to forward our plans, or to discuss them with you in person if you would prefer.

We would also like to invite you to attend one of our London-held meetings at some convenient date this summer. We are in the process of improving ZZ9 to include an off-set litho'd magazine-newsletter and mounting a nationwide advertising campaign, helped by many of the SF bookshop proprietors. We would very much like to know your reactions to our plans, and to make you an Honarary Member if you would consent to this?

I think that's all for the present - a newsletter will be on its way to you shortly along with details for the improvment of the club. I hope that you will be able to respond to this letter in the near future and look forward very much to hearing from you.

Sincerely for the ZZ9 committee,

Elaine Thomson *Elaine T.*

If Hitchhiker's Anonymous (see previous page) was the first, the second and longer-running *Hitchhiker's* fan club is 'ZZ9 Plural Z Alpha: the Hitch Hiker's Guide to the Galaxy Appreciation Society', which is still going. In May 1982, the original president and founder Elaine Thomson wrote to Douglas, having failed to contact him by phone, to ask him for his approval on the notion of her and another club member writing a 'Making' or 'History' of the *Hitchhiker's Guide* and inviting him to come to a London meeting and take honorary membership of the Club. Douglas accepted his Honorary membership, but sadly never attended a formal ZZ9 event.

This letter is from Shelley Page, a graphic designer who later became a Disney artist, working on movies such as *Who Framed Roger Rabbit* (1988). Douglas was intrigued by her beautifully written letter and invited her out for a drink. Shelley says they enjoyed a short-lived relationship. Sadly, she has lost Douglas's letter of reply.

ANSWERED

86 Holland Park
London W.11
727 3408
Jan 1st 1980

Dear Douglas Adams –

I am a freelance illustrator (airbrush, editorial, publishing etc.) ~ which along with scriptwriting, cab-driving and journalism must be one of the most anti-social jobs in existence – and here I am, true to form, at 1.00 a.m. on New Year's Day, with two perfectly good parties to go to, stuck at home with an airbrush, a radio and an impossible deadline for company!

As you might imagine I'm feeling pretty bloody – Kenny Everett's over, all my friends are out having a good time and I have to finish a poster of John Garfield & Lana Turner before morning!

The single thing that makes life bearable at this moment is my trusty, much-thumbed copy of the 'Hitch-Hiker's Guide to the Galaxy'!

You may find it ironic that, as a girl much given to panic most of the time – I find the words 'Don't Panic' on the cover, it stared at for several minutes, most re-assuring! Life mimics fiction!

So what I wanted you to know is that at moments like this, when I seriously consider chucking it in and getting a steady job like war correspondent or digital watch assembler, I reach for your book and mentally hitch a lift with Ford, Zaphod & Co. and somehow the world doesn't look quite so bad when I get back!

I suppose this is really a fan letter, although I freely admit that at the moment (1.15 a.m.) it feels more like a complaint to the world in general and magazine editors in particular! So please accept my compliments on the 'Guide' and my best wishes for future efforts.

Also, as a devoted fan of Dr Who since the days when I used to hide behind the sofa when the Daleks appeared, thanks for re-vitalizing the series – in the words of another science-fiction character – may both you and the Doctor live long and prosper!

There is one thing that I most urgently would like to know – is there to be a sequel to the 'Guide'? I cannot believe that you could leave a perfectly good starship, cast of characters and devoted public (me) stranded in Hyperspace! Please let me know – much as I love the 'Guide' – and however many times I can happily re-read it – I know how it ends! – so – it lacks that element of suspense!

Well, I have to get back to Lana Turner – Happy New Decade – may it heap more laurels upon you – or something!

Yours appreciatively –

Shelley Page

P.S – if you ever need a really snappy piece of airbrush illustration at 3.00 in the morning ....!

1.

64 STATION RD
KINGS HEATH
BIRMINGHAM
B14 7SR
Tel: 021 444 7712

ANS

Dear Douglas*/Mr Adams*/Hoopy Frood*/Genius*/Ravenous Bugblatter Beast of Traal* – [Delete whichever is not applicable].

Hi there! You don't know me and I don't know you either, but I'm writing to inform you that you have most probably saved me from the depths of manic depression. I had applied for an M.A at a Polytechnic which shall remain nameless, namely Manchester, and after having been rejected I decided that life was no longer worth living — but, something deep inside made me put on "The Hitch-Hiker's Guide to the Galaxy" L.P. After listening to someone who was even more miserably depressed than myself and the hilariously hysterical version of the Vogon poem, how could I feel bad?

I would dearly love to know if there are any plans for more radio episodes apart from the repeats, for which the BBC is renowned? I watched "Ask Aspel", a few weeks ago and Mark Wing-Davey was on much to my delight; he mentioned the fact that another TV series would appear on our screens sometime next year. Frankly (or maybe Douglasly), I just cannot imagine how that could ever come about because all the episodes from the radio, Books, L.Ps and T.V have already been very mixed up. Although, Mark did say that it will begin and end at a cricket match — the mind boggles!

I would love to know how you chose the actors for the parts because Mark seems to be an ideal Zaphod, even though he's got blond hair. [If you ever meet him, can you ask him if he remembers a guy called Rodney Haigh – cuz I know his wife]. Why did Geoffrey McGivern not continue with the role of Ford Prefect?

MARY QUANT

2.

Actually I'm glad that David Dixon is playing Ford Prefect, because he is just how I imagined Ford to look and he's got fabulously blue eyes! [My favourite colour]. If you've got any spare photographs of the characters floating about [the photos I mean] – is there any chance of me acquiring them – autographed if possible. [N.B – I will stoop to almost any level to get them].

I think Arthur [Simon Jones] is so fantastic that I cannot praise him enough – so I won't; I mean he's just so "not with it". I have a teddy bear called Arthur, but I called him that before I knew of the "other" Arthur, because that name actually means "The noble bear man" – very original! I also have a little blue fluffy rabbit who's called Peter, but that means "a rock" – so where did I go wrong?

One of my many hobbies is collecting names, their origins and meanings, so if you've any spare ones up your sleeve.... ...... Actually, names are funny things if you ever look up their meanings – Douglas, for instance means – "from the dark stream" – are you? Ford, means "the river crossing" [pretty obvious wasn't it?] and Marvin, would you believe, means "famous friend" – I couldn't find out what Zaphod and Slartibartfast mean.

I am a Graphic Design student in my final year at Birmingham Polytechnic [don't laugh – I would love to know what's so funny about that place]. Anyway I will soon be unleashed onto an unsuspecting and unprepared world — so watch out! I was recently doing a project and much to my surprise, I found that the typeface I was using was and still is, called "Marvin", of all things. I'm also doing a poster for "Hitch-Hiker", so if you would let me know what your address is, I will send you a print of it. My sister was wondering where she could get a jacket like Ford's and

MARY QUANT

3.

I was wondering if I could sort of borrow Zaphod's jacket to wear at my final show, because I'm going to miss one episode of "Hitch-Hiker" because of the show. Could I have the real head with it, so that I'll have someone to talk to – The Degree show will be open to the public on the 2nd and 3rd July from 10am – 8pm and on the 4th July from 10am – 4pm. and you'd be very welcome, if you decided to come. I'm very glad that there's a "Hitch-Hiker" convention in Birmingham this year – is there any chance of ensuring that I could definitely get there? What exactly does one do at such a convention – I've never been to one before. Anyway, it's been great writing to you – I don't expect you'll have time to write back but I'll wait with great anticipation.

Yours hopefully

Ewa Kuczynski [Miss].

P.S – I'll try to see you at the convention, but if not, I shall find some other way.

P.P.S – Give my thanks to Marvin for being more depressed than I was.

P.P.P.S. Could you possibly tell me how, when and where Zaphod, Ford and Arthur shave?

P.P.P.P.S – I'm not married, have no children and do not live in Surrey either.

MARY QUANT

DOUGLAS ADAMS

Dear Ewa,

Thanks for your letter. Sorry about the enclosed sheet, hope you understand.

Geoff McGivern wasn't available when the t.v. show was being cast – he was in "The Dresser" in the West End.

I'm afraid I think it's highly unlikely that the BBC would hire out Zaphod's costume – but you could always ask them.

Best wishes

Douglas Adams

London N1

6th June 82

Dear Ewa Kuczynski,

Thank you for you letter. I'm not sure I'm going to be able to answer all your questions as I have an enormous pile of correspindence to catch up with now that I have finally finished Life, the Universe and Everything - which is coming out in August. That book will answer some of them for you I hope anyway.

Here are a few answers though. David Dixon is not Dave Dixon, and his eyes are not that colour either - he was wearing contact lenses for the show. The reason for the change in hairstyle is, I'm afradi, quite simpy a continuity lapse. The first programme was made a concsiderable time before the rest, and that was a detail which went wrong. Come to thin of it that's not quite right. No, the continuity lapse was between the filmed sections which comprised the first half og the programme, and the studio videotape sections which formed the second half of the show. The point is the same though - there was a considerable time lapse between the two and somebody slipped up.

My connection with Doctor Who was that I was the script editor for a season 79/80. I also wrote some episodes. They are unlikely ever to be published because I don't think I'll ever have time to do them, and I wouldn't let anybody else do it.

I suggest you call your duck The Duck With No Name, which will give it a certain cachet amongst other ducks. It will seem like a duck with an interesting past. The two baby ducks should be called Duck With An Interesting Future A and Duck With an Interesting Future B.

Must go now,

Best wishes,

Douglas Adams.

Another letter (opposite), in a beautiful hand, from a graphic designer called Ewa Kuczynski, then a Manchester Polytechnic art student, who lived in Birmingham. In the letter, she refers to a poster she mocked up to promote the *Hitchhiker's* TV series (overleaf). Douglas replied to her more than once – the first time was a short handwritten note on yellow cards, accompanied by a photocopied standard letter (see page 179). However, when Ewa wrote again (a letter that's now sadly missing), Douglas responded with a fuller, typed letter about the gap in continuity of Ford's hair in the TV series (above and right).

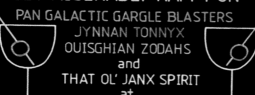

SEE THE MARVELS OF THE UNIVERSE
for less than thirty Altairian dollars a day

HOLIDAYS IN THE SUN
FOR SOLAR FLARES
AND REAL SUNBURN

VISIT THE UNCHARTERED BACKWATERS OF THE UNFASHIONABLE END OF THE WESTERN SPIRAL ARM OF THE GALAXY

DROP IN ON AN UTTERLY INSIGNIFICANT LITTLE BLUE GREEN PLANET WHOSE APE DESCENDED LIFE FORMS ARE SO AMAZINGLY PRIMITIVE THAT THEY STILL THINK DIGITAL WATCHES ARE A PRETTY NEAT IDEA .....

THE RAVENOUS BUGBLATTER BEASTS OF TRAAL OFTEN MAKE A VERY GOOD MEAL OF VISITING TOURISTS

GET MISERABLY HAPPY ON
PAN GALACTIC GARGLE BLASTERS
JYNNAN TONNYX
OUISGHIAN ZODAHS
and
THAT OL' JANX SPIRIT
at
THE EVILDROME BOOZERAMA

THE MAXIMEGALON MUSEUM OF DISEASED IMAGINATION proudly presents

THE HOOLOOVOO

a super-intelligent shade of the colour blue

PLUS

many other

BAROQUE MONSTROSITIES

DON'T PANIC

MEET
ZAPHOD BEEBLEBROX
EX-PRESIDENT OF THE IMPERIAL GALACTIC GOVERNMENT
OFTEN THOUGHT TO BE
COMPLETELY OUT TO LUNCH!

PLEASE REMEMBER TO BRING YOUR TOWEL!

MAGRATHEA

THE MOST IMPROBABLE PLANET THAT EVER EXISTED

[contact SLARTIBARTFAST]

ALL MATTRESSES GROWN IN THE SWAMPS OF SQUONSHELLOUS ZETA
ARE VERY THOROUGHLY KILLED AND DRIED BEFORE BEING PUT TO SERVICE

For more details watch
THE HITCH HIKER'S GUIDE TO THE GALAXY
starting Thursday June 4th at 7.55 on BBC I

Ewa Kuczynski's poster art, loosely based on the graphics used for the *Hitchhiker's Guide* TV series. She refers to the poster in her first letter to Douglas, reproduced on page 176.

Highbury, London N5.

I'm sorry to have to send you this photocopied letter, but I don't employ a secretary, and if I try to answer every letter individually I simply don't get any writing done. Since I find I am answering the same questions fairly often, here are the answers to those questions.

1) I'm afraid I don't have any photographs of myself. My mother says she has one of me she took in her garden five years ago but I've seen it and it's not very good. The focus is all wrong.

2) My doctor has warned me not to attempt any further explanations or rationalisations of the plot of Hitch Hiker.

3) The books are different from the radio series because the series were written serially and I didn't know what was going to happen next. The books were written with the benefit of hindsight and I tried to make better use and sense of the material.

4) There will not, after all be a second television, not for the time being at least. Please don't write and ask me why, a)because it's a secret and b) because...

5) I am busy writing a third book. This will be called LIFE, THE UNIVERSE AND EVERYTHING, and will be all new. It will continue where the first two books left off and should be published round about late spring next year.

6) There may be a new record album but I don't know what will be on it.

7) There may yet be more Hitch Hiker on radio, but I'm not even thinking about it till next year.

8) There is a very good chance that there will one day be a Hitch Hiker feature film, but all that I know about it is contained in this sentence.

9) For news of Marvin's career as a solo recording artist write to the Marvin Depreciation Society, 2 Whitechurch Lane, London E1.

I hope this covers what you want to know,
Best wishes,

Douglas Adams.

This is a copy of the standard reply many people got from Douglas once the demands on his time became too great and the fan letters too numerous for him to reply personally every time.

Fwd.

23-27 TUDOR STREET, LONDON EC4Y 0HR

Telex LDN 265863 (Unipapers) Telephone: 01-583 9199

16th September 1974

Douglas Adams, Esq.,
Fraser & Dunlop (Scripts) Ltd.,
91, Regent Street,
LONDON, W. 1.

Dear Douglas:

I'm sorry to be so long in replying to your letter, but I've only just returned from a fortnight away, to find it.

There was no way that the show could not have come in for punishment from me. I have to review programmes without discrimination as to their provenance, and without deviating from values I maintain. Once a critic falls into the trap of saying, for example, "Crossroads is moleshit, but, given what it sets out to be, it is good moleshit" he might as well take his hat and open a tobacconist's somewhere on the South Coast. It may make me appear hard, but I care hardly at all for what a thing sets out to be; I concern myself only for what it is. Thus, it may have been that the Footlights show was of a very high amateur standard, that it worked better in a Cambridge environment, or on the stage, or before the hacks took their shears and glue to it, but that is minimal business of mine. I have to say: Should it have been on television/ Was it worth watching when it got there?

None of this means I don't sympathise with the horrors you detail and your suffering from them: I have written much telly myself, and have seen filet turned to Wimpey. All I would say to you and to anyone involved with good amateur stuff originally beamed at a very

PUNCH PUBLICATIONS LTD. Directors: A V Caudery N A Whinfrey K N Holt W Davis B P Knox-Peebles R Tookey
Registered office: 23-27 Tudor Street London EC4Y 0HR Registered in England No. 797363

-2-

specific or local audience is: when They come to you and offer the big time, don't jump at the offer. It matters very little to promoters or TV companies if they try an experiment on and it flops disastrously, because tomorrow is another day. But it matters very much to those who were hoping to make their contribution to the thing the beginning of a writing, or acting, career. "What have you done?" subsequent employers/publishers/producers will ask, and you will say "I was involved in That", and they will say "Oh, that That?" and may very well add a rider to the effect that they will let you know. I have known a lot of talent that rushed a novel out prematurely, or a play, or had a showof pictures because a gallery owner thought there was an outside chance of a succes comique, and a lot of that talent works for ICI these days, or teaches O-level Spanish.

I hope my review does no-one any permanent damage; I'm sure the genuine talent will survive such tiny onslaughts. But the blame for any setbacks lies fairly squarely with the BBC, and, it must be said, for those whose heads were turned by their offer. To be fair to all of us, let me say that at twenty, my own would probably have spun like a top; but fifteen years on, I know better, and there's no point knowing it unless you pass the knowledge on.

My best wishes,

Alan Coren
Deputy Editor.

Of course, not all of Douglas's letters represent fan mail. Douglas, disappointed by some harsh criticism in *Punch* magazine regarding the May Week revue's TV broadcast in 1974 (for which Adams-Smith-Adams had written many of the sketches), seems to have complained by letter and got the following response from critic and satirist Alan Coren. He encourages Douglas not to lose heart from the negative review, nor to accept offers of the big time from TV executives too readily.

23-27 TUDOR STREET, LONDON EC4Y 0HR

Telex LDN 265863 (Unipapers) Telephone: 01-583 9199

Douglas Adams
110a Highbury New Park
London N5 2DR

Oct 29 1979

Dear Douglas,

Dept of Low Improbability; friend of mine used to live at 114 H N P, name of Duncan Campbell. I cashed in your voucher for two cases of bubbly. Well, to be accurate, for a picture of two cases of bubbly, which we have all enjoyed.

I have now finished the book, and would like to say that you have done the bookification extremely well. In fact, I'll say it. I resented finishing it.

Alan Coren says over my shoulder, Why doesn't Douglas write something for us ? So if you have any very small 45 rpm you wish to turn into a smash hit article, or if you have any idea floating loose in the souter space of your mind, don't forget that Punch ranks second only to an RT cover.

yours

Miles

PUNCH PUBLICATIONS LTD.

Registered office: 23-27 Tudor Street, London EC4Y 0HR Telephone: 01-583 9199 Registered in England No. 797363

In 1979, a few years after Douglas received the letter from Alan Coren (opposite), Coren's colleague Miles Kington wrote praising Douglas for his 'bookification' of *Hitchhiker's Guide*. Coren himself also gets a mention – generously offering Douglas the opportunity to submit material to their magazine.

EIGHT
Fame, Flying and Awards

Douglas's first formal book signing was in October 1979. He told people it was so well attended that he had trouble getting out of the taxi, through the crowds and into the venue. Whether or not that's true, fame had certainly come knocking: the invitations to speak and enthral flooded in, and he was even honoured with his own portrait (above) in the National Portrait Gallery, London.

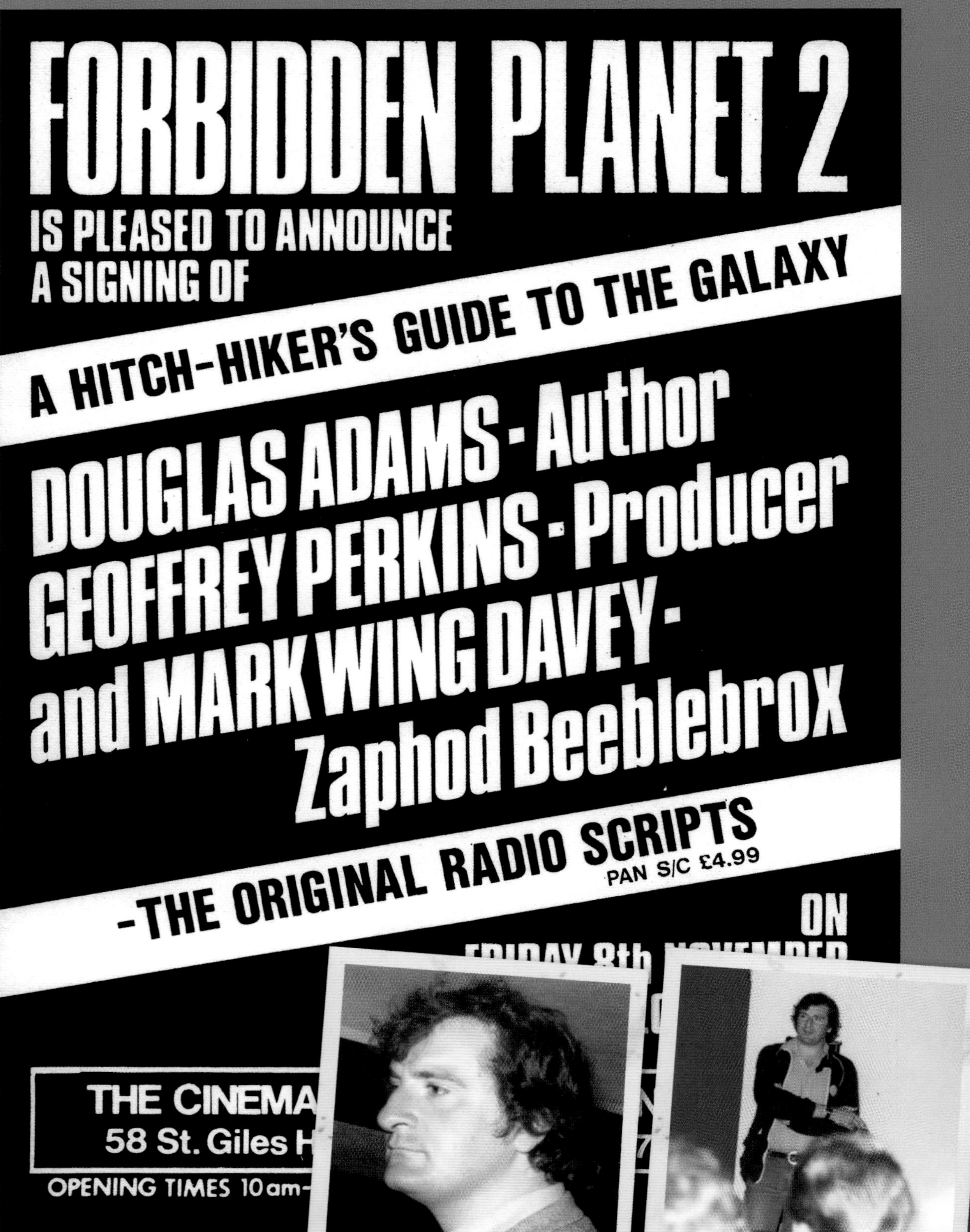
FORBIDDEN PLANET 2
IS PLEASED TO ANNOUNCE
A SIGNING OF
A HITCH-HIKER'S GUIDE TO THE GALAXY
DOUGLAS ADAMS - Author
GEOFFREY PERKINS - Producer
and MARK WING DAVEY -
Zaphod Beeblebrox
-THE ORIGINAL RADIO SCRIPTS
PAN S/C £4.99
ON
THE CINEMA
58 St. Giles
OPENING TIMES 10am-

In September 1980, Douglas flew up to Glasgow, Scotland, to be guest of honour at Hitchercon One (so far the only convention of its kind). Douglas delivered his speech and judged the fancy dress. The flier is for another of many signings that Douglas attended over the years. This one was in 1985 for the launch of the *Radio Scripts* book.

Pacing around

Fib

Not here to talk about technology –

— HHGG interface – Microsoft

Instead I thought I'd try and answer the two questions that writers get asked all the time.

Where do you get all your ideas from?

Does your hand hurt yet –

Don't know what they think ~~we'd~~ we all do all day, but that is what people ask.

And the time they ask it, of course, is when you're doing signing sessions. Signing sessions are the

Douglas's notebooks are filled with jottings of what were clearly intended to become speeches. We have no idea whether this speech ever made it in front of an audience but it is an insightful musing on the problem of the same question faced by an author at his or her book signing. The notes are transcribed overleaf.

bane of a writer's life, because the second worst thing that can happen is that dozens, scores, even hundreds of people can turn up, each wanting you to write something really personal and different and witty in their books. And the very worst thing is that no one turns up at all

But they are mostly friendly cheerful people who turn up. They know there's not going to be much of a chance for a chat, especially if there are going to be lots of people, but they want to be able to say something friendly and cheerful as you're sitting churning away at one friendly personal signature after another, so they say 'Does your hand hurt yet?'

And you smile and say no, it's bearing up fine, and thanks for asking.

The trouble is that people have usually figured out that they are going to say that before they actually get to the bookstore, and one of them is, of course, going to find themselves first in line. So he's all ready to ask if my hand hurts yet, but he's first in line. So he thinks 'Damn! Damn' and then thinks I'll say it anyway. So, in a very friendly cheerful way he says, illogically and out of nowhere 'Does your hand hurt yet?'

And the person in the line behind him thinks 'Damn! That's what I was going to say'

Pacing around.

(A6, or Fl6?)

Not here to talk about technology –

HHGG interface – Microsoft.

Instead, I thought I'd try and answer the two questions that writers get asked all the time. 'Where do you get all your ideas from?'

'Does your hand hurt yet?'

Don't know what they think we all do all day, but that is what people ask. And the time they ask it, of course, is when you're doing signing sessions. Signing sessions are the bane of a writer's life, because the second worst thing that can happen is that dozens, scores, even hundreds of people can turn up, each wanting you to write something really personal and different and witty in their books. And the very worst thing is that no one turns up at all.

But they are mostly friendly cheerful people who turn up. They know there's not going to be much of a chance for a chat, especially if there are going to be lots of people, but they want to be able to say something friendly and cheerful as you're sitting churning away at one friendly personal signature after another, so they say 'Does your hand hurt yet?' And you smile and say no, it's bearing up fine, and thanks for asking.

The trouble is that people have usually figured out that they are going to say that before they actually get to the bookstore, and one of them is, of course, going to find themselves first in line so he's all ready to ask if my hand hurts yet, but he's first in line. So, he thinks 'Damn, Damn!' And then thinks I'll say it anyway. So, in a very friendly cheerful way he says, illogically and out of nowhere, 'Does your hand hurt yet?' And the person in the line behind him thinks 'Damn! That's what I was going to say.'

Concorde.

Brown peeling fablon on the front passenger bulkhead.

Little windows with bubbles in the glass.

Defense de fumer Attachez Ceintures.

On the pushbuttons for calling the stewardess are little pictures of a stewardess's head. They are not great works of graphic art. They are 3/4 views, and look as if they were done by an ancient Egyptian fresco designer, and were the major reason why he decided thereafter to stick to doing profiles.

The face looked as if it had been assembled out of the bits of plastic children make faces out of by sticking them in potatoes.

They looked like an example of the work of a potato faces.

Magazine – British Airways High Life.
" " Concorde Supersonic Sales.

Magazines in racks in glossy white covers with the title of the magazine printed according to its own logo, but in dark blue.

During the 1980s, Douglas's success coupled with his passion for cutting-edge technology perhaps contributed to his preferred use of Concorde when he needed to cross the Atlantic. But the plane's interior décor was already looking a bit tired by 1984, when Douglas jotted down the observations above and over the following pages (and transcribed on page 191). Some of the other passengers weren't immune to his close scrutiny, either!

Old American businessmen in brand new clothes, ~~...~~ faces full of finely burst blood ~~vessel~~ vessels finely scraped and patted with something pungent, nodding off with the exhaustion of having spent a ~~year getting to~~ lifetime getting to look like that.

Elderly American women elaborately and palely dressed looking rather sombre about something on ~~their~~ little fold down table.

Reading a large new straw coloured hardback ~~bestseller~~, holding it rather elegantly with pincered fingers, and peering at it over half moon glasses as if it was something rather precious ~~that~~ might get broken.

— as if it was a pair of their husband's underpants.

Elegant young ladies, daftly perfectly made up and dressed in something grey with a stripe in it.

Concorde gallery

Continual chaos of things being tipped over and smashed.

Mach Meter, blue moulded plastic with the smart gold margin and the smart white letting rather heavily rubbed away and faded.

Lots of grubby little marks and cracked plastic.

Cold waiting for something or someone on a hillside.

Description of the alien who can't bear the cold, sitting miserably holding his little hands up to his mouth and blowing fumes over them, while all his scales rattled. The little devices or drinks. There weren't enough to go round. Little squabbles broke out about whose turn it was on the after-breather.

(But an important point is to make this a normal level. Not absurdly cold, because ~~these~~ I always try and overdo things – make things too big, ~~too~~ hot too absurd – relax the style a little.

There's a man sitting across the aisle from me who is the man I was trying to describe earlier – an elderly businessman, dressed in a smart grey lightweight suit, with ~~a~~ fine dark socks and fine black leather moccasins, a fine thin gold watch, a ~~chin like a frogs~~ a neck like a frog's, ~~the~~ heavy tortoiseshell glasses, fine, dry skin with dark freckles on the back of his hand and delicate fingernails, and on his face, a fine sense of gaping wonder (incomprehension?) as if, for the first time since he was a child he wondered, and wondered till his fine thin grey hair tingled, what he was doing here –

(gaping with a fine sense of incomprehension)

The man on my left is very serious, refuses all drinks, and reads about India. ~~Has g~~ heavy glasses.

I had the feeling that he was about to lean over, pat me on the hand with his fine dry ~~loose f~~ loose-skinned fingers, maybe gape, and say "Young man, are you describing me?"

The sun shone brightly through the window, refracting, and doing designs from the fifties on the ~~brow~~ peeling brown fablon.

resembles nothing so much as a frog, who, at the end of his life is strangely bewitched

The pale brown, yellow ochre, repeating design on the matt plastic walls seemed to be ~~based on something~~ a kind of extravagant fantasia based on something gynaecological and the ~~re~~ remains of a kipper.

Window shutter. Plastic window shutter

Here's my current argument about my poor book -

- That if ~~my course is~~ I knew that my course is wrong, I seem unable to correct it until it goes wrong, till disaster strikes!

We are currently travelling at Mach 2

Concorde

Brown peeling Fablon on the front passenger bulkhead.

Little windows with bubbles in the glass.

Defense de fumer. Attachez Ceintures.

On the pushbuttons for calling the stewardess are little pictures of a stewardess's head. They are not great works of graphic art. They are ¾ views, and look as if they were done by an ancient Egyptian fresco designer and were the major reason why he decided thereafter to stick to doing profiles. The face looked as if it had been assembled out of the bits of plastic children make faces out of by sticking them in potatoes.

They looked like an example of the lid of a box of potato faces.

<u>Magazines</u>

British Airways High Life.

" " Concorde Supersonic Sales

Magazines in racks in glossy white covers with the title of the magazine printed according to its own logo, but in dark blue.

Old American businessmen in brand new clothes, faces full of finely burst blood vessels finely scraped and patted with something pungent, nodding off with the exhaustion of having spent a lifetime getting to look like that.

Elderly American woman, elaborately and palely dressed, looking rather sombre about something on their little fold-down table. Reading a large new straw-coloured hardback bestseller, holding it rather elegantly with pincered fingers, and peering at it over half-moon glasses as if it was something rather precious and might get broken.

as if it was a pair of their husband's underpants.

Elegant young ladies laden, perfectly (darkly) made up and dressed in something grey with a stripe in it.

Concorde galley

Continual chaos of things being tipped over and smashed.

Mach Meter – Blue moulded plastic with the smart gold margin and the smart white lettering rather heavily rubbed away and faded.

Lots of grubby little marks and cracked plastic.

Cold waiting for something or someone on a hillside.

Description of the alien, who can't bear the cold, sitting miserably holding his little hands up to his mouth and blowing fumes over them, while all his scales rattled. The little devices or drinks. There weren't enough to go round. Little squabbles broke out about whose turn it was on the after-breather.

(But an important point is to make this a normal level. Not absurdly cold, because I always try and overdo things – make things too big, too hot, too absurd – relax the style a little.)

There's a man sitting across the aisle from me who is the man I was trying to describe earlier – an elderly businessman, dressed in a smart grey lightweight suit, with fine dark socks and fine black leather moccasins, a fine thin gold watch, a neck like a frog's, heavy tortoiseshell glasses, fine, dry skin with dark freckles on the back of his hand and delicate fingernails, and on his face, a fine sense of gaping wonder (incomprehension?) as if, for the first time since he was a child he wondered and wondered, till his fine, thin grey hair tingled, what he was doing here.

(gaping with a fine sense of incomprehension.)

The man on my left is very serious, refuses all drinks, and reads about India through heavy glasses.

I had the feeling he was about to lean over, pat me on the hand with his fine dry loose-skinned fingers, maybe gape and say, 'Young man, are you describing me?'

The sun shone brightly through the window, refracting, and doing designs from the fifties on the peeling brown Fablon.

The pale brown and yellow ochre repeating design on the matt plastic walls seemed to be a kind of extravagant fantasia based on something gynaecological and the remains of a kipper. [Marginalia: Resembles nothing so much as a frog, who, at the end of his life is strangely bewildered.]

Window shutter. Plastic window shutter.

Here's my current argument about my poor book.

– That if I know that my course is wrong, I seem unable to correct it until it goes wrong, till disaster strikes.

We are currently travelling at Mach 2.

That done, we could finally relax about the baggage and start seriously to worry about the state of the plane which was terrifying. Mark told me that Merpati bought their planes 2nd hand from Uganda Airways, but I think he was joking. The door to the pilot's cockpit remained open for the duration of the flight, or might actually have been missing entirely.

I have an oddly reckless and cheerful view of air travel. It rarely bothers me at all. I don't think this is bravery, because I am for instance frequently scared stiff in cars, particularly if I'm driving, but once you're in an aeroplane everything is completely out of your hands so you may just as well sit back and grin manically about the grinding and rattling noises and the turbulence which threw the plane all over the sky like a leaf.

Not all of Douglas's plane travel was quite as luxurious as he might have found on Concorde (see previous pages). During his trip to Africa for *Last Chance to See* (see pages 240–51), his experience was quite different. This page from his notebook sets out some of his observations of a rusty light aircraft displaying a dubious-looking state of repair.

AND THE WINNER IS...

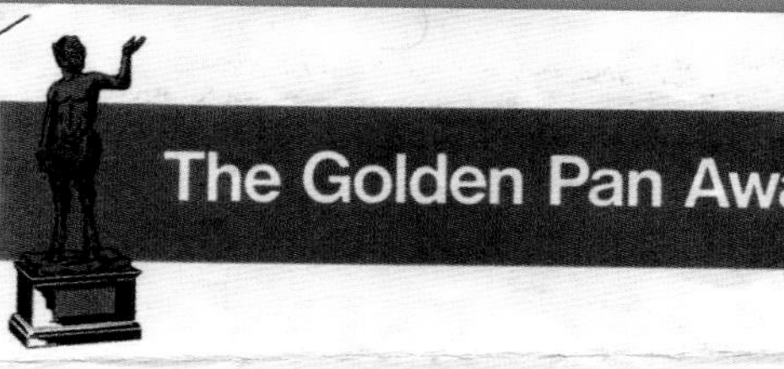

On 12 January 1984 Douglas Adams becomes - at 31 - the youngest author to receive a Golden PAN for THE HITCH HIKERS GUIDE TO THE GALAXY which is also the first PAN Original title to reach sales of one million copies.

* * * * * *

The idea for THE HITCH HIKER'S GUIDE TO THE GALAXY first came to Douglas Adams some years ago while hitch-hiking around Europe using a copy of the PAN Hitch-Hiker's Guide to Europe. Drinking the local wine and gazing up at the stars in a camp site, he conceived the idea of a HITCH HIKER'S GUIDE TO THE GALAXY. The idea lay dormant until Simon Brett, who was the producer of the Radio 4 series, called Douglas and asked if he could write a comedy science fiction drama for radio ...

* * * * * *

* The radio series was first produced on Radio 4 in March 1978 attracting a large cult following. It has been repeated numerous times since.

* THE HITCH HIKER'S GUIDE TO THE GALAXY was published by PAN in October 1979. It went straight to Number 1 in the bestseller lists and appeared in the list for a total of 46 weeks.

* The Restaurant at the End of the Universe, the sequel to THE HITCH HIKER'S GUIDE TO THE GALAXY, was published a year later in December 1980. It was Number 1 for 3 weeks and in the bestseller lists for 19 weeks. Sales now stand at over three quarters of a million copies.

* Life, the Universe and Everything was published in August 1982. It was Number 1 for 7 weeks and in the bestseller lists for 15 weeks. Sales to date are fast approaching three quarters of a million copies.

Pan Books Ltd., Cavaye Place, London, SW10 9PG
Telephone: 01-373 6070 Cables Pandition London SW10

/2 ....

/2

* So Long, and Thanks for the Fish - the fourth book, will be published by PAN in hardback in November 1984

* There have been three stage shows based on THE HITCH HIKER'S GUIDE TO THE GALAXY, two produced by Ken Campbell at the ICA and The Rainbow Theatre and one produced by Theatre Clwyd.

* The 6-part TV series of THE HITCH HIKER'S GUIDE TO THE GALAXY was shown originally on BBC 2 in January 1981 and repeated almost immediately on BBC 1.

* There have been two successful LPs based on the books.

* A major film, scripted by Douglas Adams, is in development in America.

* The Meaning of Liff by Douglas Adams and John Lloyd, published in November 1983, is currently at Number 5 in the bestseller lists where it has been since publication. The Meaning of Liff was one of PAN's bestselling titles over Christmas and has already sold well over 100,000 copies.

The Directors of Pan Books request the pleasure of your company to celebrate the presentation of a Golden Pan to

DOUGLAS ADAMS

to mark the sale of One Million copies of

THE HITCH HIKER'S GUIDE TO THE GALAXY

in the Pan edition alone

Please bring this invitation with you

RSVP
Clare Harington
Pan Books Ltd
18-21 Cavaye Place
London SW10 9PG

6.30-8.30pm
Thursday 12 January 1984
The Roof Garden
99 Kensington High Street
London W8
Entrance at 99 Derry Street

Douglas was presented with his first (of several) Golden Pan Awards at a ceremony in the sparkling mirror-tiled nightclub venue of the Kensington Roof Gardens, London. The publisher, Pan Books, was keen to celebrate the company's first ever million-selling Pan Original and the fact that Douglas was the youngest author ever to sell a million copies, aside from Anne Frank. Douglas received a little golden statuette of the cloven-hoofed Pan to mark the occasion and took the microphone, saying, 'I've known about this award for a while, and I'm glad to say my acceptance speech is very nearly ready' – a nod to his legendary lateness when it came to writing. Douglas's personal guests at the ceremony included his younger siblings Jane (in the photo right, holding the statuette) and James (far left), his mother Janet and his step-father Ron Thrift.

On ‘Bop Ad’

Even as a callow youth, it seems Douglas was practising his autograph for some future starry purpose. In July 1980, as part of his warm-up video before the first screening of the TV pilot of *Hitchhiker*, Peter Jones (‘The Voice of the Book’) cracked the joke about Douglas having signed so many copies of the paperback that an unsigned copy was now worth more than one with the author’s mark. The notion was later applied to other authors who were also prodigious signers, such as Terry Pratchett. It’s fair to say Douglas did enjoy a good signing tour. He travelled the globe, meeting his fans and scribbling like crazy, so it seems inevitable that his signature would eventually shrink, saving on ink and a very tired left arm. For a man who did not really like being called ‘Doug’, it seems funny that after many iterations, his distinctive signature ended up being a squiggle that fans in ZZ9 Plural Z Alpha: the Hitch Hiker’s Guide to the Galaxy Appreciation Society (see page 174) adopted as their hero’s unofficial nickname – ‘Bop Ad’.

A trawl through the archive reveals this shortening went one step further... a medical inoculation form (when Douglas was about to tour the world seeking out some of its most endangered species for his book *Last Chance to See*; see pages 240–251) proves that a cursory ‘D.Ad-’ would sometimes also suffice. Here are some of the fuller iterations of Douglas’s signature.

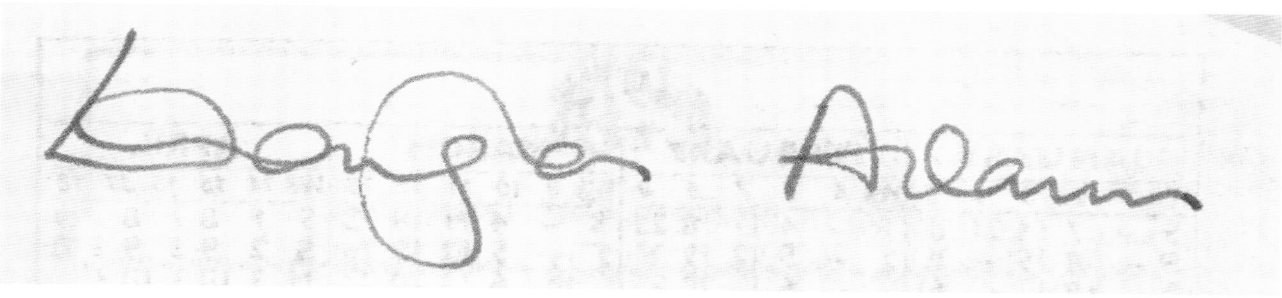

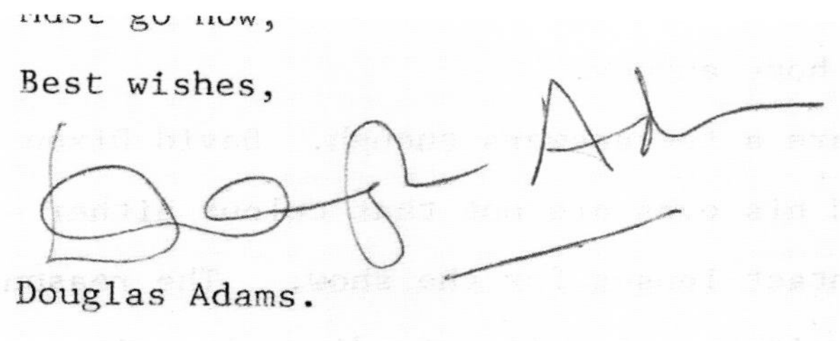

must go now,

Best wishes,

Douglas Adams.

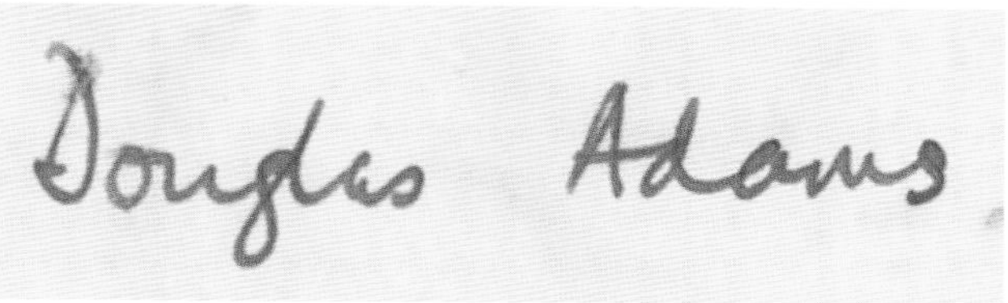

REHEARSAL SCRIPT

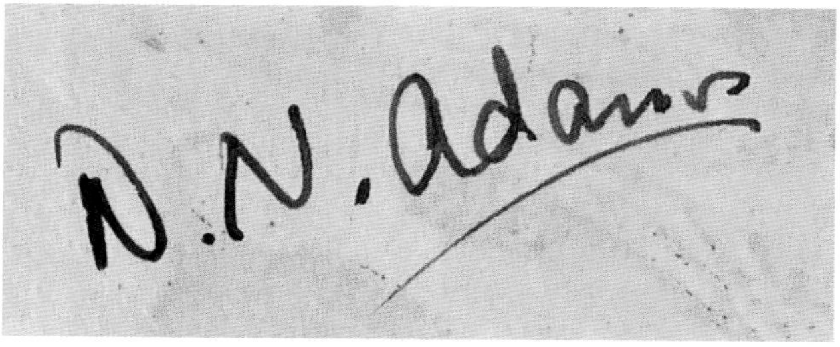

NINE

Later Invitations to Collaborate

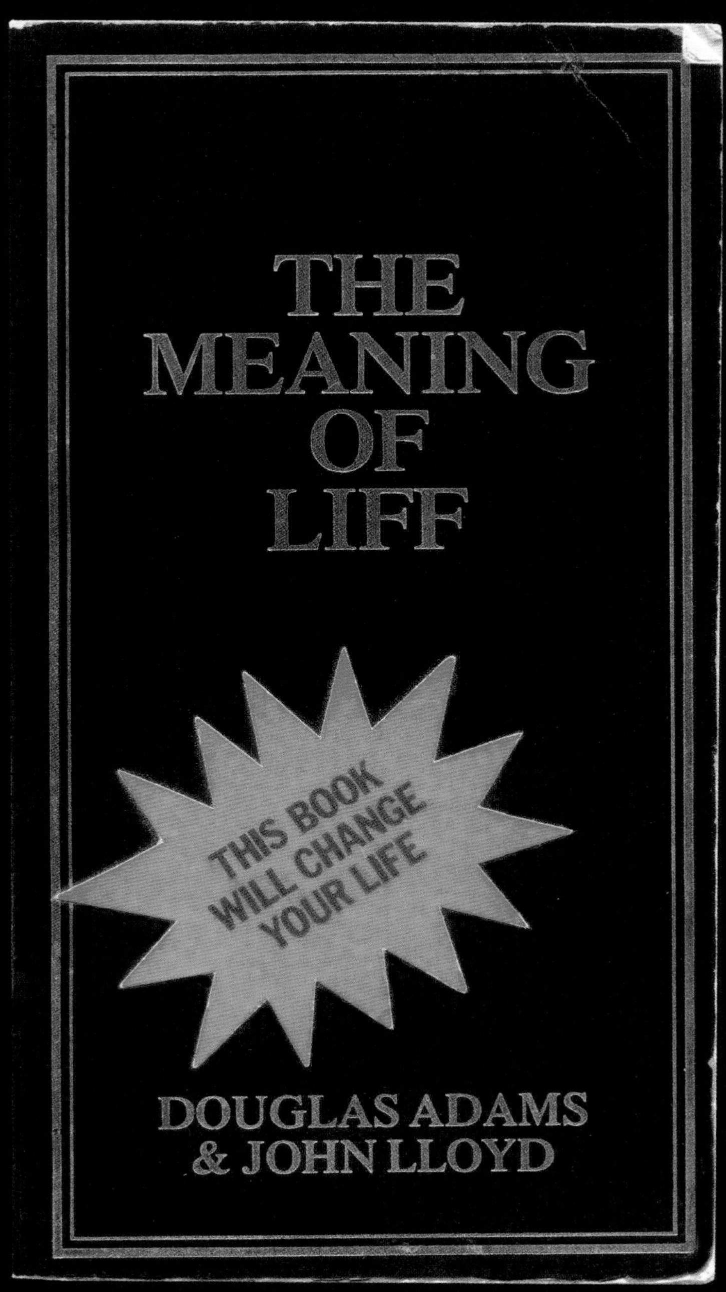

As Douglas's success with *Hitchhiker* grew, so others sought the fruits of his writing talent. Some of those collaborations were with long-standing friends and colleagues (*The Meaning of Liff* with John Lloyd being a case in point), but the archive also points to new ventures with some perhaps more unexpected famous names.

FOOTLIGHTS PANTO

BBC radio LIGHT ENTERTAINMENT
presents

BLACK CINDERELLA TWO GOES EAST
or
CONFESSIONS OF A GLASS SLIPPER TRYER ONNER

The show that will do for pantomime what Mozart did for fluid mechanics. Starring, in order of alphabetical importance:
RICHARD BAKER TIM BROOKE-TAYLOR ROB BUCKMAN
JOHN CLEESE PETER COOK GRAEME GARDEN DAVID HATCH
MAGGIE HENDERSON JO KENDALL JONATHAN LYNN
RICHARD MURDOCH BILL ODDIE JOHN PARDOE MP
Music by the Nic Rowley/Nigel Hess Difficult Listening Band.
Script by Rory McGrath and Clive Anderson.
Lyrics by Jeremy Browne.

★★★★★★★★★★★★★★★★★★★★★★★★★★★★★★★

This show will be transmitted on Christmas Day at 1.30 p.m. and New Year's Day at 12.30 p.m. Radio 2.

smerrychristmasmerrychristma
chrismasmerrychristmasmerryc

BLACK CINDERELLA T
or
CONFESSIONS OF A G
TRYER ONNER

RICHARD BAKER — DAVID HATCH
✓TIM BROOKE-TAYLOR — ✓MAGGIE HENDERSON
ROB BUCKMAN — JO KENDALL
JOHN CLEESE — ✓RICHARD MURDOCH
✓PETER COOK — ✓BILL ODDIE
✓GRAEME GARDEN — ✓JOHN PARDOE

all

starring in alphabetical importance, with others too numerous to mention

MUSIC BY
THE NIC ROWLEY & NIGEL HESS DIFFICULT LISTENING BAND

SCRIPT BY
RORY McGRATH and CLIVE ANDERSON

LYRICS BY
JEREMY BROWNE

PRODUCTION (and torn hair) by: DOUGLAS ADAMS

RECORDING: SUNDAY 17 DECEMBER 1978 : PARIS STUDIO : 1930-2100
REHEARSAL: 1000-1930
R.P.REF.NO: SLN51/143G430
TRANSMISSION: MONDAY 25 DECEMBER 1978 : R2 : 1330-1430
REPEAT: MONDAY 1 JANUARY 1979 : R2 : 1230-1330

12.15.
3/4 hr.
SPEECH ON X-PAIR
SONGS ON SHURES
Cues on musi Handel
horseps etc.

BBC broadcaster and executive David Hatch recruited Douglas in early 1977 as a radio producer. Although Douglas's output was frequently disorganized and less than prolific, the immediate success of *Hitchhiker's Guide* in March 1978 had earned him a certain kudos. That year Hatch appointed Douglas to produce the 95th anniversary Footlights pantomime (ticket, inset), the star-studded *Black Cinderella Two Goes East or Confessions of a Glass Slipper Tryer Onner*, from a script by Clive Anderson and Rory McGrath. Getting Peter Cook and John Cleese to appear must have been something of a casting coup.

Larger problem to begin with.

DOCTOR SNUGGLES AND THE PEANUT SOLVING MACHINE

Douglas Adams and John Lloyd.

PART ONE

The kitchen. Dr Snuggles is talking to Miss Nettles about the forthcoming birthday for eight of the mice. Miss Nettles is preparing eight birthday cakes. Nobby listens. He is sitting on top of a machin designed to deliver really fresh eggs straight to the mixing bowl. At the top of the machine is a hen with a long ~~xkxxxx~~ winding chute ~~x~~ leading to the bowl. Miss Nettles needs two eggs for the mixture, so she pulls a lever which moves a feather duster to tickle the hen under the chin. The hen is pleased and lays an egg. The egg trundles down the chute, catches Nobby's feet, and he has to barrel run it down the chute. At the last moment he is flung off and the egg cracks and breaks into the bowl. Nobby, flying through the air, grabs the lever which tickles the hen who lays another egg.

Miss Nettles machines

Dr Snuggles tells Miss Nettles that he is going to send off to Uncle Bill in the Amazon for a special treat for each of the eight birthday mice, whose favourite food is peanuts. Meanwhile Miss Nettles tugs hard on the lever of another machine which is very large and ~~xxxxxxx~~ complicated. It buzzes and whirrs and sends off clouds of smoke and eventually picks up a small pinch of salt and puts it in the mixing bowl. Snuggles makes a moue at the machine - he's not very happy with it. He goes off to Ricketty Rick with Nobby who complains about not being part of the birthday party. It's not his birthday explains Snuggles.

In Ricketty Rick Snuggles gets out the peacock writer to send off a message. The Peacock ~~Wix~~Writer is a bird with a music stand strapped on his head and a fan of feathers at the back which work like the types of a type writer, slapping forward in turn to print a message on the piece of paper.

Snuggles tells the peacock he wants the message "Dear Uncle Bill,

The *Hitchhiker's Guide* on radio had caught the ear of the Irish actor and writer Jeffrey O'Kelly, who sought out Douglas and John Lloyd for help with his TV cartoon series *Doctor Snuggles*. The two turned in several outlines and a couple of scripts that were actually made. This material for *Doctor Snuggles and the Peanut Solving Machine* is one of several pieces for the series that survives in Douglas's archives.

RUPERT AND THE FROG KING

(FILM STARTS WITH STILLS LIKE FRAMES FROM THE COMIC STRIP, OVER WHICH WE HEAR THE VOICE OF A NARRATOR)

STILL: MR. BEAR DIGGING IN THE GARDEN.

NARRATOR: Rupert is helping his father dig the garden.

ANOTHER STILL MR. BEAR (AND RUPERT MAYBE) BEING BOTHERED BY FLIES.

NARRATOR: "There are a lot of flies around" says Mr.Bear. I wonder what's happened to all the frogs? There are usually plenty of them at this time of year to keep the flies under control."

That's funny, says Rupert. There were plenty of them in the garden yesterday. I wonder where they've all gone?

Rupert decides to see if there are any frogs in the stream that runs by Bill Badger's house.

On the way there, he is surprised to see a strange object flying overhead. "Why! It's just an ordinary paper dart" exclaims Rupert. "Where has it come from and why doesn't it fall to the ground ?"

STILL OF RUPERT WALKING ACROSS THE COMMON.

SUDDENLY A PAPER DART (ANIMATED) FLIES SLOWLY THROUGH THE AIR.

RUPERT(ALSO ANIMATED FOR THE FIRST TIME) TURNS HIS HEAD SLIGHTLY TO WATCH. OTHERWISE THE PICTURE REMAINS QUITE STILL. IT'S NOT REALLY FULL ANIMATION THIS TURN OF RUPERT'S HEAD BUT A KIND OF "ONE-FRAME-A-SECOND" JERK.

WHEN THE DART HAS FLOWN RIGHT THROUGH FRAME, CHANGE TO ANOTHER NEW STILL: WE SEE RUPERT ARRIVING AT BILL BADGER'S.

NARRATOR: Rupert arrives at Bill Badger's to find his friend and PODGY playing with paper darts, and excitedly he tells them about the mysterious dart he has just seen.

In October 1981 Paul McCartney's company MPL and Douglas's literary agent Ed Victor struck a deal for Douglas to write (with Terry Jones and John Lloyd, who were also asked) an animated short involving newspaper cartoon character Rupert the Bear – McCartney had held the rights to a film of the character for some years. These first two pages show how the film might have developed from static frames, as per the original newspaper comic strips, into fully fledged animation. The film eventually became known as the award-winning short *Rupert and the Frog Song* (1984).

"Oh it was probably one of mine" says Bill. "Thgy're very good. Watch thiis"

STILL: BILL THROWS A DART.

SECOND STILL: THE DART FALLS TO THE GROUND A FEW FEET AWAY.

"No it wasn't like that...it was more like..."

A PAPER BIRD (ORIGAMI STYLE)

AT THIS MOMENT XNXXXXXXXXXXXXXXXXXXXXX FLIES IN THROUGHX THE WINDOW THE BIRD IS ANIMATED, AND AS IT FLIES INTO THEIR LINE OF VISION THE TWO FRIENDS' HEADS TURN AS WELL TO WATCH THE BIRD AS IT CONTINUES TO HOVER IN THE AIR IN FRONT OF THEM

The friends stare in astonishment at the odd creature. Suddenly they hear a laugh behind them and turnx to discover Tigerlilly the conjurer's daughter.

STILL OF THE FRIENDS SEEING TIGERLILLY.

NEXT STILL IS TIGERLILLY UNFLODING THE PAPER BIRD.

"This is my bird" says the Chinese girl."It's made with magic paper that my father has just invented."

"Was that your dart I saw flying across th common?" asks Rupert.

"Yes," says Tigerlilly. "It was going to pay my gas bill.X Xxx xxxxx xxxxxxxxxxxxxxxxxxxxxxxx You just write on the magic paper where you want it to go, and it will fly straight there."

XXxxxxxx The Chinese girl offers to let Rupert try a piece for himself.

"I know," says Rupert, "I'll send it to find the missing frogs."

STILL OF RUPERT WRITING ON THE PIECE OF PAPER.

STILL OF RUPERT LAUNCHING DART.

XXXXXXXXXX CUT TO OUTSIDE THE HOUSE. THE DART STARTS TO FLY OUT...

ANIMATED THIS TIME.

Today's new word
from the Oxtail English Dictionary.

Blerup (noun) Publishing and printing term.
All books, but especially reference books are designed to contain at least one blerup. When you flick through the book looking for a page number or a key word, as soon as you get near the page you want your thumb jumps and a great fat wad of pages jumps across making you start your search again. This wad is correctly called a 'blerup'.

Today's new word
from the Oxtail English Dictionary.

Bastable (adjective) The corridors of British Rail trains are designed to be bastable – that is 'not quite impassable'.
They are rendered bastable by British Rail bastabling clerks whose job is to stand in the narrowest part of the carriage looking after three rucksacks, a folding pram and a large sea-trunk.

Today's new word
from the Oxtail English Dictionary.

Tarshle (noun) That part of a screwhead which breaks off when you try to remove a screw from a door-hinge. Can also be used as a verb, as in 'Oh bollocks, I've tarshled the screw'.

Today's new word
from the Oxtail English Dictionary.

Furfle (verb) The impossible business of trying to keep your farts down to a reasonable level of decibels when in a lavatory in easy listening distance of lots of other people.

While in Corfu with John Lloyd and Mary Allen in the summer of 1978, Douglas would inevitably take long breaks from writing *The Hitchhiker's Guide* to spend the time with his friends. During these breaks, they would occasionally play a game based on an English lesson Douglas had enjoyed when he was 12: the class had to give meanings or definitions to ordinary place names. John Lloyd, ever the producer, had the sense to write a few of these ideas down and then, in late 1981, used them when writing the second tie-in book to his hit comedy TV sketch show *Not the Nine O'Clock News*. In that volume (a page-a-day calendar called *NOT 1982*), these definitions, and more by a few other writers, were known as 'new words from the Oxtail English Dictionary'. *NOT 1982* sold well enough for another edition the following year, but in the meantime the publishers suggested a whole book full of the satirical definitions. Douglas and John Lloyd started by pasting existing cuttings from the *NOT* book on to index cards. These are just a few that survive in Douglas's archive.

A safe place where you put something and then forget where you put it

Trying to pull chain + finishing pee at same time — column of water, pee that doesnt make it

trying to find the RIGHT thing to read in the lavvy

Muthill: — credit Wimbledon.

KIRBY MISPERTON:
Pedestrian run/shuffle when erossing road to slowly to make you not slow down- half hearted and useless attemot to help impression of hurry.

PITSLIGO: sweaty bit under arms.

retracing memory steps.

Thirlspot:
EDGWARE — cf. kitchenware / ar aware.

DOONA — stifled fart, inverted fart one you hope people are going to be talking after.

BAGSHOT — to be within bagshot of something.

Pop of coffee / clean sheets — short-lived freshness.

SUNSNEEZE

Breathing through your nose in a lift.

Moment: in between closing of lift door and when it actually moves.

Pantrymime
Looking for scissors, tin opener — dangaction instead.

Wit of Loftus.

NUBISM

During September and into October of 1982, John Lloyd and Douglas, holed up in singer-songwriter Donna Summer's luxury beachfront villa in California, compiled quite a lengthy list of place names and other words and their definitions, written in notebooks or typed on further index cards. An array of these notes, added to by both men, from various notebooks, index cards and computer printouts, is reproduced above and over the following pages.

Person who owns a horse which pisse
water into your whisky.

✓ Person who owns a horse which pisses water into your whisky.

✓ To turn vegetables over so that the bruised side is underneath.

✓ The pleasant smell of an empty biscuit tin.

✓ A kind of poltergeist which specialises in stealing new copies of the A-Z from your car

✓ One who skies down a mountain in a blue funk, and then rips down the little slope just in front of the bar like a victorious slalom champion.

✓ One who washes everything up except the frying pan.

To wake up in the night and write down a mnemonic which the following morning you can't remember what it means.

Something left over from a meal futilely saved in the fridge knowing it will never be consumed.

Bit at the end of a phone conversation when you can't get off the line

saved in the fridge knowing it will never
consumed.

Of barristers, to clean a filthy stiff collar with a toothbrush until it is clean enough not to be ashamed to send to the laundry.

One who is proud of a bespoke suit which actually looks like something from an Oxfam shop.

✓ The drawer your mother keeps her paper bags in.

Of writers, never to have a pen.

Intelligent person who cannot spell.

The state of a barristers flat greasy hair after wearing a wig all day.

To get a laugh with someone elses joke (to tell someone elses funny story while they are present.

Of barristers, to put bands on inside out.

The stuff that falls out of a hairbrush when you finally get round to cleaning it.

Morning after an Indian meal – clean teeth but garlic is still killing your houseplants

FANGFOSS n.

A traditional false beard of just more skin-thickness which allows Iranians and Palestinian terrorists to appear with a permanent five-o'clock shadow – as their religion demands.

~~[illegible]~~

ALDWINCLE n.

The fake antique plastic seal attached to a pretentious gin bottle.

Sinister.

HENDRA.

~~[illegible]~~

EPHAM.

WAPPING

3990400

(213) 456 - 8841

OSWESTRY n.

(OLD SAXON)

Ancient word for a road where three times as many carts pass by in the opposite direction to the one in which you are travelling.

Also, the name of a London Underground station. A connection is unlikely. (Especially during rush hours).

PADUCAH n.

(YIDDISH)

The bloody-minded determination to continue a boring story to the finish.

FRANT n.

Measure. The legal minimum distance between two trains on the District and Circle line on the London Underground. A frant, which must be not less than 122 chains (or 8 leagues) long, is not connected in any way with the adjective "frantic" which comes to us by a completely different route (as indeed do the trains).

ABERLOUR vb.

(Of bus queues) To glare with mild anger and disappointment at a distant ~~ly~~ approaching bus knowing by its shape that it doesn't have your number on it.

20590

EVERCREECH n.

The look given by a group of polite, angry people to a rude, calm queuebarger

ADLESTROP n.

That part of a suitcase which enables your underwear to spill out all over the conveyor belt at an airport.

DORCHESTER n.

A throaty cough by someone else which obscures the crucial part of the amusing remark you've just made.

26 /26

DULEEK (n.)
Sudden realisation, as you lie in bed waiting for the alarm to go off, that it should have gone off an hour ago.

DULUTH adj.
The smell of a taxi out of which people have just got.

DUNBOYNE (n.)
The moment of realisation that the train you have just patiently watched pulling out of the station was the one you were meant to be on.

DUNCRAGGON (n.)
The name of Charles Bronson's retirement cottage.

DUNFERMLINE (n.)
The length of thread by which a silver button is separated from a blazer which has seen better days.

DUNGENESS (n.)
The uneasy feeling that the plastic handles of the overloaded supermarket carrier bag you are carrying are getting steadily longer.

DUNTISH (adj.)
Mentally incapacitated by a severe hangover.

This list of *Liff* entries is from a printout dating from 1983. A secretary called Mavis Kenney was employed in November 1982 to type John and Douglas's notes into an early word processor. This is but one page of many reams of folding computer paper she produced.

YARBOROUGH noun.

The point at which two people approaching each other from opposite ends of a long corridor recognise each other but pretend they haven't noticed each other because its going to be horribly embarrassing to have to continue doing so the whole length of the passage.

CHARING vb.

'Charing' is what people do to you when you ring up a company, and a whole string of people say 'Can I help you?' listen for ten minutes to exactly what it is you want before saying its someone else you should be talking to.

BERMONDSEY adjective.

If you are walking down the street and someone comes towards you shouting "Hallooooo !" and smiling and holding out their right hand, and then (when you've just taken your right hand out of your pocket and begun to smile) the other person sweeps past and greets someone directly behind you, then you will probably feel a bit 'bermondsey'.

VENABLES noun.

Venables are a strain of prefectly healthy rodent (eg mice, rats,guinea pigs) which develop cancer the moment they enter a laboratory.

FINCHLEY adj.

A man entertaining a girl at a restaurant which is just a bit out of his price range is said to appear 'finchley' when he tastes the little dribble of wine the waiter pours out for tasting, and tries to look sauve and sophisticated when he hasn't the faintest idea whether the wine is any good or not.

TRING noun.

The little shuddery feeling a girl gets when a man puts a hand on her newly shaved leg.

SCARBOROUGH noun.

A speechless warning glare directed at someone who just has, or is just about to, embark on a whole series of frintons, fulbourn -s or wigans.

SNAPE noun.

(RARE) There are believed to be no more than eight snapes in the whole of the British Isles.
This increasingly rare form of municipal tunnel, which,it is believed,may become extinct by the early 1980's,is one in which no-one has pissed over the concrete during the preceding night.

FRINTON noun.

The expression on your face when you've just said that someone's a cunt,and then realise they're standing right next to you.

The Meaning of Liff was published in late 1983 (simultaneously by Pan Books and Faber & Faber) in a small pocket-sized volume with an orange sticker on the front proudly asserting 'This book will change your life' (see page 197). What Douglas and John admired about the design was that it didn't say anywhere on the front that it was meant to be funny. Douglas's archive contains quite a few rejected draft ideas that didn't make the original book and its later update *The Deeper Meaning of Liff* (1990). A few of those rejected entries are arranged above and on the opposite page.

Zebrarianism, the mystic philosophy which teaches that this is the one true path. Unlike other religions it holds that the road is both long and winding and straight and narrow depending where you are, but in any case it should be contemplated. In this it differs from Moonieism, which teaches that where the road is narrowest it is easier to stop innocent passers by and bore them with your life story, or from the Hare Krishna Sect which believes that to pass down the road is hard, and should be made harder by hopping up and down it making a lot of noise in an orange bedspread in the company of other adepts.

RISBOROUGH noun.

A hateful look directed out of the back of your neck.

Risboroughs are often employed when you have just, only just, by pushing and shoving managed to be the last person to squeeze into a rush-hour compartment so closely that you have to bend your head when the doors start closing. You then feel part of the club, and when the train stops at the next station and there are more people waiting, you zap them with a powerful risborough and say between gritted teeth "If anyone else gets on this train....."

UTTOXETER noun.

A small but immensely complex mechanical device which is essentially the "brain" of a modern coffee machine.. The uttoxeter enables the machine to take its own decisions without the need for human intervention.

On receiving the coin, and the command "coffee", the uttoxter decides which of the following courses of action to take; It may (a) shoot the plastic beaker down upside down and pour coffee all over the bottom of it (b) shoot the plastic beaker straight out of the hatch and onto the floor and pour coffee down the grating (c) shoot the plastic beaker down the right way up and then fill it with cold oxtail soup (d) shoot the plastic beaker down and do nothing at all, with(optionally) (e) wait till you put your hand inside to investigate then pour coffee all over it (f) gurgle a bit and then take the rest of the afternoon off.

CLOPTON noun.

An insane housewife.

During any consumer shortage(bread, sugar etc) hundreds of cloptons can be seen queuing outside the shop which sells whatever it is there isn't any of. ~~in the hour before dawn.~~

The remarkable thing about cloptons is that they will readily starve their family of food, water and clothing in order to buy something which there is a shortage of even if it is a shortage of long-handled, quill-bristle Peruvian funt-brushes and they'v already got a wardrobe stuffed with them.

When in 1973 it was announced by the Kenyan Government that there were hardly any white rhinos left in Africa, a queue of more than two thousand cloptons beseiged the London offices of the World Wildlife Fund, who were only able to avert a riot by announcing that white rhinos were now completely extinct.

MIDWICH noun.

This is the moment of false recognition in a long corridor encounter. Though both protagonists are perfectly well aware that the other person is approaching, and they know that they know, they have to pretend the opposite. They now look up, smile glassily with mouths gaping, and as if having seen each other for the first time gasp out "HaaaalllooooB!" as if to say "Good GRIEF! YOU...HERE.!! Well I never! Coh! Stap me hearties etc"

LUBBOCK noun.

A large mouthful which makes it impossible to hear what the speaker is saying.

Lubbocks are in common use by British Rail, the major lubbock-importers in this country. Every station tannoy-announcer is supplied with a daily stock of lubbocks (usually made of surgical lint or wads of corrugated cardboard), enabling them to easily make such remarks as "Will ALL passengers harwarble burdle aqum amorditraber curgy afar: eeg in one minutes time please."

LIFF ON TV

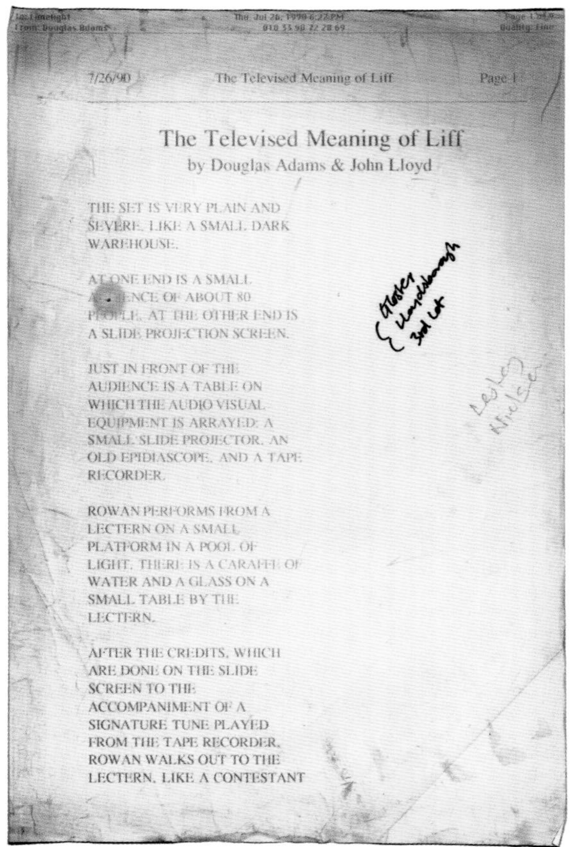

To: Limelight From: Douglas Adams — Thu, Jul 26, 1990 — 010 33 90 72 20 69 — Page 1 of 9 — Quality: Fine

7/26/90 The Televised Meaning of Liff Page 1

The Televised Meaning of Liff

by Douglas Adams & John Lloyd

THE SET IS VERY PLAIN AND SEVERE. LIKE A SMALL DARK WAREHOUSE.

AT ONE END IS A SMALL AUDIENCE OF ABOUT 80 PEOPLE. AT THE OTHER END IS A SLIDE PROJECTION SCREEN.

JUST IN FRONT OF THE AUDIENCE IS A TABLE ON WHICH THE AUDIO VISUAL EQUIPMENT IS ARRAYED: A SMALL SLIDE PROJECTOR, AN OLD EPIDIASCOPE, AND A TAPE RECORDER.

ROWAN PERFORMS FROM A LECTERN ON A SMALL PLATFORM IN A POOL OF LIGHT. THERE IS A CARAFE OF WATER AND A GLASS ON A SMALL TABLE BY THE LECTERN.

AFTER THE CREDITS, WHICH ARE DONE ON THE SLIDE SCREEN TO THE ACCOMPANIMENT OF A SIGNATURE TUNE PLAYED FROM THE TAPE RECORDER, ROWAN WALKS OUT TO THE LECTERN, LIKE A CONTESTANT

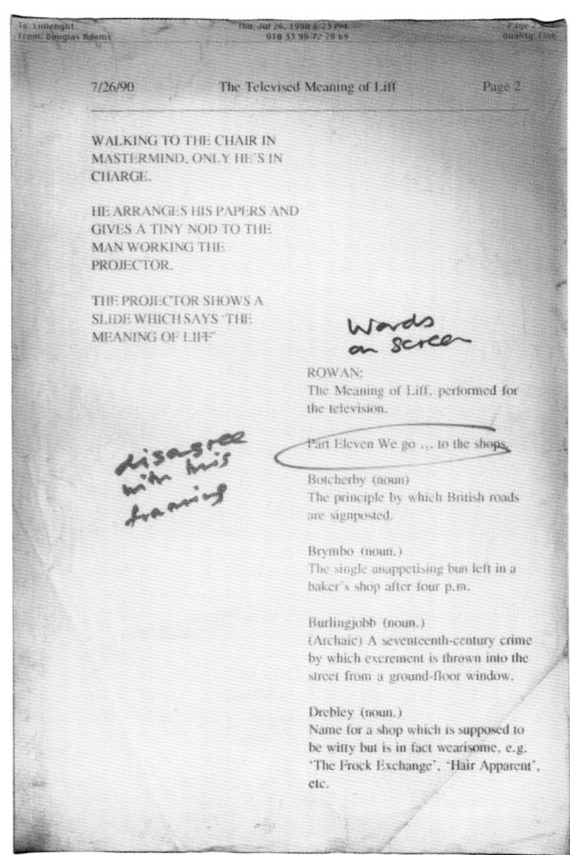

To: Limelight From: Douglas Adams — Thu, Jul 26, 1990 — 010 33 90 72 20 69 — Page 2 — Quality: Fine

7/26/90 The Televised Meaning of Liff Page 2

WALKING TO THE CHAIR IN MASTERMIND, ONLY HE'S IN CHARGE.

HE ARRANGES HIS PAPERS AND GIVES A TINY NOD TO THE MAN WORKING THE PROJECTOR.

THE PROJECTOR SHOWS A SLIDE WHICH SAYS 'THE MEANING OF LIFF'

ROWAN:
The Meaning of Liff, performed for the television.

Part Eleven We go ... to the shops.

Botcherby (noun)
The principle by which British roads are signposted.

Brymbo (noun.)
The single unappetising bun left in a baker's shop after four p.m.

Burlingjobb (noun.)
(Archaic) A seventeenth-century crime by which excrement is thrown into the street from a ground-floor window.

Drebley (noun.)
Name for a shop which is supposed to be witty but is in fact wearisome, e.g. 'The Frock Exchange', 'Hair Apparent', etc.

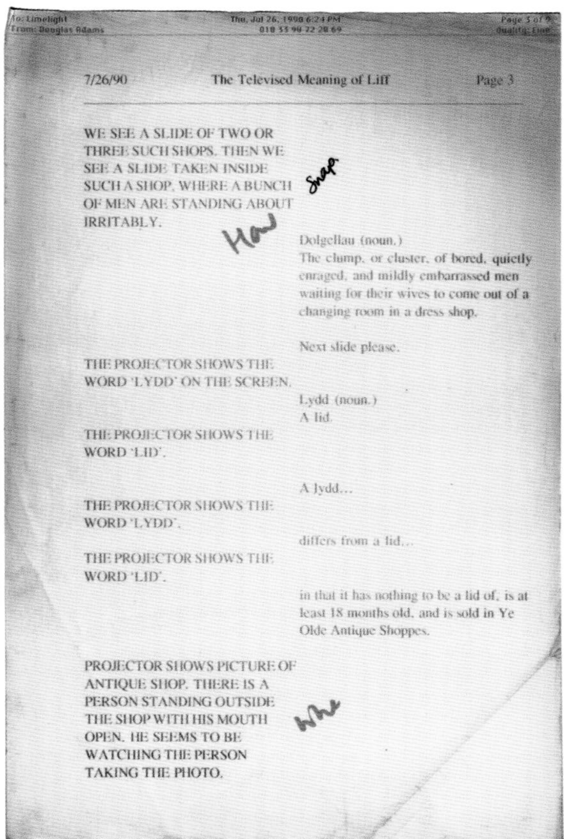

To: Limelight From: Douglas Adams — Thu, Jul 26, 1990 — 010 33 90 72 20 69 — Page 3 of 9 — Quality: Fine

7/26/90 The Televised Meaning of Liff Page 3

WE SEE A SLIDE OF TWO OR THREE SUCH SHOPS. THEN WE SEE A SLIDE TAKEN INSIDE SUCH A SHOP, WHERE A BUNCH OF MEN ARE STANDING ABOUT IRRITABLY.

Dolgellau (noun.)
The clump, or cluster, of bored, quietly enraged, and mildly embarrassed men waiting for their wives to come out of a changing room in a dress shop.

Next slide please.

THE PROJECTOR SHOWS THE WORD 'LYDD' ON THE SCREEN.

Lydd (noun.)
A lid.

THE PROJECTOR SHOWS THE WORD 'LID'.

A lydd...

THE PROJECTOR SHOWS THE WORD 'LYDD'.

differs from a lid...

THE PROJECTOR SHOWS THE WORD 'LID'.

in that it has nothing to be a lid of, is at least 18 months old, and is sold in Ye Olde Antique Shoppes.

PROJECTOR SHOWS PICTURE OF ANTIQUE SHOP. THERE IS A PERSON STANDING OUTSIDE THE SHOP WITH HIS MOUTH OPEN. HE SEEMS TO BE WATCHING THE PERSON TAKING THE PHOTO.

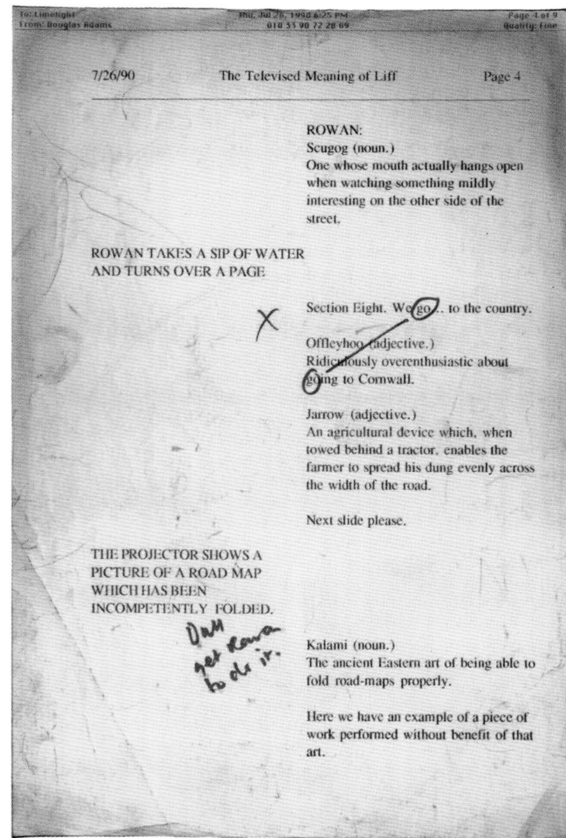

To: Limelight From: Douglas Adams — Thu, Jul 26, 1990 — 010 33 90 72 20 69 — Page 4 of 9 — Quality: Fine

7/26/90 The Televised Meaning of Liff Page 4

ROWAN:
Scugog (noun.)
One whose mouth actually hangs open when watching something mildly interesting on the other side of the street.

ROWAN TAKES A SIP OF WATER AND TURNS OVER A PAGE

Section Eight. We go... to the country.

Offleyhoo (adjective.)
Ridiculously overenthusiastic about going to Cornwall.

Jarrow (adjective.)
An agricultural device which, when towed behind a tractor, enables the farmer to spread his dung evenly across the width of the road.

Next slide please.

THE PROJECTOR SHOWS A PICTURE OF A ROAD MAP WHICH HAS BEEN INCOMPETENTLY FOLDED.

Kalami (noun.)
The ancient Eastern art of being able to fold road-maps properly.

Here we have an example of a piece of work performed without benefit of that art.

In 1990, Douglas and John Lloyd worked up a short sample script for a potential TV pilot based on *The Meaning of Liff* and its sequel *The Deeper Meaning of Liff*. Lloyd had been producing TV for over a decade with actor Rowan Atkinson, first with *Not the Nine O'Clock News* and then the historical sitcom *Blackadder*, so Atkinson was a natural choice as presenter.

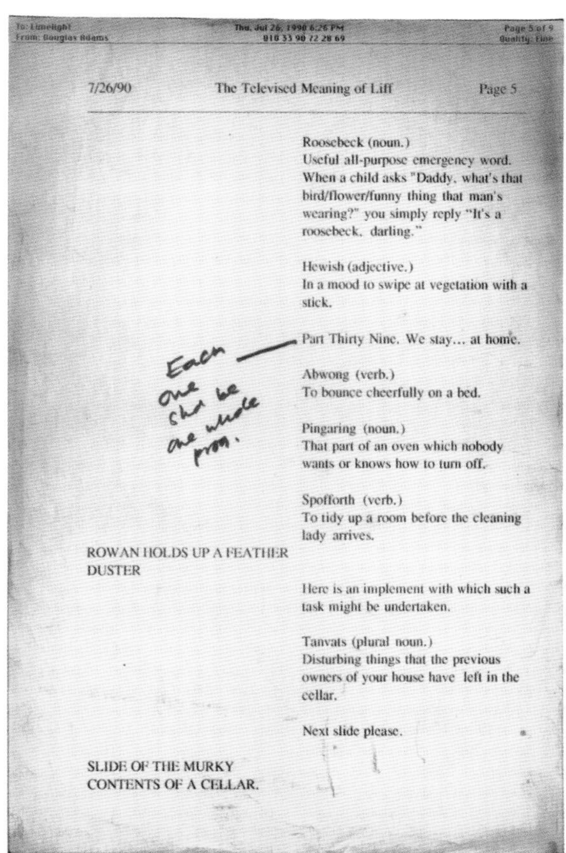

To: Limelight
From: Douglas Adams
Thu, Jul 26, 1990 6:26 PM
010 33 90 72 28 69
Page 5 of 9
Quality: Fine

7/26/90 The Televised Meaning of Liff Page 5

Roosebeck (noun.)
Useful all-purpose emergency word. When a child asks "Daddy, what's that bird/flower/funny thing that man's wearing?" you simply reply "It's a roosebeck, darling."

Hewish (adjective.)
In a mood to swipe at vegetation with a stick.

Part Thirty Nine. We stay... at home.

Each one shd be one whole prog.

Abwong (verb.)
To bounce cheerfully on a bed.

Pingaring (noun.)
That part of an oven which nobody wants or knows how to turn off.

Spofforth (verb.)
To tidy up a room before the cleaning lady arrives.

ROWAN HOLDS UP A FEATHER DUSTER

Here is an implement with which such a task might be undertaken.

Tanvats (plural noun.)
Disturbing things that the previous owners of your house have left in the cellar.

Next slide please.

SLIDE OF THE MURKY CONTENTS OF A CELLAR.

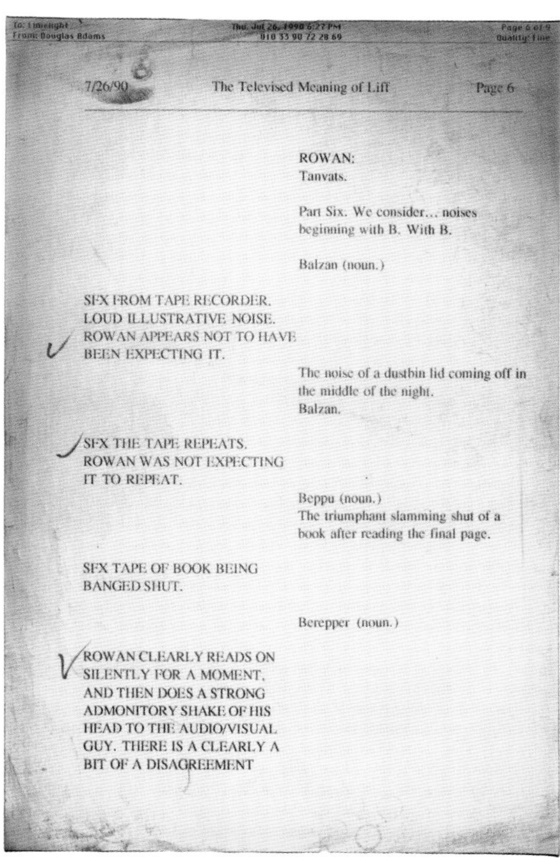

To: Limelight
From: Douglas Adams
Thu, Jul 26, 1990 6:27 PM
010 33 90 72 28 69
Page 6 of 9
Quality: Fine

7/26/90 The Televised Meaning of Liff Page 6

ROWAN:
Tanvats.

Part Six. We consider... noises beginning with B. With B.

Balzan (noun.)

SFX FROM TAPE RECORDER. LOUD ILLUSTRATIVE NOISE. ROWAN APPEARS NOT TO HAVE BEEN EXPECTING IT.

The noise of a dustbin lid coming off in the middle of the night.
Balzan.

SFX THE TAPE REPEATS. ROWAN WAS NOT EXPECTING IT TO REPEAT.

Beppu (noun.)
The triumphant slamming shut of a book after reading the final page.

SFX TAPE OF BOOK BEING BANGED SHUT.

Berepper (noun.)

ROWAN CLEARLY READS ON SILENTLY FOR A MOMENT, AND THEN DOES A STRONG ADMONITORY SHAKE OF HIS HEAD TO THE AUDIO/VISUAL GUY. THERE IS A CLEARLY A BIT OF A DISAGREEMENT

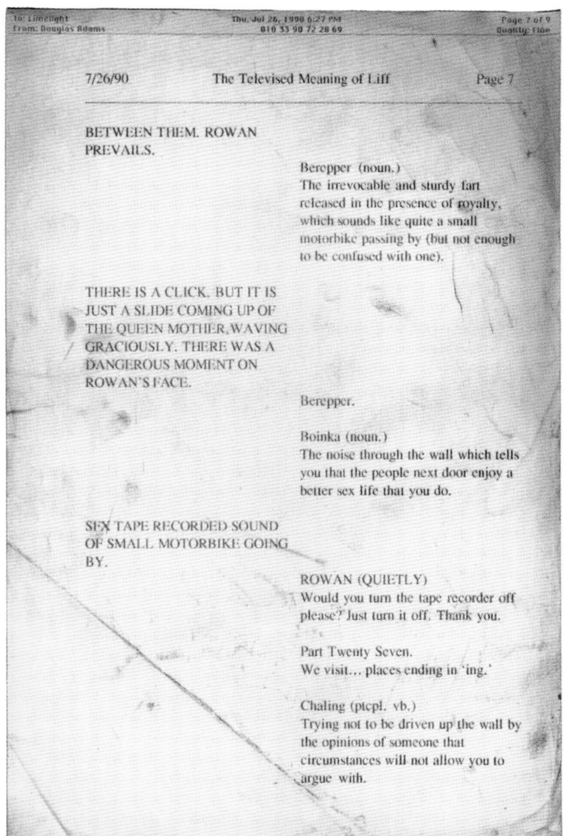

To: Limelight
From: Douglas Adams
Thu, Jul 26, 1990 6:27 PM
010 33 90 72 28 69
Page 7 of 9
Quality: Fine

7/26/90 The Televised Meaning of Liff Page 7

BETWEEN THEM. ROWAN PREVAILS.

Berepper (noun.)
The irrevocable and sturdy fart released in the presence of royalty, which sounds like quite a small motorbike passing by (but not enough to be confused with one).

THERE IS A CLICK, BUT IT IS JUST A SLIDE COMING UP OF THE QUEEN MOTHER, WAVING GRACIOUSLY. THERE WAS A DANGEROUS MOMENT ON ROWAN'S FACE.

Berepper.

Boinka (noun.)
The noise through the wall which tells you that the people next door enjoy a better sex life that you do.

SFX TAPE RECORDED SOUND OF SMALL MOTORBIKE GOING BY.

ROWAN (QUIETLY)
Would you turn the tape recorder off please? Just turn it off. Thank you.

Part Twenty Seven.
We visit... places ending in 'ing.'

Chaling (ptcpl. vb.)
Trying not to be driven up the wall by the opinions of someone that circumstances will not allow you to argue with.

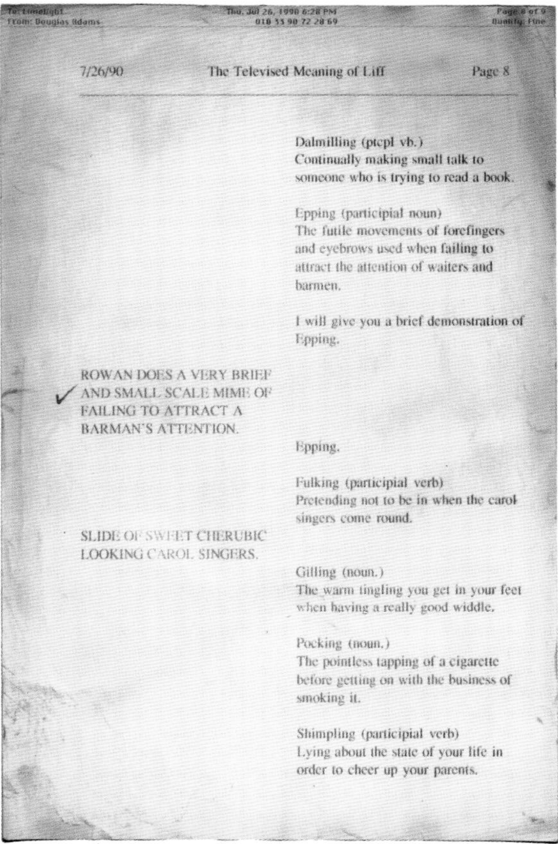

To: Limelight
From: Douglas Adams
Thu, Jul 26, 1990 6:28 PM
010 33 90 72 28 69
Page 8 of 9
Quality: Fine

7/26/90 The Televised Meaning of Liff Page 8

Dalmilling (ptcpl vb.)
Continually making small talk to someone who is trying to read a book.

Epping (participial noun)
The futile movements of forefingers and eyebrows used when failing to attract the attention of waiters and barmen.

I will give you a brief demonstration of Epping.

ROWAN DOES A VERY BRIEF AND SMALL SCALE MIME OF FAILING TO ATTRACT A BARMAN'S ATTENTION.

Epping.

Fulking (participial verb)
Pretending not to be in when the carol singers come round.

SLIDE OF SWEET CHERUBIC LOOKING CAROL SINGERS.

Gilling (noun.)
The warm tingling you get in your feet when having a really good widdle.

Pocking (noun.)
The pointless tapping of a cigarette before getting on with the business of smoking it.

Shimpling (participial verb)
Lying about the state of your life in order to cheer up your parents.

This fax to Limelight Productions (rather faded in real life, but brought back to readability here) sets out the intention. Sadly, the programme was never made, but for anyone who knows Rowan Atkinson's work, it's easy to imagine the actor rolling the vowels. John Lloyd has himself more recently performed extracts to great audience acclaim at various Douglas-related events.

UNUSUAL OFFERS

DOUGLAS

(P I L O T)

"THEY'LL NEVER PLAY THAT ON THE RADIO"

Presenter
DOUGLAS ADAMS

Written by
JON CANTER

Produced by
PETE ATKIN

Interviews:
GRAHAM FELLOWS
ERIC STEWART

REH/REC: SUNDAY 22nd AUGUST, 1982: 1000-1400: B11
PROG.NO: FLG289Y768
TAPE NO: SLN34/289Y768

- 7 -

1. DOUGLAS: CONT: And Phillips Records heard the songs and saw that they were good and said:
"Fab, wow, terrific, wouldn't it be great if we released your songs as an album, large brandy please waiter and some water for the Sister."
Verily, they released an album, changing her name to Soeur Sourire - Sister Smile - because that's very much the kind of thing record companies do.
They also released a single. "Dominique", dedicated to the founder of the Dominican order,
And, lo, at a time when Cliff Richard was pagan and Born Again was a Swedish tennis player, it sold a million.
Dominique by Soeur Sourire, better known as The Singing Nun....

2. TAPE: SINGING NUN: "DOMINIQUE"

3. DOUGLAS: "On the highways and in the towns, he spoke only of the good Lord, he spoke only of the good Lord".
There she was, up in the Top Ten, cheek by wimple with The Beatles and "I Want To Hold Your Hand".
"Dominique", like The Singing Dogs, They're Coming To Take Me Away, Jilted John and Neanderthal Man, was a one-off.
But if there's one thing better than a one-off, it's a two-off, so Phillips released "Tous Les Chemins" as the next single.
Did that dent the charts?
No, it didn't.
Did that ever-so-slightly-so-you-can-barely-see-it-scratch the charts?
No it didn't. DOUGLAS CONTINUED OVER....

- 1 -

1. ANNOUNCEMENT FROM CONTINUITY

2. DOUGLAS: (WINNINGLY)
Shakin' Stevens, Barry Manilow, Sheena Easton, and The Nolans. Just some of the exciting chart acts you won't be hearing in this programme - which is about bizarre and unexpected hits that spring out of nowhere and make you go "What?".

3. TAPE: PAT A CAKE/THREE BLIND MICE FROM "SINGING DOGS"

4. DOUGLAS: That was 'Pat A Cake' and 'Three Blind Mice' from 'The Singing Dogs Medley', which got to number 13 in 1955.
According to the sleeve, the band consisted of "King, Caesar, Dolly, Pearl and Pussy", which is a little suspect, but I assure you they were 100% canine.
Not a lot has been heard of them since, but you know what it's like when you become a rock star...the kennel in Weybridge...the spaniel-eyed spaniels who'll do anything for you...snorting marrowbone jelly by your lamp-post shaped swimming pool... you get heavily into non-productivity.
Our next artist, and I use the word wrongly, was last heard of running a smoking accessories company in Philadelphia. Yellow fingers, yukky lungs, that kind of thing.

/CONTINUED OVER......

- 8 -

1. DOUGLAS: And I'm sorry, but this is beginning to get me down, because, actually, personally, I think The Singing Nun is at least as good as Toyah Willcox.
All right, she doesn't have an interesting haircut. She plays accustic guitar, manually, which doesn't compare with playing synthesizer by computerised laser. But she does have the kind of gentle charm you don't often find on Top Of The Pops. So, write to Phillips Records of Brussels - you'll find them in The Belgian Yellow Pages under "restaurants" - and ask them to re-release "Tous Les Chemins" by The Singing Nun.
Maybe it'll be a hit this time round. Apart from anything else, I'd love to see the video.

2. TAPE: SINGING NUN: "TOUS LES CHEMINS"

3. CLOSING: ANNOUNCEMENT FROM CONTINUITY

You know what this needs to make it a hit don't you?

Douglas was asked to present a radio pilot programme of novelty records and one-hit wonders with a script by his former flatmate, comedy writer Jon Canter. This short draft of *They'll Never Play that on the Radio*, with Douglas's own annotations, is in his archive. Pete Atkin, director at BBC Light Entertainment, made the recording and was pleased with it. He then submitted it to the department's Direction Group, who, somewhat to Atkins' bafflement, decided it was too unusual for Radio 4 – it never aired.

I think that ~~I~~ Jon has done a very good job on this script

The only reason I'm writing ~~this, though~~, is just to try out the nib on this pen and see what it feels like. I'm becoming increasingly dyslexic I think. Every word I write involves going back and filling in the missing letters

This note is among the archive material for *They'll Never Play that on the Radio* (opposite) – Douglas trying out a new nib and musing on his need to go back and fill in missing letters!

Dark Ride Notes

1 **EMBARKATION AREA.**

As passengers are waiting a recorded voice assures them that there is nothing to be worried about...

..."Absolutely nothing at all. Rumours that may have leaked out to the effect that there is a terrifying alien monster called Xarstradon from the planet Glartalfury hiding out in the complex, to which our passengers are being sacrificed, are completely fanciful, highly exaggerated and probably not even true.
No spaceships have crashed in the area at all, and nothing nasty whatsoever has crawled out of it. And it certainly isn't demanding human sacrifices. Absolutely not.
I can state quite categorically that under ***no*** circumstances would the management of Chessington Zoo be prepared to allow its paying customers to be eaten by any giant green slavering alien life form, with laser beam eyes and razor teeth, even if we were all scared witless by it, which we aren't because it doesn't exist.
So - no need to worry on that score.

Other things you don't need to worry about are **this** noise...

(SFX TERRIBLE ROAR)

... which has been dealt with, and won't be troubling anybody any more.

(SFX EVEN WORSE AND LONGER TERRIBLE ROAR)

Just ignore it. Now I want you all look to your left please. Your left! I insist that you look to your left. There is nothing to see to your right whatsoever!

As the train pulls in to the embarkation point (from the right) it is full of steaming skeletons with a few scraps of clothing clinging to them. A large arm comes down and quickly clears them out of the way.

In one of Douglas's more unusual collaborations, he met with Ian Hanson, former sculptor, then Head of Studios at the Tussaud's Group. Famous primarily for its waxworks, Madame Tussaud's was developing a new space-themed Dark Ride at their Chessington World of Adventures theme park in Surrey, UK. However, the offer of a huge advance for his Dirk Gently novels meant that after devising the first notes (above and opposite), Douglas pulled out. Nonetheless, he gave the company permission to use anything he'd already talked about. Apparently, Douglas had suggested getting the cast of hit comedy *The Young Ones* involved, but nothing came of this.

You sit in the seats. The train moves off. It looks as if it is going in one direction - you see the start of the advertised dark ride - and the rails appear to lead in that direction, but as you approach them the train is (or appears to be) diverted and starts to climb the ramp, surrounded by a revolving tube of laser light.

You hear voices and alarms indicating an emergency. The voices are shouting urgently that another train (i.e. yours) has been diverted! What are they going to do? They must shut the ride!"

"No!" insists another, "we can't afford to close it down!"

"Stop the train!"

Terrible throbbing grinding noises and lights indicate suggest that one force is trying to pull the train back down while another is inexorably pulling it up.

The voices in panic say they'll have to let this train go, but they must now close the ride and stop anyone else coming in. Send them all off to (*some other attraction in the Park)*.

As you approach the top of the ramp you see that you are entering the broken side of a terrifying spaceship. There is a huge gash in it, broken pipes and wires and lots of smoke, with electrical sparks playing through it. The train goes through this.

2 **FIRST AREA**

The end of a pitched battle. You are just in time to see some shapes retreating into the smoke.

A very ancient hobbled space pirate with a robot vulture on its shoulder hobbles into sight with a smoking Stunderbuss. He is appalled to see you.

Whereas a traditional pirate has a false arm and a false leg, Cap'n Long John Silicon is now nearly all mechanical, the only thing he has left is his own original arm and leg.

"You fools!" He berates you "I've only just managed to escape! What in the name of the spacedevil's knees do you think you're doing here! You haven't a quark's chance in a particle accelerator of getting out of here alive!"

The train moves forward a little anyway.

"If you won't stop you're going to need a friend" he mutters. He muses. "Well I some news for you. Some good news for you, and also some bad news. Would you like to hear the good news?"

You have to get him to give you the news.

"The good news is, that you have a friend. The bad news is - it's me."

He introduces himself, and also his pet robot vulture that sits on his shoulder. He used to have a parrot, "but what with one thing and another decided that a vulture would probably get more out of my particular lifestyle. Waste not want is what my mother used to say to me. Bet you're surprised to think I had a mother aren't you? Not half as surprised as my mother was, God rest her soul!"

The vulture peers at the passengers and remarks that perhaps he will have to start his diet tomorrow instead.

Meanwhile, one of the shapes that fell to the ground in the smoke starts to revive behind the pirate. It is a horrible looking alien soldier. It begins to rise to its feet, with a fearsome weapon in his hand.

The passengers will be bound to make some kind of noise at this point.

The pirate leans forward to the passengers and says "What? You'll have to speak up? What? I can't hear you."

This will encourage the passengers to shout out more.

Pirate: "All you seem to be saying is... " [tape loop plays back a snatch of the noise the passengers have been making]. "...Doesn't make much sense to me."

At the last moment the pirate reacts by spinning round and firing at the alien soldier, who dies spectacularly.

The vulture flies down to the body of the soldier and starts to peck at it. Horrible stuff begins to ooze out of the body.

The vulture goes "Yeeuuuurch!" in disgust and flies back to the pirate's shoulder where it gazes longingly at the passengers once more.

The pirate explains that the monster Xarstradon is the single most violent and hungry creature this side of the Horsehead nebula, and the only chance they have is that there is one thing it likes as well as eating people, which is a nice tune.

He suggests that they break into the ship's computer music room.

The train moves on.

3. **Area Two**

The Computer Music Room.
You pass through a short tunnel into this area in which lights and noises suggest that you are being analysed and reduced to a computer program yourself.

You then emerge into an unreal looking computer interior.
In here, all the noises that you make are fed into a synthesiser, looped, distorted, manipulated by computer and fed back to you.

All around you as well will be strange looking electronic instruments. When the train stops, light beams spring up in front of the carriages (NB they don't need to be lasers of course, they can work like burglar alarms). Passengers can reach out and break any of the beams. Each one causes one of the instruments to make a noise, or alter a noise, so that the train as a whole can make, well, music - of a kind.

The music is continually sampled and looped by the synthesiser computer, and at the end the pirate records a part of it onto his hand accordian. The accordian produces the brief snatch of sound whenever he plays it.

The plan has gone terribly wrong, he says. The monster likes a *nice* tune. The Pirate gives it as his opinion that this is an exceedingly horrible one. Still it will have to do.

General scheme of remainder and problems.

We want to end with something that explains why the skeletons are put on the train.

Ghosts, robots.

4. **Area 3**

Armaments area. General idea is that this is where your train acquires its armaments for fighting the monster. As much as possible should be interactive. The various things you see demonstrated might be a little like the traditional "Q" scenes from James Bond movies.

A recent discovery of original soundtracks by The British Theme Park Archive revealed that some of Douglas's ideas on these few pages of script made it to fruition in the ride known as 'The Fifth Dimension'. Not only that, but *Hitchhiker's Guide* veteran voice artist David Tate ('Hi there, this is Eddie, your shipboard computer') played the newsreader-style announcer on video as you entered the ride. Sadly, the ride was grossly simplified and re-vamped after just six months, and Douglas's witty script was given the chop.

PETE TOWNSHEND

FIRST SEGMENT

BLACK AND WHITE WHITE "DISTRESSED" FILM, TO GIVE THE LOOK OF A TWENTY YEAR OLD DOCUMENTARY.

AN INTERVIEWER SPEAKS TO CAMERA. THE INTERVIEWER IS OF THE CLIPPED, PATRONISING TYPE FAVOURED BY THE BBC.

INTERVIEWER Good evening. Tonight on Face The Face, my first guest is Mr Peter Towhsnend. Not as you may think Group Captain Peter Townshend the former consort of Princess Margaret, but someohe whom younger viewrs might recognise as the leader of a popular new beat combo, called, rather enigmatically, the Who.

CAMERA REVEALS PETE 1. HE IS 20 YEARS OLD, WEARING A UNION JACK JACKET.

INTERVIEWER: Peter, welcome.

PETE 1 NODS CURTLY.

INTERVIWER: Good. Well, your latest platter, currently soaring up the national hit parade is called "My Gee Gee Eneration. Tell me, have you always been interested in horses?

PETE 1: No, you got it wrong. It's G..G.. generation. It's a stutter.

INT: I see. So your lead singer suffers from a speech impediment, is this it?

PETE 1: No, he just couldn't read the words properly.

INT: (GIVES LITTLE LAUGH, THINKING THIS IS A JOKE. CUT TO PETE NOT LAUGHING. IT'S NOT A JOKE.) Nevertheless, the words are very interesting. Do you think

In the summer of 1985, Douglas was asked to contribute to a charity event, The Snow Ball Revue, for that Christmas (this was also the year of Live Aid). He drafted a linked series of sketches for Pete Townshend (of rock band The Who) that would be filmed and screened between live performances. Pete's wife, Karen Townshend, chaired the organizing committee, and Lynne Franks (the inspiration for Edina 'Eddie' Monsoon in *Absolutely Fabulous*) handled the PR. The impressive cast list included David Frost, Joanna Lumley, Midge Ure, Bill Wyman, Gary Kemp, Mike Batt, Rik Mayall, Ian Dury, Rowan Atkinson, Terry Jones, Michael Palin and Steven Berkoff. Townshend played as part of his Deep End Band, with Pink Floyd's Dave Gilmour and others.

4th SEGMENT FACE TO FACE

P2	Look, one thing I'd like to bring up.
P1	Yeah?
P2	Just a piece of advice. Friendly advice.
P1	I'm not interested in advice from anybody. Particularly not anyone your age.
P2	Well, it's fanny you should say that. It's just this line you P1 – LA wrote wrote, you know the one, about 'Hope I die before I get old'. Just an artistic point, really, I'm not sure how well it scans.
p1	(VERY SUSPICIOUS) What do yo mean, scans?
P2	Doesn't sort of flow right, in the song. How about, let's think, supposing we modified it slightly, so it wemt 'Hope I get old beofre I die.' Just goes better I think.
P1	Modify it?! That's the complete opposite!
P2	Just a shift of emphasis. The rhythm's better.
P1	That's camp. It doesn't even rhyme. 'Things they do seem awful cold, hope I get old before I die..."
P2	Well, we can look at that other line. It could go 'Things they do seem... er... like apple pie.' That could work.
P1	What!
P2	Trust me on this one. I speak with the expeience of twenty years.
P1	That's exacly why I never take advice from anyone your age.

CUT TO MUSIC

INT:	Well, someone who does know for sure is my last guest tonight on Face the Face, brought here tonight at vast expesne to the laws of physics, succesful publisher, film producer, novelist and farmer, may I introduce Lord Townshend of Twickenham.
PETE 3	ENTERS. HE IS NOW A OLD MAN IN A WHEELCHAIR WITH WHITE HAIR AND GLASSES AND A WALKING STICK AND A BATTERED OLD TWEED SUIT. HE IS VERY GENIAL AND PLEASANT AND BEAMS A LOT. HE IS OBVIOUSLY VERY CONTENT AND OLD AGE SUITS HIM WELL.
INT:	Welcome, your Lordship.
PETE 3	Thank you. Thank you very much. (HE PATS PETE 2 ON THE BACK) Not sure about the line either you know. I think it should go "Hope I get really old and then die peacefully in bed with all my gr[illegible]en gathered arouhd me." It'll slow the song up a bit, but that's no bad thing is it?
INT:	Sir, looking back on a long and illustrious career as both a musician and man of letters, you've done so much, accomplished so much, tell me, is there anything you still have left to do, any ambition unfulfilled?
PETE 3	Well, not really. I have had a pretty full life. Not everything has gone exactly the way I would have liked, but it's been very interesting, full of rewards and... (HE LOOKS AROUND) well, in fact, I suppose there is one thing that, now I've reached this age, I still hanker after.

INTERVIEWER:	And what is that?
PETE 3:	(REACHING FOR HIS STICK) May I?
INTERVIEWER:	(PUZZLED) By all means...
	PETE 3 GETS UP, AND STARTS TO SMASH UP THE SET WITH HIS STICK. HE CREATES TERRIBLE DEVASTATION + SMOKE, FIRE ETC. THIS IS FILMED IN OVERCRANK, SO THAT THE VIOLENCE BECOMES BALLETICALLY SLOW. PLAY OVER IT A GENTLE SONG. SUGGEST 'BLUE, RED AND GREY' WITH ALL THE BITS ABOUT 'I LOVE EVERY MINUTE OF THE DAY'.

IN AID OF
THE CHISWICK FAMILY RESCUE
AT
THE DOMINION THEATRE
TOTTENHAM COURT ROAD, LONDON W1.
ON SUNDAY 22ND DECEMBER 1985
AT 7.30 PM

SCRIPTED BY IAN LA FRENAIS AND FRIENDS AND STARRING
JOANNA LUMLEY, DAVID FROST, PETE TOWNSHEND, MIDGE URE, BILL WYMAN,
ANDY SUMMERS, STEPHANIE LAWRENCE AND FRIENDS.

Douglas's film scripts demanded Townshend play himself aged 20, in his mid-40s and in old age, riffing on his infamous 'Hope I die before I get old' lyric. The middle-aged Pete (page 2 in the script) tries to give advice to the brash young Pete (page 1), who famously smashed up his guitar and amps on stage. The future elder statesman Townshend, though genial, still harbours fantasies of trashing the place. There's no known existing filmed record of these interludes, but luckily some drafts (reproduced opposite and above) survive.

On the Desktop

As a fan and fore-thinker of technology, it's not surprising that Douglas was keen to experiment with word processing in the early days of home computing. His forays are documented in his notebook from early 1984, when he was still working on the first (ultimately abortive) *Hitchhiker's Guide* movie script for Columbia. The phrase 'KW-ing' appears, which probably hints at use of word-processing software WordStar on an IBM machine. Douglas clearly wasn't confident in the technology yet, jotting down handwritten notes as to where in the machine's memory he's storing certain blocks of his precious text. ('Joe' in the notes is most likely Joe Medjuck, who was working for producer Ivan Reitman.)

Reconstruction of plot as explained to Joe.

They arrive on Magrathea to discover that the Answer is due.

---

16 Jan 84

Finished the scene on Damogran

used the Heart of Gold Imp Drive speech.

KW-ing the wake up scene onto the end of Damogran, which means that Damogran will be more up to date than MV1-UNF.

17 Jan 84

Getting rid of the Vogon bit for the while, dumping it into BIN.

Description of Vogon cabin in BIN2

Ford's travel plans can be peppered throughout the script.

Planetarium section in BIN 3.

It's going to be hard to learn to love that robot, Zaphod.

Where does the Babel Fish go, then?

Babel Fish section KW in Babel.

I'm KW-ing all of MV1-UNF from the original first sight of HOG bridge ("Who are they Trillian?") to the end of the Deep Thought section into a new file which will continue directly from the end of Damogran.

This is DAM 2

MV1-UNF up to the point where DAMOGRAM would take over (xxx) is 34 pages long.

Feb 22nd

Have been fiddling with comms between TRS-80 100 and Rainbow.

The TRM file on K user 3 and K user 12 (identical) works with the pair, though it maybe that there is problem with line feeds coming into the Rainbow.

It works perfectly well transferring stuff To the TANDY.

For some mysterious reason, when transferring stuff to the TANDY with MITE it sends about 5 x-offs and then gives up.

No idea why.

In an article for *MacUser* magazine in December 1987, Douglas recalled his first meeting with a Macintosh computer, beginning a continuing fascination with all things Apple. He wrote that what he 'fell in love with was not the machine itself, which was ridiculously slow and underpowered, but a romantic idea of the machine. And that romantic idea had to sustain me through the realities of actually working on the 128K Mac, then the 512K Mac and even (let's be honest, now that the MacII is here) on the MacPlus'. He persevered through all those iterations, though, and ultimately became an advocate for the brand, invited to speak at conferences about Apple itself. It's now a matter of legend that Douglas was the first to buy a Mac in the UK (and his friend, the actor, comedian, writer and director Stephen Fry, the second). This is an image of one of Douglas's AppleMacs, now housed in the Cambridge Computer Museum, UK.

TEN
Holistic Detective

In November 1985, Douglas's agent, Ed Victor, landed Douglas a huge advance and a two-book deal that would become Dirk Gently and his holistic detective agency. It took Douglas a while to identify how best to describe his new books, but his papers give insight into the evolution of the character and stories.

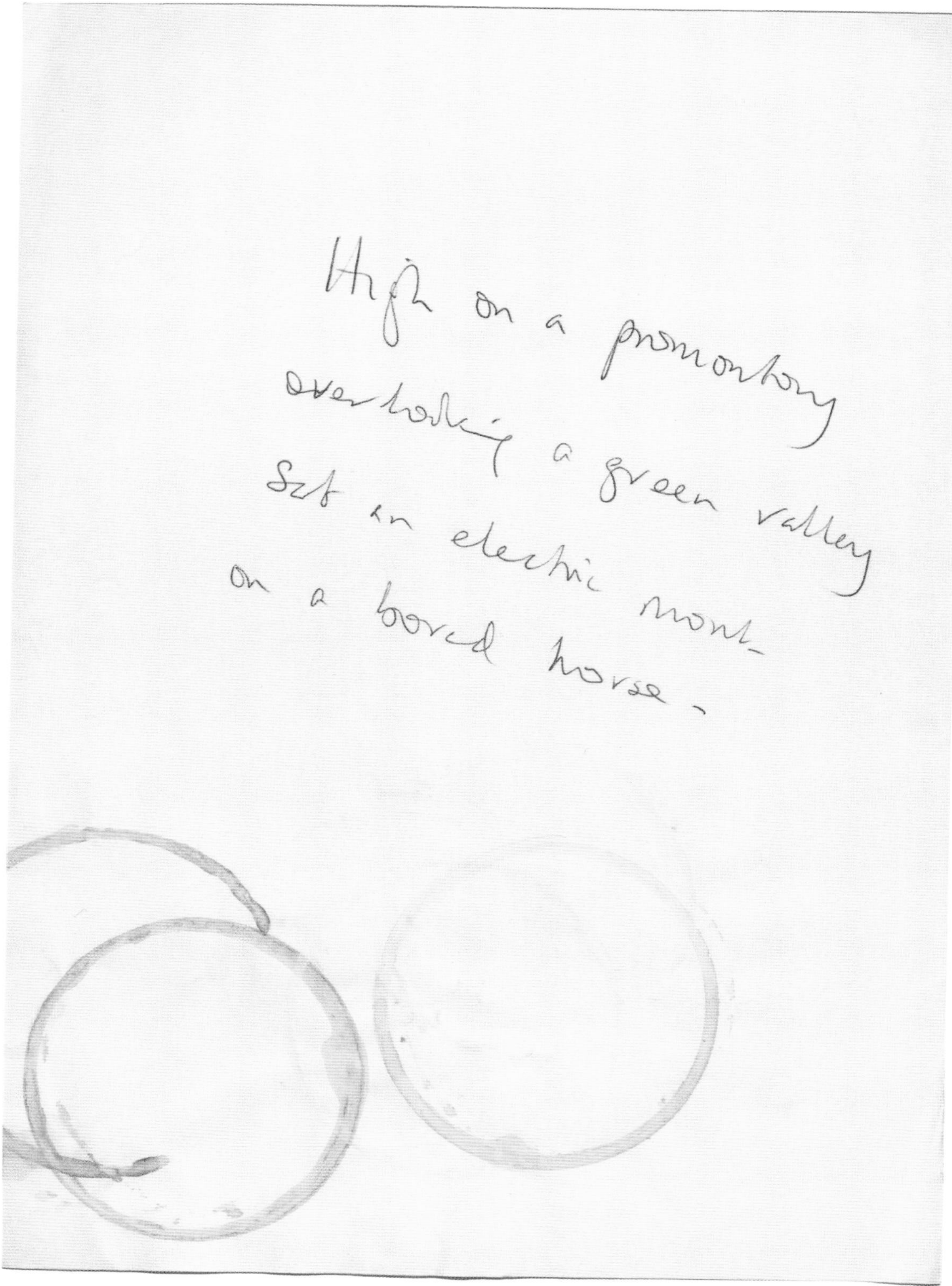

High on a promontory
overlooking a green valley
Sat an electric monk
on a bored horse.

The mug-stained note above is where *Dirk Gently* began – a random, intriguing line jotted down on a piece of paper that Douglas would rediscover and further ponder. The line was originally intended for a continuation of the *Hitchhiker's Guide* storyline (opposite, top).

The second *Dirk Gently* book was *The Long Dark Tea-Time of the Soul* (1988), which concerned itself with the fate of the Norse gods. Douglas had played with this notion in the early 1970s, in a 'mockumentary' script about Zeus (opposite, bottom).

THE HITCH HIKER'S GUIDE TO THE GALAXY SHORT STORY.

High on a rocky promontory sat an electric monk on a bored house. The monk was an electric one because beleiving anything at allthese days is so difficult that it's easier to get a machine to do it for you, and the horse was bored becasue ~~it had had nothing to do all day other than sit there overlooking a valley while this cowled machine sat him motionlessly believing things that were palpably untrue.~~
nothing was happening. ~~He, the horse,~~ [It] had been standing there all day while this cowled machine had sat on top of ~~him~~ [it] motionlessly beleiving things that were palpably untrue, even to a horse.

C.U. Zeus.

Of course, one can't help feeling bitter at times, just at times though, I mean life still has its pleasures – a few perks, I did a commercial for a brand of cooking oil last month – it's easy to scoff and say I'm just a has been, and the thing is, I have moved over, I've let others move up ~~into~~ my place but it still creates problems when you're immortal

[CAPTION ZEUS, KING OF THE OLYMPIAN GODS]

VO – Tonight on Mocumentary – we look at the Immortals, and we ask, Where are they and what are they doing now?

Cut to WAS hilly countryside – blustery day. Small tent in the distance.

Tent – drink.

Archaeologist has run off with my money.
Inflation.
Equity

This time there would be no witnesses.

There was instead just a rumble of thunder, a buffet of wind, and the onset of that interminable light drizzle from the north east by which so many of the world's most momentous events seem to be accompanied.

This time there would be no witnesses.

This time there was just the dead earth, a rumble of thunder, and the onset of that interminable light drizzle from the north east by which so many of the world's most momentous events seem to be accompanied.

This time there would be no witnesses.

This time there was just the stormy darkness of the night, and away in the distance the looming blackness of the tower.

This time there would be no witnesses.

This time there was just the darkness of the night, and the tower. The night was hot and full of rain, the tower a short and blackened stump supported by squat ungainly butresses. Each slash of rain was made momentarily particular by the dim light that flickered redly from deep in the structure's interior. The shadows of its heavy butresses veered wildly in the dying light.

This time there would be no witnesses.
The evening sky settled like lead on the land. The grey light of the moon was blotchy with storm clouds, hot and heavy with rain.
There is a structure standing here, a sort of tower. It stands there no longer, of course, but its shadow remains, immensely long and immensely dark. At first the tower seemed more insubstantial in the fading gloom, but soon the only light that still played on it was the dim red flicker from within it, and its own shadows came out to play. the shadows of its great buttresses veered wildly and the structure assumed monstrous proportions that danced, loomed and fled, loomed and fled again, leaping into the night.
No witnesses.

This time there would be no witnesses.
This time there was just the darkness of the night, and the tower.
The night was hot and full of rain. It beat about the tower's blackened stump, and each slash was made momentarily particular by the dim red light that flickered from deep in its interior. The shadows of its heavy butresses veered wildly in the dying light.
No witnesses.
No figures floundering desperately through the stinking mud.
Silence, and the thunder of the rain.

Tue, Nov 4, 1986 *The Big Resource* *Page 21*

Perhaps there is also the sound of voices, it is hard to tell above the raging of the wind as it screams through the huge buttresses.

Primeval earth.

A spaceship - a sort of tower, explodes, after which a lot of time passes.

TIME MACHINE NOTES

Time Machine - Interior.

This is the Professor's room in Cambridge, full of decrepit sofas and so on.

All the various pictures in it all over the walls, pictures of boat teams, prints of King's college chapel and Sidney St Bridge transform themselves into VDUs monitoring the progress of the ship.

The controls, such as they are are all located within the top of his dining table/desk which is always covered with huge piles of books and papers which have to be moved off in order to use it.

It's a quantum wave function. The desk is either a desk, or it is a control suite for manipulating the temporal spatial vectors and quantum wavefunctions of its flight. Either way it has a pile of books on it which have to be cleared off.

A nice scene might be an emergency get away during which

At some point it would be nice if we discovered that it could respond to a MIDI interface, so that time travel could be controlled by a MIDI sequencer in an emergency.

Dirk- Messy divorces a speciality.

Yes, thank you Mrs Sunderland, not that messy.

The time machine runs on extremely low power.

Advertisements.

The research and development on the machine was in large part sponsored by companies in return for advertising.

The effect of this is whenever the machine arrives somewhere it generates adverts for the sponsoring company in its immediate vicinity. These will be generated in such a way as to blend in carefully with the surroundings. In a

Getting under way was a problem for Douglas. In the past he'd had a habit of writing or typing the same bit over and over again, honing and shaping the flow of the words, without advancing very much further. Once he began working on a computer, the same habit persisted, even though word processing meant that it was no longer necessary. In his archives are over a dozen hard copies of these variants of the first page for *Dirk Gently*. Maybe he just liked to print out each version, just because he could. Or, perhaps he was trying to solve the conundrum of his complex plot by reinventing it over and over again.

Dirk Gently's Holistic Detective Agency /Douglas Adams

WHAT IT IS:
A ghost/horror/detective/time travel/romantic comedy epic.

VITALLY IMPORTANT BACKGROUND STUFF:
The story begins many many millions of years ago, before the first spark of life ever appeared on this planet. Ten minutes before, to be precise.

The last remnants of an embattled and evil race, the Straglaxans, have landed on a barren young planet, to build a vast refuge for themselves. Their ship is crippled. They take a finely calculated risk in trying to restart the ship's engines.

Against huge probability the risk fails.

The engines explode.

The ship and its crew are blown into gamma rays, and send a pulse of energy into the rich primeval slime, triggering the beginning of Life on Earth.

MEANWHILE...
A large number of millions of years go by.

The world we know and recognise emerges.

An odd world, some would say, a world that we, its inhabitants, have continually peopled with imaginary Gods and Devils, to explain the inexplicable.

These annotated notes (above, opposite and overleaf) are drafts for the book's press release, attempting to explain the genre, plot and characters.

And there seems to be an awful lot that is inexplicable.

Amongst the things that we most constantly try to explain to ourselves are death, guilt, evil, a persistent sense of loss and headaches.

NOW:

Dirk Gently is, as he is fond of telling his friends, (of whom he has many, some of which he has kept for as long as a week), a Professional Charlatan. He makes a living by having silly ideas and then finding people stupid enough to believe them.

His current one is Dirk Gently's Holistic Detective Agency.

As a result of a popular science book he read recently he has decided to try and apply the principles of Quantum Mechanics to the finding of lost pussy cats.

His theory is that they are not lost, but that their wave form has temporarily collapsed and must be restored.

This is, of course, complete tosh.

At least, it might as well be for all the cats he finds.

Probability

Instead, in the course of the story he stumbles unwittingly on a force that has powerfully interfered with and haunted life throughout human history, which is the collapsed quantum wave form of the very strong probability that in primeval times the Straglaxan ship's engines did not explode.

Like all waves interfering with other waves, it has peaks and troughs, times when it is very powerful, times when it is very weak.

When it is powerful it causes a huge increase in violence, irrationality, and paranormal activity as our world passes into the grip of the Straglaxan ghosts. – are the ghosts in some way generating the probability wave as a way of retrieving the situation?

At its most dangerous, it takes possession of people, makes them the puppets of an evil race, lost in time.

Richard Macduff?

Matthew Winkworth is a man with a problem, which he makes the great mistake of confiding to Dirk Gently.

His problem is that he has left a message on somebody's telephone answering machine about which he is now extremely embarrassed. It was just asking Eve Bairstow out for dinner, but he made a complete mess of talking to her machine and doesn't want to appear a complete fool at this early stage of what he hopes will be their relationship.

with the prop

What to do?

Gently proposes a very simple answer - break into the house, wipe the tape.

It's worth noting here the many wonderful actors who have played Dirk in various adaptations over the years. Douglas's friend and occasional collaborator Michael Bywater appeared in scenes for a *South Bank Show* documentary in 1992; comedian Harry Enfield was a lugubrious Dirk Gently on BBC Radio in 2007 and actor Stephen Mangan played a more sparky Dirk on BBC TV in four episodes, beginning in 2010. The longest-running version to date starred Samuel Barnett as Dirk (with Elijah Wood as his sidekick 'Todd') for two series on BBC America, in 2016/17.

SOME CHARACTERS:

Dirk Gently:

There is a long tradition of great detectives, and Dirk Gently does not belong to it.

There are those who say that he hardly belongs to the most minor tradition of human beings, but the only people who say that are people who know him, which leaves a good 3.9 billion people who have no particular reason to loathe him. Yet.

A typical Dirk Gently bill:

To:

Finding cat (deceased) - £50
Detecting and triangulating vectors of interconnectedness of all things - £150
Tracing same to beach on Bahamas, fare and accomodation - £1500
Struggling on in face of draining scepticism from client, drinks - £327.50

Dirk Gently's Manservant:

- believed by Dirk Gently to be the smallest, ugliest man who ever lived, and often used by his employer to break the ice at sèances. He is cantakerous, wilful, goes completely insane at weekends for relaxation, and usually refers to himself as "Mr Gently's Creature". He is also known as "The Nameless Horror", or "Nameless" for short.

Joyce Stickley:

Dirk Gently's lank and ratlike girlfriend.

Matthew Winkworth:

A computer software designer who does not deserve the things that happen to him in this book.

Samuel Taylor Coleridge:

Well known Romantic poet, drug abuser and unwitting stumbler upon sensitive architectural plans.

The Regius Professor of Chronology at St Cedd's College, Cambridge, or "**Reg**" for short.

A kindly old duffer, widely thought to have been brilliant in his day, though no one's quite certain as to when exactly his day was. A minor character to begin with who begins to assume greater importance as more facts come to light about him. For instance, Matthew Winkworth discovers that he appears to have been living in the same set of rooms in College for over three hundred years. The nature of Cambridge academic society is such that no one has seen fit to call attention to this.

"Reg" is in fact a retired time traveller.

It is through his intervention that our heroes are eventually enabled to fight a battle to the death in the primeval swamps of Earth...

Hello,

You have reached the offices of Dirk Gently's Holistic Detective Agency. Or rather, you have reached an advertisement for it. Or at least, an advertisement for the book of the same name. If you'ld like to leave a message after the beep, you can't. There isn't going to be one.

This is Douglas Adams speaking, and Dirk Gently's Holistic Detective Agency is my new book.

When I wrote the Hitch Hiker's Guide to the Galaxy books I was only mucking about really, seeing if I could get the typewriter to work. Well, it did, all except for the letter "B" as anyone who reads them carefully will quickly realise.

This time I decided to do the job properly. What the world needed, I could see was a thumping good Ghost Horror Detective Whodunit Time Travel Romantic Musical Comedy epic with a decent cookery supplement at the back. Well, it's not going to get it, I'm afraid, because I'm a lousy cook. But I think I've managed to cram the rest in.

Dirk Gently's Holistic Detective Agency. Published by Heinemann on June15th. I can't remember what price it is off hand, but it's a keen one. Dirk Gently's Holistic Detective Agency. The first ever fully realised Ghost Horror Detective Whodunit Time Travel Romantic Musical Comedy Epic. Certainly the first one ever to beginning with the word 'this.' Read it, and find out why.

In a script for an answer phone message to plug the book upon release, Douglas came up with a neat explanation for his new genre of novel (above, inset).

DIRK GENTLY'S HOLISTIC DETECTIVE AGENCY

Dear Bookseller,

When I wrote **The Hitch-Hiker's Guide to the Galaxy** books I was only mucking about really, seeing if I could get the typewriter to work. Well, it did, all except for the letter "B", as anyone who reads them carefully will quickly realise.

Well, this time I decided it was time to really get down to it, roll my sleeves up, and do the job properly. What the world needed, I could see quite clearly, was a thumping good Detective – Ghost – Horror – Whodunit – Time-Travel – Romantic – Musical – Comedy Epic with a decent cookery supplement at the back. Well, it's not going to get it, I'm afraid, because I'm a lousy cook and always manage to burn the spinach, but I think I've managed to cram the rest in.

I would like your help in this. In the past I've seen **The Hitch-Hiker's Guide to The Galaxy** displayed under "Travel" and **The Restaurant at the End of the Universe** featured next to Egon Ronay and the Good Food Guide, and this is a trend I would like to encourage. There is no section of a bookshop in which will **Dirk Gently's Holistic Detective Agency** will not happily sit, and from which it will not, I hope disappear pretty smartly too. Except for the cookery section. Please don't put it there, it will only confuse people. Wait for my next book. My publishers are begging me not to call it me **Dirk Gently Makes the Perfect Spinach Soufflé**, but they're going to have to buy me a lot of lunches if they want to change my mind.

I've really enjoyed writing this book, more than any since my first one. I hope you enjoy selling it. Good luck with it.

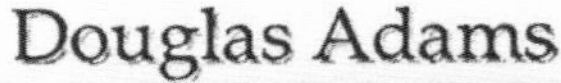

Portrait of an author who just finished his new book at 4.00 o'clock this morning.

A 'Detective – Ghost – Horror – Whodunit – Time-Travel – Romantic – Musical – Comedy' was how Douglas described the book – here in a letter to retailers, as well as to every newspaper or magazine reporter, TV host and reviewer ever afterwards.

Kubla Khan

In Xanadu did Kubla Khan
A stately pleasure-dome decree:
Where Alph the sacred river ran
Through caverns measureless to man
    Down to a sunless sea.
So twice five miles of fertile ground
With walls and towers girdled round:
And there were gardens bright with sinuous rills,
Where blossomed many an incense-bearing tree;
And here were forests ancient as the hills,
Enfolding sunny spots of greenery.

But oh! that deep romantic chasm which slanted
Down the green hill athwart a cedarn cover!
A savage place! as holy and enchanted as e'er
Beneath a waning moon was haunted
By woman wailing for her demon lover!
And from this chasm, with ceaseless turmoil seething,
As if this earth in fast thick pants were breathing,
A mighty fountain momently was forced:
Amid whose swift half intermitted burst
Huge fragments vaulted like rebounding hail,
Or chaffy grain beneath the thresher's flail:

And 'mid these dancing rocks at once and ever
It flung up momently the sacred river.

Five miles meandering with a mazy motion
Through wood and dale the sacred river ran,
Through caverns measureless to man,
And sank in tumult to a lifeless ocean:
And 'mid this tumult Kubla heard from far
Ancestral voices prophesying war!
    The shadow of the dome of pleasure
    Floated midway on the waves;
    Where was heard the mingled measure
    From the fountain and the caves.
It was a miracle of rare device,
A sunny pleasure-dome with caves of ice!

    A damsel with a dulcimer
    In a vision once I saw:
    It was an Abyssinian maid,
    And on her dulcimer she played,
    Singing of Mount Abora.
    Could I revive within me
    Her symphony and song,
    To such a deep delight 'twould win me,
That with music loud and long,
I would build that dome in air,

That sunny dome! Those caves of ice!
And all who heard should see them there,
And all should cry, Beware! Beware!
His flashing eyes, his floating hair!
Weave a circle round him thrice,
And close his eyes with holy dread,
For he on honey-dew hath fed,
And drunk the milk of Paradise.

And Kubla sternly gazed once more
Upon on the emerald valley's floor
Where Alph† in newly bubbling flood
Began to flow with crimson blood
And like a garnet† ribbon wound
About the woods and rocky ground.

And cries of fight and cries of woe
And steely clash of foe on foe
That mingled with the women's yell
Conjoined to sound the very blast of hell.

He watched his people die like cattle
Amidst the slaughter of the battle
In war's infernal charnel shed
Ten thousand people all lay dead.

† Early references to Alf Garnett, it would seem

Thrice struck the muffled passing bell of thunder
Through wood and dale the hollow echo ran
Through caverns measureless to man,
While flowed the bloody boiling river under.
And 'mid this tumult Kubla heard the sigh
Of ancient voices weeping from on high!
    Then tumbled down the dome of pleasure
    And sank in ruins through the waves;
    And hark! the shrill and shrieking measure
    Of the melting of the caves.

And Kubla Khan was watching still,
He hung his head and hid his eyes,
As standing on the rocky hill
The sun was darkened in the skies.

That sunny dome! Those caves of ice!
And all who hear can only grieve
And all who see cannot believe
How Man such glory could achieve
Yet lose it in a thundrous trice.
Now all lies under desert sand:
Now dust the city, dry the land
And sour the milk of Paradise.

Samuel Taylor Coleridge-ish. 1797-1987

The alternative timeline in the *Dirk Gently* story gave Douglas the opportunity to flex his literary muscles and create new verses for Coleridge's famous poem 'Kubla Khan'. Douglas's section begins halfway down the third page, from 'And Kubla sternly gazed…' to the end. It's worth noting Douglas's acknowledgement at the end (in the '-ish' and the dates) that the authorship wasn't entirely authentic!

the Country Fresh Farmhouse Churn butter which comes in tiny hermetically sealed vacuum-formed ~~plastic~~ packs

•

It's amazing how much paper you can cover if you have a certain facility with words and no great impulse to make any of them mean anything.

•

At the very beginning of the book we follow the course of a meteorite that is travelling through the solar system towards the planet Earth. We may update it from time to time during the course of the book.

Then, towards the end of the book Dirk will be in a desperate situation, confronting a deadly adversary, and at the critical moment the meteorite will strike the enemy down. This will outrage and deeply upset Dirk, because he will be convinced that he was capable of winning through using only his wits. This might be doubtful, which is what makes him particularly angry. He bitterly resents the fact that.

-

I'm beginning to get used to the place in a resigned sort of a way, but I was pretty appalled when I first got here. If I tell you that even the palm trees on the beach have Muzak pumped out of them you'll probably be able to fill in the rest of the picture from your own imagination, but in case you can't, here are a few more details.

The place is full of what I assume are typists from whatever the Australian equivalent of Bromley is. Every evening there are theme parties during which I sit in my room and read or watch tv in order to avoid seeing lots of fat drunken Australian cavorting around the place

in grass skirts or cowboy hats or whatever the theme of the evening is. Yesterday I spent lunchtime sitting getting slowly sozzled on tequila sunrises and listening to the conversation at the table next to me which for three quarters of an hour was exclusively concerned with stories about road accidents involving heavy goods vehicles. Most of the rest of yesterday I spent like this – I woke up at about eight, but didn't summon up the energy to get up till about 1 o'clock. This represented a good five hours of solid trying and continual failure. I hadn't realised quite how tired I was after the tour until faced with the prospect of being able to stay in bed as long as I wanted to. I then had the tequila sunrises and then went and sat purposefully by the pool. By about 7.00pm I realised that the time for swimming had effectively passed and retired exhausted to my room and spent the evening listening to maddened drunk Australians rampaging through the night in grass skirts and watching what I eventually deduced must have been one of the Mad Max films on tv. That too featured a lot of road accidents, at least one of which involved a heavy goods vehicle.

Scuba diving-

At least they don't pump the muzak under the water and none of the fish attempt to tell you about road accidents, they merely bite your leg off.

I can hardly bear to describe what has just happened. I am sitting by the pool. A walking band of happy people playing accordians and maraccas has walked past playing happy jolly having-fun-type music. With them were lots of little girls wearing Tahitian flowered skirts with flowers in their hair. And behind them were four bronzed Australians wearing Hawaiian print shirts, shorts and white socks, smiling and carrying two dead pigs on poles.

The setting here is really very beautiful which is why I particularly hate all those things which the brochure describes as "superb" or "sophisticated" and "international", i.e. the muzak and the talent contests and all the other trappings of that international, superb and sophisticated dump, Butlins.

I was talking to an Australian couple on the boat. My general line of introduction is "Hello, my name is Douglas, don't you hate the muzak?" This couple didn't as a matter of fact. They thought it was very nice and international and sophisticated. They lived on a sheep farm some 850 miles west of Brisbane where all they ever heard, they said, was nothing. I said that must be very nice and they said that it got rather boring after a while, and a little light muzak was balm to them. They refused to go along with my assertion that it was like having spam stuffed in your ears all day and after a while the conversation petered out.

It is now 6.20pm and already quite a lot of big beefy australians are resolutely plodding around in their Hawaiian grass skirts, so I'm starting to tuck into some Tequila sunrises to help myself cope with it all.

A rather callow Australian youth has just walked past wearing a Hawaiian print shirt, grass skirt, shark's tooth necklace and two cups of tea. I can only imagine that he feels very embarrassed to look as stupid as that, or that his brain is dead. What is the matter with the world?

Over the following pages, concluding this collection of artefacts on *Dirk Gently* from the archive, are some highlights from the notes for Douglas's third, unfinished *Dirk Gently* novel, which was published posthumously in 2002.

He appeared to live in another world, which would have been good news for all concerned had it been true, but unfortunately his body had taken up solid, or at least flabby, residence in this one. He was a record company executive, a job that suited him terribly well because it gave a tremendous vantage point from which to affect to despise everything, including the record company which paid him to be a vile toady – redundant payment, since he would have done it for free since he had been doing it for free all his life. It was part of his affectation not to know what bands his record company currently had signed, what records they had released, what they sounded like, or even what they looked like. If asked, he would instead talk in a whiney drawl about Baudelaire about whom he also knew nothing.

•

The cathedral.

The towers throng with cows and hippos. One of the gargoyles at a low level by the entrance is a gargoyle beneath which is a bearded saint driving a sword into its belly in a reverend manner.

People built this.

Guillaume, le maître charpentier, couvrier, mason, sculptor, etc.

Inteconnectedness with the past. By being ignorant of the past we cut outselves off from a lot of what we are and open ourselves to Coca Cola advertsing and blah.

"He is a little timid sir. It is my opinion that were you to introduce him into the company of a goose and invite him to say boo to it, he would be unwilling to comply with your request."

"Thank you for sharing your views with us."

"And if I might be permitted to continue on the goose topic for one further moment sir..."

"Yes, Nameless?"

"To say that I despise the creatures sir. That is all that I wished to add. Rarely do I see a goose standing in that preposterous way that they have, sir, like a pair of insolent and partially dismembered bagpipes, when I am not tempted to perform violence on it. On one particular occasion, sir, I succumbed to temptation. I thank you, sir, for your indulgence." So saying, he withdrew.

•

The thing about Nameless is that he claims to be a lot nastier than he is.

But he takes out most of his real rage on his animals and plants.

I imagine him hosing them down with neat Baby Bio, in a kind of desperate rage of caring. They are all wilting, sick and bedraggled, stained and dripping with neat Baby Bio.

"I mean look at these plants. I just wish they'd say what they want, I'd give it to them. But what is it? More water? Less water? I give them more water and less water till I'm blue in the face. Sun? Food? More sun? Less food? They just sit there and wilt and sulk. Most of them die, I think they do it out of spite. Everything I try they react the same way. I water them they wilt. I don't water them they wilt even quicker. I'd do anything if they'd only respond. Just show a little willingness to meet me halfway. Talk to them. By God I talk to them. Plead with them. Scream at them. They just sit in their pots and sulk. Pots I gave them! Little bastards."

•

Pot death.

Cyclamens are the worst. They die. That is all they do. They just allow you to buy them in order to sit there and die at you. Well, this one is not going to make me feel guilty. I'm not going to give it the chance to wither up and wilt at me. Your fun finishes here, buddy!"

With a twist of his shoulders he delivered a massive thwack of the spade against the cyclamen pot. It hurtled through the greenhouse, shattered against the rear brick wall, and dribbled in heavy bits to the ground. Elegant little flowers peeked brokenly out from under the clods of over-watered earth in silent reproach. Nameless stamped on them, ground them with his heels, slapped the earth off his hands and hobbled ferociously from the room.

•

I think that Nameless is, after all, Dirk's manservant, a sort of deranged and malformed Jeeves. His back is all twisted about. I have constant back troubles which weaken me, they weaken me terribly. Just picking up a teapot makes him clench his entire face. You wouldn't, would you sir, think that I was as strong as an ox."

"Well, it would depend on which ox..."

Anyway, on one occasion he gets attacked by some villain, who gets Nameless into a half nelson. When he increases the pressure something deep in Nameless's back goes crunch, click, and his spine ripples back into shape.

A look of stunned shock crossed Nameless's face, and passed rapidly on to the face of his assailant, who hardly had to time to start working out why he was suddenly hurtling through the air before he had to start wondering instead why he was slowly sliding up a wall that when he had last looked at it had been at least ten feet away, and also why so many bits of him were hurting so much. His head continued to slide up the wall until it made severe contact with the ceiling, which at the last moment suddenly turned out to be the floor instead. The sheer quantity of conflicting data that suddenly needed to be processed unexpected data processing required by all this caused his brain to go 'bing' and he spent the next two minutes dreaming happily of seal pits in Suffolk for reasons which it is not the purpose of

•

Conversation between two people who habitually daydream tends to involve a lot of sudden and radical changes of subject as each speaker tried vainly and at short notice to remember what it was the other was speaking about.

•

Mind-witheringly explosively astoundingly blisteringly dull

•

Postcard: I've marked a room with a cross completely at random. It's not the one I'm staying in.

•

from le Cep restaurant in Beaune.

Couple in restaurant, very shyly not talking to each other. He was a young and slightly overweight American who wore a small and tightly fitted smile as if to suggest that he had his own reasons with which he was quietly pleased for not saying anything at this time. She was a blond and fragile English rose. She sat blinking and delicately clutching the fine stem of her wine glass, furiously conscious of her upbringing which said that she must make conversation. From time to time a half formed thought would break nervously from her lips. The American would lean forward slyly and say "pardon?"

The smile would broaden with suprise and relax whenever the conversation went on for one more rally

He would occasionally have his attention distracted for a moment by some event at a nearby table – the chink of a glass, the arrival of another course, and he would glance around with his smile to check it out. "Oh yes," his smile would say "they have chinked their glass. Well, that's exactly the sort of glass that would chink, of course, and they are exactly the sort of people who would chink it in that way. Exactly what one would have expected."

The smile would tighten its grip by a notch and his glance would then swivel back and fasten itself on to his own glass.

By the end of the evening their glances had hardened in directions other than each other, and bed tonight was going to be a perfunctory business punctuated by animal cries addressed to their respective mothers, saying "Look what I got" and "look what you got me into."

"I think I'm going to have that. That's framboise. That's raspberries or sump'n."

•

The food.

The ingredients had the air of being rather startled at being introduced to each other in public and struck up a rather uneasy relationship on the plate.

The sauces all had that slightly granular quality which suggests that things haven't gone entirely calmly in the kitchen.

•

Very rich person – has lots of money which they don't understand how they have. They

Relate to rhino

Smell is a much more primitive and powerful sense than sight or hearing. Sight and hearing are the senses that the modern world uses. All communication that we hold to be of any account is by those two senses. We read, we write. We talk, we watch television. We listen to the radio. We listen to arguments, we listen to music. There are hugely developed parts of the brain continually ready to process sight and sound, to sift meaning out of them.

Smell we do very little with. It tells us if the toast is burning or the milk is off. Otherwise it is a language we simply don't know, which is why it can catch us so fearfully off our guard, and suddenly smelling again the soap you were washed with as a child roars through like out emotions like a

•

You work very hard at being succesful in order to be loved, and then expect people to love you for yourself rather than for your success.

Take the Sword of Courage, buckle unto yourself the Shield of Integrity, stride forth and do battle with the Salmon of Doubt

•

This should be a phrase used by somebody that Dirk encounters. It should be someone who thinks that they lend literary depth to their speech with by filling it with metaphorcial images. Unfortunately most of them are completely preposterous, as is this one. However, Dirk decides it is strangely appropriate and deliberately adopts it, quoting it frequently.

Among the great qualities of human beings are how wrong we can be, and also how quickly we forget.

On visiting a restaurant:
"Imagine the finest, most delightful meal you have ever tasted..."
"Yes..."
"And keep thinking of it. It may help sustain you through the horrors of the meal you are actually about to eat."

This idea is drawn from my telling Richard's producer that I didn't like Quest For Fire (he produced it) and his director that the Return of the Jedi was too much like the Muppet Movie (he directed the Muppet Movie).
It's just a thought about a plot device for a book.
We have a scene in which someone makes just such a dreadful faux pas as one of the above, and then says "Well, I think I'll just jump out of this window"
Meanwhile, we have been following another strand of plot in which something is going to happen on a particular street at a particular time. Later we discover in parenthesis that the person concerned is in hospital, and also that the event, whatever it was, was disturbed by having someone jump out of the window on to it.

At the end of the book the whole of California sinks into the sea taking with it x million people who 3 million years later became useful as fuel.
During the course of the book we will visit the far future and hear something about a wonderful new form of fuel, which is actually, as we discover at the end, several million anciently dead Californians.

"If he is a typical example of the man in the street, then I have to say that the next lunatic who goes beserk in the the street with a sub-machine gun does so with my blessing."

Truth is anything which can be proved by a clever lawyer.
•
Muzak: the drab and monotonous horn-line that lulls the listener into a false sense of despair.
•
When the sun leaves the desert it seems to take the whole world with it, and to make a point of leaving you, personally, behind.
•
It really was enough to make a nun say fuck.
•
He awoke to discover that he was a dog.
He didn't realise straight away because he always felt a little muzzy in the mornings, and it was, after all, a completely unexpected turn of events. He lay there, and slowly pieced the evidence together.
•
In my head is the perpetual brrrr brrrr rhythm of the phone ringing waiting for the real sound to fill it.
•
There were certain onions sitting unneeded, sour and furry in the bottom of a pickle jar in a dusty corner of the larder. They had been there for many years, gathering grime and offensiveness, unthought of. He only thought of them now because suddenly he knew how they felt.

"I would like some coffee," I said. I got up and went wearily over to the percolator in which yesterday's coffee was being kept hot and viscous. I poured some into a polysterene mug, tipped in a little creamer powder from another, looked for a clean pencil to stir it with, took a tiny sip, and then poured it down the sink instead.

Dear Douglas

ARVIND ETHAN DAVID

Dear Douglas

The first time I wrote to you was nearly 30 years ago, in 1994. I was an 18-year-old undergraduate student at Oxford, and I had wanted your permission to adapt your novel *Dirk Gently's Holistic Detective Agency* into a stage play.

After some time, a response came from your wonderful agents at the Ed Victor Literary Agency. I wish I still had a copy of that letter, but I remember what it said:

'Douglas does not believe that his novel *Dirk Gently's Holistic Detective Agency* is suitable for adaptation for the stage, or indeed, for any other medium. But he will not stop you from trying.'

So we tried. We tried to reinvent your complex, brilliant, baffling novel, with its multiple timelines, time-travel, ghosts, aliens, ghostly aliens, murders and horses into something that could work on stage.

Incredibly, some months later, you came to see the results.

I remember with bowel-clenching clarity, sitting two rows behind you, watching you watch our version of your creation. I remember my despair when you didn't laugh at all for the first 10 minutes, and then the relief when you did, and that your big honking laugh was a tonic to the whole company. I remember when you took out a pencil and made some notes in your program.

I also remember the dinner afterwards. Terrified, I asked you what you thought. You tilted your giant head to one side and said, 'Well, you know, you've made me think for the first time that maybe there is a TV show in Dirk Gently, and maybe I should get around to making it...'

You never did, one of many tragedies of your early death. Twenty years later, I made it for you, starring Elijah Wood and Samuel Barnett. Netflix and Hulu and BBC America released it to millions of people, introducing a new generation to the incomparable Dirk Gently, and they came to love him as much as I did.

I wish I could have watched you watch it. I'm certain your pencil would have come out again.

Thank you for not stopping me from trying.
Arvind

Arvind Ethan David is a writer and producer who has made (so far): eight feature films, three television shows, two musicals, five graphic novels, two table-top games, three Audiodramas and one perfect daughter. His career started, continues and will probably end with the work of Douglas Adams. The illustration above is by Ilias Kyriazis, and is an imaginative piece of the night when Douglas Adams came to see Arvind Ethan David's stage adaptation of *Dirk Gently*.

ELEVEN
Last Chances

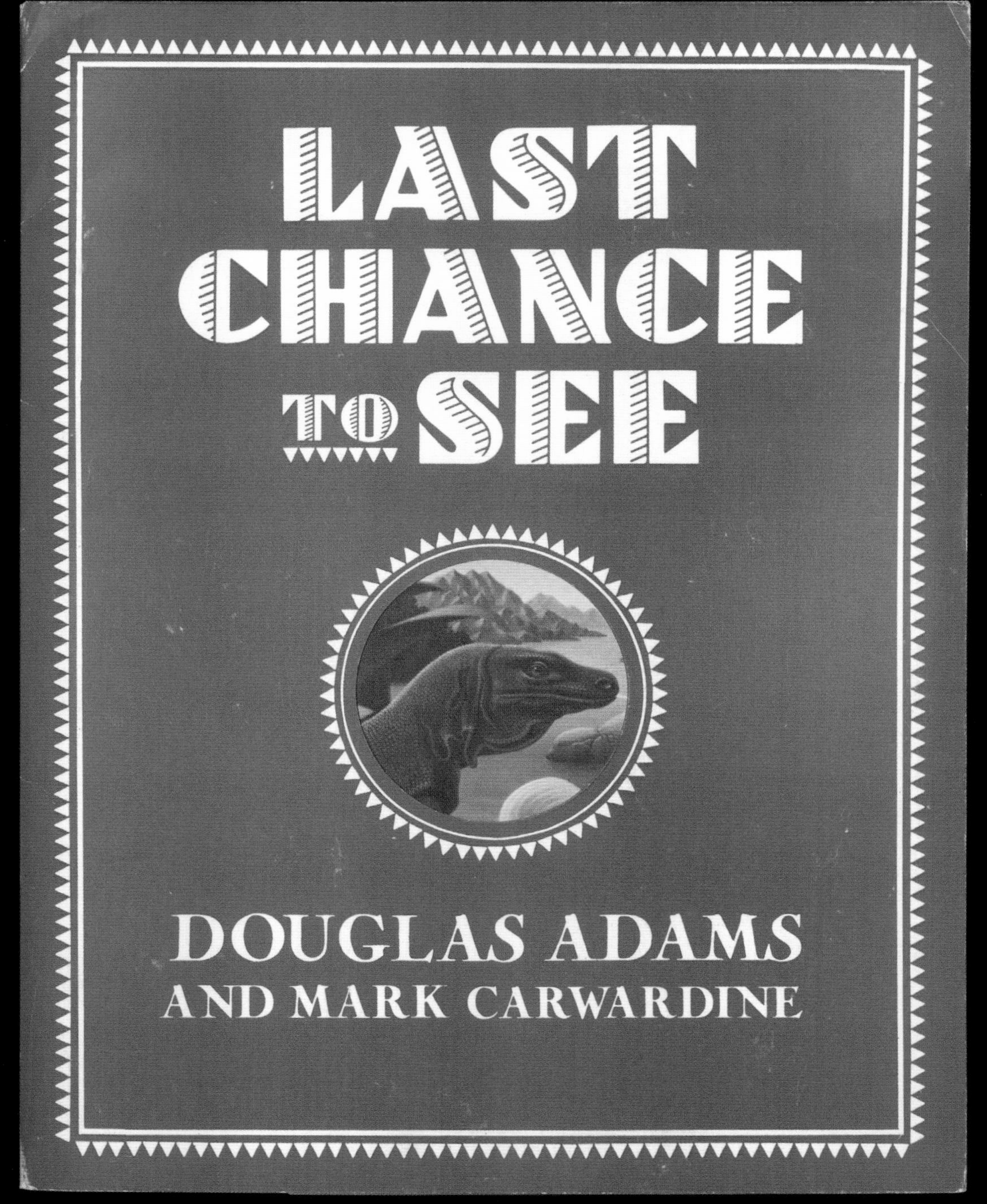

Last Chance to See took Douglas and Mark Carwardine to far-flung places in search of species on the brink of extinction and producing both a radio programme and a book. This, and later Douglas's work for Save the Rhino (also featured in this chapter), became a firm passion and source of pride for him.

PLANNING THE TRIP

From: Gaynor Shutte, Producer, Features, Arts and Education

Room No. & Building: 110 HWH **Tel. Ext.:** 5307/7687 **date:** 29th April 1988

Subject: "LAST CHANCE TO SEE"

To: H.F.A.E.R.

It might be helpful to you if I put down on paper as much as I know about this project to date.

First of all the series itself. It will consist of six half hour programmes each of which will tell the story of an expedition to search for an exotic and endangered animal. Much of the tone of the project will come from the fact that **Mark Carwardine** is an extremely experienced and widely travelled Zoologist, and **Douglas Adams** is an extremely ignorant non-zoologist to whom virtually everything will come as a complete surprise (sounds a bit like Ford prefect and Arthur Dent).

Some animals they will find, some they probably won't, but its the adventure of the search which the programmes will illustrate as well as the people they meet, the difficulties they overcome (or don't) and the other wildlife they encounter.

The history of the series so far is that Douglas Adams went to see CR4 to discuss the trip and the possibility of making a radio series from it. Douglas Adams and Mark Carwardine are making the trip to collect material for a book they are jointly writing about these endangered creatures, for which Heinemann has given them a half-million pound advance. For each individual trip they have budgeted and planned for three people. Originally they were going to take a professional photographer and attempt to record the sound themselves, but when Michael expressed interest, and I think partly as a result of his advice, they decided to make the "third" person a sound engineer. At this point Michael called and asked if I would like to produce the series and suggest a good S.M.
Group 5 would be happy to release an S.M. for the trips (not necessarily the same S.M.) - which as you will see from the attached itinerary - would not require the third person to be away from base longer than three weeks at a time. Douglas and Mark would pay for the S.M.'s travel and subsistance.

The six expeditions are as follows:

Cat. No. 6916
AS/20

Publishers Heinemann paid an advance of £500,000 towards a book by Douglas and Mark that would fund their trip. They needed other sponsors, too, and Douglas asked the Controller of BBC Radio 4 if the station might like to consider sending along a few sound recordists. And indeed they did: producer Gaynor Shutte shared duties with Steven Faux and Chris Muir.

EXPEDITION CHECKLIST

Travel
Passport(s)
Visa/entry permit
Immunisation certificates
Ticket(s)
Spare passport photos
International driving licence
UK driving licence
Insurance details
Numbers

Money
Local currency
Sterling
Dollars
Travellers cheques
Credit cards
Neck purse
Money belt

Paperwork
Letters of introduction
Business cards
Notes, information
Pens, paper
Field and travel guides
Phrase book/dictionary
Map(s)
Addresses

Miscellaneous
Washing powder
Swimming goggles/snorkels
Water purification tablets
Paracord
Torch
Plastic bags
Glasses/sunglasses
First Aid Kit
Compass
Watch
Penknife/survival knife
Food/sweets
Water bottle
Gifts (inc cigarettes)
Malaria tablets
Loo roll
Reading books/magazines
Matches/lighter
Candle
Rucksack(s)
Mosquito spray/headband
Mosquito coils

Clothes
Hat
Shoes
Walking boots
Socks, pants, hanks
Headover/gloves
Shorts
Trousers
Shirts
T-shirts
Flip-flops
Tie(s)
Sweaters
Jacket/suit
Zoot suit/coat/umbrella
Swimming trunks
Khaki gear
Pyjamas

Camera equipment
35mm camera bodies
Polaroid camera
Compact camera
Photography belt
Lenses/converters
Tripod/monopod/tree bracket
Lens hoods
Flash gear
Spare batteries
Underwater gear
Film
Equipment bag(s)
Padlock
Motordrives
Infra-red remote control
Tissues/clean air
Extension bellows
Silicagel
X-ray bag

Other equipment
Binoculars/telescope
Dictaphone (+ tapes)
Shortwave radio
Sony Professional (+ tapes)
Laptop computer (+ discs)

Overnight
Sleeping bag/cobra bivi bag
Mosquito net
Toiletries
Towel
Alarm clock
Tunnel tent

Douglas and Mark purchased some new camera gear. After much consulting of diaries and other deliberations, they were ready to go in the summer of 1988. Accounts vary, but Douglas may have been advised that, for tax reasons, it might be a good time to spend much of the year out of England! His friend Stephen Fry moved into Douglas's Islington home, minding it for the duration of the trip. He recalls using Douglas's enormous bath and taking calls from him in far-distant time zones, at odd times of the night.

LAST CHANCE EXPEDITIONS (1988–89)

The purpose of the trip was to raise awareness of the plight of certain endangered animals, and this Douglas and Mark managed admirably, with the radio programmes and in the book. Each man brought their expertise to the projects: Mark explaining the animals and their habitats to Douglas and he, in turn, revealing these truths in an easily accessible – and memorably hilarious – way. Douglas's observations and his chronicling of the more human aspects of air travel (dodgy old aircraft, mad pilots, corrupt customs officials), or by boat on choppy waters, or across rough terrain in a Land Rover, and then roughing it in some of the worst sleeping conditions, are often the funniest parts. These excerpts are good examples of that. This piece (below and opposite) is about an impromptu minibus tour on Bali after an extra stay overnight due to intransigent officialdom at the airport.

Our guide was Gusti Madenik Swastika. The "Gusti" is the family name. 'Made' is the name given to the second child of a family. There are four different names given to the children of a family according to the order in which they were born. Since most Indonesian families run to more than four, they then cycle the names around once more, sometimes sticking 'nik' on the end to distinguish them from their elder siblings.

Month
Date
day
PAGE

The last name, Swastika, was the one name that was given to a child as a given name – what we would call a Christian name, but it was by no means clear who ever called them by this name.

Gusti was a man of immense good humour and charm, bubbling with laughter and enthusiasm for everything that happened and everything we said.

He explained about the gradations of the Hindu temples – there are four different types – the domestic temple for the home, the tower temple dedicated to Brahmah, Vishnu & Shiva, the functional temple for regulating the growth of crops and so on and the big public ceremonial temples.

We visited one temple and had a look around it. We took photographs of a priest who prayed and chanted devoutly whenever you waved a camera at him for which he expected a tip – and relaxed with a cigarette whenever you put your camera away.

I took one group of photographs of him for which he bowed and prayed devoutly, smiling serenely and murmuring chants under his breath. He made it clear he expected a tip for this, which I was happy

DON'T MAKE LIGHT OF YOUR LIFE.

Month
Date
day
PAGE

to give him. He accepted this with devout bowing and murmuring and smiling and stuffed it into a side pocket from which he then drew a pouch of tobacco. He teased and sorted the strands and then patted them into wads and carefully inserted them between his lower lip and gum. I had been watching him surreptitiously and then suddenly noticed that my flash had been at the wrong setting (it's remarkable how much of the time that we were in Indonesia we had insufficient light) I had to take the photos again. Hurriedly the priest hid the tobacco pouch, shoved the wad to the back of his mouth and became beatific once more. I took some more pictures and then there was more murmuring and nodding and chanting and smiling. He then seemed to abandon his tobacco wad in favour of a cigarette. This seemed to give him trouble however, because every time we happened to turn in his direction he had hurriedly to hide the cigarette and resume his praying posture. We had to avoid looking directly at him, or at least to avoid making it look as if there was the slightest danger

IT IS WRONG TO TELL A LIE.

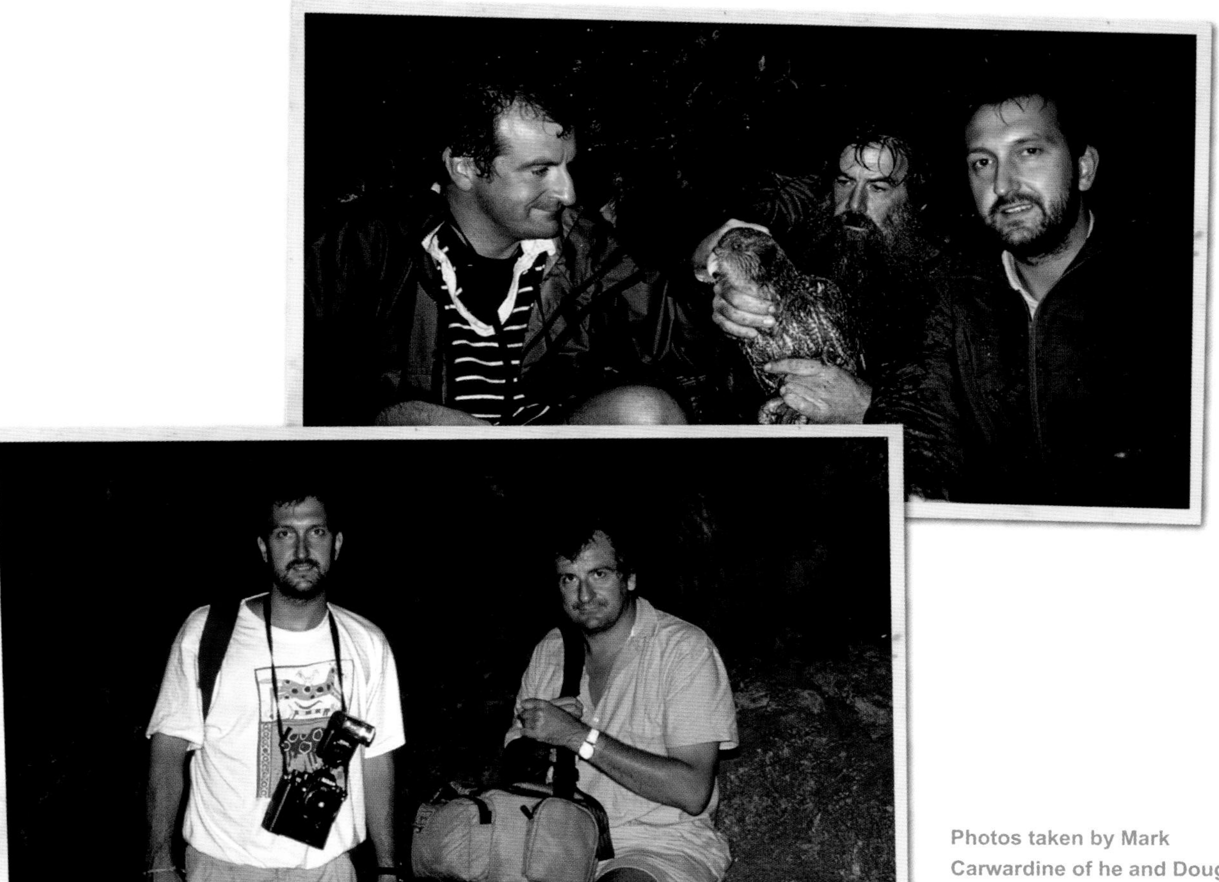

Photos taken by Mark Carwardine of he and Douglas on their expedition for *Last Chance to See.*

Our guide was Gusti Madenik Swastika. The 'Gusti' is the family name. 'Made' is the name given to the second child of a family. There are four different names given to the children of a family according to the order in which they were born. Since most Indonesian families run to more than four, they then cycle the names around once more, sometimes sticking 'nik' on the end to distinguish them from their elder siblings. The last name, Swastika, was the one name that was given to a child as a given name, what we would call a Christian name, but it was by no means clear who ever called them by this name.

Gusti was a man of immense good humour and charm, bubbling with laughter and enthusiasm for everything that happened and everything we said. He explained about the gradations of the Hindu temples – there are four different types – the domestic temple for the home, the lower temple dedicated to Brahmah, Vishnu & Shiva, the functional temple for regulating the growth of crops and so on, and the big public ceremonial temples.

We visited one temple and had a look around it. We took photographs of a priest who prayed and chanted devoutly whenever you waved a camera at him – for which he expected a tip – and relaxed with a cigarette whenever you put your camera away.

I took one group of photographs of him for which he bowed and prayed devoutly, smiling serenely and murmuring chants under his breath. He made it clear that he expected a tip for this which I was happy to give him. He accepted this with devout bowing and murmuring and smiling and stuffed it into a side pocket from which he then drew a pouch of tobacco. He teased and sorted the strands and then patted them into wads and carefully inserted them between his lower lip and gum. I had been watching him surreptitiously, and then suddenly noticed that my flash had been at the wrong setting. (It's remarkable how much of the time that we were in Indonesia we had insufficient light.) I had to take the photos again.

Hurriedly the priest hid the tobacco pouch, shoved the wad to the back of his mouth and became beatific once more. I took some more pictures and then there was more murmuring and nodding and chanting and smiling. He then seemed to abandon his tobacco wad in favour of a cigarette. This seemed to give him trouble however, because every time we happened to turn in his direction, he had hurriedly to hide the cigarette and resume his praying posture. We had to avoid looking directly at him, or at least to avoid making it look as if there was the slightest danger of our raising our cameras.

This is a draft of a letter to Jane Belson (then his live-in girlfriend, later his wife) written by Douglas in a plane over Africa during the expedition.

2 Feb 89.

Darling Janey,

Excuse the paper, it's all I have with me. We are currently in a small 16-seater twin engined plain flying over the Great Rift valley with Mt Kenya to the right and Kilimanjaro off to the left, heading down first to Tanzania and the up to Bukavu in Zaire. It's a tiny charter airline run by missionaries, which meant that the flight started with a brief prayer, which is something I found rather startling. I could do without the feeling of being asked to commit our souls to God before take off. There is such a suffocating air of goodness on the plane that I wish I had some chewing gum which I could evilly stick under the seat. Still, it was the only flight we could get and we were lucky to get it.

Although ~~we~~ we were on different flights

going by different routes, Mark + Chris and I arrived at Nairobi airport almost simultaneously because ~~their~~ their flight was almost two hours late. We got stuck in almost immediately – Mark lived in Nairobi for six months once and knows it well. We borrowed a Land Rover belonging to some friends of his and we drove off ~~into~~ Nairobi National Park. Just at the gate of the Park someone pointed out to us that we had a puncture, which was incredibly lucky. Ten minutes later and we would have been deep inside it in Lion country and unable to get out of the car.

2 Feb 89.

Darling Janey,

Excuse the paper, it's all I have with me. We are currently in a small 16-seater twin engine plane flying over the Great Rift Valley with Mt. Kenya to the right and Kilimanjaro off to the left, heading down first to Tanzania and then up to Bukavu in Zaire. It's a tiny charter airline run by missionaries, which meant that the flight started with a brief prayer, which is something I found rather startling. I could do without the feeling of being asked to commit our souls to God before take-off. There is such a suffocating air of goodness on the plane that I wish I had some chewing gum which I could evilly stick under the seat. Still, it was the only flight we could get and we were lucky to get it.

Although we were on different flights going by different routes, Mark & Chris and I arrived at Nairobi airport almost simultaneously because their flight was almost two hours late. We got stuck in almost immediately – Mark lived in Nairobi for six months once and knows it well. We borrowed a Land Rover belonging to some friends of his and we drove off into Nairobi National Park. Just at the gate of the park someone pointed out to us that we had a puncture, which was incredibly lucky. Ten minutes later and we would have been deep inside it in Lion country and unable to get out of the car.

After several days on Mauritius and a trip to Round Island, the team eventually arrived on Rodrigues Island to finally see the much-anticipated 'world's rarest fruitbats'. This was a notably brief bit in the book (though slightly more expanded in the radio show). Douglas's notebook reveals why his mind wasn't on the topic, and it began when they were met by a driver called Henri (below, and transcribed on page 251).

Count the cockroaches
Count the geckos again
~~Count~~
See if there's any change
Doze.
Show off the camera to an Italian.

Henri — fat, sleek, badly dressed, with ill fitting old jeans tucked up under his paunch and a grimy baseball hat pulled down over his long brushed back hair. Long disgraceful sideboards and a ~~thick~~ disgraceful moustache cheerful with Sir.

The Caves

Much more dramatic than we expected.
The watchman was drunk. This seems not to

have been a coincidence. His three sons conducted us through the caves. Normally the watchman prevents his sons from accepting tips. So they arrange to pre-invest in getting him drunk so ~~that~~ they can take tourists into the caves and accept their tips.

They wrap an old sack around a ~~s~~ metal rod, pour petrol ~~of~~ over it and set fire to it.

Afterwards we went to the forest to look for the bats.
The main consequence of this (apart from the fact that we succeeded in seeing the rarest fruitbat in the world) was that I got bitten by about ~~the~~ 200 mosquitos. This was in the time ~~that~~ it took for me

to discover that I had forgotten to bring my own insect repellent and wait for Mark to finish applying some to himself and then borrow his. To be honest the consequence of this was that I didn't give a fig about the fruitbats once the bites had started to take effect. If there was a button I could press which would permanently rid the world of all its mosquitos in a moment I would hit the button, and let the ecological results fall where they may. That, at least is my reaction at the moment as I sit writing this on the following evening after a terrible seething night of feverish scratching and clawing at the air in a vain attempt to stop myself continuing to scratch. Then a day on the boat to the Ile de Coco, again trying desperately hard to stop myself scratching and continually failing. My legs are a great mass of red lumps each of which seethes at me, and gives me just a brief relief while I'm actually scratching at the thing but then feels as if its on fire as soon as I stop.

On the island, after exploring we had some lunch and then lay ourselves out on benches and chairs to get some siesta – during which ~~[illegible]~~ my bites seethed at me relentlessly. When we arose again ~~it happen~~ we went for a swim – which was pretty pathetic, about two

and a half feet of water ~~sit~~ with a sandy bottom and few desultory bits of brown seaweed.
Emerging from the ~~sea~~ and towelling myself I was approached by an enquiring mosquito, at which point I achieved in an ~~instant~~ the highest pomb of hatred ~~that~~ I think I have yet attained in my life so far and would cheerfully have machine gunned the bugger.

Otherwise Île de Coco was an idyllic island. It looked not so much like a tropical tree lined island as a modish hairstyle set in an azure sea.
Two very rare birds ~~the~~ Noddy – found in

Henri – fat, sleek, badly dressed, with ill-fitting old jeans tucked up under his paunch and a grimy baseball hat pulled down over his long, brushed back hair. Long disgraceful sideburns and a thick disgraceful moustache cheerful with sin.

The Caves

Much more dramatic than we expected. The watchman was drunk. This seems not to have been a coincidence. His three sons conducted us through the caves. Normally the watchman prevents his sons from accepting tips, so they arrange to pre-invest in getting him drunk so they can take tourists into the caves and accept their tips. They wrap an old sack around a metal rod, pour petrol over it and set fire to it.

Afterwards we went to the forest to look for the bats. The main consequence of this (apart from the fact that we succeeded in seeing the rarest fruitbat in the world) was that I got bitten by about 200 mosquitos. This was in the time that it took for me to discover that I had forgotten to bring my own insect repellent and wait for Mark to finish applying some to himself and then borrow his. To be honest the consequence of this was that I didn't give a fig about the fruitbats once the bites had started to take effect. If there was a button I could press which would permanently rid the world of all its mosquitos, in a moment I would hit the button and let the ecological results fall where they may. That, at least, is my reaction at the moment, as I sit writing this on the following evening, after a terrible seething night of feverish scratching and clawing at the air in a vain attempt to stop myself continuing to scratch. Then a day on the boat to the Ile de Coco, again trying to stop myself scratching and continually failing. My legs are a great mass of red lumps, each of which seethes at me, and gives me just a brief relief while I'm actually scratching at the thing but then feels as if it's on fire as soon as I stop.

> **...we had some lunch and then lay ourselves out on benches and chairs to get some siesta – during which my bites seethed at me relentlessly.**

On the island, after exploring, we had some lunch and then lay ourselves out on benches and chairs to get some siesta – during which my bites seethed at me relentlessly. When we arose again, we went for a swim – which was pretty pathetic, about two and a half feet of water with a sandy bottom and a few desultory bits of brown seaweed. Emerging from the sea and towelling myself, I was approached by an enquiring mosquito, at which point I achieved in an instant the highest point of hatred that I think I had yet attained in my life so far and would cheerfully have machine gunned the bugger.

Otherwise Ile de Coco was an idyllic island. It looked not so much like a tropical tree lined island as a modish hairstyle set in an azure sea. Two very rare bids – the Noddy – found in...

Things to take on next trip -

Suitcase with built-in wheels
Mandarin Duck bag
Zoom lenses.

Douglas's final note regarding the expedition...

RHINO CLIMB (1994)

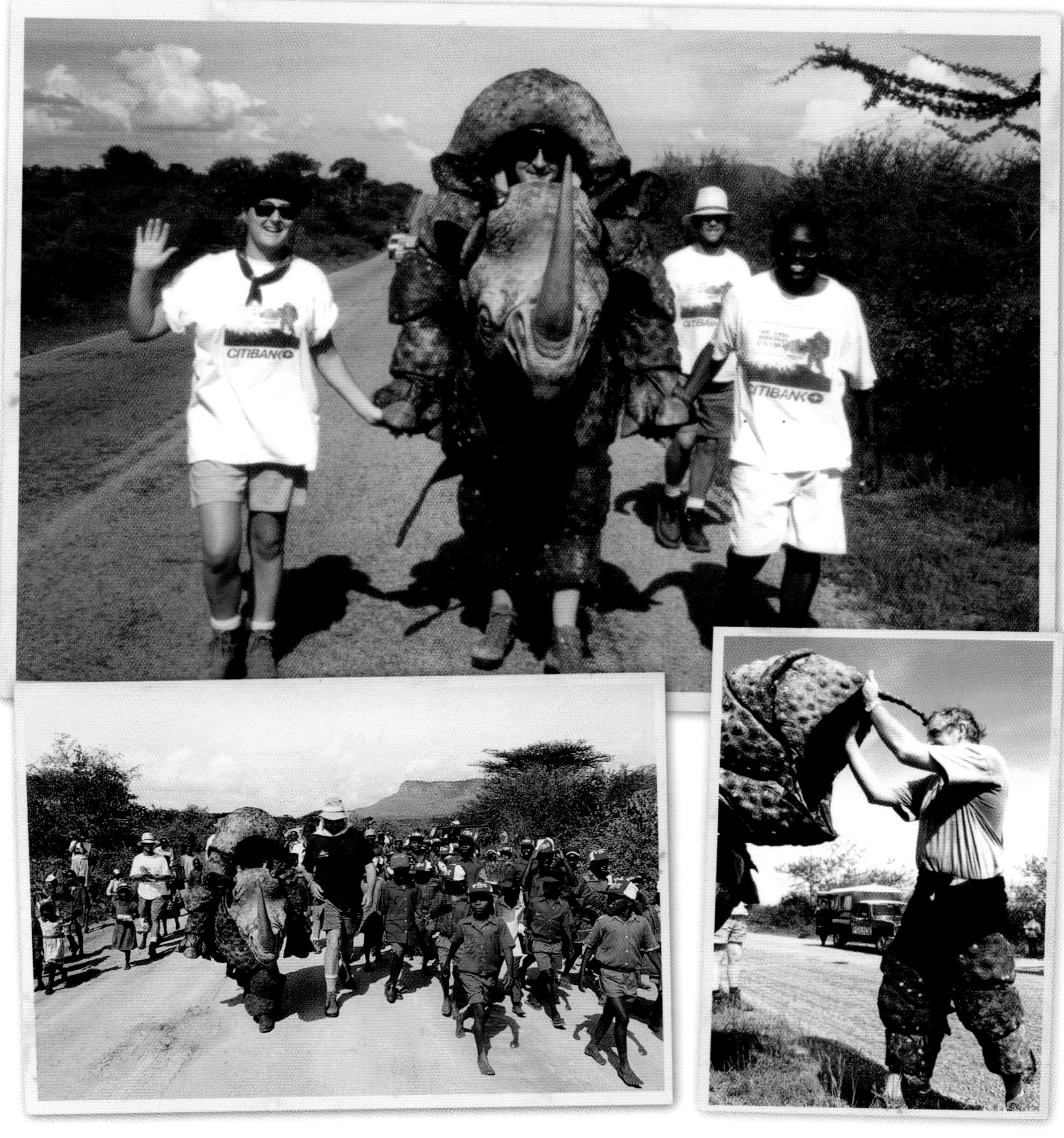

Perhaps inevitably after the *Last Chance* trip, Douglas became a passionate advocate for natural causes. This famously included the plight of the rhino. In 1994, employees from the London offices of Save the Rhino International co-opted Douglas into their trek to raise awareness. Making their way 320km across part of east Africa, from Mombasa, Kenya, to the summit of Mount Kilimanjaro in Tanzania (lying 5,895m above sea level), the main rhino team consisted of James Hersov, Tom Kenyon Slaney, Johnny Roberts, Will Stanhope, David Stirling and (taking care of the essential rhino costume) William 'Todd' Jones, known for his creature performances in film and theatre. Todd said that Douglas and his sister Jane joined them near the Tsavo National Park and took their turns in the rhino get-up, too (above top, and bottom right).

Douglas's presence, and later an article that appeared in *GQ* magazine documenting his involvement, successfully raised the profile of the endeavour and – as a consequence – the plight of the rhinos. The positive influence of the expedition was such that when the Tanzanian parliament called a vote intended to allow the reshaping of the national parks so that more licenses would be available for shooting wildlife, the Minister for Parks was disappointed – the result went against his expectations.

TWELVE

Fan of Science and Technology

THE NEW YORK ACADEMY OF SCIENCES

PRESENTED TO

Douglas Adams

IN RECOGNITION AND CERTIFICATION OF BEING ELECTED

AN ACTIVE MEMBER

OF THIS ACADEMY

FOUNDED 1817

June 1993

Cyril M. Harris

PRESIDENT AND CHAIRMAN OF THE BOARD

SECRETARY - TREASURER

A man fascinated by technology, Douglas Adams was both an advocate for conservation and a forward-thinking innovator, whose ideas, such as they might pop up in his writing, articles and speeches, were often arguably ahead of their time. This chapter collects some of the evidence for his inventive talents.

SCIENCE AND CHAOS THEORY

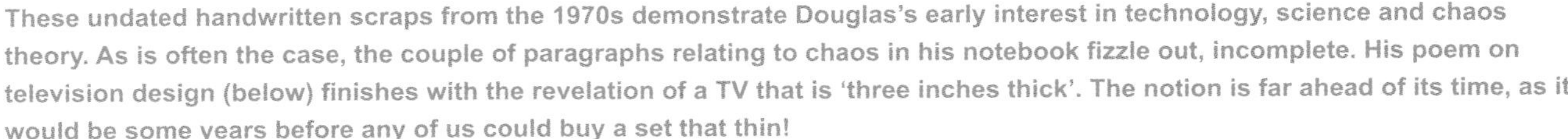

These undated handwritten scraps from the 1970s demonstrate Douglas's early interest in technology, science and chaos theory. As is often the case, the couple of paragraphs relating to chaos in his notebook fizzle out, incomplete. His poem on television design (below) finishes with the revelation of a TV that is 'three inches thick'. The notion is far ahead of its time, as it would be some years before any of us could buy a set that thin!

The man who designed television sets

I have a secret inside me
Cleverly rolled up in a tight little ball
Screwed packaged and tight
And I like to roll it when no one is looking.

Whenever I pass a television shop
(And I pass a television shop at every opportunity)
I take note of how the people stop to watch
The televisions in the window.
I peer over their shoulders awkwardly as if in ignorance
But they don't know my tight rolled ball, I think
They don't know that those televisions at which they are
So anxiously peering
To them the latest and most beautiful
To me are
Pretty poor stuff.
I design televisions.
My latest one is three inches thick.

The short transcript below is from a fragment ripped from a handwritten couple of paragraphs in Douglas's notebook. It gives his take on how much humankind has to learn in order to make sense of the world.

We live in a simple chaos – a chaos caused by our inability to understand the extreme, baffling simplicity of the rules by which our universe is governed, a simplicity so fundamental that it becomes blurred beneath the complexity of its own efforts.

Early man had an awful lot to learn, an awful lot. Everything. However, there were certain things that were self-evidently true – they didn't require any argument or analysis.

This undated piece is post-1998, as it mentions *Starship Titanic* as a 'CDDB of the world'. The gag towards the end (about *Being Douglas Adams*) suggests 1999 or 2000, after the movie *Being John Malkovich*. Douglas was already wondering how the internet would affect developments in the CD-Rom industry, in which he was working. H2G2 was the eventual website (very like a prototype for Wikipedia) developed at The Digital Village, the company he set up with like-minded friends in 1996.

Let's look a long way out for a moment.

What I would like to feel we have built, fifty or a hundred or two hundred years from now, is a soft model of the world. The Dataside of the world – for those who remember back to the early days of Starship Titanic. A database of the world. A cddb of the world. So that every object in the real world has its counterpart in the soft world. Except that every object in the soft world has a wealth of information attached to it – what it is, how it works, what its history is, what people think of it, what their experience of it is, and the myriad ways in which it is connected to the billions of other objects in the soft world.

Devices we use as Guides will essentially be windows through which the hard world and the soft world – the matterside and the dataside – view each other and connect with each other.
In the real world the most potent and powerful connection between any two objects is physical proximity. In the soft world it can be any connection that anybody can imagine.

In the real world if you want to know what the view from the top of the Eiffel Tower looks like you have to go there.

In the soft world you can ask the Guide to show you what it looks like from the top of the Eiffel Tower. Maybe it can show you the view through a webcam there. Or maybe it can construct a VR view for you in real time based on everything it knows about everything that can currently be seen from the top of the Eiffel tower. First thing you see is a lot of virtual graffiti, some of it quite naughty, being French. You wave it away.

And as you look down at your virtual view you ask it how many of the cars you can see from your current vantage point are British. For a moment you think it's not working. Then you say, OK, how many of them are Peugeots – the view lights up with thousands of moving dots. OK – how many of the cars you can see currently have some Bach playing on their in-car stereos. A few dozen. Oh, there's one playing your favourite recording of the Schübler preludes. Do they have their flag up? Yes! She'll talk to you – but only because the only thing you'd asked about her was what she was listening to. Anything else and her flag would have been down for you. You chat for a bit about the music and quickly discover a tremendous rapport.

What about having dinner together? OK... but she has a gluten problem, which restricts where she can eat. And you like turbot. A couple of restaurants light up in the view. One of them looks great for a romantic tryst, lots of alcoves and dim lighting – but some of the people who've eaten there tonight have left notes saying that they're obviously understaffed in the kitchen tonight and the food has been coming out cold or reheated. The other place gets raves about the food, but it's a bit bright and noisy. You decide that good food is the thing to go for. Then you remember – damn! You're not actually in Paris, you're in New Delhi and got a bit carried away.

That's alright, says your new friend, I'm actually in Albuquerque. I'm a music squatter.

Meaning?

She just monitors the network for anybody who's looking for someone who's listening to that recording. The real occupant of the car had his flag down and wasn't talking to anybody, so she intercepted your query and really enjoyed talking to you. And now she's going out to dinner. Locally. Bye.

You track which restaurant she's going to and send a Margarita to her table to say thanks. But she's annoyed that you tracked her and turns connection off. Oh well, you go back to your day job, erecting advertising hoardings on Mars. Soft Mars, that is, which has recently been added to the Soft Solar System. It was quite an expensive project because you can't rely on millions of people feeding back millions of snippets of information every day, which is what keeps the Soft Earth going so well.

The mapping data from Mars has been acquired the expensive way, which means that if you want to visit Soft Mars – which is either a fully immersive environment at your local Trumbullarama, or a lower res one on your own headset, you can either pay for it and see it in its pristine state, or explore it for free and put up with all the billboards advertising new movies, such as 'Being Douglas Adams' about people who pay for the experience of banging their heads on doors a lot.

2/20/01 GSM Page 1

GSM

- I'm very glad to back in Europe for a few days. I currently live in a rather technologically backward part of the world called California.
- We've hardly got any electricity there, let alone decent cellphone coverage.
- When we first moved there a couple of years ago we were in a rented house. The third time we called out the washing machine service man he sat us down and said "There's something you need to understand. I can tell you're from Europe, and things work differently there. There, you have washing machines to wash the dishes for you. Here in America, you have to wash the dishes for the dishwasher."
- We live in Santa Barbara, ~~which is~~ a beautiful little town on the 101 Freeway, which is one of the main thoroughfares between Los Angeles and San Francisco. If you drive up and down the 101 you get a very intermittent signal. If you have a GSM phone, one of the areas you definitely won't get a signal is within a one mile radius of our house.
- At Christmas we went to Fiji. We had a wonderful time. Scuba diving. One day we rented a boat and sped across the ocean to the island where they filmed the movie Cast Away. It's called Mondriki, and it is the perfect tropical desert island. Sun. White sand. An infinite surround of blue ocean. A single rocky hill. A clump of palm trees. And perfect cellphone reception.
  - Why was there perfect cellphone reception? Apparently it was in Tom Hanks's contract that there had to be.
  - Now what we want to do is try to persuade Tom Hanks to do a road movie on the 101.
- But at least in California we have free local calls and we do have DSL and it actually works. So it's fair to say that in California we're so backwards in rolling out communications technology that the only thing we're actually ahead of is British Telecom.
- You remember when a few months ago, BT started to make some claims based on some old patents that appeared to cover hypertext links, which are the building blocks of the world wide web.
  - The thing that astonished me was that they could claim to have invented the web without even a hint of embarrassment about having not done a damn thing about it.
- Cellphones are technology. And technology, as Danny Hillis pointed out, is our word for stuff that doesn't work yet.
- How do we know it's technology?
- Typically it will come in a box with a registration card, the way that – for instance – a bunch of flowers doesn't.

Increasingly, over the years Douglas was called upon to give talks at tech conferences, with sometimes quite influential names in the audience. On this and over the following pages are his speech notes, in full, for such an event – the Global System for Mobile Communications (GSM) convention in February 2001, in Cannes, France.

- It probably comes with a sheaf of brightly coloured leaflets for you to give to the garbage man who in turn buries it in the ground for future generations to grow things in.
- It will also come with a manual, the way that, for instance, a teacup doesn't, or a chair doesn't.
    - Unless it's one of those office chair with levers and locks and tension springs all over it. Like most things designed to enhance your productivity, playing with it all day is much more fun than actually working.
- If it's a cellphone, one of the things your manual will tell you about is how to spend 17 hours straight programming your telephone numbers into it with a matchstick. This despite the fact that you already did this with the last cellphone you bought only six months ago. And despite the fact that what both of these things are is communications devices. And despite the fact that you've already got all your names or phone numbers on your computer which is also, guess what, a communications device.
- Yes, you can make them all communicate with each other. Provided you kept the little cable. And provided the cable fits both of your cellphones. And provided the software runs on your computer. And provided you kept the manual and have got nothing better to do with your life than read it.
    - And provided, of course, that the reason you're replacing your old cellphone is not that you've lost the damn thing.
- Another thing technology comes with is a power adapter. Now electricity is a fairly commonplace item these days, unless you live in California, but it comes in more flavours than Haagen-Dazs, Baskin Robbins and the iMac put together.
    - And one adapter will not fit another device. We've all got drawers full of little orphaned black bricks.
- And the in-car handsfree kit for one cellphone will certainly not fit another one either. Not even a later model from the same manufacturer.
- I understand that there is an economic imperative behind this - you don't make money on the phones, but you can make money on the accessories. But the result is that we mostly don't bother with the handsfree kits any more. We just career down the highway with the phone clamped to our ear, peering at the tiny screen, and prodding one-handedly at the buttons. Ah, so that's why evolution gave us opposable thumbs.
- On the 101 people race from one pool of reception and another and then drive as slowly as they can while they're in one, weaving around the road trying to operate their phones with their thumbs.
- So this is a sales strategy that is not merely inconveniencing its customers, it's actually killing them off.

- But's it odd how patient we are with this stuff, as if we actually expect it to be clunky and awkward, which is why people put up with Microsoft Windows.
- We invent and invent and invent.
- Sometimes we get things right, more often we get things wrong and have to try again.
- Sometimes we can't help but try again even when we've already got it right once.
  - The bathroom tap for instance. Once upon a time this was a very simple device. Now you go into the bathroom in an airport or hotel and you approach the washbowl with caution. Do you turn the water on or do you push something? With your hand or your foot? Is it meant to come on automatically? Do you have to wave at it? And when you're finished, who's responsible for turning it off? You or it? Will it know? Or do you have to find somebody?
- Of course the fact that we continue to tinker with stuff that already works perfectly well echoes our own nature as evolved beings. Every act of conception is a new throw of the dice, a unique new mix of genes, some mixes more successful than others. It's the key to our adaptability. Anything that really is an improvement will tend to proliferate, and we wouldn't have got to it if we hadn't kept reshuffing and making mistakes with stuff that already seemed to be working.
  - There's a new generation of smart office chair beginning to arrive which makes a virtue of doing away with all the knobs and levers. All the springing and bracing we've learned about is still there, but it adjusts to your posture and movement automically without you having to tell it how to.
  - Here's a prediction for you. When we have software that works like that, the world will truly be a better and happier place.
- Many years ago I invented a thing called The Hitchhiker's Guide to the Galaxy. I never meant to be predictive science fiction writer in the mode of, say, Arthur C Clarke. My reason for inventing it was purely one of narrative necessity, which is that I had lots of extra bits of story that I didn't know what to do with. I didn't know anything at all about technology in those days, and didn't think twice about any of the issues. So I just made it a bit like things I was already familiar with. It was a bit like a pocket calculator, a bit like a TV remote. It had a little window at the top and lots and lots of little buttons on the front. And if you wanted to know about anything you had to look it up in an index, find the right number, tap it in and wait for the entry to come up on the tiny screen. I'd invented WAP! But as I say, I didn't know anything about technology. I didn't know about Xerox Parc, I didn't know about the dynabook, I didn't know about user interfaces. That's my excuse. What's yours?
- Of course, whenever we invent something new, we always base it on something we're familiar with.

- That's why the first movies were just filmed plays, proscenium arches and all.
- That's why we originally thought that a phone is something that would be used to alert you that that someone was bringing round a telegram.
  - Much the same way we now phone someone to tell them we've sent them an email.
- That's why first designed computers as a kind of super adding machine with a long feature list.
- Then as a typewriter with a long feature list.
- Then as a television with a typewriter sat in front of it.
- Now, with the coming of the world wide web, we've reinvented the computer as a kind of giant brochure.
- The computer is none of these things, but they're all things we're already familiar with, and we model them in the computer in order to make the computer usable.
- The mistake we make, of course, is to build in the limitations of the thing we're modelling along with its usefulness. That's why a word processor models the process of typing and doesn't model the process of *writing,* which is a very different thing.
- We've all had the experience of going into a shop and saying "That's nice. Have you got it in blue?" to which the answer is 'no'. End of story. Nobody at the other end of the retail chain ever discovers that you - and who knows how many other people - wanted it in blue. The exact same thing happens on websites. If you come looking for something they haven't got there is a null transaction. I wanted this movie on DVD but it's only on VHS. I wanted these jeans in a 36in leg and you only go up to 34. Nothing happens. But the easiest thing in the world would be to redesign the software so that it made a record of what it was the customer actually came looking for. The reason we don't think to do that is that there was no easy way of doing it in bricks and mortar shops, and bricks and mortar shops is still the model we're working from.
- So the new thing we've modelled in the computer is the telephone. And it's got a long feature list. Lots of extra bits that we've gradually tacked on, most of which are buried deep in menus that the average user never even finds. Same as Microsoft Word. Did you know that over half the features that Microsoft Word users ask for are already there in the program? You just can't find them, or if you can they're too much bother to use.
- So if the computer isn't a typewriter or a television or a telephone or any of these other things we've modelled in it, what actually is it?
- Well, obviously, it's a modelling device.

- We can model in it anything we care to imagine. And since it's also a communication device, the possibilities are endless. Any of your modelling devices can communicate with any of your other modelling devices and create more powerful and more complex models. Notice, that's complex, not complicated. An eye is complex. A digital camera with its boxful of manuals and cables and software installers, is complicated.
- So what should we model in our computers?
- Well, one thing it would good to get some kind of handle on is the *world*, so let's model that.
- It's a big job, but then there are a lot of us, and a lot of computers. Many more than Thomas Watson ever imagined. You may remembered that he it was who, as the head of IBM commissioned a study to find out how many computers the world would actually need. The answer came back six, and Watson was determined that IBM would build them all.
  - That was back in the old top down, Big Brother view of the world. What we failed to foresee was that the world would not be dominated by one or a few giant computers sitting at the top of the hierarchy, but rather it would be *informed* by millions and millions of tiny little brothers and sisters and cousins, all down at the bottom of the hierarchy, where the information is. And that as a result we might gradually not even need a hierarchy.
- So let me say again - there are a lot of us and a lot of computers, and they are all handling information all the time, and could handle a very great deal more if we had the wit to let them.
- Let me give you an example. There are an enormous number of CDs in the world. Creating an entire discography of every CD ever recorded would be a daunting task. But a rather bright company called CDDB.com, now gracenote.com, figured out that since people frequently put cd's into their computers' cd rom drives and since computers are often connected to the internet it would be possible to create such a discography automatically. Any time that any one person happened to get their hands on an absolutely brand new recording which wasn't in the discography yet, all they had to do was spend two minutes typing up the track listing, and nobody would ever have to do it again. And if they didn't do it, someone else would.
- It only needed one person to do it. And then anybody who put a copy of that CD into their CD-rom drive anywhere in the world would be immediately presented with that track listing. It doesn't originate from the CD itself, because the CD format was specified before we thought of adding digital information to the tracks. It has come from the shared network which has recognised the CD from the exact number of bytes on it, which, like a fingerprint, is unique. So gracenote.com has a comprehensive discography of every CD recording in the world which is self-updating.

- That's just CDs.
- Imagine if every piece of information we ever generated about the world that passed through a computer, whether it's
  - a restaurant typing up its menu for the evening, whether it's
  - a shop maintaining its stock list, whether it's
  - a car noticing what speed it's going, how much petrol it's got left and where the nearest service stations are and what prices they are charging, or whether it's
  - someone measuring the wingspan of an african swallow, or
  - writing down where and when their grandmother was born, or whether it's
  - someone taking a digital photo from the top of the Great Pyramid, or just
  - of a flower that's bloomed early this year.
  - Or late. Or the settings on your thermostat and when it turned on or off.
  - Or if every time you took your child's temperature the network remembered.
  - Imagine all of that gradually creating a shared software model of the world. Just imagine.
- The one thing I did get right when I came up with The Hitchhiker's Guide to the Galaxy was that it would know where you were and would come up with information appropriately. And that, of course, is the thing that makes the crucial difference to everything in that list above. If every piece of information knew the when of itself and the where of itself, so that the virtual world we created fitted over the real world like an invisible glove.
- And these devices, that we currently think of as telephones or PDAs, would be the devices that made that invisible world visible, the things which both generate the model and make it appear to us. They become windows from the real world into the virtual world, which is everywhere around us.
- Of course, they won't be like this. These are just telephones with bits added on. These will disappear. The next big wave of technology that will hit us in a very few years is nanotechnology, and it's coming a lot faster than people realise. The difference will be that instead of making computers out of stuff, we will make stuff out of computers. We will be making dumb matter smart. Instead of little screens, our displays will be sheets of paper, windows, mirrors, pools of water anything nearby that can hold an image. Sound will radiate at us from any live surface.

many of you are saying 'Yes, cellphones are all very well, but all this stuff is g
bit far?'
I've come up with a set of rules to describe this phenomenon.

- How many people here find this idea either horrifying or at least very disturbing? How many of you are saying 'Yes, cellphones are all very well, but all this stuff is going a bit far?'
- I've come up with a set of rules to describe this phenomenon.
  - It comes from watching my six year old daughter grow up in a world of email, cell-phones and DVDs and all those things that frighten my mother.
    - Rule 1 - Anything that's in the world when you're born is normal and ordinary and just a part of the way the world works.
    - Rule 2 - Anything that's invented between when you're fifteen and thirty-five is new and exciting and world changing and you can probably get a career in it.
    - Rule 3 - Anything that's invented after you're thirty-five is against the natural order of things.
- Let me quote a friend of mine, the molecular engineer Brosl Hasslacher. He says "The Romans believed that there were little gods in local things like fountains, trees, that's basically what the world will look like soon because there will seem to be little gods in there but its basically sets of computers lying around in paint or in plastics, but there will be enlarged functional spaces attached to them, paint won't be paint it will be listening, it will be recording, it can interactive. That's a very confusing world, but one of the things we learn about confusing worlds is that young people get used to them very quickly."
- OK, let's come down to earth for a moment, because all this stuff I'm describing is still months and months away.
- What can we do now?
- Well, we should remember that these are communication devices. Let them be smart about what's around them and let them find ways of communicating with them. No cables. No configuration. Let's see how far Bluetooth can take us. Let phones communicate easily with computers, with televisions, with radios - oh and particularly with cars. I want my car radio to become a hands free phone device by the mere action of carrying my phone into the car. That way I can hope to get to Los Angeles without having to drive through the mangled wreckage of other phone users.
- And we can start to build this database that is a model of the world. Insert ←
- This is an idea I've been pursuing for a while, and since it grew out of The Hitchhiker's Guide to the Galaxy I called it h2g2 and started it out as a community website, a community, that is, of voluntary researchers starting to build the very guide that they would then be able to use. A collaboratively built guide, just as gracenote.com is a collaboratively built CD database. It's in its infancy, though it has already built up

Hitchhiker's Guide to the Galaxy I called it h2g2 and started it out as a commu
website, a community, that is, of voluntary researchers starting to build the ver
that they would then be able to use. A collaboratively built guide, just as gracen
is a collaboratively built CD database. It's in its infancy, though it has already b

a hugely enthusiastic group of researchers pouring stuff into it. And before we could even get more than a couple of steps along the way of building the kind of infrastructure we needed to make the thing start to self-organise and self-propagate, guess what, like every other website on the planet we ran out of resources. Or money, as we call it.

- However, I am very pleased to announce that as of today it is to rise reborn. The rights to the h2g2 website have been acquired by a bunch of guys you may have heard of, called the BBC, which to me seems highly appropriate since that's where Hitchhiker was first born. I'm very hopeful that with the BBC driving it we can begin to turn it into the most extraordinary resource. Please go and look at it. If you don't like it, add something to it to make it better. You can't do that to the Nine o'clock News.
- I hope that one day it can begin to form the basis of something which brings my original vision of The Hitchhiker's Guide to the Galaxy as a mobile, personal, collaborative guide to real life.
- Meanwhile, I'd be happy just to get cellphone reception around my house.

1

Not because we expect to get all of it of course, but because we can hope to close the gap considerably and sell many more books.

Eighty five or 90% of what a reader pays to read what an author has written does not go to the author who wrote it.
This 85% is of intense interest to authors.
So there's an awful lot of dead wood in there, quite literally, that we can – to everybody's profit get rid of by some form of electronic distribution,

How will elec. distribution change the way that the book as we know it is distributed, and how will it change the very nature of the book. ~~And~~

How will the author get paid?

There have been many attempts at electronic books in the past, and they've all failed pretty much because the technology hasn't been there.
My own experience – Voyager expanded books.

Lot of resistance to the idea of ebooks from the public. Particularly all those people who 10 years ago said they couldn't see any point in typing on a computer.
I believe this resistance will gradually disappear as the electronic book itself improves and becomes smaller, lighter, simpler, cheaper, in other words, more like a book.
One other crucially important area in which it must improve radically and I think this is the key one. A book, typically, has a resolution

SMYTHSON OF BOND STREET

These three pages of notes are Douglas's thoughts on the future possibilities of electronic books and publishing. Dating from the late 1990s, the musings are well ahead of Kindles and other ebooks. Douglas, having years earlier predicted this industry with *The Hitchhiker's Guide* itself, would sadly not live to see the concepts actually realized in the kinds of devices we all now take so much for granted. The notes are transcribed over the page.

2

of between 600 and 2400 dpi. A computer screen has about 74. It's not comfortable to read. When I've finished a day's work on the computer I print the stuff out and go and sit ~~on~~ the sofa to read it.

When resolution improves, that, coupled with the fact ~~that~~ the screen is back-lit will, I believe change a lot of attitudes very quickly.

People say they love the feel of a book the smell of a book. This may be true, but I'm sure a lot of people said that about the horse when the motorcar was first invented. We have managed to change our allegiance.

I said that the device has got to become more like a book, and this is important.

Alan Kay - electric motors.

The thing will be ~~the d~~ a descendant of the book, not of the computer.

But we don't need to carry this too far. I'm not sure that we need to model virtual page turning in an electronic book any more than ~~this~~ you needed to put reins and stirrups into a car.

Essentially the book, as we know it is approximately 100,000 words of text ~~organised~~ ~~linearly~~ that tell a story with ~~with a~~ ~~beginning~~, a beginning, a middle and an end, and the device we read it from has just got to offer us the cleanest simplest access to that material. It can also let us

SMYTHSON OF BOND STREET

do some things that books don't. Anyone who spends much time on computer has experienced that frustration when reading a book when you want to remind yourself who a character is or what they last said or did and it takes you ages to track it down. ~~the~~ If you're a computer user you expect to be able to do a search for it. And if you're doing research you may want to be able to search across several related books. In the digital domain the boundaries between entities tend to disappear. It's like rivers flowing into an ocean, You still get currents but you don't get river banks anymore.

So the devices must be very simple. They are not computers, they are books which have computers in them. They should also be powerful though. ~~They~~ They need to be able to communicate. I imagine early models will need to dock to computers, but to my mind the real electronic book will be a standalone device which connects wirelessly to the net. ~~The net is the thing which changes everything~~.

The net is the thing which changes everything.

~~Au~~thors are used to feedback loops which are so long as to be almost meaningless.

Kurt Vonnegut. , immediacy.

Eighty five or 90% of what a reader pays to read what an author has written does not go to the author who wrote it.

This 85% is of intense interest to authors. So there's an awful lot of dead wood in there, quite literally, that we can – to everybody's profit get rid of by some form of electronic distribution.

(Not because we expect to get all of it, of course, but because we can hope to close the gap considerably and sell many more books.)

How will elec. distribution change the way that the book as we know it is distributed, and how will it change the very nature of the book.

How will the author get paid?

There have been many attempts at electronic books in the past, and they all failed pretty much because the technology hadn't been there.

My own experience – Voyager expanded books

Lots of the resistance to the idea of ebooks from the public. Particularly all those people who 10 years ago said they couldn't see any point in typing on a computer.

I believe this resistance will gradually disappear as the electronic book itself improves and becomes smaller, lighter, simpler, cheaper, in other words more like a book.

One other crucially important area in which it must improve radically and I think this is the key one. A book, typically, has a resolution of between 600 and 2400 dpi. A computer screen has about 74. It's not comfortable to read. When I've finished a day's work on the computer I print the stuff out and go and sit on the sofa to read it.

When resolution improves, that coupled with the fact that the screen is backlit, will, I believe change a lot of attitudes very quickly.

People say they love the feel of a book *[and]* the smell of a book. This may be true, but I am sure a lot people said that about the horse when the motorcar was first invented. We have managed to change our allegiance.

I said that the device had got to become more like a book, and this is important.

Alan Kay, electric motors

The thing will be the descendent of the book, not of the computer.

But we don't need to carry this too far. I'm not sure that we need to model virtual page turning in an electronic book any more than you needed to put reins and stirrups into a car.

Essentially the book, as we know it is approximately 100,000 words of text that tell a story with a beginning, a middle and an end and the device we read it from has just got to offer us the cleanest, simplest access to that material. It can also let us do some things that books don't. Anyone who spends much time on computers has experienced that frustration when reading a book. When you want to remind yourself who a character is or what they last said or did and it takes you ages to track it down. It you're a computer user you expect to be able to do a search for it. And if you're doing research you may want to be able to search across several related books. In the digital domain the boundaries between entities tend to disappear. It's like rivers flowing into an ocean, you still get currents but you don't get river banks anymore.

I'm not sure that we need to model virtual page turning in an electronic book any more than you needed to put reins and stirrups into a car.

So the device must be very simple. They are not computers, they are books which have computers in them. They should also be powerful though. They need to be able to communicate, I imagine early models will need to dock to computers, but to my mind the real electronic book will be a standalone device which connects wirelessly to the net.

The net is the thing which changes everything.

Authors are used to feedback loops which are so long as to be almost meaningless

Kurt Vonnegut, immediacy…

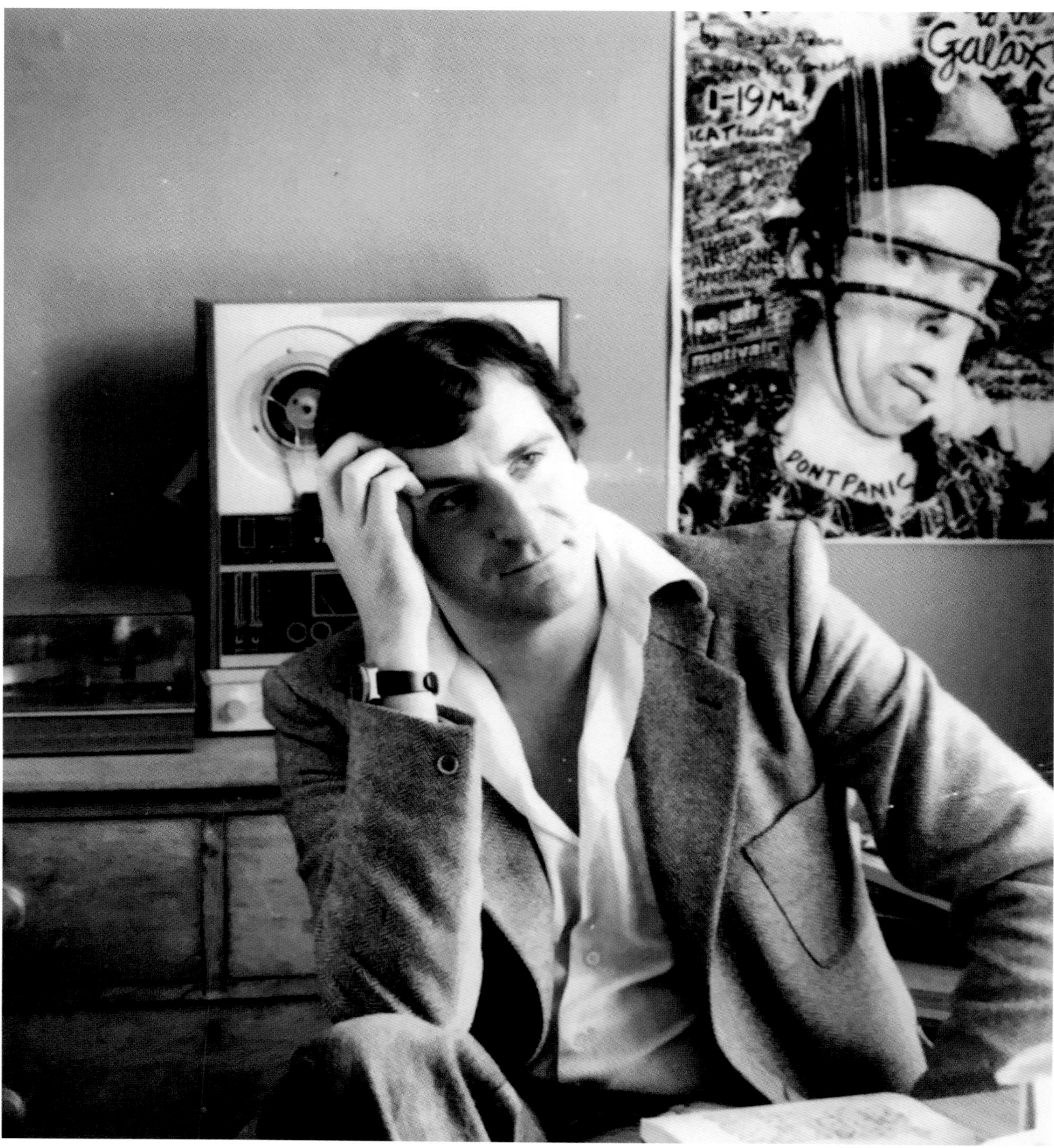

Once he had the money, Douglas was known to indulge his passion for high-end tech. In late 1985, he told Susie Corfield of *The Sunday Telegraph Magazine* that he owned a Bang & Olufsen television and a Panasonic video recorder, although he hardly ever watched TV and was far more interested in audio equipment – he had a Linn Sondek turntable, a Naim amplifier, Linn Isobarik speakers, a Nakamichi tape deck and a Yamaha compact disc player. In his study, he had a Nad amplifier and tuner, Boston acoustic speakers and a Mission compact disc player. This photograph, taken by Mark Gerson in 1979, shows Douglas seated in front of audio equipment that, at the time, would have been state of the art as far as Douglas's budget allowed. Gerson's letter to Douglas after the photoshoot, and further images on the contact sheet are reproduced on the opposite page.

24 Cavendish Avenue
St John's Wood
London NW8 9JE
telephone 01-286 5894

Mark Gerson
Photographer
FIIP

Oct. 12th. 1979.

Douglas Adams,
Highbury New Park.

Dear Doug,
It was very pleasant photograhing you, the colour looked particularly good and was collected by PENTHOUSE messenger yesterday, a duplicate of the b/w contact proof sheet is with Jacqui Graham at PAN BOOKS.

Please keep this contact sheet with my compliments, if any magazine contacts you direct and wishes a photograph in a hurry, they can always get in touch with me, if you so desire.

Best regards,

Sincerely,

Mark Gerson, FIIP.

Reg. office
Mark Gerson Photography Ltd
27, John Street, London, WC
Reg. No 626 230

This page of early notes relates to the infamously difficult interactive fiction game of *The Hitchhiker's Guide* by Infocom. They were discovered among other notes mostly concerning work on the movie script. Douglas's involvement in the development of the game was fairly comprehensive – In 1985, he said he designed the 'shape and logic... and wrote the text' in collaboration with an 'extremely talented' game designer called Steve Meretzky.

The goal is to be Happy – but what is happiness.

If you don't play you win instantly

Have to discover the goal – goal is to discover goal.

If you become immortal you lose the game

Insult you in alphabetical order

Traal – fight the Beast

Improbability Drive

PGGB – you get drunk

Cause and effect goes wrong.

Marvin.

Cocktail Party.

Database – Guide.

Time Travel.

Cheating is part of game – extra points.

Towels – problem solving.

/ Bureaucracy – wrong address.

1

Bureaucracy

At the beginning you are feeling extremely chipper. You've just moved into a new house. It's a bit of a mess at the moment, everything's lying around in boxes, but it's a really nice house, which you are able to afford because you've got a new job at double your previous salary, and apart from some silly nonsense from the bank, everything is terrific. That will sort itself out, no doubt. You sent them your change of address card weeks ago. Best of all, you've got a couple of weeks holiday before you start, and your new employers have been very nice to you and given you a return plane ticket to Paris to enjoy yourself for a while.

First problem is the phone. It keeps ringing and you suppose you ought to answer it. Getting to it amongst all your boxes is a problem.

Also in your boxes are various other things you are going to want in the next few days, and finding them without damaging them is going to be a problem. There is your Boysenberry computer, for a start, with its built-in programming language that even an idiot could use, and probably only an idiot would want to. There are all kinds of programs for it which you have to find amongst your boxes. You thought, when you got a computer that it would save you from the usual mess you get yourself into which was having piles and piles of unidentified pieces of paper hanging around. Now you find that you have piles and piles of unidentified floppy disks lying around.

There are check-book balancing programs, loan amortising, eclipse predictors, recipe programs, communication programs, spreadsheets, etc., etc.

A delivery man arrives at the door with something with (what - more programs? A stereo?) something. You have no recollection of ordering it. It turns out that there is someone else with the same name as you living in the street. The delivery man says that things are always getting misaddressed around here, drives him batty.

You are able to take delivery of thing if you like, but you would have to pay by credit card. (He prompts you that he accepts US Excess or Beezer.

You discover that your US Excess card is past its expiry date. You are close to your credit limit on your Beezer card, but can just afford to buy this thing, if you want it.

There were plans for a *Hitchhiker 2*, but a new game called *Bureaucracy* was clearly more urgent in Douglas's mind and there was a reason for that. It was based on a recent real-life experience he'd had while buying his new apartment in Islington. Frustrated with his own bank failing to recognize the new address they were helping him to purchase, and despite his sending of two change of address cards, they kept replying to his former address. After a final stiff complaint, the bank replied in writing, promising to get it right in future – but guess where they sent the letter?

Dear Douglas

NEIL GAIMAN

Dear Douglas

I remember the day I learned you were dead.

I was in Wisconsin being interviewed on the phone by a journalist in Hong Kong, and something that was obviously silly clickbait about Douglas Adams dying went across my computer screen. I snorted, unimpressed. I clicked on the link. I found myself staring at a BBC news screen, and saw the news.

'Are you all right?' said the journalist in Hong Kong.

'Douglas Adams is dead.'

'Oh yes,' he said. 'It's been on the news here all day. Did you know him?'

'Yes,' I said. Of course I knew you. We carried on with the interview, and I don't know what else was said. The journalist got back in touch several weeks later to say that there wasn't anything coherent or at least usable on the tape after I learned that you were dead, and would I mind doing the whole interview again?

When we die, we become whole things, and all the times of our life become one. I remembered the last time I saw you, in 1998, when you were in Minneapolis touring with *Starship Titanic* the game, and I remembered it beside the first time I saw you, when you opened the door to me to your flat in Upper Street, Islington, in 1983.

You were 30 and I was 22. You had just returned from Hollywood, where you had had a miserable time trying to make the *Hitchhiker's Guide to the Galaxy* movie. You were welcoming and kind and very funny. You gave me a book of yours I didn't have and you signed it for me. You were tall, and slightly awkward. You explained that only people who don't know where their towels are would have come up with knowing where your towel is as an attribute of cool. You were so many things, and none of them were ever cool.

I kept interviewing you over the next few years, and running into you, and eventually I wrote a whole book about you. (You were bemused but kind about helping me with that. And you said nice things about the eventual book, too, even if you had me write your blurb for it.)

I wish I could get to our emails. I was on Compuserve back then, and our correspondence is long-lost. I loved being able to help, when you'd ask me things; I was at my happiest (because you asked) and my saddest (because I could not do it) back then when you wrote to ask if I would write the radio adaptation of *Life, the Universe and Everything.* There was no time.

(I'm so glad I said no. The job went instead to Dirk Maggs, who made magic with it, and carried on on the life course that meant that he and I would eventually work together making radio dramas.)

You were unique. Which is true of all of us, of course, but it's also true that people come in types and patterns, and there was only ever one Douglas Adams. No one else I've ever encountered could elevate Not Writing to an art form as you could. No one else has seemed capable of being so cheerfully profoundly miserable. No one else has ever had your easy smile and crooked nose, nor the faint aura of embarrassment that surrounded you like a protective force field.

After you died people asked me about you. I told them that I didn't think that you had ever been a novelist, not really, despite having been an internationally best-selling novelist who had written a bunch of books which are now seen as classics.

I said I thought that perhaps what you were was something we don't even have a word for yet. A Futurologist, or an Explainer, perhaps. You were able to explain the world to itself in ways that the world won't forget. You could dramatise the plight of endangered species as easily (or at least, as astonishingly well, for nothing you did that involved writing was ever exactly easy) as you could explain to an analog race what it means to find yourself going digital. Your dreams and ideas, practical or impractical, were always the size of a planet, and you carried us along beside you.

We were lucky to have been here when you were writing. I wish you were still here. I want to know what you would say or think about the world. You'd just have turned seventy. That's not even that old, is it? Not any more.

I miss talking to you, miss strange emails and unexpected phone calls. I miss the whole phenomenon that was you.

From wherever I am to wherever you are,

Neil

Neil Gaiman first met Douglas, in 1983, as a 22-year-old journalist sent to interview him (above; Neil on the left and Douglas on the right, with the guitar). They became friends. Since then he has written award-winning, bestselling comics and books, including *The Sandman*, *American Gods*, *Neverwhere*, *Stardust* and (with Terry Pratchett) *Good Omens*.

THIRTEEN

Exploring the Digital World

The Secret Empire
The Colonisation of Space has already begun

THE DIGITAL VILLAGE

We just don't know about it yet...

created by

Douglas Adams

Strictly Private & Confidential
Controlled Distribution

Draft 1.0 19 April 1996

'I would have loved to have been a software designer... and work in computer systems. It sounds terribly dull, but actually it's dealing with information and how we shape information, and how we understand it, how we deal with it, what we mean by it – at the most fundamental level. I find it profoundly exciting.' – Douglas Adams

Central Productions Ltd
46 Charlotte Street
London
W1P 1LX

Telephone 071-637 4602
Telex 291721
Fax 071-580 7780

Home
081-567-0617

9 May 1991

Mr. Douglas Adams
22 Duncan Terrace
London N1

Dear Douglas

I just wanted to write and thank you very much for giving us so much of your time when we met a few weeks ago.

I have been thinking much about your cave man/antler mentality analogy. I have sent you a copy of the outline of our History of the World in 52 minutes idea, because it is about cave men and antlers although I had never articulated it like that.

It seems to me that once upon a time we did understand both our cave and the world that our cave looked out on. We sat and stared at the stars, heard the wind call and the animals cry and did not feel separate from them. Gradually we developed our antlers and one day they had become so sophisticated that they began to glow. As they glowed ever more brightly they began to shut out the natural light from outside the cave and we started to forget what was out there. We became experts on our cave and saw ourselves as its masters, painting it, living in it and all the while it grew smellier and smellier.

The question now is whether or not we have the nous to move the antlers outside the cave and use their power effectively to understand the world outside and regain a more fitting sense of proportion about our cave and ourselves.

Exploring that idea is the reason for wanting to make the history of the world in a single accessible story. As you can see from the brief synopsis the project should have a considerable interactive element, which is integral to what I see as a multi media project.

Registered Office: Central House, Broad Street, Birmingham B1 2JP. Registered in England and Wales, No. 2422952

Robbie Stamp, then a producer at Central TV in London, wrote to Douglas in May 1991, thanking him for a recent meeting (above). This meeting seems to have been thought-provoking enough for them to meet many times afterwards, forming a close friendship and a working relationship that culminated in the creation of a multimedia publishing company, The Digital Village (TDV). In the early days of the company, TDV meetings took place in the offices of Douglas's literary agent Ed Victor, who once said: 'Douglas believed that we were in the middle of, not a digital revolution but a digital evolution. He thought that the planet was evolving from an analogue to a digital planet.'

The project is a long term one. I would greatly appreciate the opportunity to talk to you about it.

Yours Sincerely

Robbie Stamp

Robbie Stamp
Producer Features Group.

This portrait photograph of Douglas has been hanging in Robbie Stamp's study at home for many years, a testament to and reminder of their firm friendship. The artwork (above, right) is the stylized logo for the 'h2g2' website (it remains the logo today), created at The Digital Village and designed by Jack Kriendler. Then, and even now, h2g2.com was a big deal – Robbie Stamp describes it as a 'plan for the "Earth edition" of the *Guide* – the thought that there was more to say than *Mostly Harmless*'.

DOUGLAS ADAMS

STARSHIP TITANIC

7/26/96

(a) the speech cen
the mouth

(b) the speech cen

i) the ears an
the mou

ii) the nose ar
the mo

iii) the eyes ar
the mo

(5) If all the pieces
the mouth wi

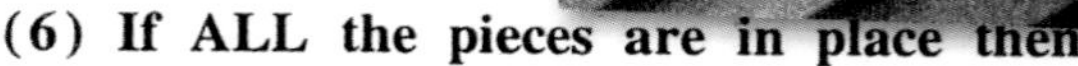

(6) If ALL the pieces are in place then
Titania wakes.

2. Titania Wakes.

All of the head gradually animates. The eyes and mouth move intelligently. The face comes to life.

An image slowly forms in front of the head. It is of the girl in the photo. She is a beautiful, shimmering hologram. Her head is bowed. Gradually she raises it. She looks at you and blinks.

Titania: Are you from the insurance company?

(you communicate with her via the chatterbot on the statue. We assume you say something to the effect of 'No').

She tells her story briefly. The ship was going to be scuttled. It had cost way too much to build. It was unfinished as it was. Massive fraud. The Manager and the Accountant arranged for the ship to be destroyed on its maiden voyage. But they had to shut down and completely disassemble the ship's intelligence (i.e. her) in order for that to happen. The Architect (who knew nothing of this, and was emotionally wrapped up in his creation) discovered

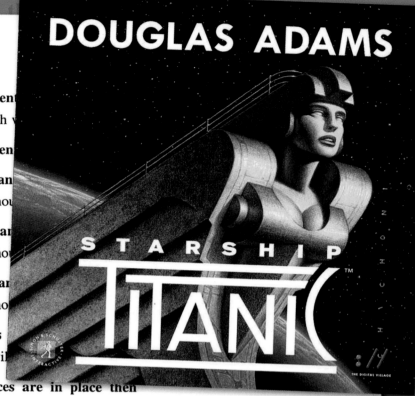

One of The Digital Village's earliest projects, and one of the two biggest projects the team undertook (the other being h2g2.com), was the computer game *Starship Titanic*. This is a sample from the draft script of the game.

what was going to happen. There must have been a terrible fight. But by that time Titania was disassembled and unconscious.

She does not know where the ship has been. She says that if you know the nightsky above your planet then you can navigate your way home. She will authorise the opening of the door to the Bridge. (When you go there, the inner door will open to you)

She believes that the Architect must have left the ship when it landed on Earth. If you will take the ship back to Earth so that she can look for him, then you can have the ship. Laws of salvage.

3. The Bridge

(you enter this from beside the Arboretum. The inner door will now be open)
The Bridge is very sweepy and beautiful, but surprisingly simple.
The Captain's chair faces out into the huge hemispherical window, through which you can see a starscape, very slowly shifting and swinging. It has a big beautiful curvy console in front of it, divided into three main areas.
There is one single (but very large) button in each area.
One reads 'Stop', one reads 'Go' and the third reads 'Cruise around a bit'
The chair is empty. There is a heavy ornament resting on the 'Cruise Around a bit' button, holding it down.
If you take the ornament off the 'Cruise Around' button, the starscape will settle to a steady (but slow) forward motion.
If you press the Stop button, motion will stop and sound will die away.

If you press the Go button a little panel within the button will light up saying 'Go where?'
At the same time there will be a beep and a light flashing from the navigator's chair which is is a little below and to one side of the Captain's chair.

The Navigator's chair is an altogether more elaborate business.

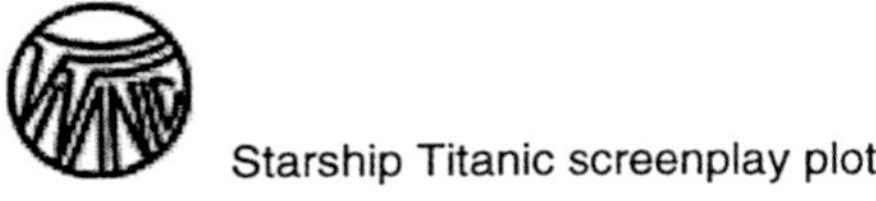

Starship Titanic

At the centre of the Galaxy, on the world of Blerontin, a vast civilisation of which we know nothing is preparing for an event of epic proportions, the launching of the greatest, most gorgeous, most technologically advanced starship ever built – the Starship Titanic.

Snapshot scenes: Bustle to get it ready. Technicians, crewmen, workmen. It is berthed in a giant gantry. We get a sense of enormous size, but no clear view - yet. Journalists hustling to get extra angles on the story. Reports, interviews, hurry, last minute checks.

Disasters have plagued the project, mostly financial. Building it has brought financial disaster on virtually everybody involved, including one entire planet, who have sent along a deputation to protest, but there is one thing that everybody is certain of – the Starship Titanic is the greatest technological achievement of this or any other age, and is utterly indestructible.

The interior of the ship is extraordinary. An Earthman seeing it would think it was a mixture of the tomb of Tutankhamen, the Chrysler Building and Venice. But anyone a little less provincial would recognise it as being the style of Leovinus, the galaxy's most renowned architect. He is an old man now, and the design of the Starship Titanic is the crowning achievement of his career.

Is it ready? Really ready?

'Yes,' says Leovinus the architect, with deep pride.

'Yes,' says Brobistigon the manager, smoothly.

'Yes,' says Scraliontis the accountant, with a sly look at Brobostigon, 'everything is ready...'

The Digital Village's computer game of *Starship Titanic* had a tie-in novel, written by Douglas's friend Terry Jones, formerly of Monty Python fame. There were also plans for a movie to follow later, and a draft storyline was found among the archives. These two pages were part of a much longer document that set out the screenplay plot.

The day before the launch.

Leovinus is being feted by the media, and he's enjoying it. It's only slightly spoilt by one particular journalist asking unpleasant, probing questions about alleged irregularities, but there's always one isn't there? Of course there have been problems along the way, but they have all been solved. No, there is no question of corners having been cut, no conspiracy, no one has been bought off. The ship is not about to fall out of the sky. Yes it's a terrible pity about the collapsed economy of Yassacca, but he's an artist not an economist. He gets quite heated. He is clearly passionate about his ship.

That night he goes to have one last look around it. On his way he bumps into the annoying journalist. He probes some more. He asks if it is true that the standard of workmanship has dropped since the building of the ship was moved from Yassacca to Blerontin to save on costs? Leovinus rises to the bait. He insists that the standard of workmanship is the highest possible, and says that he will personally show him round the ship to prove it.

A few workmen are here and there on the ship putting some finishing touches; they are just leaving.

The ship is magnificent, astonishing. From the centre of the ship two great canals lead off, one to the fore, one to the aft. These partly have the effect of cooling the engines, but are also elegant recreational facilities: gondolas ply their way up and down them. Between them lies a deep well, which forms the gigantic keel of the ship. The Staterooms, 1st Class, 2nd Class and SuperGalactic Traveller (or Riff Raff) class are ranged in corridors round the inside of the well. There are bars and restaurants, art galleries, music rooms...

But there *are* anomalies. With mounting alarm Leovinus begins to find more and more things that are not right. Unfinished things, cybersystems that are not working correctly, robots that are, frankly, colliding with doors. The whole of

The First Series:

The first series focusses on two people in particular, and we discover the magnitude of the enterprise through the eyes of each of them.

One is **Robert Darwin** (distant, co-lateral relation). We meet him right at the beginning of Episode One.

He is a computer games designer who owns his own company and is extremely wealthy. He is British, but has mostly worked in America. He now lives in a large and extraordinary hi-tech ranch on the coast of north Queensland, Australia. He loves the Great Barrier Reef, and modern communications means he can run his business from there. (This will be a major location)

He only happened into computer games by accident. He's not really interested in products as such, more in the ideas that give rise to them. He made his fortune not out of great ambition, but as an incidental by-product of his natural intelligence. For him, running something well is more interesting and less trouble than running it badly. A deep understanding of game theory helps. He's forty, good-looking and unmarried. He has an illegitimate daughter, now 19 and at Cambridge. They get on very well.

The second is **Jenny Tchao**, a Japanese-American journalist. She wants a story on Robert Darwin. There have been many, of course, but she wants something better. She will do anything to get close to him, even, it transpires, to the extent of sleeping with him. This is not merely professional ruthlessness, though. She finds him extremely attractive – which complicates things for her.

They both, in very different ways, discover about the Secret Empire – he at the beginning of the first series, she at about Episode 13.

Here's how:

Page 12

Secret Empire was a concept for an elaborate science-fiction TV series spanning thousands of years of human colonization of space. Douglas had ideas he wanted to explore in a similar fashion to author Isaac Asimov's *Foundation Trilogy*. These few pages from April 1996 represent the tip of an enormous project that might have resulted in a very expensive series. Brillstein Grey Entertainment of Hollywood had outlined the potential TV deal in a fax to Robbie Stamp at The Digital Village in June 1998. Sadly, though, the project never came to fruition.

:// THE DIGITAL VILLAGE

SERIES STRUCTURE:

The series is planned as a long running epic story of Earth' s colonisation of our Galaxy, starting today. Or, as we discover, starting twenty years ago and conducted in the utmost secrecy. Our actual story starts in the present day, at a moment of crisis in the project.

Basic outlines have been created for four seasons of The Secret Empire, with ideas for the fifth season under consideration.

Each season will consist of 22 episodes, each to fill an hour slot – except for the first episode of each season, which will be a feature length episode. This will move the time frame of the story forward one or more centuries. However a plot device which is central to the series concept will ensure that we continue to tell the developing story of a central core of characters, with whom the audience can continue to engage from one series to another.

The movie length establishing episode will introduce the new environment which the characters inhabit, providing appropriate and consistent scientific backgrounds. If the The Secret Empire is successful, the establishing episode will become a significant event in its own right as viewers wait to see what has happened to their favourite characters and what stage humankind's colonisation of space has reached. This approach will allow the writers to focus on story lines within a clearly defined "world" with its own clearly defined set of rules.

Each establishing episode will be set on or around New Year's Eve, in 1999, 2099, 2299, 2599......

Within each series, each episode will tell a self-contained, stand-alone story, but will also form part of a continually developing narrative.

Typical stories will deal with

- explorers having adventures out at the edge of the Empire's expansion, discovering new worlds and facing unknown hazards.
- settlers trying to establish themselves on new worlds, dealing with the challenges of diverse and conflicting human and alien cultures, ecologies and physical environments
- the evolution of the human race in previously unimagined ways, through the proxies of its machines and ideas
- scientists and test pilots trying to break new technological, psychological and biological barriers.

Draft 1.0,
19 April 1996

Page 5

:// THE DIGITAL VILLAGE

- rising political tensions and eventually battles between newly established worlds.

In every case, the struggles and adventures of the pioneers will be overseen and intervened in by our cast of regular characters: there are seven of them, and their role is to manage the expansion of the human race throughout the galaxy. Their role is not so much to be leaders they are more like orchestrators, philosophers, games players. They manage with the lightest possible touch, working to engineer the smallest difference that makes a difference (the 'butterfly' effect). They are The **Difference Engineers**, and the relationship between them and the pioneers and settlers is like that between chess players and their pawns – except that the chess board is infinitely large and complex, and the opponent is the unknown future.

The group will consist of an Historian, a Mathematician, a Soldier, a Musician, an Evolutionary Biologist, a Journalist and a Games Theoretician

The ways in which they are able to intervene will develop from series to series as technologies, distances and their own physical natures change dramatically over time.

Hence each episode will be able to take as its theme an issue that may be historical, philosophical, technological, political, cultural or moral, but the actual story will usually be an adventure drama set in space or on one of the worlds colonised by the Empire.

Note on technology: There are very real ideas to be explored in the fields of machine intelligence, nanotechnology, game theory, evolutionary theory, complexity theory, virtual reality etc. It will be the aim of The Secret Empire stories to be as literate as possible in these areas, so that as the series develops and the technologies involved become more and more fantastic, they will nevertheless be built onto a strong logical structure.

SERIES ONE

Episode I (Movie Opener): The **Exmundia** project is now twenty years old. Our ships and bases are now throughout the solar system, but the project is plagued with problems and disasters. How will it survive? A remarkable man is sought to turn it around: Robert Darwin. Like Yul Brynner in the Magnificent Seven, he in turn chooses and assembles the strange and eclectic group of talents he thinks, he will need – and one he thinks he probably should have done without.

On New Year's Eve, 1999, a day which mankind spends in an orgy of fear, superstition and exhilaration, he finds himself standing on the moon watching the Earth rise. This is the millennium in which, ready or not, the human race will move out of its cradle.

Draft 1.0,
19 April 1996

Page 6

:// THE DIGITAL VILLAGE

Other–story ideas: The discovery of a startling new technology – Matter cannot travel faster than light but – it appears – information can. A pair of identical twins is discovered who seem, effectively, to have two halves of the same brain, and it doesn't matter how far separated they are from each other: communication between them is instantaneous. One of them is sent out to a construction action base in the outer reaches of the solar system over one light hour away, the other remains on Earth.

Between them they form a channel of instantaneous communication. Other twins with this ability are sought. However, it turns out to be putting an intolerable psychological strain on them and starts to drive them towards violent nervous breakdowns. Can the effect be understood and reproduced technologically before something terrible happens? Isn't it immoral to subject them to these pressures? But the benefits to humankind etc. ... ?

The spaceside twin is about to be brought home when an accident occurs to another spaceman. Can he be rescued in time? Saving him is utterly dependent on real-time communications with Earth. The twins become nearly psychotic but stick with it: the spaceman is saved and the effect is understood. It should be possible to reproduce it technologically... This leads over time to the development of a new type of secret commuter – people who live on Earth, live perfectly normal home lives, but who for eight hours a day work on the outer planets, and moons by telepresence.

The discovery that faster than light communications exist causes great arguments about another project: the colony ships. Colony ships are being built out in the vicinity of Jupiter, which will take large groups of colonists at speeds of around one tenth of the speed of light to other stars. They will take many decades, maybe centuries to arrive. The debate:

- Wouldn't it be better to wait till faster-than-light travel can be discovered rather than subject these people to such a journey? No, because faster than light travel will never be discovered. It is a physical impossibility.
- But faster than light communications was thought to be a physical impossibility, and now it is well understood .
- That's different!

So, two competing projects are in hand on the outer edges of the solar system: one is the building of the colony ships, based on the assumption that faster-than-light travel will never come about. The other is a project to break or circumvent the light barrier: a group of radical scientists creating technologies that are being flown by reckless daredevil test pilots amongst whom the mortality rate is desperately high.

Draft 1.0,
19 April 1996

Page 7

:// THE DIGITAL VILLAGE

The inherent contradictions between the two projects, let alone the gruesome loss of life, cause enormous, political tensions in **Exmundia**.

At last the slow colony ships are launched. Not long afterwards, the light barrier is successfully breached – but it's a terribly long way from being a technology that can be easily and safely applied. The faster than-lighters seem to have lost the argument by winning it.

Over time it becomes clear that most of the conflicts and struggles that occur out in the field are both embodied and resolved within the group of the **Difference Engineers**. Their continued existence seems to become more and more essential to the long term success of the project. As the end of the 21st century nears, the DE's are all well over a century old, but this process can't go on for ever something more radical needs to be done...

SERIES TWO

'**Episode I (Movie Opener):** The technology now exists, in experimental form, to map a human brain into a machine. If this can be done, then it will be possible for the minds of the **Difference Engineers** to persist forever.

But the implications of this are enormous. How on earth can a human and survive in a machine? And what about the original mind, still in its original body? The exact same person now exists in two different locations, though from the very first second of the experiment, of course, the two 'persons' will be diverging. (Of course, if the mind in the machine is copied to another machine, you then have yet a third person. What are the moral and philosophical problems of just doing a back-up?)

Robert Darwin, the leader of the **Difference Engineers**, volunteers to be the first guinea pig. His mind is copied into a machine. He wakes up inside it. The experience is terrifying. He calms down, he is kept artificially calm, but it's clear that something is terrible wrong and that he will quickly go mad if something isn't done. The problem is that 'mind' isn't an abstract thing. The mind evolved as an organ of the human body, wired to a specific set of receptors (eyes, ears, tongue etc. ...) with control over sensitive and responsive limbs. The world exists as a model in the mind, and information about that world flows interactively along physical nerve pathways. The mind in the machine has urgently to be given physical things to respond to and manipulate or it will collapse into madness.

No sooner than they manage to address some of these problems than appalling news arrives. The original person, Robert Darwin's original human form has been murdered. The only form in which he now exists is as this machine entity. Machine/Darwin is utterly devastated – and terrified for his own safety. Who would have murdered him and why? Will the murderer also

Draft 1.0,
19 April 1996

Page 8

THE MILLENNIUM STORY (WT)

The project has three components:

Part one:

Most of the television projects planned for the closing years of the 1990's, understandably focus on the history of the twentieth century (sixteenth century archive is thin on the ground). But the change to a new millennium also gives us a chance to reflect on the whole course of both the planet's and our own history.
The Millennium Story will therefore comprise 365, two minute films, to run through an entire year, spanning the course of history from planetary evolution, to the development of life on earth, and the emergence of humans; from the development of language and writing to the Internet: from the first human dwellings in caves to the Sky Line of Manhattan, from the sled pulled by humans to the Space Shuttle.

Each film would be a mixture of location filming, paintings, photographs, animation and computer graphics and a simple voice over.

The series would be divided into 28 themes with about thirteen films per theme. At the end of the year in which they were shown, the short films could be edited together and the producers would also therefore have created 28 half hour documentaries. Each theme could involve the work of world renowned graphic artists, animators, cinematographers and directors.

The films would also be turned into a book, CD ROMs and very importantly distributed on line via The Digital Village Web Site on the Internet.

Whatever the bandwidth situation, by the time these films are ready to be broadcast, downloading two minutes of video is manageable and as indicated above by The Digital Village Web Site. Indeed the site could provide further information, on line conferences with experts in the themed areas, more graphics etc. It could become *the * site to discuss issues relating to the Millennium - everything from the wilder excesses of millenarianism to serious philosophical and cultural debate. Indeed choosing the themes in the first place could be done as part of a promotional competition.

Little is known of this series concept, which once again suggests Douglas's fascination with human evolution and our relationship with technology. A series in short component pieces might not make for smooth-flowing longer segments, but Douglas's intention is clear. The Digital Village was certainly a fertile ground for letting his imagination run wild.

Producing short films in this way, gives broadcasters all over the world the maximum chance of being able to schedule all or at least a part of the series. The films would be easy to version for any broadcaster in the world as there will be no one screen host, only a voice over, the voice over would therefore simply need to be translated. The ease of re versioning should lead to sales to many broadcasters.

As the films are already carefully "themed" it will be relatively easy to reversion them into the 28 half hour documentaries, which are then available to broadcasters and cable and satellite stations around the world.

Significant economies of scale in production would occur provided that in pre-production, each film is carefully story boarded as a commercial would be, then all African, Asian, Chinese, Indian or South American filming done in large blocks covering a number of films and themes.

Part Two

The Second Component is to use the same research effort and database to produce an IMAX or IWERKS film, focusing on the birth of our planet and the development of life on earth, to run in the growing number of IMAX/WIDE screen formats around the world.

Part Three

The Third Component is a road show featuring Douglas Adams and, possibly members of Pink Floyd performing a History of the Universe Show in a number of fantastic venues around the world. The show would mix film, holography, music and narration to provide a cathartic experience as the human race moves from one millennium to another.

This would lead to an Album and further TV coverage for the sponsor.

The possibility of a Douglas Adams/Pink Floyd 'History of the Universe' roadshow sets the mind reeling, but perhaps his ambition would have outstripped the genuine feasibility?

Dear Douglas

ROBBIE STAMP

I miss you still.

I am sure that many other friends will have started their letters in the same way, for I am sure that it remains true for all of us who were lucky to be touched by your friendship and your genius.

You really were the most fantastic company and the last lunch we had together began at lunch time (logically) and finished well past tea time. Those hours felt precious then, how much more so now? I'm not sure that a day goes by when I do not summon to mind an idea of yours, a conversation, an insight, especially about your endless fascination with perspective. What if there was a Super Intelligent Shade of Blue? How does a Rhino experience her world? What if we truly had paranoid AI?

I have just done my first word check for this letter. You will be glad to know that I am still of course using Macs and that Pages (no accident of course) has used the Number 42 for its word count number icon!

I know you were more than a little ambivalent about the way that 42 followed you around – one of my favourites is the fact that there are 42 'Negative Confessions' in the Papyrus of Ani.

These include

39. 'I have not harmed the bread rations of the gods'

42. 'I have not slain sacred cattle'

Maxims I know you lived by…

My father died the day before you did and on the night I came back from the hospital we talked, as we so often did after your move to California, your morning and my evening.

Earlier in the week, as it became clear that my father was gravely ill, you had called the house and found my mother-in-law looking after my children and with such care and concern, spent more than twenty minutes talking to her, although you had never met. It genuinely still brings tears to my eyes (I know, I know, I don't set a high bar here!) when I think of that call with Sylvia all these years later.

On our call, I sat in the chair in the kitchen and you listened to the story of the previous days and there are few better things you can be for a person who is bereaved than to be 'present' in conversation and to hear the story of a loved one's final hours. We later turned, as we so often did in happier moments, with good red wine and champagne and margaritas, to ideas and imaginings as you sensed that I wanted to be in some other spaces too that evening.

Why have I chosen to write of this again? I told this story at your Memorial and many years have passed since. I think it is because it speaks to your kindness and to friendship and care for family and indeed to the love I felt for my friend and the love I still feel.

You see, I still miss you.

Robbie Stamp (above in 1995 with Douglas) was a television producer when he met Douglas. Together they formed The Digital Village, the company that produced h2g2.com and *Starship Titanic* (see pages 279 and 280–83). He is currently the chairman of Bioss International Ltd.

On ‘The Division Bell’

Douglas was friendly with David Gilmour of Pink Floyd, close enough to hear an advance copy of their new album, released in March 1994 as *The Division Bell*. As a 42nd-birthday present (and as a reward for suggesting that LP title, in this draft letter to Gilmour) Douglas was invited to play guitar on stage with his music heroes in October that year, for two numbers: ‘Brain Damage’ and ‘Eclipse’.

David Gilmour
from Douglas Adams

Dear Dave,
I’ve listened to the album a lot over the last few days. First of all I think it’s terrific. The tracks that really stand out to me are High Hopes, Where were you? and Wearing the Inside Out. I especially like the rhythmic trick you play with the bell on High Hopes. When we hear a tolling bell we instinctively hear it as tolling the barlines, so to speak, so using it to toll the half-beat before the bar creates great internal tensions in the song. When it comes back at the end, there’s a great sense that all of our effort is in vain because the bell’s own rhythm inevitably reasserts itself. Incidentally, have you thought of calling the album itself ‘The Division Bell’ rather than High Hopes? I feel that pulling an image from inside a song rather than just repeating a song title gives a feeling that the focus is within the album rather than on its surface. It’s a very strong image as well, and one that I’m sure Storm will have a happy time circumventing. (Another great phrase, by the way, is ‘Magnets and Miracles’ – I think either of those would be stronger than High Hopes)
So far I’ve had a just few combing and rinsing type thoughts on the lyrics, which are pretty minor. For instance, I think the second line of A Great Day for Freedom should be ‘They hurled the blocks to the ground’ – for several reasons.
I noticed you were uncertain about ‘locks’ and wanted to change it to ‘chains’, but I think you get the same problem - it’s quite a well-worn image, and it is only an image. ‘Blocks’ gets you the same sound as ‘locks’, so it conforms to your first musical instinct (which is usually the right one) plus it has the advantage of being a picture rather than an image. It was, after all, blocks (of concrete) that were being thrown to the ground.

m...' My instant top-of-head thought (before I even knew wha
g was about) was that it could be something like 'As you lo
und my life...' Then I wondered what I meant by that, and s

I prefer 'they' rather than 'we' but this is just a personal feeling: I remember the day the wall actually came down. We all celebrated and felt very self-congratulatory, but it struck me at the time that we hadn't actually done anything, they had. We had just raised our glasses to it. Now, a few years later, we still haven't actually done anything, and all the new opportunities that flew up in to the air have dropped back to the ground. So, now we are organising a big charitable bash for Bosnia at which we will all be raising our glasses again. It's a poor substitute.

I think 'to' will work better than 'onto'. As you sing it, the stresses go 'onto' which goes against the way we normally say it. If you just sing 'to' instead you can do more with it, give it more a sense of heaving something.

There's a similar point on the last line of the (Dylanish?) Out the Door. All the words 'In the end I suppose...' are wasted when all you want to say is 'You just can't win.' Make 'em wait for it. Leave the line half-empty, then come in with 'You just can't win'.

I've got quite a few observations of this kind, but they are all tiny like this and I think it would be quic ker to go over them with you in person when I next see you.

There was one song you particularly wanted me to look at, She Takes It Back. I haven't been able to make out from the tape what all the lyrics are – except for one verse 'So I spat on her and lied to her...etc', which I think is actually one of the best verses on the album, so I wouldn't want to change it. The last verse seems to fall apart and I guess that's what you wanted me to look at. I haven't managed to come up with anything yet, because I've only just sat down and deciphered what I could of what was there! I'll see what I can do.

However, listening to that track, and listening to one of the instrumental sections of the album together gave me an idea for a whole other song. I don't suppose you're interested in more songs at the moment, but I'll show it to you anyway. It's based on that terrible US Army slogan, 'Be All That You Can Be'

Family Values

Kill all that you can eat
Eat all that you can see
Burn everything to give you heat
Be all that you can be.

Take all that you can steal
Steal everything that's free
Burn all that you can breathe, sweet baby
Be all that you can be

Drive everywhere you go
Pave everything you see
Drill everything beneath your feet
Be all that you can be

Push everything that's near
Pull everything that's far
Grab everything within your reach
That's everything you are

Rape everything you love
Beat everything you win
Kill everything you fight for, baby
Be all that you can be

I've done a rough tune for it that's quite simple, but you might not want to hear it if you were interested enough in it to do a tune yourself. I think it should have a sort of lyrical, anthem-like feel, as if it was something uplifting and heart-warming. Something they can sing along to.

I've got a structural suggestion to make. I thought that after about eight minutes of instrumental introduction that the opening line of lyric could have been stronger than 'As you look around this room...' My instant top-of-head thought (before I even knew what the song was about) was that it could be something like 'As you look around my life...' Then I wondered what I meant by that, and started wandering off on a new train of thought, which might either interest you, or might go in directions you don't want to go in

The line gave me a sense of intrusion, of being exposed. I felt like that while I was under investigation by the Inland Revenue, and there's a good friend of mine (Bywater) who spent a long period being harrassed by bailiffs and eventually went bankrupt. You really end up rigid with hatred at these little berks with pencil moustaches, dandruff and no conversation who take over your life. So anyway I sat and wrote another lyric (at end of letter). It's in standard 12 bar blues format – which is not something I can remember having heard on a PF record. There may be some specific reason why you feel that a 12 bar blues is not th e right sort of thing for a Floyd album, but I think that if it was done with the rich, thunderous, many-layered sound of Floyd it could be extremely effective.

If you like the idea at all, then I have a specific idea of where it might go. I mention this slightly nervously, because what I'm suggesting may seem to you like a radical disruption of something that is already exactly as you want it to be, in which case please just ignore it. Here's the idea in any case. You split the opening instrumental section just an instant before the piano comes in. A few bars before the split you start to scatter a few rhythmic hints and rumbles that something's coming. Then you open the song with a pounding blues riff. You do the song. You end the song fairly abruptly on 'embrace'. Just the lead guitar plays out its last line, fading into the distance, without the drums, bass etc. Immediately underneath the last couple of phrases of disappearing guitar you bring in the piano part and the whole quiet, lyrical mood resumes, though now, of course, there's a slight sense of paranoia and anger and things not being quite what they seem that's hanging in the air for it to play off. Then, when the opening lines of 'What do you want from me' arrive, they've got an added resonance. Well, see if you like it.

Some other comments: You mentioned that the fade ins and outs were just cobbled together roughly at the moment and were subject to change. Well, I think that it might be a good thing to cut down a bit on the synth whistling sounds, only because anybody with a synth can do those now. Since you can call on much greater resources than just a synth and a mixing desk I think that you could do something much more effective using dramatic and unusual recorded sound. Send someone out with a DAT machine to get the sound of huge rocks dropping into the sea, or cars crashing or aeroplane propellers. Or ambient sound from unusual locations – I've got some tape of a raucous Shanghai traffic jam, and another tape of 200 hippos belowing in a pool with a high curved river bank behind them. etc, etc.

Another thing you mentioned was that the orchestrated play out of High Hopes was a bit bland at the moment. A thought that occurred to me when I listened was that you could lay in a manic, swirling harpsichord part that doubles time from one repeat of the chord sequence to the next. I've always wondered why nobody (at least, nobody that I've heard) has ever used a real, full-blooded, play-it-with-a-welding-mask-on harpsichord going full-tilt on a rock album before. Put a howling lead guitar part over it and you might end up with something really wild. I can play you some examples of what I mean when I get back from St Croix if you're interested.

Anyway, I could go on like this for pages, but don't want to waste my time and yours if it's not useful. The only reason I have to time to write song lyrics at the moment is that I have incredibly pressing work of my own waiting to be finished.

En¨joy skiing,
love to Polly,
Best,
Douglas

Mr Philips

Mr Philips, Mr Philips
Is on my case
Mr Philips, Mr Philips
Is on my case.
Don't know why he's picked on me
Five billion people in the human race.

Mr Philips, Mr Philips
Shouting through my letter box
Mr Philips, Mr Philips
On his knees down at my letter box
Every time I go out
Seems I have to change the locks

Mr Philips, Mr Philips
Going through my bank accounts
Mr Philips, Mr Philips
Snooping through my bank accounts
Can't understand what he's after,
Searching for very specific amounts

Mr Philips, Mr Philips
Nosing through my garbage pails
Mr Philips, Mr Philips
Crawling through my garbage pails
Prove what he wants with that garbage
Prove that I'm the Prince of Wales

Mr Philips, Mr Philips
Is on my case
Mr Philips, Mr Philips
Away somewhere and on my case
So I'll just stay and amuse myself,
In Mrs Philip's warm embrace.

Dead for Tax Reasons

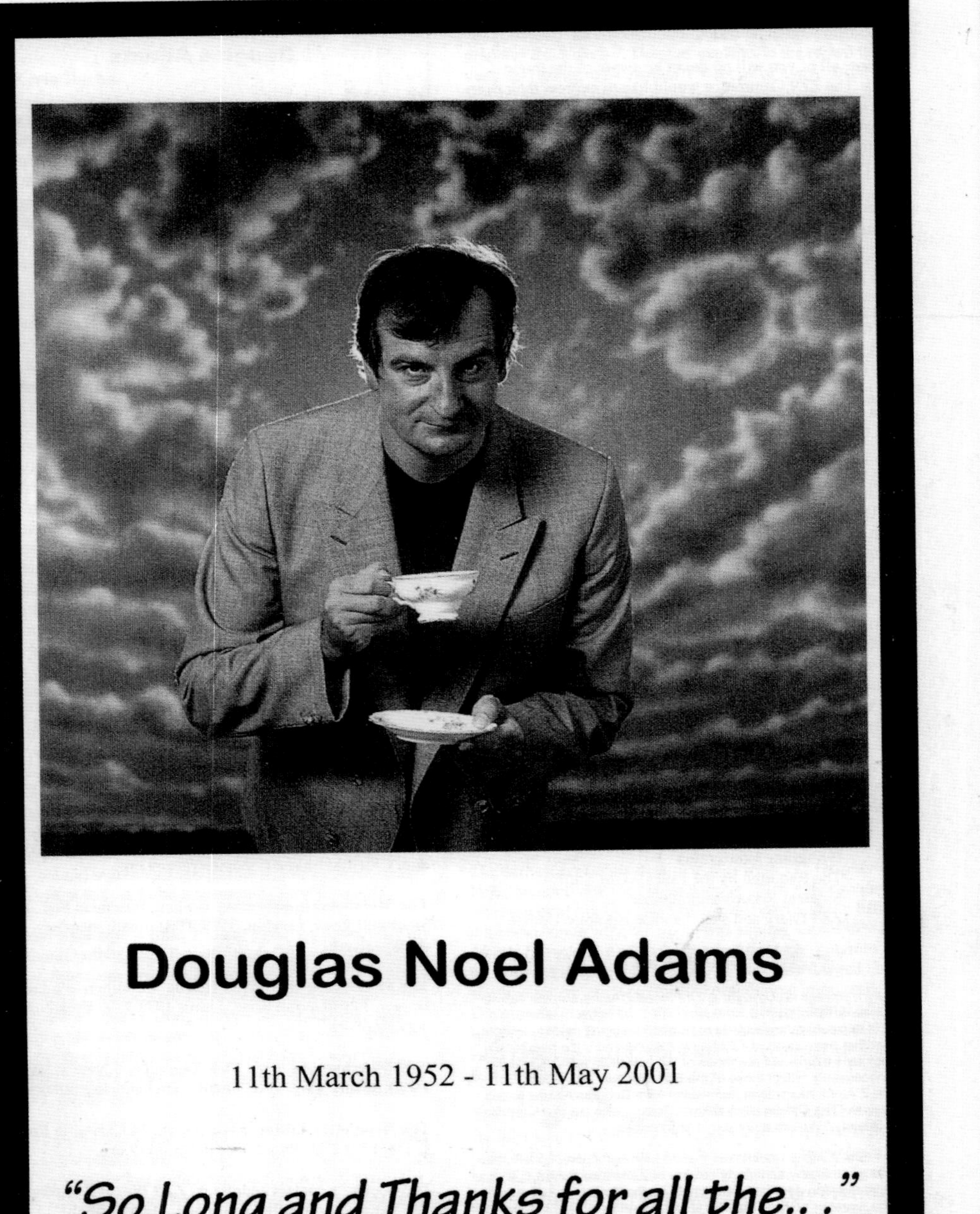
Douglas Noel Adams

11th March 1952 - 11th May 2001

"So Long and Thanks for all the.. ."

Douglas died unexpectedly, aged 49, after a workout in his local gym in Montecito, California. The world was rocked by the news on Saturday 11 May 2001. The official appreciation society ZZ9 (see page 174) made this tribute issue (above) of their regular fanzine *Mostly Harmless*.

Douglas Adams was a six-foot-five-and-a-half, left-handed man and struggled to live in an altogether smaller more right-handed world. I think that contributed to his keenness to keep blowing it up.

'I love deadlines,' said Douglas Adams. 'I love the whooshing sound they make as they whistle past.'

When I first met him, he was six months past the final, beyond which the sky will fall, deadline for *Dirk Gently's Holistic Detective Agency*. He had been at it for over three years and had written one sentence. It was a brilliant sentence, an authentic Douglas Adams sentence. It was 'High on a rocky promontory sat an electric monk on a bored horse.' Thirteen words down, seventy-nine thousand nine hundred and eighty-seven to go and three months to do it. It marked the start of the cat and mouse game that was the crazy joy of being Douglas Adams' editor. Waylaying Douglas, and teasing him in to writing his book was not for the faint-hearted, requiring total focus and all the Machiavellian sneakiness that one could muster. But the results of being invited to share Douglas's imagination were worth anything.

Douglas would not always share everything though. Near the beginning of the *Long Dark Tea-Time of the Soul* there are strange references to a single banana in a small bowl on a hospital bedside table. When I read it, I asked him what the banana was about. 'Wait and see,' he said with a mischievous grin. So I waited. Shortly after the book was published, I remembered the unresolved banana mystery and asked him about it. Douglas reminded me that since the banana episode he had let several cats out of the bag, some of them had gone off and had kittens and it had proved rather difficult to round them all up again; then confessed that he had completely forgotten what the banana joke was, but he was sure it had been a good one. From time to time over the years I asked him if he had remembered yet, the last time was only a few weeks ago. Now I will never know. And I cannot bear that.

Sue Freestone, May 2001

A version of this piece about Douglas – by Sue Freestone, his long-suffering book editor (and great friend) – was published in *The Bookseller* after Douglas's untimely death.

Afterword by Kevin Jon Davies

There's the mad housefly-cum-fruit-bat-*thingy* called Agrajag that confronts Arthur Dent in *The Hitchhiker's Guide to the Galaxy*. The creature's lifeline zig-zagged with that of our bewildered hero, as mine has regularly intersected with that of Douglas Adams and his works. For years, Douglas and the cast members of various *Hitchhiker's* productions have kindly tolerated this fly-on-the-wall documenting their craft with enthusiasm.

I never could get the hang of Thursdays, apart from 9 November 1978. The day I met Douglas and first shoved a microphone under that magnificent nose. He'd just joined *Doctor Who* as script editor, after *Hitchhiker's* had debuted on Radio 4, and was fast becoming a mini-industry. 'I'm doing a book version for Pan,' he revealed, 'Out late next year, assuming I manage to finish the bloody thing!' Of course, with hindsight I would tell him, 'Stop what you're doing and finish that book!' It would be the real start of his fortune and fame.

One year later and I'd joined a little animation company in West London called Pearce Studios, run by my talented, BAFTA-winning boss, Rod Lord. My chance meeting with producer Alan J.W. Bell led to a contract for us providing graphics for the TV series of *Hitchhiker,* and I was thrust into Douglas's professional orbit.

I recorded further interviews with him on video, spoke at fan conventions where he was guest of honour and, in 1993, sat nervously while he watched my final edit of *The Making of Hitchhiker's Guide* for which he'd generously allowed me to write new scenes for his precious characters. Later that year, he invited me to art direct the big sliver book, *The Illustrated Hitchhiker's*, using early digital compositing techniques, in the days when nobody had yet heard of Photoshop.

The last time I saw him, he'd just made a speech at the Public Awareness of Science Drama Awards in December 1998. He was mobbed as he came off stage and so I waited to see him at the wine and cheese party afterwards, but he went home. The following year he emigrated and that was that. The day we heard in 2001 that he'd died, so tragically young at 49, we all felt bereft.

Being asked by Unbound to dig through his personal archives has been a delight, an honour and a challenge. What to include, what to leave out? We've concentrated on the paperwork, for he did his most famous stuff in the days before computers. His handwriting and terrible typing feel like precious artefacts now, and oh how we wish he was still here. Mind you, I'm acutely aware that if he were, he wouldn't want me or anyone else poking about in his unfinished pages and seeing the agony it took to write down his ideas and craft those sentences. I hope you've enjoyed this collection for its unique perspective on a startling and wildly intelligent mind. Thanks, Douglas, it's been a blast.

KJD

PS I'd also like to thank Douglas's family, the team at Unbound, Kathryn and Adam at St John's Library, Cambridge, my wife Elaine and my son Liam, who have all been on this journey with me.

ABOVE: Kevin Jon Davies on Towel Day, which is celebrated in honour of Douglas Adams every year on 25 May.

OPPOSITE: Douglas Adams' teddy bear, complete with its own towel draped around its shoulders, displayed in the St John's College Library, Cambridge.

OVERLEAF: A teenage Kevin Jon Davies with Douglas Adams on set in 1980.

Sorry to have missed you,

Best wishes

[illegible signature]

Acknowledgements

Kevin Jon Davies should like to thank the following individuals and organizations.

For content, information, reference and support:

Sue Adams, Polly Adams, Will Adams, Steve Arnold, Alan J.W. Bell, Steve Broster, Neil Carruthers, Ken Clark, Daniel Cohen, John Cleese, Adam Crothers, The D.A.C., Roy Evans, Jill Foster, Neil Gaiman, Galactic Hitchhikers, Dave Haddock, Berry Healey, Nigel Hess, Penny Howard, Elaine Jackson, William 'Todd' Jones, Chris Keightley, Ewa Kuczynski, David Learner, John Lloyd, Marie McGuire, Kathryn McKee, Susan Moore, Anna-Maja Oléhn, Shelley Page, Norah Perkins, Marc Platt, Griff Rhys Jones, Jem Roberts, Save the Rhino International, Alison Scott, Gaynor Vaughn Jones, M.J. Simpson, Martin Smith, Robbie Stamp, Theatr Clwyd, James Thrift, Jane Thrift, Roger Tomlinson, Nick Webb, Gary Wild, ZZ9 Plural Z Alpha.

For friendship and encouragement:

Daniel Aguila, Mark Ayres, David Beasley, Howard Berry, Chris Cassell, Anthony Martyn Clark, Peter Cox, Gavin French, Derek Handley, David Graham Hicks, Stephen La Rivière, Alistair Lock, Tony Luke, Dirk Maggs, Stephen Mansfield, Ralph Montagu, Marc Montoya Castro, Andrew Pixley, Jonathan Saville.

For love:

Julie Bissett & Adam Davies
Elaine Davies & Liam Davies

Permission Credits and Thanks

The Publisher and the Editor should like to thank the following individuals and organizations for their permission to reproduce their photographs, artefacts and written material in this book.

Every effort has been made to trace copyright holders. The Publisher and the Editor should like to apologize for any errors or omissions, which are completely unintentional. They will, if informed, make corrections in any future editions of this book.

The archive images used are by permission of the Master & Fellows of St John's College, Cambridge. All images, artefacts and facsimile text © Completely Unexpected Productions Ltd, except:

page 2 © Rod Lord/Pearce Studios Ltd (www.rodlord.com); page 6 © Cliff Pinnock; page 9 © PA Images/Alamy (photographer: Ian West); page 10 photo kindly supplied by Sue Limb (photographer unknown); page 11 © Mike Cotton, former Varsity Photographer 1972–4. Now Mike Penhaligon (mike@penhaligon.org); page 26 (top) kindly supplied by Mike Jordan (photographer unknown) / (bottom) kindly supplied by Completely Unexpected Productions Ltd (photographer unknown); page 35 © Completely Unexpected Productions Ltd (photographer James Thrift); page 53 (bottom left) © Nigel Luckhurst / (bottom right) kindly supplied by Completely Unexpected Productions Ltd (photographer unknown); page 54 letter © and permission from John Cleese; page 57 (top) © Nigel Luckhurst; page 65 (poem text) © Completely Unexpected Productions Ltd and Chris Keightley / (inset) © KJD; page 70 (centre left & right bottom) © Mike Cotton, former Varsity Photographer 1972–4. Now Mike Penhaligon (mike@penhaligon.org); page 71 © Mike Cotton, former Varsity Photographer 1972–4. Now Mike Penhaligon (mike@penhaligon.org); p.75 kindly supplied by Completely Unexpected Productions Ltd (photographer unknown); page 100 (bottom) © zz9.org/Darrel Bevan; page 101 (top) © Cliff Pinnock; page 106 © Jill Foster, with her kind permission; page 115 © Stephen Mansfield, with his kind permission; pages 138–9 © Immediate Media Company; page 140 © Mitch Davies/Science Fiction Theatre of Liverpool; page 141 (top left) © Theatr Clwyd / (top right) © Theatr Clwyd (Michael Grensted) / (bottom left) © Cyranoid Publishing Corporation Ltd / (bottom right) © David Beasley; page 150 (top, and left bottom) © Cliff Pinnock / (centre left) © KJD / (bottom right) © David Learner; page 151 (all) © Rod Lord/Pearce Studios Ltd (www.rodlord.com); page 160 (all) © Michael Dare; page 161 (left top & bottom) Michael Joseph/KJD / (top right) © KJD; page 163 © Ken Humphrey; page 172 (letter from Robin Hill) © Penny Hill, with her kind permission; page 173 (letter and photo) © André Willey; page 174 © Elaine Jackson (née Thomson); page 175 © Shelley Page, with her kind permission; page 176 (top right and left, and bottom left) and page 178 © Ewa Kuczynski, with her kind permission; page 180 © The Estate of Alan Coren; page 181 © The Estate of Miles Kington; page 183 © Brian Griffin (www.briangriffin.co.uk); page 184 (inset left and right) © Michelle Drayton-Howard, with her kind permission; page 197 © PanMacmillan Publishers/Reproduced with permission of the Licensor through PLSclear; page 198 (inset top) © Andy Hollingworth; pages 212–13 © Completely Unexpected Productions Ltd and Jon Canter; page 219 (inset) © courtesy of The Centre for Computing History, Cambridge, UK; page 237 © Ilias Kyriazis; page 240 © Gaynor Vaughn Jones; page 243 (all) © Mark Carwardine; page 252 (all) © Save the Rhino International; pages 270–71 (all) © Mark Gerson; page 275 © John Copthorne; page 279 (inset portrait) kindly supplied by Robbie Stamp (photographer unknown); pages 288–9 © Robbie Stamp (photographer: Jill Furmanovsky); page 292 courtesy of ZZ9 © ZZ9.org (cover image photographer unknown); page 293 © Sue Freestone, with kind permission; page 294 © Master & Fellows of St John's College Cambridge; page 295 © KJD; pages 296–7 © David Beasley; page 320 © Griff Rhys Jones, with his kind permission.

Also with thanks to:

Will Adams and Martin Smith for their kind permission to reproduce all work relating to the collaborative genius of Adams-Smith-Adams.

John Lloyd, whose many collaborations with Douglas Adams leave a lasting legacy in many of the works featured throughout this book.

Robbie Stamp for his kind permission to reproduce work from The Digital Village.

And to: Margo Buchanan (page 34), Arvind Ethan David (page 236), Stephen Fry (page 8), Neil Gaiman (page 274), Dirk Maggs (page 162) and Robbie Stamp (page 288) for their letters to Douglas, written specially for this book.

A Note on the Editor

Born in 1961, the son of a librarian and a millwright, Kevin Jon Davies grew up enthralled with the BBC's *Doctor Who* and *The Goon Show*. In 1978, *The Hitchhiker's Guide* radio series seemed to combine the best of both, so he sought out its then little-known author Douglas Adams, for a fanzine interview. After two years at art college instead of sixth form, Davies joined Pearce Studios Ltd as a teenage trainee, working for animator Rod Lord on the award-winning TV graphics for *The Hitchhiker's Guide* (BBC, 1981) and Gerry Anderson's *Terrahawks* (LWT, 1983). A year spent as an Effects Animator at Walt Disney UK on *Who Framed Roger Rabbit* (1988) led to five more at Passion Pictures Ltd, blending 'toon' characters with live action for international TV commercials.

Davies turned director in 1993 with two BBC retrospectives, *The Making of the Hitchhiker's Guide* and *Doctor Who: More Than 30 Years in the Tardis*. He designed *The Illustrated Hitchhiker's Guide* (1994), conducted celebrity interviews at Sci-Fi Channel (Europe), helmed film dramas *Shakedown, Return of the Sontarans* (1994) and episodes of *Space Island One* (Sky, 1998) and produced DVD extras for such BBC classics as *Adam Adamant Lives!*, *Blake's 7* and *Dad's Army*. In 2003, Davies first met director/adapter Dirk Maggs, shooting promo films for his many Adams-related projects, including the latter four *Hitchhiker's Guide* radio series and the *2012/13 Live Tour*, all starring the original radio cast. Davies first dipped into Adams' personal papers at Cambridge for unused scraps to include in the final radio series, *The Hexagonal Phase* (2018). This led to his recent deep-dive through those same archives, for this book. Davies is a visiting lecturer for the Film & TV Production MA course at The University of Hertfordshire.

Unbound is the world's first crowdfunding publisher, established in 2011.
We believe that wonderful things can happen when you clear a path for people who share a passion.
That's why we've built a platform that brings together readers and authors to crowdfund books they believe in – and give fresh ideas that don't fit the traditional mould the chance they deserve.
This book is in your hands because readers made it possible. Everyone who pledged their support is listed below. Join them by visiting unbound.com and supporting a book today.

3.14a, 4érémie 2uerra, A dull shade of orange, A N B, Konrad A., Henrik Aasted, Dror Ben Abba Amiel, Odin Abba-D'Souza, Billy Abbott, Hazel Abbott, Ian Abbott, Nijaz Abdulgalejev, Cerise Abel-Thompson, Richard Abela, Tom Abell, Matthew Abercrombie, ABF, David Abigt, abnqeut (aka Daan Bos), Clara Abrahams, Karl "Krazy" Abrahamson, Tomasz Abramowicz, Stephen M Accetta, Steve Acheson, Jörg Henry Ackermann, Caroline Acton, Michelle Acuña, Randall Adam, Charles Adams, Geoff Adams, Holly & Patrick Adams, Jack Adams, Jonathan Adams, Paul Adams, Peter Adams, River Maria Adams, Sophie Adams, Ted Adams, Will Adams, Roger Adams Reed, Rich Adase, Becky Addis, Sheila Addison, Adel, Adam M. Adler, Patrik Adolfsson, adrianminde@gmail.com, AEF, Mike "Mutant" Affourtit, Manjul Agarwal, Roger Agburn, Aaron Agee, Reggie "Grinzy" Agee, Ole Ahlgreen, Aria M Ahmed-Cox, Joe Ahrens, Kevin Aitchison, Frank E Akaiwa, Bronwen Aker, Raschad Al-Khafaji, Alan, Fernando Alas, Albendon, Kristine Albert, Steffen Albert, Allen Alberti, Teresia Albertsson, Wyndham Albery, David Albin, Dan Alcalde, Dave Alcock, Isabella Alcorn, Ignacio Alcuri, Alder Family, Graziano Aldrovandi (Bracco), Gillian Aldus, Ale, Paul Aleixo, Alessio & Erika, Ian Alexander, Pam Alexander, Wilma Alexander, Alexander, Micahel Alexenko, Imran Ali, Alissamoon, Andrew S. Allan, Chris Allan, Karen Allan, Verity Allan, James Allard, Mattias Allared, Brett Allen, Craig S. Allen, Darren Allen, Jon Allen, Judy Allen, Louise Allen, Mark Allen, Myles C. Allen, Peter J. Allen, Robyn Allen, Sally Allen, Shane Allen, Tina Allen, Charles J Allen IV, Thomas Allen Sollars, Rob Alley, Stuart Allison, Faisal Almana, Jim Alt, Ciro Altabás, Alumiere, Enrico Alvares, Sulaiman Alwahid, Basem Aly, Andrew Amaral, Gene Ambaum, Amber & Matt, Gui Ambros, Amisha, Robert Amling, Gabriele Ammermann, Karen Amoudry, Amy and Carlos Fred, S Amzalak, Ssieth Anabuki, Ondra Anderle, Alec Anderson, Charlie Anderson, Claire M Anderson, Clifton (spaceman) Anderson, Corey Anderson, David Anderson, James Anderson, Jay Anderson, Jeffrey Anderson, Josh Anderson, Keith Anderson, Larry Anderson, Mark Anderson, Nikki Anderson, Phillip Anderson, Shawn Edward Anderson, Toby Anderson, Trevor Anderson, Henry Anderton, Keef Andrew, Phil Andrew, Andrew and Mary, Brandon Andrews, Hunter Andrews, John Andrews, Matt Andrews, Nicholas Andrews, Paul & Rhian Andrews, Shawn Andrews, Vanessa Andrews, Alex Andronov, Igor Andronov, andykisaragi, ANE/ZWNBSP, Angela the Paranoid Android, Bernard Angell, John Angle, Tony Anjo, Rob Annable, Kirk Annett, Libby Anson, Lauren Anthone, Brett Anthony, SK Antoniak, Uwe Apel, Austin C Appleby, Matt Appleby, Jenna Appleseed, Peter Appleton, Simon Appleton, Phoenix Nest Arcade, Carol Archard, ArchibaldPusterwitz, ARCJones, Christoffer Arehorn, Richard Arends, Stephanie Aretz, Francis Arickx, Karina Arlind, Katharine Armitage, Chris Armstrong, Franny Armstrong, Caitlin Armstrong Clark, Joseph Arnhold, Charlotte Arno and Chris Bradbury, Alexander Siryk Arnold, Laurence Arnold, Steve Arnold, Tobias Arntsson, Craig Arnush, Marc (JIFFY) Arrand, Dave Arter, Frazier Arthur, Joyce Arthurs, Nick Arthurs, Jim Artillus, ARTLUNG, Sabrina Artus, Henry Arundel, Christine Asbury, Dave Asebrook, Tommy Åsén, Heather & Brierley Ash, Martin Ashby, Adrian Ashton, Keith Ashton, Matt Ashton, Robert Ashton, Robin Ashurst, Charles Askew, H David Askins, Christian Goos Asmussen, Kate Aspinall, Mark Aspinall, Peter Asquith, Pax Asteriae, MATS ÅSTRÖM, Mark B Atherton, Richard H Atherton, Alexander Atkin, Vance Atkins, Audrey Atkinson, Daniel Atkinson, Iain Atkinson, Karen Atkinson, Kevin Atkinson, Mike Atkinson, Timothy Atkinson, Byron Atkinson-Jones, Colin Attrill, Paul Attryde, Grace Atwell, Abraham Aucamp, John Auckland, Benjamin Auerbach, Paul Auerbach, Mike Ault, Aurora My Favorite Marie Castiglia, Matthew Austin, Austin, Austin Loomis never asked Douglas who the "Oh ah" fellow was., Jeff Autor, Rosalind Aveling, Allison & Michael Avella, Nicholas 'Aquarion' Avenell, Ben Avery, Simon Avery, Inbar Aviezer, Jennie Avila, Kathie Avital, Avivana, Charles Awdry, Michael Aydeniz, James Aylett, Darryl Aylward, J. Marc Aynardi, Richard Ayoade, Bob Ayres, Mark Ayres, John Ayton, Lorena B, Alana B-H, Tom B., Willem B., Wayne B. and Evan T. Williams, Quintin Baas, Babou, Peter Bachler, Alex Bacon, Chaz Baden, Oliver Baeck, Megan Baehnisch, Daniel Bagel, Sheena and James Baggaley, Ian Baguley, Dave Baguley (the), John Bagwell, David Bailey, Duncan Bailey, Matt Bailey, Simon Bailey, Loïc Bailliard, David Baillie, Matthew Bain, Chris Bainbridge, Caroline Bainbridge & Michael Harris, Martin Baines, Roy Baines, Steve Baines, Gordon Baird, Katharine Baird, Richard Bairwell, Clinton Baker, Craig Baker, Jedediah Baker, Kelly Baker, Nicholas Baker, Ross Baker, Victoria Baker, Lila Bakke & James Giantomasi, Jeroen Bakker, Lennard Bakker, Hynek Bakstein, Marin Balabanov, Ian Bald, Carol Baldi, Paul Baldowski, Tom Baldwin, Geoff Ball, Jim Ball, Carl Ballard, Nancy Ballard, Simon J. Ballard, Derek J. Balling,

Enrique Balmes, Adam Balogh, Etan Balogh-Kerner, Matthew Balyuzi, Carl Bamber, Ross Bamford, Nick Banbury, Dhruba Banerjee, Jens Bang, Bangerturner, Oliver Banister, Ben Banks, Simon Banks, Amos Bannister, Dave Bannister, Marko Banušić, Mike Banyard, João Baptista, Alex Barber, Alison Barber, Christopher Barbour, Paul Barbour, Bernard Barcz, Dominique Barcz, Johan Bard, Iain M Barker, Simon Barker, Jason Barkla, Jonas Barklund, Jem Barnard, Andrew Barnebey, Nic Barnes, Nicholas Barnes, Nick Barnes, Paul Barnes, Ryan Andrew Barnes, Michelle Barnett, Nigel E Barnett, Marc Barnhill, Danny Barnhoorn, Gordon Barr, Karen Barrass, Ali Barratt, David Barratt, Josh Barratt, Luke Barratt, Mark Barratt, Alexander Barreto, Andy Barrett, James W. Barrett, Ken Barrett, Michael Barrett, James Barrett-Bunnage, Brian Barrier, Eric Barrington, Brian Barris, Chris Barron, Steve Barron, Jimmy Barrow Vargon Poet, Caitlin Barta, William Bartell, Bjørn Peare Bartholdy, Alex Bartholomew, Vinnie Bartilucci, Jon Bartlett, Michael J Bartlett, Paul Bartlett, Rod Bartlett, Chris Bartley, Daniel C Barton, Lewis Barton, Nikki Barton, Philip Jerome Barton, Jacob Bartynski, Thomas Bartz, Uri Baruchin, Mary Barzee, Simon Basher, Sara Basso de Marc, Sanjay Basu PhD, Anna Batchelor, Claire Bateman, Gary Bates, Gemma Bates, Ronald Batey, Michael Batista, Simon Batistoni, Philipp Batman, Allen Batson, Becky Batt, Zoe Battiscombe-Scott, Kate Baty, Andreas Christoph Bauer, Justin Baugh, Dagmar Baumann, Mark "MarkWHO42" Baumgarten, John Baumgartner, John Bavington, Fiona Bawden, Alasdair Baxter, H. Baxter and R. Jackson, Francesca Baylis, Emma Bayliss, Andrew Bayly, Anthony D Baynes, Val Bazaras, Birdie Be-Nites, Richard Beach, Nick Beadman, Ziplock Beaglefrocks, Kirsty Beagley, Helen Beal, Lisa Beale, Jeff (not that one) Beamish, Christopher Bean, Rosemary Beardow, Mark Beards, Steve Beardshaw, Shaune Beattie, Andrew Beatty, David Beaumont, Eilis Beaumont, Bob Beaupre, Glenis Beaven, Pete Beck, Lane Becker, Dan Beckford, Justin L. Beckham, Jacques Beckman, Addie Beckwith, Brian Beckwith, David Beddingfield, Rachael Bedlington, Katarina Bednarikova, Zaphoid Beeblebrox, Matt Lee Beeblebrox (No relation, probably), Mark Beecham, Peter Beecham, Lucas Beef Chief Sorbo, Beefyonder, Andrew Beehag, Dave Beer, Sandra Beermann, Dave Beesley, Stephen Beggs, Rick Behl, Elizabeth and Jason Behnke, Gert Behrmann, David Beitey, Donna Bekendam, TraciandBrian Belanger, Marc André Bélanger, Fernando Belaza, John Belgrove, Jerry Belich, Alex Bell, Andrew Bell, David Bell, Graeme Bell, Martin J. Bell, Ted Bell, Tim Bell, Douglas Bellak, Neil Bellamy, Rob Bellin, David Bellinger, Michelangelo Bellini, Adam Belmonte, Lisa G. Belt, Todd Bemis, Ben42, Ronnie Bendall, Hennes Bender, Nathalie Bending, Jon M Benedict, Wendy L. Benedict, Jeanne Adell Christensen Benjamin, Tim Benjamin, Benjamin, Mika, Hannah & Asa, Anna Bennett, Conrad Bennett, Karl Bennett, Richard Bennett, Simon Bennett, Steph Bennett, Steve Bennett, Alex @alxb Benoehr, Catharine Benson, Ewan Benson, Tara Benson, Thomas Benson, David Charles Bent, Hayden Bentley, Julian Benton, Leslie M. Bereck, Siera Berg, Jim Bergemann, Katrina Bergen, Robert Berger, Joran, Linus, and Rafael Bergh, Nick Berglmeir, Martin Berglund, Karin Bergstermann, Steve Berlin, Noah Berman, Beatrice Bernescut, Joshua Bernett, Bernhard, Rob Bernstein, Indulis Bernsteins, Greg Berry, Howard Berry, Keith Berry, Nigel Berry, Patrick Berry, Sean Berry, Simon Berry, Steve Berry, Berry, George Bertele, Sam Bertram, Nicola Best, Bart and Tig Beswick, Amy Bethell, Robert Betley, Felix Bettelheim, Joseph Bettinger, Patrick Bevington, Beware of the Leopard podcast, Isla Bezencon, Maryana Bhak, Carlo Luciano Bianco, Aimee Bias, David Bick, David Bickerstaff, John Biddulph, Matt Biddulph, Biddytoes, Flea and Jessie Bean, Brad Bidnick, David Biedenbach, Gabriel Bienczycki, Ward Bigler, Gianlorenzo & Davide Bignotti, Jakub Bijak, Ian Biles, Frank O. Billet, Kelly Billingham, Paul Billinghurst, Daniel Bimson, Charlie Bing, Jan Binge, Andrew Bingham, Donald J. Bingle, Chris Binner, Ronald Binnie, Peter Binnig, David C Birch, John Birch, Timothy D. Birch, David L Bird, Paul Bird, Stephen Bird, Wiebke Bird, John Addison Birkbeck, Simon Birrell, John Birt, Sarah Birt, Dorothy Birtalan, Marshall Bishop, Nathan "Bish" Bishop, Scott Bishop, Paul Bissett, Simon Bisson, Ludie W Bitner III, Ole Bittner, Trix Bix, F. David Bixler, Hans Bjerregaard, Mikaela Björklund, Alexander Bjorn, Gina Bjorvig, Benjamin Bl., Wojciech Blacha, Andrew C Black, David R. Black, Guy Black, Kenneth E Black, Scott Black, Bryan Blackburn, Melissa Blackburn, Mark Blackham, Craig Blackketter, William Blackledge, John, Catherine and Alisdair Blackshaw, Thomas Wowbagger Blackwell, Holly Blades, Andrew Blain, Colin D Blair, Olive Blais, Nicholas Blake, Paul Blakeley, Graham Blakelock, James Bland, Noreen Blanluet, Glenn Blauvelt, Glenn R Blauvelt, PhD, Mark Blaxter, Caron Blay, Nicolas Bleach, Simon Blears, Adrian Bleese, Sarah Blenkinsop, Richard E. Blitz, Hillary Block, Mathias Block, Philip Blom, Håkan Blomqvist, Holly Blonde, Mark Bloom, Charlie Blough, Don Blubaugh, Alexandra Blum, Lars Blumers, Neil Blumfield, Blümi, Simon Blyth, bm5k, Craig Boardman, Mike Boas, Lord Bob, Michael Bobbitt, Patrick Boch, Wes Boddie, Karl Bode, Colin Bodell, David Boeke, Dennis Boersma, Patrick Boersma, Peter Boersma, Rob Boffard, Chris Bogaars, Dimitrios "Taki" Bogiatzoules, Oliver Bogler, Tristan Bogler, Dondi Bogusky, Deanne Boilesen, Kevin Bolemon, Chris Bolton, Kieran Paul Bolton, BON COMICS, Chris Bond, Gregg "Cabe" Bond, Steven Bond, Mike Bond (HG2G Scrapbook), Collin Bonde, Vincent Bondy, Naomi Bonfield, Carlos Alberto Bonilla Pauly, Sarah Bonkat, Peter Bonnalie, Jess M Bonner, David Bonney, Shield Bonnichsen, David Book, BookLore, Annette Boon, Natalie Boon, Sean Boon, Tom Boon, Alan James Booth, Katie Booth, Stephen James Booth, Val Booth, Dan Booth & Heather Lane, Andrew Boothman, Sebastian Boothroyd, Thomas Borck, Julien Bordagaray, Chris Bordenca, Joe Borg, John Borgsdorf, Joe Bork, TR Borkowski, Meriko Borogove, Ivo Boruta, Andrew Bosch, Bryan Dillon Boscia, Katrin Bosse, Phil Boswell, Zoltán Böszörményi, John Boteler, Aron Bott, Fabian Bouché, William Boucher, John Boudreaux, Francois Boulard, Ross Bourne, Sarah Bourne, Dennis Bours, Karl Bovenizer, Thea Bøwadt, Keith A Bowden, Euan Bowditch, David V. Bowen, Jason and Sarah Bowen, Tim Bowen, Rob, Aimee, Brenna, and Ronan Bowers, Brad Bowers and Matt Armbruster, Adam Bowie, Grayson Bowler, Simon Bowler, Clare Bowman, Jack Bowman, John Bowman, Phil Bowman, Sarah Louise Bowman, Mark Bowsher, Thomas Bowyer, Alan SF Boyd, Caleb R. Boyd, J. Patience Boyd, Kate Boydell, Tony Boydell, Jeremy M. Boyle, Michael, Lauren, and Annabelle Boyle, Paul Boyns, Nikki Boys, Øivind Braaten, Carolyn Braby, David Bradbury, James Bradbury, Nick Bradbury, Dave Bradley, Ian Bradley, Kate Bradley,

Pete Bradley, Scott Michael Bradley, Bernadette Brady, David Brady, John Brainard + Jessica Bahlman, Keith Braithwaite, Matt Braithwaite, Tim A. Braithwaite, Erasto Branco, Saskia Brand, Brandeis, Ralph Brandi, Alan Brandon, Nicholas David Brandt, Dax Brannan, Alison Bransfield, Gordon Branson, Guy Brasher, Tony Braund and Catherine Hallowes, Richard W H Bray, Tristan Bray, Paul Brayford, Walt Brecht, Peter Breeden, Jim Breeds, Emma Breen, Holger Brehmann, Francisco Javier Brenes-Araya, Ruth Brennan, Martin Brennand, Tony Brenton, Orla Breslin, Arno Brevoort, Jane Brewer, Neil Brewitt, Ginny Brewster, briana. weatherholtz@gmail.com, Darien Brice Dickinson, Volker Brichzin, Steve Bridge, Jack Bridgman, Richard Bridgman, Alison Brierley, Alex Briggs, Peter Briggs, Beverley Bright, Robin Bright, Cate Brimblecombe-Clark, Chris Brimmage, Jim & Sue Brindley, Keith Brinkley, Pam Brisjar, Ben Bristow, Marland Britt, Niamh Britton, Sam Britton, Henrik Brix Kronborg, Broadbean Broadbean, Johnathan Broadley, Alice Broadribb, Thomas Broadway, NH Brobakk, Brooke Brod, Charles W. Broderick, Jesco Brodersen, Jenny Brodie, Lindsey Brodie, Janet Brodnitz, Łukasz Bromirski, Simon Bromley, Stuart Bromwich, Richard Bronze, Andrew Brook, Michelle Brook, Geoffrey Brooke, Joe Brooke-Smith, Alan Brookland, Daniel C. Brooks, Michael Brooks, Phillip Brooks, A. Brooks Hollar, Matt Broom, Philip Broomhead, Anne & Joe Brophy, Max Brosa, Chris Brosnahan, Chiappetta Bross, Rob Brougham, Bert Brouwer, The Browell Family, Andrea Brown, Andy Brown, Brian Brown, Chris Brown, Craig Brown, Dave CW Brown, Dominic Brown, Fredric Brown, Gareth Brown, Geoff Brown, Glenn Brown, Ian Brown, ID Brown, James L Brown, Katya Brown, Mark G Brown, Mark James Brown, Matt Brown, Richard Keith Brown, Simon Brown, Stephen Brown, William Brown, Olly Browne, Simon Browning, Tim Browning, Sandra Browning Nolte, Cole Michael Brownjohn, Peter Brownlow, Bru-, David Bruce, Nigel & Llewellyn Bruce, Christina Brunnenkamp, Jean-Claude Brunner, Alex Brunori, Tom Brusch, Kelli Bryan, Darryl E Bryant RT(R), MRI, Bob Bryla, Simon Bubb, Jonathan Buchalter, Gary Buchan, David Buchanan, Kevin Ian Buchanan, Stanley Edsel Buchanan, Huw Buchtmann, Richard Buckby, Jonathan Buckmaster, Grahame Budd, Andrew Budgen, Oana Budurea, Patrick Buechner, Katherine Buffington, David Bugden, Christian Buggedei, Bugz, Dorothy Bukantz, John Bull, Kate Bull, Thomas Bull, Juliet Bullimore, Erica Bullivant, Charles C. Bullock, Matt Bullock, Mark Bult, Lars Bunge, Daniel Bungert, Bernd Bunk, Tony, Gillian & Hann Bunn, Travis Bunt, Paul Bunting, Anatoly Burakov & Nadezda Issakova, Ansel and Tabitha Burch, John Burchill, Lloyd Burchill, Andrea Burden, Anthony Burdge & Jessica Burke, Scott & Shoni Burg, Alissa Burger, Michael Burgess, Neil Burgess, Tom Burgess, Bob Burgoyne, Keith Burgoyne, Charlotte Burke, Gerard Burke, Keith Burke, Kimberly D Burke, Pat Burke, Jeff L. Burke CD, David Burnett, Anthony Burns, Katy Burns, Yancy "beowuff" Burns, Dan Burraway, Angie Burrow, Chris Burrows, Kristian Burrows, Jessica Burston, James Burton, Jim Burton, Jonathan Burton, Nicholas Burton, Thomas Büsch, Dave Bush, Connally Bush Bennison, Paul Bushen, Niel Bushnell, Orson Bushnell, Christian Buss, Andrea Bustamante, Anthony Butcher, Marcus Butcher, Matt Butler, Sinéad Butler, Toby Butler, Butter, Simon Butterfield, Brian Butterworth, Rosemarie Buttery, Jerry Butts, Rik Byatt, Brian Bygland, bygrinstow, Matthew Byng-Maddick, Colin Byrne, Frank Byrne, Rob Byrne, Tony Byrnes, Scott Byron, Jason Bytheway, Kasia Bytnerowicz, Elizabeth C, C & R & A, Ian Cadwallader, Kevin Cafferty, Thomas Cagan, Jim Cain, Casey Cain Warvigilent, Ian Cairns, caitcreates, Alan Calder, Amelia Calderbank, Matthew Caldwell, S Caldwell, The Calgary Kohnens, Kate Calico, Jon Callas, Colin Callister, Neil Calton, Howard Calvert, Shane Calvert, Russ Calvert (hoopy Frood!) , Chris Cameron, David Cameron, Douglas Cameron, The Cameron Family, Dídac Caminero, Paul Camp, J Campagna, Allen Campbell, Barbara Truxal Campbell, Kate Campbell, Shirley Campbell & Richard Cherns, Rich Campoamor, Cheryl Campsmith, G. Canales, Tony Canepa, Lynne Canfield, Simon Canfield, Simon J Canham, Thomas Canning, Sara Cannon, John Cant, JD Canterbury, Brent Cantley, Richard Cantlon, Michael Cantor, Deborah Cantrell, Oliver Capon, Jonathan "4Slippy" Capparelli, Amber Caputo, Shaun Carberry, Michael Card, Edward Carey, Jessica Cargill Thompson, Robin Carlberg, William Carleton, John Carlin, Rick Carlson, Sean Carlson, Paul Carlyle, Ewan Carmichael, Paul Carnahan, Amber Carnegie, Wade Carney, Will Carney, carol@cmappassociates.com, Marie Carone, Charlotte Elise Carpenter, John Ralph Carpenter, Darren Carr, Debra Carr, Dominique Carr, Jason Carr, Liz Carr, Travis Carr, Anne-Marie Carslaw, Mick Carter, Neale Carter, Peter Carter, Stephen H Carter, Andrew Carton, Tony Carton, Ed Cartwright, Barry Caruth, Steve Caruth, Ande Case, Sean Casely, Vicki Casey, Benjamin Casha, James Casler, George Casley, Michael Casner, Caspar, Jane Casper, Ronnie Caspi, Chris Cassell, Elaine M. Cassell, Paul Cassella, Allayne Cassidy, Paul R Cassidy, George Cassie, Jacob Cassity, Andrea Acas Castiglioni, David Castle, Kari Castor, Zac Cataldo, Maris Catania, Nick Cater, Catherine, David Catley, Jelle Cautereels, Patrick Cauty, Dominic Cave, Matthew Cawson, Fenric Cayne, Irene Cencich Remley, John Ceneviva, Marta Cepek, Sasha Cepek, Rafael Ceribelli, Nancy L Cerkvenik, NJ Cesar, Lothar Cezanne, Johann Chacko, Frank Chadwick, Marie Chadwick, Warwick Chai, Elizabeth Chaldekas, Richard Chalk, Andrew Chalke, Chalky, Mike Challis, Hamon Chamberlain, Patrick Chamberlain, Tania Chamberlain, Chris Chambers, Richard Chambers, Selena Chambers, Cuauhtemoc Chamorro, Tom Champion, Sckeama Chan, Victor Chan, John Chanaud, Jac Chandross, Rich Chaney, Hyen Chang, Bryan Chapel, Chris Chapman, Kenny Chapman, Phil Chapman, Richard Chapman, Isaac Chappell, Rachael Chappell, Alex Chapple-Hyam, Andy Charalambous, Dean Charge, Alan Charles, Anthony Charles, Thalia Charles, Charles & Peggy, Karen Charlesworth, Becca Charnley, chasb, Kosmas Chatzimichalis, Dennis A Chauvey, Anne Cheesman, Tony Cheetham, Lucy Chen, Paul Cheney, Alan Chenkin, Daniel Chernick, Graham Chestney, John Chesworth, Jan Chetwynd Stapylton, Darren Chia, Chibby, Chris Chibnall, Chickadee, Dave Child, Paul Child, Beth Childs, Robert Chilton, Sterling Chin, Jhana Chinamasta, Bob Chinn, Richard Chinn, Mark Chitty, Desiree Choi, Rei Chomsky, Andrew Chorney, Michael Chouinard, David Chrichard, John Christian, Leigh 'Doug' Christian, Lars Christiansen, Ulrik Christiansen, Charlotte Christie, Maria & Summer Christie, Christine, Luke Christodoulou, Paul A. Christodoulou, Michaela Christofi, Liam Christopher, Pete Christopher, Neil Chue Hong, Susan Chun, Gemma Church, Andy Churchill, J Victor Churchill, Tony Ciak, Joslyn Cianciolo,

Mary Cigan, Kunkel Clan, Joseph Clancy, Christian Clare, William Clare, Clare, Andrew Clark, Chris Clark, Douglas A. Clark, Gordon Clark, Jason Clark, Joseph Clark, Roger Clark, Ross Clark, Steve Clark, Terry Clark, Tim Clark, Daniel Clark Jones, Amanda Clarke, Becky Clarke, Chris Clarke, Holly Clarke, Jenny Clarke, Martyn Clarke, One (for her Daddy), Nobby Roy A Clarke, Roderick Clarke, Aer Nicholson Clasby, Sigrid Claßen, Rob Clatterbuck, Gillian Claus, Laura Clayton, Neil Clayton, Lorna Clayton-Rawle, Dave Clayton-Wagner, Dominic Cleal, Lars Cleary, James Clegg, Angela L. Clemens, Nicola Clements, Jayne Clementson, Nick Cliffe, Jason Edward Clifford, Roger Clifford, Rebel Clodi, Jon Clokie, James Clover, Mark Clowes, Joel Clyne, Garrett Coakley, Lucy Coats, J. Michael Cobb, Rebecca Cockcroft, Amy Cockram, Graham Coe, Andrew Coen, Colette Coen, Paul R. Coen, Billy Coghill, Baron Cognito, Dan Cohen, Jeffrey Cohen, Matthew Cohen, Melissa S. Cohen, Norm Cohen, Adam Cohen-Rose, Jonathan Cohn, Elaine Cole, GMark Cole, Jennifer Cole, Stephen J. Cole, Karl Colella, Katy Colella, Christopher I G Coleman, Larry Michael Coleman, Max Coleman, David Coles, Jonathon Coles, Richard Anthony Coles, Jenny Colgan, Stevyn Colgan, S C Colgate, Beth Coll, Alberto Collado Gray, Ian, Sarah, Noah and Anita Collingwood Rink, Alex Collins, Frank Collins, Ian Collins, Joel Collins, Mark Collins, Michael G. Collins, Mike Collins, Nick "Tiger Bred" Collins, Russell Collins, David F Collins Jr., Alasdair Collinson, Daniel Collis, Noel Collyer Ex-President of ZZ9 Plural Z Alpha -The HitchHikers Guide to the Galaxy Appreciation Society, Colombo, Coltrey, Melusine Colwell, Jim Combes, Jenn Comfort, Chris Comley, Suzanne Compton, Gerald Conheady, Holly Conheady, Sharon Conheady, Michael Connaughton, Charlie Connelly, Chris Connelly, Brian Conner, Riff Conner, Chris Connolly, David and Mary Connolly, Jamie Connolly, Cassandra Connor, CJ Connor, Georgina Conroy, Colin Considine, Joe Conway, Lewis Conway, Peter Conway, Alan Coo, Brad Cook, Darren M Cook, David Cook, Ian Cook, Mike Cook, Steven Mark Cook, Tim Cook, David Cooke, Juliette Cooke, W Cooke, Rod Cookson, Robin Coolen, Herko Coomans, Neil Coombes, Paul Cooney, Aaron Paul Cooper, Barry Cooper, Catherine Cooper, Donald Roy Cooper, Hannah Cooper, Nick Cooper, Paul Cooper, Richard Coote, Gideon Copestake, Valentina Coppo, Matthew Copsey, Cale L. Corbett, Andy Cording, Mike & Rosie Corlett, Bill Corner, Toby Corner, Paul Cornish, Andrew Corrigall, Brian Corrigan, Bil Corry, Edward Corry, Jeffrey Corson Jr., George Cort, Jaume Cos, Jo Cosgriff, John Costello, Fiona Coster, Catherine Costigan, Francois Cote, Allen Coté, Alas and Casey Cotita, John Cotter, Mark Cotter, Nick Cotter, Martin Cottrell, Nicholas Cottrell, Isaac Coughlan, Kathryn Coughlan Baylor, Brian Coulter, Nick Coulter, Christopher Courchesne, Peter Courtney-Green, Graham Coutts, Philip Coutts, Sean Coutts, Andrew Cowan, Gene Cowan, Jai Cowan, Simon Coward, Allan Cowley, Stephen Cowley, Dylan Cowper, Alastair Cox, Anneke Cox, Dominic Cox, James Cox, Michael S Cox, Robert Cox, John Coxon, Dawn Coxwell, Mairi Coyle, Andrea 'Shand' Cozzolino, Robert Craddock, Alex Cragg, Stephen Cragg, Matthew Craig, Paul Craigie, Dylan Craine, Helen Crampton, Neil Crane, Steven Crane, Arthur J Crang, Simon Craven, Blyth Crawford, Greg Crawford, Robert Monty Humdinger Crawford, Peter Crawley, RPJ Creative, Jez Creek, Sirena Cremaschi, Dr David Crepaz-Keay, Robert Crighton, Mark Crimando, Lisa Coston Critz, Boyd R Critz V, Roi Croasdale, Angela Crocker, Kyle Crocker, David Croft, Keith Cronshaw, Deborah Crook, Tom Croom, Stephen Cropp, Iain Cropper, London Crosby, Bev Cross, Dave Cross, Penelope Cross, Neal Crossan, Michael Crouch, Alex Crouzen, Samuel Crow, Tom Crowder, Israel Crowe, Ryan Crowe, Crown Vic, LTD, Tilla 'Trillian' Crowne, Rod Crownover, Andrew Crowther, Rob Crowther, James Cruise, Bill Crum, Logan Crum, Graham Crump, Mary R. Crumpton, Kevin Culbert, Jill Cullen, Ian Adam Cullin Cunningham, Devin Cullison, Heather Culpin, Stuart Cumberland, Karen Cumming, Michele Cumming, Alys Cummings, Daniel Cummings, David Cummings, Mark Cummings, Chris Cummins, Andy Cunningham, Jo Cunningham, Ricky Curioso, Alun Curnock, Dave Curran, Jules Curran, Kevin Currie, Daniel Currie Hall, Ian Curry, A T Curtis, Deborah Curtis, Ian Curtis, Michael R Curtis, Rick Curtis, Ruth Curtis, Lesley Curvers, Stephen Cuthbert, Scott D. Cuthbertson, Daniel Cutting, Tim Cutting, Cuz, Karl Anji Oliver Cyan, Silke Caracan Czarny, A. D., James D., Michele D'Acosta, Justin D'Angelo, Justin D'Onofrio, Annie D'Orazio, Kraken D'Waggin, Matthew d'Ancona, Joseph Da Silva, Maarten Daalder, David Dack, Gustav Dahl, Christoffer Dahlblom, Thomas Dahmen, Kristian Dainton, Steve Dalby, Sarah-Jane Dale, Russel Dalenberg, Elizabeth Daley, Robert Dallas, Richard Dallaway, Sara Dallmayr, Diane Dalrymple, Charles Dalton, Jon Daly, Stephen Daly, Adrian Daminato, Dan, Dan-o, Raj Dandekar, Mark Dando, J. Daneman, Craig Danese, Paul Daniel, Paul Daniels, Geoff Dannatt, Danne, Dirk Dannemann, Danon, Donald Dansereau, Eric Danziger, DapperCyborg, Larry Darby, Stephen Darlington, Matthew Darlison, David Darts, Zachary Dashow, Fiona Dashwood, Lim Dau Hee, Graham Dauncey, C Dave, James Harold Davenport, MJM Davenport, Ruth Davenport, Kevin John Davey, Stuart Davey, Amit David, Arvind Ethan David, David, Drew Davidson, John Davidson, Beate Davies, Glyn R. Davies, James Davies, Joshua Davies, Kenvyn Robert Davies, Linda Davies, Mark Davies, Nigel Davies, Pam Davies, Rhodri Davies, Rhys Davies, Samantha Davies, Simon Davies, Rhys Davies-Thomas, Andrew Davis, Benjy Davis, Carlton Davis, D. Zoots Davis, Emma Davis, Ian Davis, Jason Davis, Josh Davis, Laura Davis, Nora & Barry Davis, Professor Jon Davis, Rob Davis, Stephanie Lynn Davis, Walter Davis, Jason Davison, Steve Dawes, Misty Dawn, Dawn, Anthony and Jane Dawson, Elizabeth Dawson, John Dawson, Paul Dawson, R. Dawson Jr., Mat Dawson-Jones, Brendan Day, Evan Day, Frances Day, Tanya Day, Steven Day Clark, Lu Daynes, dbschlosser, Stephanie de Brito Leal, Roland de Bruijn, Tatiana Alejandra de Castro Pérez, Maarten de Groot, Shara De Lorme, Andrew de Lotbiniere, Victoria De Maria, Tom De Mulder, Rene De Paula Jr, Thomas de Senna, José De Sousa, Mike de Vos, Patrick de Vries, Beverley De Witt-Moylan, Lisa De-Vine, Alison Dean, Brad Dean, Clare Dean, Nick Dean, Shervin Dean, Yvonne Dean, Sarah Dean & Tom Wateracre, Donald Dean McBride Jr, Andrew Deane, Christina F DeBello, Koert Debyser, Cecil Decker, Jonathan Decker, L.A. Decker, Carsten Deckert, Jeff DeClue, Hank DeDona, Chris Dee, Joanne Deeming, Rob Deere, James Deering, Chad Deeson, Jeff Del Papa, Joanne Delage, Carmella Delargy, Sebastian M Deliqué, DeltaVictor8, Alicia Jean Demetropolis, Harald Demler, Seamus den Hollander, Emma Denby, Faith Denham, Denis and Leila, Steve Denninger,

Jon Dennis, Nicholas Dennis, Kevin Denny, C David Dent, Chris Dent, Dent Arthur Dent, Samuel Rhys Dent, Ellen Derbyshire, Lyndsey Derbyshire, Kean Dermody, Magdalena Derwojedowa, Dave Derycker, Ian Desborough, Albert Deschenes, Filip Desmet, Dermot Desmond, Valeria Dessi, Paul Dettman, Patrick Deuley, Raj Deut, Alan Devine, James P. Devlin, Laura Devlin, Mike Devlin, Bob Lee Devoest, Chris Dewar-English, Sunny-Blue DeWilde, Dave Dewson, John Dexter, Morag Deyes, Anthony Dhanendran, Luca Di Candeloro y Miguel del Amo, Federico Di Gioia, Michael Di Salvo, Wayne Diamond, Diana, Craig Dibble, Phil Dibowitz, Andrew Dickens, Dayna Dickens, Robert Dickerson, Keith Dickinson, Miranda Dickinson, Roger Dickinson, Tracy Dickinson, Angela Dickson, Helen Dickson, Ian Dickson, Richard F. Dickson, Sarah Dickson, Marion Dickten, Jan Didden, Seth Diehm, Jacob Diemer, Lemon Dierks, Andrew Differ, Difool (DAC), Adriana DiFranco, Robert Dilg, Justin Dilks, Robert Dillette, Sam Dineley, Frederick Dingledy, Daniel Dion, Paul Dion, Tom Dion, Panos Dionysopoulos, Traci-Ann DiSalvatore, Brent M. Diskin, Disputandum, Dithermaster, Jeff Dittburner, Caroline Dix, Henry Dixon, Paul Dixon, Carol Dixon-Smith, Laurène DK, Maggie Doane, Nancy Dobbs, Dustin Dobransky, Gareth Dobson, Max Dobson, Edwin Docherty, James Docherty, Vincent Docherty, Cory Doctorow, Andy Doddington, Lauren Dodds, Leigh Dodds, Kelly Dodge, Gareth Doe, Jonathan M Doe, Randal Doe, Christopher Doecke, Michael R. Doehler, Martin Döering, Ren & Luke Doidge, Alana Dolan, Matthew Dolling, Juanjo Domínguez, David G. Dominick, DON'T PANIC!, Clive Donaghue, Mark David Donajgrodzki, Allan Donald, Donald and Vanessa, Sandy Donaldson $5x10^{23}$, Sean Donaway, Michael Donegan (the Manx one), Barney Donleben, Brendan Donnelly, Nigel Donnelly, Shaun Donnelly, Trevor Donnelly, Trevor A. Donnelly, Adam Doochin, Zephram Doodlebodge, Farrel Dooggg, Ben Doran, Ed Doran, Rory Dormer, Shawn K Dorsey, Cathy Doser, Rick Doten, Christopher Dotson, Ryan Dotson, Benjamin Doty, Shane "shaniber" Doucette, Linda Doughty, Jon Douglas, Paul Douglas, Teresa Douglas, Douglas, Samantha Douglass, Phil Dowell, Jonathan Dowling, Patrick Dowling, Sarah L. Dowling, Andy Down, Tim Downie, Robin Downs, Glen Downton, John Doyle, Mark Doyle, Pearl Doyle, Jelena Dragutinović, John Draisey, Anna Drake, Michail Dim. Drakomathioulakis, Tom Drapeau, Ben Draper, Joel E.P. Draper, Michaela R. Drapes, Scarlet Coralie Drayson, Justin Drew, Robin Dreyer, David Drinkwater, Norman Driskell, Dave Driver, Paul Driver, Boaz David Dror, Andrek Drouin, Aiken Drum, Graeme Drumm, Darryl S. Drury, Jill Drury, Tim Drury, Paul Drussel, Amanda Drws, DSP, Chris du Vé, Michael DuBois, Robert Dudek, Ian Dudley, Erik Due Hansen, Merlin Duff, Scot Duffton, John P Duffy, Kevin J Duffy, Peter Duffy, Phil Duffy, Robert Duffy, Carl Dugdale-Storey, Chris Duggan, Seb Duggan, Danilo Duina, Arthur Duineveld, Jan Dujardin, Paul Duley, Trevor Dummer, Courtney Dunagan, Keith Dunbar, Catherine Dunbar-Brunton, Keith Duncan, Kelly Duncan, Ross Duncan, Chris Dunford, Ian Dungworth, Robbie Dunlop, Martin Dunlop & Elizabeth Vella, Jim Dunn, Joe Dunn, Sheila Dunn, Abban Dunne, Chris Dunne, Mags Dunne, John Dunnet, Vivienne Dunstan, David Dunthorn, Michael Dunthorn, Julia Duplock, Samuel H Dupree Jr, Eric Dupuy, Jacob C Durand, Barney Durrant, Jamie Durrant, Ruth Durrant, Terry L. Durst, Tom Durst - A really hoopy frood, Russell Duston, Ant Duthoit, Jason L. Dutzy, Petter Duvander, Graeme Dyas, Greg Dyck, Shaun Dyer, William Dyer, Paul Dyett, Sarah "started with So Long" Dynan, Erik Dyreng, Richard Dyson, Mirko Dziadzka, Gary Dzidowski, Jan Dzik, Gavin Eadie, Brandon Eaker, Kate Eakins, Jack Eales, Gerald Ealy, Nigel Eames, Luke Earl, Sheila Earl, Warren Earle, John Earls, Jimm Easley, Scott Eason, Nick East, James Eastham, Terry Eastham, Lynden Easton, Mark Eastwood, Barnaby Eaton-Jones, George Eccles, Michael A Eccles, Nell Eckersley, Krista Eckhardt, Aasne Eckhoff, Nigel Eckley, Lorraine Eckman, James Edge, Michael Edlund, Michael Edmonds, Pete Edmunds, Art Edwards, Brian Edwards, Emil Edwards, Guy T. Edwards, Jeremy Mark Edwards, Martin Edwards, Nicola Edwards, Paul Edwards, Steven J. Edwards, Tim Edwards-Hart, Tim Egan, Ralph Egas, Cynthia Egbert, Philip Eggers, Michael Egginton, Matthew Egglestone, Chelsea Eggleton, Martin Eggleton, Jeremy Ehrlich, Tim EHrlich, Simon Eisner, Jonas Ekman, Elaine and JP, Andrew Eland, Michael Elder, Charles Eldridge, Brandy Nicole Eleazar, The Electric Monks podcast (A.K.A. Edward Hunter), Richard Elen, David Eliahou, Chad Elish, Rob Elisha, Elizabeth, Ardan, John Kerl, Trevor Elkin, The Elkin-Brams, Jayson Elliot, Craig Elliott, Matt Elliott, Sarah Elliott, Toby Elliott, Christopher Ellis, Duncan Ellis, James Ellis, Jonathan Ellis, Richard Ellis, Robyn Ellis, Robert Ellsmore, Jim Ellwanger, Brett Elmendorf, Klas Elmgren, Alexandre Elsayad, Stephen Elsden, Ashley Elsdon, Michael Elson, Richard Elson, James Eltringham, Robin Elvin, Sue Elwood, Elyk and Erin, Eric P. Emerson, Helen Emerson, Matt Emerson, Andrew Emery, Jackie 'Frogstar' Emery, Neil Emery, Zachary Emil, Barbara Eminger, Andrew Emm, Gregg Emmel, David Emmerson, Jennifer Emmerson, Robert Emmett Reeves III, Keiichi Endo, Rudi Endresen, Enesthi, Megan & Jason Engel, Kai Engelbrecht, Frank Engelhardt, Wolfgang Engels, Emilio Englade, Eve England, Ian Engleback, Cwytch Englebright, Miss Skye Englebright, Paul Engler, Joshua R. English, Martin English, Brian Enigma, Jamas Enright, Emily Eowyn Hoppe, Vic Eppler, Joshua Epstein, Zedd Epstein, Dr. Michael Erdmann, Stefan Erhardt, Ian Ericson, Pamela Erikson, Richard Eriksson, Tomas Eriksson, Eunice Ermovick, The Erringtons, Corinne Erwin, Michael Escolme, Tim Esler, Vanessa Espinoza, Michelle Esquivias, Ramsey Ess, Tommy Esson, Miguel Esteban, Chuck Esterbrook, et42, Delia Ettere, Alan Etzel 101010, Eulialia, Aron Evans, Cath Evans, Colby Evans, Eugene Evans, Geraint Evans, Idris Evans, Jeff Evans, Kellie Evans, Mark Evans, Matthew Evans, Phil Evans, Rhianna Evans, Sarah Evans, Vicky Evans, Zack Evans, Danie Evans & Shawn Hardt, Harry C. Evans III, Stephen Evans-Howe, Jim Evarts, Mark Eveleigh, Morten Evenbye, Katie Everdyke, Chris J Everett, Lynne Everett, The Everists, Paul Ewing, Jess Ex, Richard Eyre, Luca Fabbri, Paolo Fabbri, Rainer Fabianski, Mikołaj Fabjański, Guy Fabron, Pete Fagan, Harley Faggetter, Tony Faiers & Gerry Miles, Robert R. Fairbairn, John Fairhurst, Orsolya & Alex Faisst, Dave Falconer, David Falconer, Keith Falconer, Stephen Falconer, Sergey Faldin, Andrew Falenski, Julian Falk, Mattias Falk, Sarah Falk, Jens Fallesen, Jones Family, McIlroy Family, Mirbach Family, Whyte Family, Noah Fang, Fant, Michael W. Farb, James Farmer, Farnaby, Jonathan Farr, Finbarr Farragher, Andrew Farrell, David L Farrell, Kate and Sean Farrell, Stefan Farrenkopf, Byron Geoffrey Farrow, Peter Fasciano, Aaron Fasel, Jonas Fast, Fat Boy Ginge, Laura Fathauer, Angela Faunce Leaf, Sarah Faust, Pete Favelle,

Tina Fawcett, Joshua FB, Gavin Vincent Fearnsides, Barry Featherston, Cliff Feddema, Sara Fedeli, Dominic Fehling, Tracy Fehr, Brandon Feist, Zsolt Fejer, Henrik Feld, Thomas Feld, Arlen Feldman, Daniel Feldman, Robert Feldman, Paul Fellenberg, Martin Feller, Paddy Fellows, Peter Fellows-McCully, Rob Felvus, M. Fender, Adam Fenn, Ian Fenn, David Fennell, Patrick Fennell, Michael Fennelly, Jack Fenwick, Jason Fergus, Andrew Ferguson, Helen Ferguson, Stephen Ferguson, Jose Fernández Gil, Martijn Fernhout, Douglas Edwin Ferrebe Trafford, David Ferreira, Anthony, Elena and Saša Ferretti - Genuine Towel Enthusiasts, Jodie Ferries, Cameron Ferstat, Matthew J Fessey, Jenora Feuer, Steven Fice, Jeff Fichter, Laura & David Fichtmüller, Paulien Fiechter, Alex Fielder, Guy Fielding, James Fielding, Martin Fietz, Brook Figgins, Jason Filiatrault, Christy Filipich, Robert Filkins, Loz Fillmore, Angus Findlay, Larry Fine, Amy Finegan, @finisfunny, Toby Finlay, Elizabeth Finley, Thomas Finnerup, Finnian, Steve Fiori, Artie Firth, Carl Firth, Janet & Peter Firth, Erwin Fischer, Smarter Fish, Tony Fish, Deborah Fishburn, Andrew Fisher, Anthony Fisher, Charles Fisher, Kay Fisher, Keith Fisher, Michael Fisher, Mike Fisher, Paul Fisher, Shauna Fisher, Margaret Fisher & Miles Fisher, Roy & Lesley Fishwick, Alex Fitch, Fitz, Tom Fitz-Hugh, Mike Fitzgerald, Ben Fitzgerald-O'Connor, Peter Fitzpatrick, Joe Fitzsimons, Fixate, Fizzlewick Napoleon Orpheus Roarty Daedalus, Mari Flaata, Brett N. Flaherty, Jennifer H Flaig, Bréan Flanagan, Avi Flax, Julian Fleetwood, Katherine Fleming, Mark Fleming, Andy Fletcher, Dick Fletcher, Julian & Heather Fletcher, Matt Fletcher, Molly Fletcher, Sky Fletcher, Michael Flett, John Flint, Kathryn Flint, Flint, Philip Florian, The Flotenberger, Dr Chris Flowers, Gretchen Floyd, Flubber2kool, Nick Flügge, Thea Flurry, Kelan Flynn, Paul Flynn, Wendy Foad, Michael Foggin, T.J. Follmer, David Folsom, Carl Foner, Patrick G Fontaine, FoolSinc, For Martin; brain the size of a planet, For my beloved kids Lova & Leon Magnusson, Amy Forbes, Jean Forbes, William Forbes, Tim Forcer, Riley Ford, Rob Ford, Bette Forester, Chris Forman, Sharon Forman, Luiz Formiga, David John Fornari, Dan Forrest, Diane Forrest, Matt Forrest, Wilf Forrow, Simon Forster, Fiona Forsyth, Amy Fort, Laura Fortman-Jones, Gordon Forton, forty2, Geoff Fortytwo, Carlyle Foss, Chuck Foster, Frances Foster, Hilary Foster, John "JAF" Foster, Chris Foster-White, Aaron Fothergill, Andrew Fothergill, Elina Foui, Foundassion Limited - Next Wave Network - Shahrooz Bhopti, Four Corners Collectibles, Devin & Colter Foutz, Matthew Fowle, Daniel Oolon Fowler, Rhianna Fowler, Rob Fowler, Rosalind Fowler, Adam Fox, Angus Fox, Charles B Fox, Kyle Fox, Emily Fox-Green, Tia Foxon, Melanie Foxton, Scott Fracul, Luisa Francia, Dan Francis, Nicholas Franco, Brian Frank, Erica L Frank, Nick Frank, Jerry Franke, Miles Frankel, Daniel Frankham, Jonathan Franklin, Michael L Franklin, Helen Franklin Bell, Duane "Dewey" Franklund, John Franks, Peter Franks, Hanne Fransen, Johan Franzén, Bryan Fraser, Nikki Fraser, Oonagh Fraser, Shona Fraser, Susan Fraser, Daniel W. Frazier, Timothy Freakley, Dave Frear, Freddie & PGOAT, George Frederick, Sean Fredrick, Alison Freebairn, John Freeborn, Mike Freed, Alexander H Freeman, Jason Freeman, John Freeman, Matthew Freeman, Skeet Freeman, Luke Freiler, Adam French, Dan French, Kenneth French, Solomon French, Marc Fresko, Cheryl Fretz, William Frewin, Kerry Frey, Federica Frezza, Neal Frick, Ulrich Fricke, Brian Fried, Chris Fried, Hilary Fried, Gary Friedlander, David Friedman, Jason Friedman, Eleya Frields, David Friend, Thomas Fries, Martin Friese, Anders Frihagen, Adrian Frisicaro, Bernhard Fritsch, Joe Fritz, John Fritz, Michael Frogley, Luke Frost, Samuel Frost, Cynthia Fry, John Fry, Fuchsi, Nick Fudge, Paula Fulga, Christopher Fullbrook, Jon Fuller, Steve Fuller, Stephen Fulljames, Rob Fulton, Rob Funk, Richard Funston, Pauk Furgunson, Joshua Furman, Annaliese Furnas, Antony Fussey, Grant G, Olly G, G:Puchas, Kay G., Vanessa G., Fanni Gabnai, Onno Gabriel, Jameson Gagnepain, Colin Timothy Gagnon, Peter Gahlinger, Robert Gaimari, David Gaipa, Deane Galbraith, Sarah Gale, Kameron Gale Covall, Brian Gallagher, Helen Louise Gallagher, Josh Gallagher, Matthew Kavan Gallagher, Rachel Gallagher, Alessandro Gallo, John Galvin, Luca Gambetti, Tim Gambrell, Red Raccoon Games, Amanda Gammon, Andrew Gamwell, Sean Gandert, Bryn Gandy, Laxman Gani, Joshua Gans, Thomas Ganter, Garax, Garch, Kevin Garcia, Luis Garcia, Mark Garcia, Paco B Garcia, Daniel Garcia Usobiaga, Andrew Garden, Paul Gardiner, Samuel-Louis Gardiner, Iain Garioch, Sheila Garl, Belinda Garland, Brian J. Garland, Nick Garland, Stephen C. Garland, Wayne Garmil, Paul D Garmon, Sarah Garnham, Hannah Garrett, Owen Garrett, Paul J. Garrett, David Garrison, Conal Garrity, Nev Garven, Gary & Racquel, Annabel Gaskell, K. Gavenman, Paul Gavin, George Gearing, Hannah Geble, Erik Gedeon, David E C Gee, Guy Geens, Philip Sebastian Geiger, Stefan Gemzell, Chris George, Joe George, Jonathan George, George, Jack George-Turner, Georgi, Michael J. Geraghty, C.M. Gerard, Alexander Gerhardt, Hannes Gerl, Adam J. Gerstein, Thomas Gewecke, Hannah Geyik, GGK, Sassan Gholiagha, Ali Ghorashi, Seeta Ghowry, Joseph J.M. Gianessi, Matt Gibbins, Tony Gibbons, Alexander Gibbs, Andy Gibson, Clendon Gibson, Clinton Gibson, Julie Gibson, Rebecca & Alex Gibson, Stuart Gibson, Lucy Gibson from Geoff Burton, Oliver Giggins, Caroline Gilbert, Dan Gilbert, James Gilbert, Lauren Gilbert, Nigel Gilbert, Wendy Gilbert, Cyrus Gilbert-Rolfe, Tim Gilchrist, Adam Giles, Julie Giles, Chris Gill, Nick Gill, Jaspal Gillar, Jay GIllespie, Joe Gillespie, Harriet Gillian, Richard Gillin, Neil Gillon, Andrew Gilpin, Gina, Marcus Gipps, Mike and Ali Gipson, Tobias Gissler, Joe Gitter, Matt Gittins, Attilio Giue, Damien Glancy, Katrin Gläsmann, Martin Glassborow, John K Glasscock, Jordan Glassman, Walker Glassmire, Matthew Glastonvill, MaryAnne Glazar, Michael J. Gleason, Charlie Gleek and Kate Schmitt, Craig Glenday, Will Glendinning, J. Glenn Künzler, Cooper Glodoski, Jacob Gloor, David Glover, Lee Glover, David Glover-Aoki, glumjamesbrown, Mark Glynne, Krista Goalby, Steve Goaley, Bruce Goatly, Mark Goblowsky, Francis Godawski, Matt Goddard, Paul Goddard, Mark Godenho, Richard Goedeken, Paul L. Goelz, Jennifer Goertz, Matthias Goessler, Uwe Goetzke, Seth Goldberg, Damian Golding, Elizabeth Goldman, Nick Goldman, Dr Simon Goldman, Anna Spiteri, Robin Diane Goldstein, Chris Golightly, Daniel Golombek, Charez Golvala, Richard W. Gombert, Alison Gomm, Attila Gonda, John Gonsalves, Kyle Gonyea, Andres Gonzalez Mancera, Kyle Good, Ben Goodale, Jeff Goodall, Keren Goodblatt, Brendan Goodbody, George Goodfellow, Paul J Goodison, Andrew Goodman, Gilad Goodman, Roger Goodman, Susan Goodridge Carter, Daryl Goodwin, David Goodwin, Mark Goodwin, Richard Goodwin, Nick Goolsbee, Pete Goosselink, Sunil Gopalakrishna, Dennis Goransson,

Adam Gordon, Claire E. Gordon, Craig Gordon, Damian Gordon, Janet Maria Gordon, Keegan Gordon, Michael Gordon, Niall Gordon, Peter Gordon, Bryson Gore, Glen Goreyography Emil, Ian Gorman, Patrick T. Gorman, Thomas Gorman, Stacy Gormley, Richard Gorodecky, Jamie Gorrod, Jesse Gortarez, Andrew Gothard, Adam Gotlieb, Stephen Gough, Jane & Jonathan Gould, Joshua Goure, Stephen Gowing, Robert Goza, Daniel M Grace, Mike Grace, Fabian Graf, David Graham, Drew Graham, Gordon Graham, Guy, Christine, and Chloe Graham, Ian Graham, Jacqui Graham, Kas Graham, Matthew Graham, Scott Graham, Grahams, Edward Grainger, Justin William Gramm, Carlo Grancini, Austin Grant, Craig Grant, James Grant, Jan Friderik Grant, Lee Grant, Ruby Grant, Patrick Grant Sullivan, Rosemary Grant-Muller, Rachel Imogen Grant-Waters, Grattan, Peter C. Gravelle, Carsten Gravgaard, Bruce Gray, Cary Gray, Christopher Gray, Dennis Gray, Doug Gray, Jonty Gray, Mark Gray, Matt Gray, Michael Gray, Neil Gray, Gary Graybill, Danny Graydon, Edward Greathead, Martin Greaves, Heiko Grebing, Kristopher Greek, Clementine Greeley, Tim Greeley, Bill Green, Dan Green, Deb Green, Dwayne Green, John Green, Karen Green, Mark Green, Matthew Green, Nic Green, Paul Green, Richard Green, Sue M Green, Tom Green, Frank G. Greene, Dr Nick Greenwood, Georgia Greer, Greg Greg, Katherine Gregory, Keith Gregory, John Greig, Pascal Greilach, Doreen Greubel, Ken Grier, Chris Griffin, James Griffin, Neil Griffin, Susanne Griffin, Josie Griffin-Roosth, Matthew Griffith, Nathan Griffith, Stuart Griffith, Christopher Griffiths, David Griffiths, Mark Griffiths, Natalie Griffiths, Rhys L Griffiths, Stephen Griffiths, Tom Griffiths, Guido Grigat, Sarah and Andy Grigg, Henry Griggs, Harm Grijpstra, S & S Grimes, J. Eric Grimm, Michael Grinko, James Grinnell, Adam Grochowski, Jed Grodin, David Grogan, Alexander Grønning, Groo42, David "ishotjr" Groom, Mel Groom, Steve Groom, Charles R. Grosvenor Jr., Kevin Grove, Minty Grover, Derham Groves, Nick Gruff Smith, Martin Grund, Thomas Grundberg, Anthony J Grzesiak, Adam Grzesiczak, Pedro Lucas Guedes, Dave Guerin, Everett Guerny, Tin Guerrero, Simon Guerrier, Paul Guest, Tino Rick Gugger, Lia Guillaumet, John Guillemette Jr., David Guinane, Guinny, David Guiot, Kyle Guisewhite, Jon M Gulliksen, Cliff Gunderson, Craig Gunderson, Alison Gundy, Brendan Gunn, Cathy Gunn, Walter Gunzburg, Björn Günzel, Aobo Guo, Gürkan Gür, Ali Güracar, Nicholas Gurr, Matthew Gushta, Jordan M Gustine, D.A. Gutierrez, Altay Guvench, Eric Gwaltney, Owen Gwilliam, Liz Gwynne, Mariann Györke, Sascha Gysel, Alexandar P Gyurov, Anna H, Ben H, Edd H, Judi H, Terra H, Matti Haack, Anders Haagen, Kristian Haapa-aho, Kathy Haas, Gideon Haberkorn, Margit Regine Habusta, Jean Hackett, Brianna Hackler, David Haddock, Paul Hadfield, Julie Hadley, Jack Hafeli, D K Haffenden, Matthew J. Hagan, Sofia Hagberg, Jan Hagelskamp, Libby Hagen, Eileen Hagger-Street, Erling Hagland, Cynthia Hagstrom, Howard Hague, Patrick Hahn, Paul Haigh, Jamie Hailstone, Alastair Haines, John Haines, Marc Hairston, Scott Hajek, Tuomas Hakkarainen, Tepfer, Hal., Boaz Halachmi, Joseph Halamek, Simon Hale, Joshua Hale Fialkov, Gareth Halfacree, Dorothy Halfhide, Allison J. Hall, Dani Hall, David Hall, Eileen Hall, Ethan Hall, Jack Hall, Jon Hall, Justin Hall, Marc Kevin Hall, Matthew D Hall, Pete Hall, Erik Hällblad, Daniel Halliday, Padraic Hallinan, Joe Halliwell, Leah Halloran, Rob Halloway, Manu Hallowes, David Hallows, Peter Halls, Dave Halperin, Dave Halsey, Dan Hamamura, Ashley Hambrook, Mishra "Nemo" Hamelin, Jane Hamill, Andy Hamilton, Claire Hamilton, Ian Hamilton, Maz Hamilton, Melissa Hamilton, Robert W. Hamilton II, Dr. William J. Hamilton III, Bo Bomuld Hamilton-Wittendorff, Chris Hamley, Cathy Dobson, Maddy Hamley, Freya Hammar, Vincent Hammarin, Lee Hammerton-Walsh, Damian Hammond, Ian Hammond, Steven Hammond, Richard Hammond Smith, Lee "Snags" Hampton, William L Hampton, Joon S. Han, Mona Hanafi-Reiss, David & Denise Hancock, James Hancock, Jeremy Hancock, Paul Hancock, Mark Hancox, Michael Handelzalc, Derek Handley, Sam Handley, Camal Handor, Tibor Hanis, Fenja Hanisch, Michael Hanish, Douglas Hanke, Rüdiger Hanke, Tim Hankey, Jeremy Hanks, Ryan Hanlin, Matthew Hanlon, Séamus Hanly, Iain Hannah, Irene Hannah, Toby Hannam, tim hannigan, Christopher Hanning, Claire Hannon, Karl Hansell, Barb Hansen, Chris Hansen, Jay and Melinda Hansen, Kristian Hansen, Michael Hansen, Robin Hansen, Scott Hansen, Alex Hansford, Brian Ch. Hanson, Christopher M. Hanson, Elizabeth Hanson, Sara Hanson, Juliën Hanssens, Martin Hanstead, Bonita Hanwright, Melanie Harari, J Harasta, Michael Harder, Samyogita Hardikar, Tim Harding, Andrew Hardman, David & Alison Hardman, George Hards, Kevin Hards, Simon Hardy, Jason Hares, Harf, Matthew Harffy, Andy Harfoot, Alex Hargrave, Anita M Hargrave, Michael Hargreave Mawson, Paul Hargreaves, Pat Harkin, Ryan Harkin, Mike Harland, Doug Harley, Carolyn Harlow, Julie Harlow, Christian Harms, Steve Harms, Gerald Galvin Harniman, Kim Harning, Ulrik Harnisch, Jordan Harper, Lucas Harper, Mark Harper, Simon Harper, Mr. Gwyn Harries, Amy Harrington, Benjamin L. Harris, Carl Harris, Duncan Harris, Ian Harry Harris, James Harris, Jamie Harris, Jim Harris, Kirsten Harris, Molly Harris, Richard M Harris, Sondra Harris, Steve M J Harris, Susi Harris, Toby Harris, Olivia Harris Wing, Graham Harrison, Jason Harrison, Paul Harrison, Richard Harrison, Sharon Tracy Harrison, Simon Harrison, Allix Harrison-D'Arcy, A.F. Harrold, Chris & Briget Hart, Keith Hart, Kimberly Hart, Michael JD Hart, Michael R. Hart, Victoria Hart, Louisa Hart and Douglas Hart, Heather Hartel, Maximilian Hartl, Simeon Hartland, David C. Hartley, Ned Hartley, Suzanne Hartley, Veronica Hartley, Ian Hartley., Björn Hartmann, Michael Hartmann, David Hartnell, James Hartshorn, Dana Hartsock, Neil Hartwell, Carl Harvey, Colin Harvey, Conrad Harvey, David Harvey, Jon Harvey, Mike Harvey, Peter G Harvey, Sam Harvey, Stephen & Eleanor Harvey, Will Haseltine, Jen Hasenauer, Nate Hasiak, Simon Haslam, Sherief Hassan, Andreas Hasselgren, Karen 'Squeak' Hasselo, Tim Hastings, Anya Hastwell, Shelli Haswell, Hatti, Richard Hatton, John E. Haubenreich, C. Hauck, Terry Haughin, James Haughton, Hauke, Patrick M. Hausen, Ruth Hauser, Arno Hautala, Kim Haverblad, Nathan Hawes and Caroline Fitzgerald, Mike Hawk, Andy Hawkins, Benjamin Hawkins, MiKi Hawkins, Vivian Hawkins, Thomas Hawksworth, Tom Hawkyard, John Hawley, Nathaniel Hay, Meredith Hayden, Alexandra Hayes, Alys Hayes, Joanne Hayes, Nigel Hayes, Phillip Hayes, Simon Haynes, Monty Hayter, Brian Hazelett, Chris Hazelton, Grant Hazelton, Aaron Hazelwood, Paula Hazlehurst, David Head, Robert Head, Rachael Headrick, Christina Healey, Andrew Hearse, Emma Heasman-Hunt, Ian Heath, Joe Heath, Lawrence Heath, Lois Heath, Karen Hecht Brown, Barry Hecker, Niall Hedderley, Linus Hedenberg, Kez Hedges, Robin Heemstra,

Sean Hegarty, Heike, Lucas Heil, Dieter J Heimlich, Bardur Heinason, John E. Heinlein, Lukas Heintschel, Verdi Heinz, Tapio Heiskari, Colin Helb, Joost Helberg, Mark Hellkamp, Christer Hellström, Gabriel L Helman, Nick Helweg-Larsen, Lloyd Hemming, Michael Hempel-Jørgensen, Jan Roger Henden, Andrew Henderson, Cathy Henderson, Jim Henderson, Paul Henderson, Simon Henderson, Stephen Henderson, Sarah Hendrickson, Dr Colin Hendrie, Grady Hendrix, Ross Hendry, Benjamin Hendy, Kenna Henkel, Jason Henriksen, Anne Henry, Cynthia Henry, Patrick Henry, Mark Hense, Jon Henson, Elizabeth Henwood, Andreas Herberger, Gigi Herbert, Nicole Herbert, Sandy Herbert, David Heremans, Simon Herlihy, Eileen Sabrina Herman, Hannah Herman, William Hern, Michael C. Hernandez, Gonzalo Hernández, David Hernly, Signe Herping-Hansen, Lilian Herrena, Kayta C. Herring, Richard Herring, Mick Herron, Brian Heselden, Theo Heselmans, Patrick Hess, Robert Hession, Janicole Hetleif, Eugene Hetzel, Rhian Heulwen Price, Christian Heuser, Felix & James Hewison-Carter, Daniel Hewitt, Dr Craig D Hewitt, Russ Hewson, Anna Heym, Alexander Heyne, Catherine Heywood, Fergus Heywood, Hi Rob - thanks for everything, Philip Hibberd, Mark Hibbett, Robert Hibbitt, Adrian Hickford, Lee Hickin, Amanda Hickling, Andrew Hicks, Gary Hicks, Leanne & Andy Hicks, Ben Higginbottom, Chris Higgins, Darran Higgins, Kurt Higgins, Sean Higgins, Stu, Katherine and Izzy Higgins, Nick Higham, Highfin, B. Hightower, Heather Higinbotham Davies, Alice Hildreth, van Beijnum Hilje, Abigail Hill, Adam Hill, Antony Hill, Darrin Hill, Dean Hill, Greg Hill, Joe Hill, K Hill, Mathew Hill, Matt Hill, Richard Hill, Robin Hill, Stephen Hill, Woodrow Hill, J. J. Hillard, Kara Hills, William Hills, David Hilton, Simon Hilton, Ed Hind, Thomas Hinde, Chris Hines, Nick Hines, Mike Hinford - #LetsTryUBI, Ryan Hinks, Richard Hinton, Samuel Scott Hipp, Kai Hirdt, Adria Hirsch, Forbes Hirsch, Volker Hirsch, Michael Hirschman, Amy Hirst, Mike Hirst, Michael Hirtz, Paul Hiscock, Daniel Hiscox, Sid Hiscox, HistorySmith, Alan Hitchin, Michael Hitson, Yi-Sung Oliver Ho, Lucien Hoare, Fiona Hobbes, Martin Hobbs, Richard Hobbs, Adam Hobson, Ian Hocking, Daniel C. Hodges, Jason Hodges, Mary Ruth Hodges, Paul Hodges, Robin Hodges, Ryan Hodges, Danya Hodgetts, James Hodgins, Sanborn Hodgkins, Treve Hodsman, Guido Hoeberechts, Henning Hoenicke, Matt Hofer, Sebastian Hoffback, Andrew James Hoffman, David Hoffman, Michael Hoffman, Arne Hoffmann, Rob Hoffmann, Rob Hofker, Edward Hofman, Derek Hofmann, Jessica Hogan, Roel Hogervorst, Elizabeth Hogg, Richard Hoggett, Dan Hoizner, Ella Holden, Stephen Holder, David Holder-Twomlow, Dave Holets, Martin Holeyšovský, Holger, Bill Holland, Ivan Holland, James Holland, James C. Holland, Rob Holland, Samantha Holland, Steve Holland, Greg Hollett, Daniel Hollick, Paul Hollingdrake, Cathy Hollingworth, Les Hollis, Roy S. Hollis, Wayne Hollis, David Sheldon Hollister, Richard Holloway, Robin Holloway, Daniel Holman, John Holman, Eileen Holmes, Iain Holmes, Jim Holmes, Paul and Cathy Holroyd, Jeremy Holstein, Andrew Stewart Holt, Helen Holt, Ken Holt, Lacey Homan, John Homer, Dan Hon and Robin Ray, Jenny Honeyman, Josh Honomichl, Gerrit Jan Hoogeland, Erik Hooijmeijer, Karen Hooper Blaney, Mike Hooton, Richard Hope, Andrew Hopkins, Christopher Hopkins, Jonathon Hopkins, Matthew Hopkins, Mike Hopman, William Hopp, J.F. Hopse, Finn Hopson, Richard Hoptroff, Geir Horgen, Jochen Horn, Laura Horn, Malcolm Horn, Kenneth J Hornak Jr, George Hornby, Mike Hornby, Jeff Horne, Mike Horne, Shaun Horner, Thomas Hornigold, Dave Horoschak, Dudley Horque, Graham Horrobin, Neil Horsburgh, Athena Horsten, Tracy Horstmann, Catherine & Nick Horton, Heather (TheRamblingRabbit) Horton, Kevin Horton, Robin Horton, Elmer Horvath, Ian Horwill, Jerry Horwood, Lara Hosier, Michelle Hoskin, Jeff Hoskinson, Wolfgang Hößl, Tom 'mostly harmless' Hostler, Nick Hotalling, Neal & Sam Houghton, David House, Stephen Houston, Lynda Howard, Mark Howard, Mark J. Howard, Martin Howard, Paul Howard, Simon Howard, J Howard Roberts, Catherine Howard-Dobson, Philly Howarth, Hannah Howden, Michele Howe, Sarah Howe, Graeme Howell, Samuel Howell, Syd Howells, Matthew Howlett, Debby Howrie, Teri Howson-Griffiths, Russell and Mom Hoyer, Benjamin Hrach, Drea Hubbard, Nick Hubble, Joe Huber, David Hubert, Helen Hubert, Marijn Hubert, Gerhard Hübner, Matthias Hübscher, James Huckaby, Brian Huddleston, Paul Hudson, Trey Hudson, Stephan Huebner, Andrew F. Huff, Allen C. Huffman, Paul Huffman, Jennifer Huggett, Cory Hughart, Brian G. R. Hughes, Chris Hughes, Gary Hughes, Jimmy Hughes, Judith W Hughes, Paul Hughes, Paul D Hughes, Richard Hughes, Peter Hugosson-Miller, Gijs Huisman, Changa Huksy, Stephen James Hull, Richard Hulm, Tim Hulsizer, Charlie Hume, Lee Hume, Alison Humphrey, Amber Humphrey, Bruce Humphrey, Jos Humphrey, Will Humphrey, Peter Humphries, Sharon Humphries, Adrian Humphris, Andrew Hungerford, Adam Huninik, Jeremy Hunsinger, Adrian Hunt, Andrew Hunt, Bernie Hunt, David Hunt, Nik Hunt, Pamela Hunt, Paul Hunt, Stuart Hunt, Daniel R. Hunter, Donald Hunter, J. Colin R. Hunter, Keith Hunter, Linda Hunter, Rowan Hunter, Steve Hunter, Benjamin Hunting, Paul Huntingford, A. Huntington Griffith, Gunnar Hunzelmann, Ralph Huppin, Barry Hurford, Cait Hurley, Cindie Hurley, Jay Hurley, John Hurrell, Mark Hush, Danish Hussain, Nicholas Hussey, Paul Hussey, Alex Husted, Conrad M. Hutcheson, Danie Hutchin, Nick Hutchings, Clair Hutchings-Budd, Owen Hutchins, Lucy Hutchinson, Mike Hutchinson, Barry Hutchison, Charles Hutson, Jemal Hutson, Adrian Hutton, Allan Hutton, Richard Huw Morgan, Jörn Huxhorn, Matthew Huxtable, Neal Huynh-Richard, Caleb Hyde, Christopher Hyde, Dawn Hyde, John Hyde, Steve Hyde - So long & thanks for all the fish…, Matthew Hyland, Dan Hyman, Susan Ibbotson, Martin Ibert, Manon Ibes, Ernesto Igartua, Louise Kerr Ilett, Felix Iliff, Michael Imber, Kevin Imboden, In Memory of Arthur Duane McLemore, Ms. Indica, infrapinklizzard, Alex Ingham, Steven Ingham, Johnnie Ingram, Robert Ingram, Dave Inkersole, Jarkko Inkinen, Dark Insanities, Invariel, iopgod@gmail.com, David Ireland, James Ireland, Nicholas Irizary, Marie Irshad, Ian Irvine, David Irving, Ian Andrew Irving, Tim Irving, Matthew Irwin, Rob Irwin, Roger Isaac, Andy Isaacson, Lara Isabel, Louise Issal, James Ivey, Chuck Ivy, Ilsa Izkovitz, Juan Vicente Izquierdo, Geoff Izzard, Chris Jack, Jack, Adrian Jackson, Andrew Jackson, Chris Jackson, Elaine J Jackson, James Jackson, Jason Jackson, Karsten Jackson, Kevin Jackson, Seamus Jackson, Steve Jackson, Leri "Theattackchef" Jacobs, Jae, Prashant Jain, Dr Mark Jairaj, Ingrid Elin Jakobsen, Hana Jakoubkova, Syed Jamal, Dagon James, Ian James, Jason James, Linda James, Mike James, Mike F James, Neil James, Nicholas A James, Robin James, Russ James, James Loves Allyson a bloody lot, Aaron Jamieson, Peter Janes, Saša Janković, Chad Jannusch,

Jennifer Janson, Daniel Janssen, Bastienne Jaques, David Jarman, JaroCarstenYvonne, James Jarrett, Jonathan Jarrett, Sophie Jarvie, Anthony Jarvis, Billy Jarvis, Christina Jarvis, Laura Jarvis, Tim Jarvis, Kim Jarvis & Peter Tags, Dr Sebastian Jaskiewicz, Robert Jaspersohn, Eran Jassby, Julita Jaudzemaite, Jordan Jaunt, Ion Jaureguialzo, Howard Javes, Jay & Michelle, JB, Aaron Jean, Yoon Jeawoong, Helen Jeffries, Tim Jeffries, Craig Jeffs, Bartosz Jelenski, Peter Jelstrup, Ade Jenkins, Lloyd Jenkins, Paul S Jenkins, Rob Jenkins, Scott Jenkins & His Boys, Paul Jenner, Amanda Jennings, David Jennings, Scott Jennings, Wai-ling Jennings, Eric Jensen 42, Sean Jenson, Julia and Russell Jepson, Christopher Jerden-Cooke, Nikki Jeske, Callum Jessamine, Keith Jewell, JF, Jillian, Sergio Jimenez, Elisa Jiménez Alonso, Richard Jinks, JJ, JKH, JM, Robin Jobber, Andrew Jobbins, Mark Jobson, Jofe, Kamal Jogia, Sune Johannesson, Jared Johanning, Jacob Johannsen, Hans Johansson, johnnywalker2001@gmail.com, JohnPatrickMCP, Arlyn Johns, Pete Johns, Allan Douglas Johnson, Chris Johnson, Craig Johnson, Gustin Johnson, Jeff Johnson, Jeffrey John Johnson, Keith Johnson, Lejon A. Johnson, N A B Johnson, Nicholas Johnson, Paul Johnson, Punkeaux Johnson, R B Johnson, Sophie Johnson, Stephen Johnson, Seth Johnson & Melissa Binde, Lisa Johnston, Paul Johnston, Susan Johnston, Brian Johnstone, Peter Johnstone, Nicholas Joll, Jon and Mish, Jonas, Anna, Ragnar & Gunnar, Andrew Jones, Andy Jones, Anna Jones, Arte Jones, Barbara Jones, Benjamin C. Jones, Brian Jones, Brian P. Jones, Carol Jones, Chaz F Jones, Christopher Jones, Christopher Noel Jones, Daniel Jones, David Jones, David C. Jones, Deborah Jones, Eileen Jones, George & John Jones, Helen Jones, Ian Jones, Joseph A. Jones, Julie Jones, Kevin Jones, Mark Jones, Martin Jones, Matthew Glyn Jones, Melanie Jones, Michelle Jones, Mike Jones, mister. jones, Nicholas Jones, Nick Jones, Nigel R Jones, Peter Jones, Richard Jones, Robert T E Jones, Robin Jones, Roger O. Jones, Simon Jones, Simon & Kate Jones, Tony Jones, Virginia Jones, Henrik Jordahn, Chris Jordan, Chuck Jordan, T.M. Jordan, Harriet Jordan and Michael Olsson, Lars Jorgensen, Ole Sandbæk Jørgensen, Jørund, Elizabeth K. Joseph, Karen Josephson, Josh and crew, Josiane, Timo Josten, Charles Joy, JP, JTCC, Joy Rhiannon Julian, Julie & Rick, E.E. Jung, Sarah Jungling, Jochen Junker, Peggy Jurado, justchris, Richard JustHere4Coffee, Neal Justice, Dave Justus, Jesper Juul, Jeffrey K from NJ, Kevin K., K4-713, Tev Kaber, Adam Kafka, Susanne Kahle, Tobias Kahlenberg, Judith Kahn, Nick Kaijaks, Erno Kaikkonen, Luca Kaiser, PhD, Jasper Kaizer, Kornelis and Josepha Kalsbeek, Alan Kaltz, Andreas Kaluza, James Kalyn, Cathrin Kamphausen, Jorke Kamstra, Angelo Kanaris, David Kane, PJ Kane, Jørgen Kann, Andrew Kaplan, Len Kaplan, Michael Kaplan, Roy E Kaplan, Doc Kaps, Tasja Karapetian, Adam Karas, Oliver Karasch, Karbons, Guus Karemaker, Marilyn Karet, E Karia, Phillip Karlsson, Sydney Karnes, Karsten, Emerson Kasak, Sandy Kashmar, Aditya Kashyap, Ingo Kasprzak, Nigel Kat, Kate & Ian, Torsten Kathke, Mo Katibeh, Darius Katz, KC Katzer, Christian B. Kaufman, J.K. Kaufman, Gareth Kavanagh, Alex Kay, Michael Kay, Timothy Kay, Kaye-Panttajas, Lesley Kazan-Pinfield, David Kean, Thomas J. Kean, Peter Keane, Max Kearney, Adam Kearns, Kaffe Keating, Pete Keating, Joshua Keay, Anne Keck, Lee and Kerry Keefer, Matt Keeley, James D. Keeline, Duncan Keeling, Jon Keen, David Keenan, Janette Keene Taylor, Kees-Jan, John Keess, Derek Keevil, Darren Keig, Uwe Keim, Russell Keith-Magee, Dan Kelleher, Mike Kelleher, Arthur Keller, Beck Keller, Jaina Keller, Oliver Keller, Patrick Keller, Yvette Keller, Chris AgentSkwerl Kelley, Fina Kelley, Simon P. Kelley, David Kellum, David Kelly, Finbarr Kelly, Kate Kelly, Patrick Kelly, Trish Dish of the Day Kelly, Laura Kelsey, Steve Kelsey, Matti Keltanen (42), Patrick Kemmis, Charlotte Kemp, Kevin Kemp, Luke Kemp, Steve Kemsley, Barb Kendal, Adam Kendall, Christopher Kendall, Marissa Kender, Li Keng Ho, Maura Keniston, Andrew Kennedy, Bryan Kennedy, Dermot Kennedy, Garfield Kennedy, Helen Kennedy, Lex Kennedy, Peggie Kennedy, Scott Kennedy, William Kenney, Sarah Kennington, David Kenny, Keith Kenny, Neil Kenny*, John Kent, KT Kent, Bert Kenward, Sean Keogh, Davey Kerr, Drew Kerr, Maureen Kerr, Oliver Kerr, Elizabeth Kerridge, Paul Kerrigan, Stephen Kershaw, James Kerslake, Rolf Kersten, Kevin, Justin T Keys, Matt Keyworth, Melanie Keyzor, Ameel Khan, Aseem Khanduja, Harith Khawaja, Robert Khoe, Farokh Khorooshi, Paul Kidston, Dan Kieran, The Kift Family, Neath & Derbyshire, Terry Kildea, Andy Killin, Kadillac Kim, Bethe King, Chris King, David King, Hawken King, Jamie King, Jason King, Jennifer Rebecca King, Julian King, Matt King, Mr Simon H King, Patrick King, Philip King, Rich King, Richard King, Roger King, Tracy King, Petra Kingma, Tim Kingman, Armand Richard Kingsmill David, Rob Kingston, Jonathan Kinkaid, Kevin S. Kinney, E Kinsey, Tim Kinsey, David Kinsfather, Rob Kinsman, Bobbie Kirby, John Kirby, Judy Kirby, Dirk Kirchberg, Barry Kirchen, Liz Kirchhoff, Carson Kirk, Ed Kirk, Laura Kirk, Nick Kirk, Jackie Kirkham, David T Kirkpatrick, Vernon & Claire Kitay, B. Kitchell, John Kittridge, Taco Klaverboer, Ken Klavonic, Kelly Kleanthous, Michael Kleeman, Andreas Klein, Charles Klein, Howard Klein, Robbert Klein, Tal M. Klein, Jens Kleinemeyer, Benjamin "bizzl" Kleiner, Michael Kleinhenz, Alan Klem, Poul Klemmensen, Scott J. Kleper, Jan Klug, Graham Klyne, M. R. Kmetz, Agness Knapik, Timothy Knapman, Patrick Knapp, Michael Knauer, Christopher Knaus, Sebastian Knebel, Elinor Knechel, Jonathan Knell, Andy 'Belgium' Knight, Doreen Knight, Jason Knight, Michael Knight, Stuart Knight (blofeld), Holly Knight Spencer, Rachel Knightley, Benjamin Knorr, Julian Knott, Tom Knott, Robert Knox Miller, Bill Knutson, Kobalt the Hooloovoo, Jumana Kocache, Graham Koch, Sergey Kochergan, Mag. Georg Koe, Ryan Koechig, Paul Koerber, Dimitri Koeznetsov, Jeff Kogan, Eric Kohen, Ryan Kohl, Sharon Kohl, Aaron Kohlbeck, Anuradha Kolhatkar, John D. Koller, Dean Konenkamp, Kenny Kong, Jacob Kooter Laading, Brenden Kootsey, Kerry Kopp, David Koranyi, Barış Korkut, E. Michael Kornell, Anne Kory, Sven Kosack, Mariia Kosiakova, Carol Kosman, Lukáš Kostovčík, Kevin Kotowski & Paul Caswell, Pinelopi Kouleri, Stella Kovalchuk, Ed Kowalczewski, Anja Kowalewiez, Joe "PogieJoe" Kowalski, Timothy Jed Krafcik, Rutger Kramer, Kai Kranz, Joachim Kratochvil, Marianne Krawczyk, Uwe Kreibaum, Ray Kremer, Virany M. Kreng, Eddy Krens, Donald Kresch, Jennifer Kretchmer, Chris Kreuter, Joakim Kreutz, Eric H Krieger, J. Meryl Krieger, Gabriel Krieshok, Peter Kriesler, Craig Jonathan Kristensen, Dan Korup Kristensen, Thomas Kristiansen, Alois Kronbauer, Annike Kross, Erik-Jan Krudop, Roman Krznaric, Tareq Kubaisi, Scott Kubish, Martin Kudlac, Andrew Kuelbs & Stacy Bjorgaard, Lisa Kueltzo, David Kuhnle, Frank Kuiper, Chris Kuivenhoven, Nicholas Kujawa, Alex Kuklovsky, Brian Kulas,

Ray Kulberda, Brian E Kumanchik, Aakash Kumar, Rajiv Kumar, Svenja Kunze, Petras Kuprys, Brandi Kurr, Mark Kurta, Chris Kurzeja, Emmanuel Kusberg, Natalia Kushnir, Suzanne Kuyó et Mateo Blanc, Isa Kwan, Long Sook Kwan, Rhona Kyle, Emily Kyne, Henry L, Nicole L, Russ L, Stuart L Meek, Meike L., Michael L. and Julle F. Traver, David L.A., William L'Hommedieu, La Lettrice Vis à Vis, Stephen La Rivière, Gregory La Vance, Simon Lacey, Kai Lach, Ralph Lachmann, Seth Lachner, Kevin Lack, Nathan Ladd, Dirk Lagast, Jeffrey Lageson, David Lahner, Randy Lahrman, Olivier C. Lainesse, Ceri Laing, Steven Lainsbury, Simon Lake, Ray Lakeman, Marcin Lakomski, Abhilash Lal Sarhadi, Pierre-Antoine Laloe, Joel Lalonde, Brian Lalor, Jon Lam, On-Fai Lam, Jonathan Lamb, Jairred Lambert, jaki lambert, Susie Lambert, James Michael Lambert Jr, Richard J G Lambley, Paul Lamers, Emma Lamerton, Panagiotis Lamprakis, Nat Lancaster and Mark Moran, Barefoot Lance, Benjamin Lancum, Peter Landers, S. C. Landes, Roderick Lane, Sophie Langdon, Simon Langelier, Chris Langeluddecke, Gaëlle Langeo, Patricia Langevin, Joakim Langfjæran, Wibke Langhorst, John S. Langley, KS Langley, Benjamin Langlotz, Brandon Lanich, Jordan Lanius, Shawn & Larissa Laramie, Mark R. Largent, James Lark, Vayl Larkin, David Lars Chamberlain, Adam Larsen, Jon Larsen, John Larson, Björn Larsson, Jade Larue, David Lascelles, Lance Laskosky, Shawn Lasseter and Alexandra Miles-Lasseter, Caroline Latham, Ric Latham, Karen Latimer, Michelle Laub, Antti Laulajainen, Laura and Rob, Christian Laurberg, Emilie Laurent, Kathrine Lauritzen, Corky LaVallee, Jocke Lavett, Eyal Lavi, Tim Law, Lawjick, Tony Lawrence, Barbara Lawrie, Tom Lawry, Chad Lawson, Leonard Lawson III, Anton Lazarev, Adam Le Boutillier, Ben Le Foe, Colin Le Good, Jenet Le Lacheur, Jason Le Page, Mark Le Ray, Mark and Tom Le Surf-Hall, Daniel and Christy Leach, James Leach, Pete Lead, Joanne Leahy, Kieran Leahy, David Leake, David Leal, Simon Leaper, Julian Learmonth, David Learner, Jo Leatham, James Leavers, John Leavey, Paul and Henning Lederer, Elinor Dorday Ledoux, Matthew LeDrew, Erin Lee, Mike Lee, Steve Lee, Sze Min Lee, Shira Lee Margulies, James Leesch, David Leese, Derek Leftly, Jenny Leggat, Stephen "Don't Panic!" Legge, Ralf Legroux, Rebecca Lehman, Rich Lehman, Guy Craig and Beth Lehmann, Jonas Lehnberger, Leo Leibovici, Barbara Leicher, Rebecca Leigh, Andy Leighton, Ralph Leighton, Dr. Sebastian Leipert, Matthias Leipold, Mark Leiren-Young, Stuart Leitch, Matt Leitzen, Rodney Lelah, Christoph Lemell, Craig Lenehan, Andrew Lennard, Alba Leon, Colleen Casey Leonard, David Leonard, Ruth Leonard, Laura Lepeltier, Vincent Lequertier, Martyn Richard Lesbirel, Cosmo Lesbox, Andy Leschnik, Ilka Leukefeld, Tony Leung, Adam Leventhal, Anton Levholm, Barrie Levine, Nora Levine, Aaron Levinger, Gabrielle Indigo Levy, Kimberly Lew and John Vallejo, Marcus Lewin, Matthew Lewinski, Clive G Lewis, Darren Lewis, Joel Gethin Lewis, Katherine J. Lewis, Mark Lewis, Ross Lewis, Rupert Lewis, Tim Lewis, Wayne Lewis, Jonathan Lewis-Jones, Micha Leykum, Ralph Leyssens, Peter Li Anders, Yischon Liaw, Libby, Andy Libecki, Andrew Licudi, Stewart Licudi, Scott Liddell, Judith Liddell-King, Matthias Liebich, Dan Liebke, Alison Lievesley, Solarpunk Life, Sebastian Lifvin, Eric & Michele Light, Adrian Lightly, Eelco Ligtvoet, Lila, Ariella Lilien, Jesper Lillesø, Anthony Lilley, Mark Paul Lilley, Andrew Lillie, Duncan Lilly, Canice Lim, Chris Limb, Harmonie Limb, Erik Lind, Wells, Linda, Sofi Lindell, Adam T. Lindsay, David Lindsay, Phil Lindsay, Alexander Aerlion Lindström, George Linfield, Robert Link, Honza Linka, Claire Linney, Brian and Chrissy Linzy, Michael C. Lipcsik, Robert Lipfriend, Roberta Lippelman, The Lipperts, Lish!, Kerry Jean Lister, Gawain Little, Samuel Little, Anthony "Littonanthonylitton" Litton, Les Litwin, Michael Liu, Glen A. Livesay, Carolyn Livingston, Lisa Livingstone, Anders Ljusberg, Barry Lloyd, David Lloyd, Gregory Lloyd, John Lloyd, Richard Lloyd, Samantha Lloyd, Simon Lloyd, Peter Loats, Robert Loch, Martin Locock, Mikkel Lodahl, Gernot M. Lodemann, Jay Loden, Loek Bram Joris Karel Marijtje Mark Wiebes Mulder, Jane Loewen, Rob & Scott Loewen, Michel Loewenthal, Camille Lofters, Stuart Lofthouse, Andrew Logan, Scott Logan, Heidi Logie, Dan Logovik, Andrew Lohmann, Carlo M Lolli Ghetti, David Lomas, Steve Lomax, Beth Lombardi, Syd London, Chase London Smith, JR Lonergan, Ashley Long, CJ Long, Kirrily Long, Matthew Long, Michael Long, Matthew Longbottom, Crispin Longden, Mark Longmuir, Stephen Longstaffe, Scott Loonan, Frank R Lopez, Jonathan R. Lopez, Francisco J Lopez Garcia, Mark Lorch, Ed Lord, Gwyn Arthur Lord, Michael Lord, Lorenz, Grant Lorimer, Sebastian Loscher, Kate Losowsky, Tristan Louis, Carmen Loup, Thomas Love, Martin Lovick, Raymond Low, Justin Lowe, Martin Lowe, Stephen Lowe, D Loxton, Mario Lozza, Melissa E Lucarelli, Gavin Lucas, Richard Luciano, Federico Lucifredi, DeAnne Luck, Kelly Luck, Raymond Lucke, Steve Luckett, Michael Luffingham, Donald Lukaszewicz, Daniel Luke, Tony Luke's Family, Marco Lumachi, Monica Lumsden, Dominic Lunanuova, Jan Lund Thomsen, Nils Sonny Lundahl, Johan Lundberg, Tobias Lundberg, Andreas Lundgren, Jason Aragorn Tobias Lunn, Jeremy Lunn, Martin Lunnon, Demian Luper, Dr. Diane Luther, Damir Lutvic, Anna Lyaruu, Susannah Lydon, Andrew Lynch, Anthony Lynch, Penelope Lynch, Prof A Lynch, Conor Lynch-Jackson, Mike Lynd, Murray Lynes, Erin Lynn, Martin Lynn, Tom Lynton, Sam and Alex Lyon, Christopher Lyons, David A. Lyons, Lisa and David Lyons, Richard Lyth, D. Scott Lyttle, Christopher M, Josh M, Karina M, Miten M, Shawnee M, Paul M Lambert, Mike M., m.j.b@usa.net, Sieuwe Maas, Paul Maber-Gill, Rob MacAndrew, Geoff MacDonald, Helen MacDonald, Iain B. MacDonald, Jan Macdonald, Laura Macdonald, Alex Mace, Vladimiro Macedo, Aljaž Maček, Hamish MacEwan, Scott MacFarlane, Roddy MacFarquhar, Bill MacGillivray, Hamish MacGillivray, Anna E Macgowan, Matt Machell, Ramon Macias, Q Fiona Macintosh-Smith, Jason MacIntyre, Stewart Macintyre, Ross J. Mack, James MacKay, Graham Mackenzie, Helen Mackenzie-Burrows, Peter Mackey, Lexi Mackie, Neal Mackie, Richard Mackie, Scott Mackie, Susan Mackie, Andy MacKinnon, russell mackintosh, Alistair Macknight, Helen Maclagan, Gavin Niall MacLean, Mark Maclean, John Maclennan, Karen Macleod, Stewart Macleod, Enrico MacLøød, Bill MacMurray, Sheila MacNeill, David Macpherson, Kirstie Macqueen, Louise Macqueron, John Macready, Lauren Maddaford & Andrew Hope, Geert Maertens, Dr Willikins Mafami lover of Poplap the Brave, Martin Mager, Chris Maggs, Jane Magill, Helena Magloire, Claes Magnusson, Sigfus Magnusson, Dr Michael J. Maguire, Ed Maguire, Hannah Maguire, Liam Maguire, Csaba Magyar, Ruth Maher, Phil Mahoney, Haydn Maidment, Jessica Maisonnave, Robin Majumdar, Catt** Makin, Mal, Michael Malcangio, Ian Malcolm, Sandy Malcolm, Nick Malone, Patrick Maloney, JJ Malpas, Christopher "Chris" Man, Lex Man,

Philippa Manasseh, Mr & Ms Mancat, Ceci Mancuso, Ava Mandeville, Shubhang Mani, Stephen Manistre, Jamie Manley, Jem Manley-Buser, Kenneth Mann, Michael Mann, Simon Manning, Sasson Mansoori, Keith Mantell, Scott Mantooth, Nick Manzi, Jon C. Manzo, Charles Maragna, Saul Marchant, William Marchant, Vincenzo K Marcovecchio, Adam Marek, Alexandria Margiotta, Shaun Marin, Fred Marinello, Kevin Mark, Jay Markowitz, David Markus, Niel Markwick, Anna Marlen-Summers, Glynn Marlow, Sue Marlow, Vanda Marlow, Shanni Marmen, Andrew Marmot, Andreas Marneris, James Marnoch, Rob Marquardt, Jeffrey Marraccini, Polly Mars, Andrew Marsden, Chris "Shooty" Marsden, Graham Marsh, Jez Marsh, Nick Marsh, Richard Marsh, Craig Marshall, Dave Marshall, Graham Marshall, Ian Marshall, James & Eileen Marshall, Peter Marshall, Scott Marshall, Terrance Marshman-Edwards, Tim Marsland, Jens Marsling Bäckvall, Brian + Hayley Martel, Nicola Martelli, Alexandra Martin, Andrew Martin, Andy Martin, Frank Martin, Hannah Martin, Jackie Martin, Jacqui Martin, Liam Martin, Lori Suggs Martin, Norbert Martin, Randy & Laura Martin, Stephen Martin, Theo Martin, Robert Märtin, Michael Martine, Mark Martinico, Louis Martyn, Emma Marvel, Paul Masck, Steve Mash, Harry Maskers, Samantha Maskill, Doug Mason, Matt Mason, Alex Mason-Apps, Andy & Alison Massey, Craig Massey, Jonathan Massey, Roger Massey, Sean Massey, Thom B Masson, Denis Master, Christopher Masto, David Mather, Michael-Gemma-Alice Matherne, Duncan Matheson, Guus Mathijssen, David Matkins, Duke Matlock, Marissa Matonis, António Matos, Megan Matta, Eric Matters, Brian Matthews, Dan Matthews, John Matthews, William G Matthews, Matthias, Colin Mattholie, Michael Matulay, Matthias Maurer, Grant Maw, Tom Mawby, Richard Mawle, Adam Maxwell, Lachlan Maxwell, Glenn E. May, MaybeDuck, Emily Maycock, Dr. Philip Mayer, Monique Mayer, Phil Mayer, Adrian Mayles, Andrew Mayo, Angel V. Mayorga-Oneto, John Maytum, Eric McAfee, Shaun McAlister, Don McAllister, Ian McArdell, Sean McAuliffe, Jane McBrian, Ali & Brad McBride, Jennifer McBride, Mike McCabe, Andrew McCafferty, Racheal McCaig, Scott McCall, Janet McCallum, Patrick McCann, Dom McCarthy, Jennings, Berk, Casey & Tom McCarthy, John McCarthy, Trevor McCarthy, Neil McChrystal, Anne E McClain, Djimba Possum McCLain, Michael McCleave, Jeremy D. McClellan, Kenneth McClellan, Jed McClure, Virginia Clay McClure, Sandy McClymont, Yvonne Carol McCombie, Ryan McCormack, Una McCormack, Lisa McCoy, Craig McCracken, Christopher McCready, Lawrence McCrossan, John McCubbery, Bruce McCubbin, Rachel Claire McCue, Christopher McCune, Ed and Rita McCutchan, Andy McDade, John McDermott, Rob McDermott, Emma McDevitt, Niall McDonagh, David McDonald, Harry McDonald, Peter McDonald, Rod McDonald, Ian McDougall, Bryan McDowall, David McDowall, Liam McEneaney – dead for tax reasons, Alice McEvoy, Duncan McEwan, Fiona McFadden, Aric McFall, James C McFetridge, Daniel McGachey, Richard McGain, Jamie McGarry, Adam and Sandra McGechan, Jason McGee, Dan McGing, Craig McGinnes, Joey McGinty, Timothy McGonagle, Charles McGovern, Jeffrey McGovern, Joe McGowan, Kilian McGrath, Martin McGrath, Niall McGrath, Colleen Ann McGraw, Stephen McGreal, Jessica McGregor Johnson, Andy McGuigan, Holly McGuigan and George Walsh, Dr Martin McGurk, Austin McGwaon, Bill Mchugh, Kirsty McHugh, Craig McInerney, Cameron McInnes, Malcolm McInnes, James McIntosh, Zander McIvor, MCK42, David McKay, Greg McKee, Lauren Sara McKee, Telina McKeel, Kerry McKenna, Kevin Mckenna, Ben McKenzie, Chris McKenzie, David McKeown, Gavin McKeown, Cameron McKinlay, Steven McKinley, Frank McKinney, Alex McKinnon, Kory McKiou, Ian McLauchlin, Duane & Barbara McLemore, David McLeod Johnstone, Cheryl McLuckie, Rob McMahan, Larry McMann, Kevin McManus, Dakota McMillan, Ian McMillan, Robert McMillan, Roy McMillan, Tricia McMillan, Peter McMinn, Ryan Hugh McMullen, Kim McMunn, Shawn P. McMurray, Brob McMurrin, David McNally, Alison McNamara, David McNamee, Ciara McNeely, Graham McNicol, Razzy McPhee, Eugene McSorley, Liz McSweeney, David K McWilliams, Brian Meade, Luisa Meade, Stephanie Meade, Clarice Meadows, Paul David Mealor, Chris and Michele Means, Rod Mearing, Steven Medcraft, Justyn Paul Medd, Daryl Meechan, Sven Meeder, Richard Meehan, Cameron Meek, Leonard Megliola III, Kate Meier, Ineke Meijer, Christina Meiklejohn, David D. Meisel, Elizabeth G Melby, Jason Meldon, Emiliano Melillo, Judith Melinek, Keith Mellard, Anja Mellergaard, Ian Mellett, Ellen Mellor, Jonathan Melville, Neil Melville-Kenney, Robert Menaul, Adam D. Mendenhall, Christian Mendenhall, Scott Mendenko, Mark Mendham, Matt Mendres, Brooks Menefee, Krishna Kumar Menon, Rani Menon & Keith Amidon, Massimiliano Mentuccia, P. Timothy Menzenwerth, Matthew Mercedes, Jon Mercer, Lucinda Mercer, Treyce Meredith, Steve Meretzky, Julie Meridian, Marie Merillat, Christian Merkel, David Merrifield, Alfred Merrill, Adrian Merrington, Giles Merriott, Thomas Merritt, Panda Mery, Michael Merz, Tim Messenger, Troy Messerall, Paul Messingham, Owen Metcalfe, Christopher Meyer, Daniel Meyer, Dennis Meyer, Fred Meyer, Sam Meyer, Scott Meyer, Matthew Meznarsic, MGi, Major Miaowskis and General Whiskers, Sotiris Micallef, Manuel Miccinatti, Michael, Michaela, Dave Michaud, E.M. Middel, Benet Middleton, Gareth Middleton, Jason Middleton, Paul Middleton, Tim Middleton, Mark L Mierzwa, Migu, Frank Mikan, Sabrina Mikan PhD, Mike, Brett Milan Gajda, Jonathan Miles, Ken Miles, Milind, Blithe Milks, Alis Millar, Brian A. Miller, Dave Miller, Edward Miller, Elisa K Miller, Gary Miller, Helen Miller, Ian Miller, Jon & Cindy Miller, Kristin Marie Miller, Kurtis Miller, Patricia Miller, Philip Miller, Steve Miller, Andie Miller KE8KOY, James Miller-Argue, Robert Miller-Argue, Paul Milligan, Rachel Milloy, Deb Mills, Jon Mills, Sarah J Mills, Garry Mills / Ol'Peculier, Liz Milne, Cory Milotte, Brian Milton, Gerald Milward-Oliver, Zlatina Mincheva, Deane Miner, Dave Minter, Jason Minto, Michael Minzlaff, Julián Miranda, Luís Leal Miranda, Claire Miskell, Sonia Mistry, Bryan Mitchell, Caitie Mitchell, Claude & Audra Mitchell, Craig Mitchell, Faye Mitchell, J W Mitchell, Jon Mitchell, Peter Mitchell, Steven Mitchell, Toby Mitchell, Dean Mitchelmore, John Mitchinson, Anja Mittelstedt, John Miyasato, James Moakes, Robin Moates, Hooman Moazami, Deena Mobbs, Peter Modin, Jason Moffat, Hannah Moffatt, Jacob Moffitt, Mog, Volker Mohr, Sam Moize de Chateleux, Tracey Mold, Kat Molesworth, Peter Molinaro, Ishbel Mollison, Mark Mollon, William J. Molloy, Edward Molyneux, Paul Monaghan, Lydia Moneir, Alastair Monk, Monkey-Butt, Simon Monkman, Peter Monks, Daniel Monson, Sam Monson, House Montague for our Papa, Nobby Roy A Clarke, Jim Monteath, Pieterjan Montens, Fran Montero, Colin Montgomery, James Montgomery, Joshua Montgomery, Robert Montgomery, Cati Monti,

John Moody, Tom Moody-Stuart, Laurie Mooney, The Moont Family, Jonathan Moore, Joshua Moore, Lisa Moore, Paul Moore, Pete Moore, Ray Moore, Richard Moore, Stephen Moore, Stuart Moore, E. Moose, Adrian Mora, Jared Moraitis, Aidan Moran, Albert Moran, Andy Moran, James Moran, Jennie Moran, Katy Moran, Ray Moran, Timothy Moran, James Morden, Liz Mordue, Jeremy Morgale, Anna Morgan, Bill Morgan, Daniel J. Morgan, Dave Morgan, Gwendolyn Morgan, Gwyneth Morgan, Ian Morgan, Neal & Shelley Morgan, Nick Morgan, James Morle, Chris Morley & Angela Millard, Christopher Morlock, Nick Moroney, David Morris, Derek Morris, Don Morris, Izzy Grace Morris, Jessica Morris, Julia Morris, Pete Morris, Peter Morris, Stephen Morris, Susan Morris, Timothy Morris, James Morris Desiato, David M Morrison, Hunter Morrison, Isaac John Morrison, James Morrison, John Morrison, Kevin Morrison, Samuel J. Morrison, Thomas Morrison, Stan & Darren Morrissey, Joel Morrow, Brigit Kathleen Morse, Ian Morse, John Morse, Sam Morse, Tara Morse, Ane-Marte Mortensen, Jim Mortleman, Daryl Morton, Marcus Morton, Katrina Moseley, Brooks Moses, Cathy Mossman, Rob Mossop, Matthew 'MagpieMind' Most, Greg Mote, Paul Motsuk, Matt Mottern, Laurence Mottram, Stewart Moult, Tom Ellis/Stephen Moultrie, Ben Mountfield, Fotis Mouratidis, Michael Moutrie, Jim Mowatt, David Mowbray, Chris Mower, Mox, Theo Moye, Wayne Moyer, Alastair Moyes, Roger Moyle, David Moysen, Katie J Muddiman, Mike Muee, Andreas Mueller, Roland Mueller, Joerg Mueller-Kindt, Sarah Muff, Rob Muhlig, Francis Muir, Ari Mukamal, Jorick Mul, Sean Mulhern, Ellie Mulholland, Graham Mulholland, Edie Mullen, Michele I Muller, Cathy Nolly Mullican, Richard Mullins, Jane Mulvaney, Thomas B. Mumey, Steve Mumford, Demitri Muna, Kathryn Munden, Angus Mungal, Victor Munoz, Shane Munro, Ashley Munson, Laura Murff, Bill Murphy, Colin Murphy, Danny Murphy, Eric Murphy, Hoang Murphy, Laura Murphy, Michael Murphy, Nathan J. Murphy, Simon Murphy, Ripley Murphy Jones Rodriguez, Allan Murray, Christopher Murray, Dog Murray, Euan Murray, Ewen Murray, Fiona Murray, Joseph & Danielle Murray, Joshua "Shi" Murray, Lorna Murray, Peter Murray, Ria Murray, Richard Murray, Martin Murray 1942, Robert Musgrove, Shane Mussell, Matthew Musselman, Tami Musumeci-Szabo, Dr. Felicity Muth, Lara Muth, Preston Myatt, Hannah Myers, Chris Myhill, Myra, Hugh N, N.J.Atkins, Rhel ná DecVandé, Selena Nadav, Knut Nærum, Isaac Nagel, Julien Harry Naggar, Gerry Nagtzaam, Alan Nahum, Ashish Naik, Bala Nair, Clive Naish, Nakamoto, Phil Nanlohy, Craig Naples, Ken Napzok, Pavithra Naren, Sarah Nash, Zaxley Nash, Mo Nassar, Linda Nathan, Stu Nathan, Måns Nathanaelson, Carlo Navato, Elliot Naylor, Howard Nead, David Neal, Joshua Neal, Alison Neale, Chris Neale, Martijn Neef, Larry Nehring, Patrick J. Neill, Tony and Paula Neilson, Jeremiah Nellis, Aaron Nelson, Antony Nelson, Chris Nelson, Darek Eugene Nelson, Jeff Nelson, Kevin Nelson, Michael Nelson, Mark Nemecek, Rodolfo Nervi, Andrew Nesbitt, Jost Neßhöver, Steven Nethery, Social Netwooky, Eli Neugeboren, Konrad Neuwirth, James Neville, John New, Jonathan New, Trevor Newbery, Tim Newbury, Nathanael Newby-Kew, A. R. E. Newell, Andrew Newman, Daniel J Newman, Nick Newman, Phil Newman, Brett W. Newsom, Matt Newsome, Newt, Craig Newton, George Newton, H. C. Newton, Mark Newton, Samuel Newton, Aimee Nguyen, Nic, Joseph Nicely, Andy Nichol, Tony Nicholls, Al Nicholson, David Nicholson, Ken Nicholson, Mark Nicholson, Scott Nicholson, Sue Nicholson, Prof. Dr.Tobias M. Nickel, Cheryl Nickerson, Ken Nickerson, Caroline Nicklin, Christopher Gregory Paul Nicklin, J.E. Nicks, David Nickson, Aitch Nicol, Kiya Nicoll, Alasdair Nicolson, Jan Niehues, Erik Nielsen, Simon H.H. Nielsen, Thomas Honoré Nielsen, Harald Niesche, Nik, Nils and Lena, William Nilsen, Hayley Nilski, Jeff Nilsson, Piers Nimmo, Dan Nisbet, Akiyo Nishimiya, Oluf Nissen, Jay Nix, Robert Nixon, Shaun Nixon, Chinelo L. Njaka, Ph.D. and Paul Wright, Ph.D., Steve Noakes, Miki Noam, David Noble, John Noble, John M Noble, Jonathan Noble, Rob Noble, Nodder, Chris Nohner, Line Noise, Boris & Nadine Noll, Forrest Noll, August Nolte, Jeremiah 'Nick' Nolte, @noodlefish, AJ Noon, Jennifer Noon, Anita Norburn, Mikael Nordgren, Brian Nordmann, Helge Nordvik, Rod Norfor, Geir Norheim, Paul Norman, Peter Norman, Sophie Norman, Philip Normington, Sally Norris, Jake Norrish, Simon North, Alex Norton, Michael David Notzon, Tony Nowikowski, Joe Nunn, Mark Nunn, Yaya Nunya, Reese Nurmi, Mortimer Nutleg, Helen O, Amy O Mahony, Heather O. and Tom B., Unformed Worlds, Daniel O'Brian, Andrew O'Brien, John O'Brien, John and Deb O'Brien, Michael O'Brien, Roger O'Brien, Shane O'Connell, Angela O'Connor, The O'Day Family, John O'Dea, Alan O'Donnell, Luke O'Donnell, Steve O'Gorman, Ronan O'Hagan, Aileen O'Hearn, Bob O'Keeffe, Michele O'Leary, Kieran O'Murchu, Kevin O'Neil, Des O'Neill, Sean O'Neill, Steve O'Neill, Philip O'Reilly, A O'Riordan, Keavy O'Shea & Dom Goucher, Brendan O'Sullivan, Kate O'Brien, John F. B. O'Dowd, Mathieu Mantrant O'Dowd, Geraldine O'Farrell, Michelle O'Haren, Clara O'Shea, Alex O'Sullivan, Michael O'Sullivan, J. P. O'Toole, David Oakes, Sue Oakes, Paul (hoopy) Oakley, Tricia Oakley, Adrian Oates, David Oates, Christopher Ober, Randi & Sam Ocena, Andrej Ocenas, Max Ocklind, The Odds, Trond Ødegård, Åsa Odén, Fabrice Odero, Dominic ODonnell, Eike Oenschläger, Dennis Oestreich, Peter Offley, Matthew Ogden, Peter Ogden, Robin Ogilvie, Alan Ogilvie – Telephone Sanitizer (Level 3), Alexandra Oglethorpe, Mugren Ohaly, Evonne Okafor, Jeff Okamoto, B&K Okamoto family, Craig Okruhlica, Shakespeare Okuni, James Olander, Ole, Anna-Maja Oléhn, Micah Olguin, Patrik Olin, Alex Oliszewski, Rafael Oliveira, Dan Oliver, Mark Oliver, Nicky Oliver, Ramon Antonio Olivo, Per Ollas, Kyle Olson, Par Olsson, Kazeem Omisore, The One and Owenly, Logan ONeil, Zachary Oplinger, C & D Orlando, Lorena Orndoff, Thea Orozco, Keith Orpen, Christopher Orr, Neal D Ortego, Kevin Ørtoft Dahlstrøm, Mark Osborn, Angela Osborne, Gemma Osborne, Harley Osborne, Peter Osborne, Steven Osborne, Nick Osdale-Popa, Richard Oshea, Ed Oskiewicz, Rebecca Osterfund, Zach Ostolski, Frederick J. Ostrander, Max Ostrowski, David Oswald, Robert Otley, Benji Otto, Derek Samuel Otto, Richard Outerbridge, Jeroen Overbeek, Samantha Overstreet, Ami Lou Owen, Seanchan Owen, Shelley Owen, Stuart Owen, Nige Owen for Danielle & Emma, Ashley Owens, Tim Owens, Kate Owens-Palmer, Francis Owtram, M P, Mr P, P., Stephen Packer, Russell Pacy, Jon Padgett, Rodi Padron, Rupert Paget, Sarah Pagliaccio, Paul Paintin, John Palagyi, John Palaima, Julia Palandri, Ryan Paley, Matt Palmer, Micah Palmer, Neil Palmer, Nick Palmer, Philip E Palmer, Sarah Palmer, Will Palmer, Julian Palmers, Sveinbjörn Pálsson, Peter Paluszewski, Nicholas Pancake, Valeria Pandaciao, Eric Pankoke, Ethel Pantswetter, Daniel Paoliello, Christine Papalexis, Nicos Papandreou, Bard C. Papegaaij,

Jess Paquette, Damian Paradis, E Pardee, Kevin Parichan, Lev Parikian, Andy Park, Chris Parker, David Parker, Joe Parker, Kevin Parker, Mike Parker, Peter Parker, Rob Parker, Sophie Parker, Steph Parker, Steve Parker, Terry Parker, Tom Parker-Shemilt, Len Parkin, Chris Parkinson, Gregory Lee Parks, Luke Parks, Sheila A. Parks, William Tex Parks, Adam Parmenter, Steven Parradee, Susan Parrott, Edward Parry, Gareth Parry, Adam Parsons, Julia Parsons, Malcolm Parsons, Claire Parsons and Mark Seymour, Carl Partridge, Simon Partridge, Trudie and Michael Paschetag, Simon Passey, John Pasteur, Sascha D. Patak, Jaynesh Patel, Viral Patel, Aimee Paterson, Charlie Paterson, Colin Paterson, Craig Alexander Paterson, James Craig Paterson, Sue Patrick, Floyd Patterson, Ken and Jerry Patterson, Mathew Patterson, Walt Patterson, Niky Patyn, Gabriele Pauer, Lark Kirsten Paul, Paula and Robert Paul, Paula&Giuliano, Michael Paulick, Aaron Paulley (@AaronInNYC), Tor Hogne Paulsen, Cia Paulsson, Nathaniel Paust, Nick 'Doug' Pavis, Christopher Pavlos, Alexander Pawlak, Daniel C. Pawlak III, Spencer Pawson, Kevin Paxman, David Payne, Felicity Payne, Harry Payne, Isobel Payne, Russell Payne, Carme Paz, pcreutzberger@gmail.com, Roger Peachey, James Peak, Gary Pearce, Thomas Pearce, Lisa Pearce Collins, Matt Pearson, Nick Pearson, Rob Pearson, Kellie M. Pease, Ron Pease, Stephen Peberdy, Justin Peck, Kristen Peck, Tom Peddie, Richard Peden, Aric Pedersen, Bo Dixen Pedersen, Evan Pedersen, Viggo Pedersen, Javier Pedreira «Wicho», Luc Peerdeman, Jo Peitz, Chris Pell, Bianca Pellet, Jacques Pelletier, George A. Pelletier, Jr., Esq., Bryan Pelley, Michael Peluso, Gilbert Pena, John Pendlebury, Anja Penk, Martin Penn, Samuel Penn, Nigel Pennington, Dermot Penny, Graham Penny, Clifford Penton, David Perahia, Eli Perencevich, Dr. AvatarNirvana Perez, Samantha Perez, Lucas Pergiel, Chaz Perin, Simon Perkin, The Perkins Family, Melanie Perkins, Simon Perkins, Justin Perks, Dougal Perman, Luke Perrett, Steve Perrett, David R. Perry, Regina Perry, Shannon Perry, Lawrence Person, Andreas Persson, Tomas Persson, Ulf Persson, Riley Perszyk, Mom & Dad (Sara & Tony Perszyk), William J Pesek, Jarmo Petäjäaho, Oliver Peter, Alexander Peterhans, Michael Peterken, Carl Peters, Christopher Peters, Jan Peters-Anders, Barbara J Petersen, John Peterson, Lloyd Peterson, Sherry B. Peterson, Julian Petford, Jason Petit, Bethanie Petitpas Queen of Everything, Radoslav Petkov, Tihomir Petkov, David Peto, Ross J Petrie, Wesley Petrowski, Hilary Pettit, Terry Pettitt, Tony Pettitt, Jonathan Pettus, Ralf Pfeffer, Alwin Pfeiffenberger, William Pfeiffer, Alexander Pfeiffer-Widensky, D. Pflaume, Kevin Pham, Niklas Jan Phartiphukborlz, Dave Phelan, Tony Phelan, Phil The Sheep, John B Philip, Christopher Philippo, John Kaniyil Phillip, Andrea Phillips, Catherine L. Phillips, Colin Phillips, Fred Phillips, Gary Phillips, Heather J Phillips, Ian Phillips, Jonathan Phillips, Mark Phillips, Michael Phillips, Robert Phillips, Shane Phillips, Leon Mark Philpott, Christopher Phin, Mark Phippen, Ann Phoenix, Marie Piasecki, Martin Pickard, Dave Pickersgill, Chris Pickett, Oliver Pickles, Thomas Picton-Turbervill, John Piedrahita, Collin Pieper, Dirk Pieper, Jennifer Pierce, Pierel, Ben Pierro, Myriam Piessens, Raphael Pigulla, Tristan Pike, Jon Pike & Marcia King, Grim Pikzel, Dirk Pilat, Roger Pilgrim, David Ian Pilkington, Andrew Pilley, Haley Ann Pimental, Matt Piner, Paulo Pinho e Costa, Ivano Pinneri, Chris Pinnock, Jonathan Pinnock, Zach Pinson, Mark R. Pintar, Lydia Pintscher, Mike Piontek, Joe Piper, PipHx, Ameena Ahsan Pirbhai, Chris Piscitelli, Sampo Pitkänen, Mark Pitman, Owen Pitrone, Charles Pitter, James T Pitts, Pitxitxi, Ignasi Pizarro Blesa, Anita Pizzocchero, Herbert Leo Plankl, Simon Platt, Maxwell Plaut, Emily Player, Philip Playfair, Rachel Playforth, Harry Pledger, Nicklas v Plenker-Tind a.k.a. KingVoodoo, Rainer Pleyer, Dave Plume, Fiona Plunkett, Timothy Plymale, Bal ter sol Pnuh, Paul Pod, Robert Podd, Philip Podmore, Jeffrey Podolsky, Kevin "The Dark Ranger" Poe, Shae Poffley, Melissa Poggioli, Michael Pokorny, Gary Polak, Daniel Polinsky, Justin Pollard, Doug Pollock, Hunter Pollock, John Pollock, Jenni Polodna, Chris Pomery, Max Pommier, Pommygirl (ET), Anna Pomphret, Raymond Pompon, The Pondy-Upton, The Ponzini's, pookie, Ben Poole, Mikey Poole, Geoff Poon, Garrett Poore, Davie Pope, Emma Pope, Jason Pope, Mark Pope, Terence Pope, David Popeck, Paul Popernack, Andrew Popp, Art Popp, Tim Poppleton, Lina Porcelijn, Georg Portenkirchner, Alex Porter, Brian Porter, Jeremy Porter, John Porter, Josh Porter, Malcolm Porter, Mic Porter, Philip Porter, Jake Posner, Robert Poss, Gerard Postlethwaite, Joe Potempa, Miranda Pothiawala, potholer, Family Potjan, Ian Potter, Michael Potter, William Potter, Ronald Pottol, Silas Potts, Ben Poulos, Morten Poulsen, Darren Poulson, Mark and Nina Powell, Tristan & DeAnna Powell, James Power, Melissa Powers, Nicole Powers, Amanda Powter, Belinda Prakhoff, Joseph Pranevich, Alan Pratt, Jens Prausnitz, Travis Prebble, Alun Preece, Joe Pregracke, Ben Prescott, Mark Prescott, Paul Presley, Stephen Press, Ian Prest, Cliff & Deb Preston, David Preston, Vincent J. Preteroti, Janet Pretty, Lawrence Pretty, Michael Pretty, Grant Prettyman, Jennifer Prévost, Chris Prew, Andrew Price, Barry Price, Ben Price, Charlene Price, Jason Price, Lena Priddey, Josepe Prieto, Jammar Prince, Robin Prior, Jonathan Pritchard, Tara Pritchard, Tom Pritchard, Dave Probert, Simon Procter, Sarah Proctor, Jan Prodöhl, Mike Proskey, David Prosser, Robert Prosser, Owen Proteau, Edward Prothero, David Proud, Travis Prow, Francis Pryor, Shaun Pryszlak, Michael Psarouthakis, Gavin Pugh, Eric Puleo, Rachel Pulliam, Emily Pulsford, John Douglas Punter, Iain "Mosh" Purdie, Sean Purdy, Chris Purser, Philip Purser-Hallard, Matthew Purves, RJ Putnam, David Pye, Gary Pyke, Eric Pynnonen, Benjamin Q, Zoot Quark, Lisa Quattromini, Eric Tomas Quek, query@macraemedia.com, Helen Quigley, Nathaniel Quinlan, Thomas Quinlan, Tony Quinlan, John Quinn, Michael Quinn, Ross Quinn, Sean Quinn, Cameron R, Sophia R., RAAAAAAAAAAAAAAAY?!?, Doug "Dhomal" Raas, Bo Raber, Mark & Jay Rabinowitz, Corey Racher, Dan T. Racite, The Radcliff Family, Adam Radcliffe, M. Radclyffe, Byron Rademacher, Giles Radford, Grace Radford, Vince Radigan, SLAY Radio, Scot Radowski, Harry Rae, RAF, Daniel Rafferty, Michael Rafferty, Duncan Raggett, Timothy Raggett, Sebastian Rahlf, Karin Rahn, Dawn Zoë Raison, Harold Raitt, Adam Rajski, Erik Rakoczy, Scott V. Rakoczy, Roger Ralston, Gayle Ramage, Stephen Ramanauskas, Dananjaya Ramanayake, Jaye Rambo, David Ramey, Timothy Louis Ramey, Wilf Ramey, Ted Ramey, PhD, Kyle Ramirez, Alejandra Ramirez G, Derek Ramm, Marina Ramos, Jörg Rampacher, Matt Ramsay, Susan Ramsay, John M Ramsay - Zydeko, Jamie Ramscar, Annette Ramsden, Robin Rance, Chris Randall, Sean Randall, Beverley Randle, Blake Randle, Rands, JP Rangaswami, Matt Ranson, Jory Raphael, Eugene Rasini,

Roslyn Raskin, Matthew Rasnake, Dan Rassler, Anastasia Ratcliffe, Douglas Rath, Sandra Rath, Chris Ray, Nathan Raymond, Paul Raymond, Hannah Raymond-Cox, Martin Rayner, Paul Rayski, Angela Rayson, Chris Read, Graeme Read, John Read, Tom Read, Colette Reap, Harry Reardon, Jedidiah Reardon, Jonathan Reber, Steve Redford, Naomi Redhouse, Bryn Redman, El Redman, Erik V Reece, Aaron A. Reed, Barbara Reed, Killian Reed, Michele Reed, Mike Reed, Owen Reed-Beadle, Carl Reeder, Barry Rees, Dylan Rees, Jim Rees, Matthew Rees, Wendy Rees, Adam Rees-Taylor, Chris Regan, Keith Regan, Marta Regge, Mads Regnar, Faiz Rehman, Caroline Reich, Christian Reichhold, Thomas Reichwein, Elliott Reid, Helen Reid, Matthew Ewan Reid, Stephen Reid, Terri Reid, Tim Reid, Victor A Reid, Jeanie Reida, Anne Reifsnyder, Chris Reifsteck, Linda Reijnhoudt, Robert Reimer, Kat Reimus, Ramon Reinders, Nicholas Reineck, Alexander Reinhard Maestre Gmür, Alexander Reinhardt, Jonas Reinhardt Kopstad, Dakota Reinhart, Tom Reinhold, Travis Reis, Jason Reljac, AJ Rella, Ashlyn Remmert and Scott Richardson, Gail Renard, Josh Renaud, Steph Renaud, Mike Rende, Renfield286, Anthony & JJ Renli, John S. Rennie, Jerry Reno, David Rensin, Emmett Rensin, Alistair Renwick, Adam Resch, Jens Restemeier, Chad Restum, Gijs Reudink, Dominique Revelle, Aaron Reynolds, Dan Reynolds, Francis Reynolds, Nickolas Reynolds, Rick Rezinas, Joshua Rhoades, Gavin Rhoades & Neil Taylor, Electra Rhodes, Kevin Rhodes, Paul Rhodes, Stephen Rhys-Davies, Leigh Ribak, Michael Riben, MD, Tania Ricardo, Sonya Rice, Austin Rich, Mini-Mutant, Liz & Bill Richard, Cynthia Richards, Daniel Richards, Jean Richards, Michael Richards, Mike Richards, Neil Richards, Renée Richards, Sue Richards-Gray, Christopher Richardson, Don Richardson, Kimberly Richardson, Neil & Christine Richardson, Rhyannon Richardson, Phil Riches, Virginia Riches, Margaret Richter, Max Richter, William Ricker, Dennis Rickerson, Andrew Rickett, Elizabeth Riddington, Hamstall Ridware, Jens and Laura Riege, Craig Riehl, Jesper Riemer, Micha Rieser & Kristian D'Arienzo, Ray Riethmeier, Marc Rifkin, Nancy Rigling, Andrew Riley, Brandon Riley, Simon James Riley, Tim Riley, Jeffrey and Teme Ring, Huw Ringer, Judith Ringers, Kerry Rini, Chiara Riondino, Keith Riordan, Pierluigi Rippa, Joseph Ritter, Juliet Rix, Luke & Daniel Rix-Standing, Andrew Roach, Rob, Yuri Robbers, Fiona Roberto, Chris Roberts, Ewen Roberts, Heather Emily Roberts, Howard Roberts, Jem Roberts, John Roberts, Justin Roberts, Kate Roberts, Kirk Roberts, Laura Roberts, Malcolm Roberts, Mark Rocks Roberts, Nik Roberts, River Roberts, Shadrock Roberts, Stephen Roberts, Wyn Roberts, Anthea Robertson, Caroline Robertson, Derek Robertson, Fiona Robertson, Iain Robertson, Michael Robertson, Scott Robertson, Stephen Robertson, Stephen Robertson-Dunn, David Robeson, Harry Robins, Allyson Dylan Robinson, Andy Robinson, Brian K Robinson, Carl Robinson, Dave Robinson, Hal Robinson, Ian Robinson, Jess Robinson, John L. Robinson, JP Robinson, Nicola Robinson, Maggie Robinson-Smith, Spurious Robot, Anthony Robson, Houston Roby, Patricia Roche, Drew Rochon, Rainbow Rock, Michelle Louise Rock-Davis, Jonny Rocket, Ken Rockson, Murr Rockstroh, Christopher Rodda, Colin Rodden, Ian Roderer, Christopher Rodger, Javier Rodríguez Miravalles, Rachael Rodway, Alison Jayne Rodwell, Sym Roe, Clint Roesbeke, Kenn Roessler, Jay & Paul Roff, Molly Roffman, Markus Rogenhofer, 80sthrowback Ivan Rogers Rogers, David Rogers, Geraint Rogers, Peter Rogers, Thomas J. Rogers, Jr., Rogo of Sham, Wojciech Rogoziński, Emerick Rogul, Pierre Rohatyn, Peter George Rohde, Hendrik Rohler, Vernon Rollins, Susan Rollinson, Carrie Rolls, Janet Romain, Alex Romanelli, Martin Romankiw, Samuel Rome, Joe and Mike Romeo, Mike Romeo, Kinga Rona-Gabnai, Bryan Ronan, Gino Roncaglia, Jez Roney, David Ronicle, Jonathan Ronicle, Andrew Rooney, Rob Rooney, Frederick Roos, Carl Root, Sam Roots, Tom Roper, Charles Rose, Frank Leon Rose, Gregory Rose, James Rose, Jessica Rose, Mike Rose, Sam Rose, Sarah Rose, Paul Rose Jr, Andrew & Michelle Rosen, Michael S. Rosenberg, Pavel Rosendorf, David Rosenthal, Harriet Rosenthal, Calum Rosie, Nina Rosier, Aaron Ross, Andy Ross, Ben Ross, Craig Ross, John Ross, Jonathan Ross, Stuart Ross, Michael Rossell, Daniel Roth, Jim, Patricia & Edward Rothman, Barbara Rotondo, Jean-Yves Rouffiac, Mark Rough, Jeffrey Roulston, Angelos Roumeliotis, Peter Round, Daniel Rourke, Andy Rouse, Timothy Roustio, Anna Route, Carol Routh, Ivan Routledge, Alessandro "Sasha" Rovetta, Dan Rowe, Kenneth James Rowe, Catherine Rowlands, Andrew Rowley, Ian Rowley, Stephen Rowley, Steve Rowling, Martin Roxby, Steven Roy, Michael Rozyla, Heidy Rubin, Andrew Rubio, Eric Ruck, Lacy Rucker, Andrew Ruddle, Eric Paul Rude, Theodore Ruegsegger, Stuart Ruffell, Paul Rugg, Timothy C.W. Runge, Thilo Rusche, Paul 'Rushy' Rush, Amanda Rushton, James Rushton, Nick Rushton, Barney Russel, Benjamin Russell, Emma Russell, Henry Russell, John Russell, Matt Russell, Lisa Russell & Tim Kaye, Brian Russell Brown, Shiraz Rustom, Mark Rutherford, Ry & Dan, Hannah Ryan, John Ryan, Karl Ryan, Kian Ryan, Philip Ryan, Rob Ryan, Ryan, Robert Ryans, Timothy Ryon, Ben S, Corrie S, Katherine S, Mashilamani S, Sara S, Paul Sachs, Matt Sachtler, Neil Sackett, Ian Sadler, Nigel Sadler, Pip Sadler, Christopher Safarik, Melchor Sahagun III, Sara Sahlin, Jane Saigol, Matt Sailors, Saint, Andrew Salamy, Kami Salibayeva, Tom Salinsky, Annie Salmon, Richard Salmon, Stephen Salmon, Paul Salt, Corey Salter-Davidson, Jennifer SALVI, Sam, James Sambrook, Jean Sambrooks, Bernie Sammon, Janet Sampson, José Miguel Sancho (Barcelona), Ian Sandall, Christoph Sander, Ed Sanders, Eric Sanders, Rebecca Sanders, Timothy Sanders, David W. Sanderson, Michael Sanderson, Marc Sandham, Sajan & Chaitan Sandhu, Alec Sandison, Steven Sandor, David Sandquist, Dusty Sandrock, John Sandy, Daniel Sanger, Niraj Sanghvi, Jim Sangwine, David Santana, Carlos Santellanes, Peppe Santoro, Guilherme Santos Grise, Leo Sarsam, Eli Sasich, Coll Satchel, Jonathan Sato, Linda Sato, Michael "Zaphod" Sauder, R. Sauer, Jon Saunby, Charles Angus Saunders, Jill Saunders, Matt Saunders, Steven Saunderson, Angela Savage, Jason Savage, Keith Savage, Nicholas Savage, Sylvia Savage, Kay Savetz, Anna-Marie Savio, Sunil Sawani, Tim Saward, Michał Sawicz, Rob Sawkins, Jeremy Sawruk, Christine & Andy Sawyer, Mark Saxon, Jon Sayer, Paul Sayer, S.D. Prinz Charly zu Sayn-Wittgenstein, Claire Scadding, T Scales, Peter Scandrett, Martin Scanlan, Jeremiah Scanlon, Antonio Scaramuzzino, Andrew Scarborough, Lesley Scarles, Louisa Scarr, scauglog, Jasper Schaap, Michael Schaap, Momo Schaap, Ben Schaffer, Marc Schällebaum, Brian Schantz, Frank Schaper, Andi Scharfstein, Roland "RetRoland" Schatz, Jurgen Schaub, Torsten Schauf, Katrin Scheib, Michael Schenk, Jeremy Scherer,

Martin Scherer, Olav Schettler, Michael Scheuermann, Martijn Scheutjens, Reynir Scheving, Arthur Schiller, David S. Schilling, Markus Lorenz Schilling, Paul Nicholas Schillinger, Jason Schindler, Nichole Schlecht, Anna Schleimer, David Schlossberg, Anne-Marie Schmalz, Lina Johanna Schmerschneider, Rolf W. Schmid, Gunther Schmidl, Benjamin Robert Schmidt, Marty Eehad Schmidt, Michael Schmidt, Patrick Schmidt, Werner Schmidt, Daniela Schmitt, Sue Schmitz, Susan Schmoyer, Fred Schneidereit, Allana Schneidmuller, Christoph Schobel, Jim Scholes, Richard Scholten, Frank Scholz, Tobias Scholz, Daniel Schönamsgruber, Schondy, Jochen Schönfelder, James Schooling, Robert M. Schroeck, Ludwig Schubert, Karsten Schueckel, Zara Schulman, Mike Schulz, Phil Schulze & Helen Cawthorne, David Schulzinger, Lea Schumacher, Nicolai Schumann, Harald Schuren, Adam Schuster, Uli Schuster, Mark Schütz, Samuel Schwager, Greg "schmegs" Schwartz, Paul Schwartz, Tom Schwarz, Christopher Sciacca, Carlamia Sciberras, Peter Scoblic, Donald Scorgie, Joe Scotland, Charlie Scott, Chris Scott, Jeremy Scott, Jim Scott, Matthew Scott, Robbie Scott, Hoopy Froods W. Scott & T.J. Bandla, Robert Scott Clark, Andrew Scott Goodwin, Kishori Aaliyah Scott McCann Kareem, Matthew Scott Roren, Christopher Screeton, James Scudamore, Oliver Scull, Jimmy & Penina Scullion, Derek Scully, Mike Scully, Matt Scutt, David Seager, Karen Sealey, Alexandra Seaman, Charlie Seaman, A Seaney, Dominic Search, Jess Search, Geoff Searle, Jason Searle, Carolyn Sechler, Chuck Sedano, Tina Sederholm, Robert Sedgwick, Urban Sedlar, Tarik Sedlarevic, Andrea See, Sven Seebeck, Seebs, Michael Seeley, Catherine Seeligson, Kai Segall, Frank Seidel, Adieu-Ark-B Marketing, Glenn Seiler, Rin Seilhan, David & Reuben Sekules, Richard Selby, Mitch Seljanovski and Giorgia Stawaruk, Peter Sellars, David Sellwood, Ira Selwin, Dick Selwood, Richard Selwyn, Arna Selznick, Isaac Semko, Philippa Semper, Chris Senior & Lem, M@ Senne, Geoff & Liz Senson, Michael Sepcot, Jeremy F. Sepinsky, Seraphina, Paul & Deb Sergeant, Oleksandr Serhieiev, Matthew J Serio, Michael D. Serroul, Walter Serwacki Jr., Rade Seslija, Colin Wynter Seton, Chadwick Severn, Frank Sewald, Andrew Mark Sewell, Amy Sexton, Jeff Sexton, Sam Sexton, James Shade, Morwenna Shahani, Frank Shailes, John Shakesby, Erich Shanholtzer, Ross Shank, Jonathan Shapiro, Alex W. Sharif, Sageer Sharif, Jack Sharkey, Arun Sharma, Alexander C. Sharp, Aren Sharp, Chris Sharp, Nerys Sharp, Alan Sharpe, Sue Sharpe, Thaddeus Sharpe, Roger Sharples, Jennifer Sharpley, John Sharpley, T. J. Shartle, Hameed Shaukat, Adam Shaw, Bridget Shaw, Col Shaw, Dale Shaw, Jeff Shaw, Mark Shaw, Mike Shaw, William Shaw, Paul Sheard, Robert Shearman, David Sheehan, Josh Sheena, Isobel Sheene, Andrew Sheldon, Christopher Sheldon, Grayson Sheldon, Mark Sheldon, Peter Sheldrick and Jennifer Cutler, Edward Shelley, Ward Shelley, Wonko451 David Shelnutt, Jen Shelton, Emily Shem-Tov, Paul Shephard, Jonty Shepheard, Clare Shepherd, Cory Shepherd, Diana Shepherd, Nick Shepherd, Sam Shepherd, Vikas Shepherd, Mark Shepherdson, Lyn Sherburne, Flash Sheridan, Corinne Sheriff, Danielle Sherman, Gail P. Sherman, Shervyn, James Sherwood-Rogers, Anoop Sheshadri, Ian Shields, Justine Shih, Shilpa & Gautham, Bob Shingler, Dr Sara Shinton, John Shipman, Lesley Shires, Matvey Shishov, Tom Shivakumar Hatton, Lizzie Shoesmith, Sadie Shonrock, C R Shores, Gillian Shorter, Blake Shrode, Mark Shufflebotham, Victor Shum, Bryony Shuter, Lorna Sibbett, Colin Sibley, Daniel Sibo, Carol Siddall, Sumner Siebels, Dave & Holly Siederer, J.L. Siefers, Shannon Siegel, Richard Sievers, Gesche Siewertsen, Michael Silano, Beejay Silcox, Darren Sillett, Katie Silva, Michael Ben Silva III, Nick Silversides, Ian Silvester, Giora Simchoni, Lorna Simes, Jameson Simmons, Liam Simmons, Simon Simmons, John Simon, Neil Simon, Simon & Ashland, A. Simonds, simone.lupini2@gmail.com, simonjohnbradley@hotmail.com, Jon Simons, Rosearik Rikki Simons, Allan Simonsen, Mark Simonson, Brian Simpson, Josh Simpson, Paul Simpson, John Simpson KG4ZOW, Alan Sims, Steve Sims, Colin Sinclair, David J Sinclair, Jeremy Sinclair, Simon A Sinclair, Anjan Singer, David Singer, Hersh Singer, Briana Singleton, Andrew Singley, Alexander Sirbu, Guillaume Siret, Jerry Siskind, Katie Sisneros, Jay Sissom, Jeremy Sitnick, Phil Sivills, sixfootsixmark, Matthew Size, Adam Sjøgren, sjohnson@hexgames.com, Jan Skakle, Marcin Skarbek, SkaveRat, Michael Skazick, John Skeldon, Jane Skelly, Ant Skelton, Deb Skelton, Jerry Skelton, Simon Skelton, Steve Skelton, Reid Skibell, Jamie Skiggs, Chris Skilbeck, Michael P Skinner, Shari Skinner, Raymond Skipps, Mark J Skopczynski, Asbjørn Skovsende, Nigel Skull, Melinda Skwarok, Andreas Skyman, Elizabeth Slade, James Slade, Guy Slakman, John Slartibartfast Erikson, Rob Slatem, Martin Slater, Justin Sleep, Keith Sleight, Malcolm Sleight, Josh M Slifkin, Victor and Linda Sluiter, SMD, Jouni Smed, Michael Smeeth, Ionica Smeets, Alexander Smiding, Alan Smith, Alan C Smith, Alex Smith, Amelia & Jason Smith, Andrew Smith, Ben Smith, Benjamin Smith, Benjamin S. Smith, Brian Smith, Brian D. Smith, Colin Smith, Craig Smith, Craig and Rachel Smith, David G Smith, Derek Smith, Dr Adrian Smith, Duncan Smith, Gary Smith, Gavin Smith, Gerald J Smith, Glenn Smith, Gordon Smith, Howard Smith, Ian Smith, Jason Smith, Jeffrey James Smith, Jim Smith, Jonathan Smith, Kieron Smith, Leonie M. Smith, Libby Smith, Lisa M. Smith, Mandy Smith, Matt Smith, Meghan Smith, Micah J. Smith, Nigel Smith, Patrick Smith, Paul Smith, Philip K Smith, Raymond Smith, Rob Smith, Robert Smith, Sam Smith, Sean Smith, Shawn D. Smith, Sooz & Andy Smith, Steve Smith, Steven P. Smith, Tim Smith, Tony Smith, Trevor Smith, VC Smith, The Smith-Kane Family, Aunt Goodiebags (Dr. Nancy Smith), Ady Smivers Smith, SmokeholeNaruto, Ziggy Smolski, John Mark Smotherman, Brian R. Snape, Zoe Snape, Shannon Snell, Gareth Snelson, Brian Sniffen, Frank Snijders, Chris "Salyavin" Snook, Scott Snowden, Riatsila Snoyl, Wendy Snyder, Zach Soares, Giovanna Sociali, Drs. Bill & Tom Sodeman, Jan Söderberg, Nick Sodhi, Tom Sofa, Walter Sofronoff, David Soh (Neon), Alwin Solanky, Solidseagull, Sara Solnick, Vadim Solomonik, David Solomons, John Sommerville, Rachel Sommerville, Robert Somogyi, Daniel Sonabend, Stephen Sondheim, Jason Sonnichsen, Robert Sookochoff, Stoic Sophie, Brian N. Sorensen, Ian Sorensen, Janell Sorensen, Kurt Sorensen, Henrik Sörensen, Lennart Sørensen, Joseph Soria, Heidi Sosinski, David J. Soto, Emry Sottile, Yosefa Sotzianu, Albert Sousa, Gigi Souter, Ben Southwell, Giles Southwell, Andrew Southwick, Ben Southwood, Richard Souza, Ari Sovijärvi, Seth Sowerby, Gabriel Soxhlet, Lorenzo Spaccarelli, Brad Spachman, Riccardo Spagni, Chris Spalding, Iain Spardagus, Esther Sparrow, Paul Sparrow-Clarke, Chris Spath, Andy Speakman, Mo Spear, Thomas Spear,

Philip Spedding, Daryl Spencer, Haydn Spencer, Paul Spencer, Paul Thomas Spencer, Jesley Spenstrong, Helen Spicer, Peter Spicer, Dorothea Spille, Colin Spiller, Spinksjeremyspinks, Lord Spinner, Jon Spira, Mark Spivey, Amanda Spooner, Bernd Spörl, Dennis Spreen, John P D Sprung, Matthew Spurway, Julie Squire, Paul Squires, Daniel Sroka, St John Karp, Iain Stables, Mark Stacey, Luke Stack, Ada Stadtlander-Miller, Joshua and Eitan Stadtlander-Miller, Andrew Staff, Jessie Stafford, Tim Stahmer, Susan Stainer, Robbie Stamp, Richard John Stamper, Elizabeth Standard, Jason B. Standing, Dave (Gusty) Stanley, Greg Stanley, Neil Stanley, Chris Stannard, Vicki Stannard, George Stanton, Jon Stapley, Ben Starbuck, Trevor Starick, James Starkey, Kristine Starkey, Richard Starkings, Emily Starling, Michael Starr, Laura Starrs, Iain Stastny, Karen Statham, Mark Statham, Merv Staton, Keith Stattenfield, D. Staubitz, Mark Stay, Daniel James Stead, Stephen Stead, Drew Stearne, Markus Steck, Olly Stedall, Paul Steed, Toby Steedman, Andrew Steele, Chris Steele, Geoff Steele, Chris Steenson, R P Steeves, Vesna Štefan, Peter Stegemann, Stegga, Brendan Steidle, Jamie Steidle, Kelsey Steinbach, Jonathan Steiner, John Owen Steinhardt-Edgar, Hanna Steinhauer, Sven Steinheisser, Gabriela Steinke, Christoph Steinlehner, Dom Stellato, Gordon Stenhouse, Darren Stephens, David Stephens, Kinnon Stephens, Matt Stephens, Peter Stephens, Philip Stephens, Ted Stephens, Tyler Stephens, Benjamin Stephenson, John and Vicki Stephenson, Michael Stephenson, Peter Stephenson, Alan Stern, Joel Stern, Steven Stern, Daniel Sternberg, Fredrik Sterngren, Jason Steussy, David Stevens, Linda Stevens, Mark Stevens, Rowan Stevens, Daniel Stevenson, Emma Stevenson, Michael Stevenson, Neil Stevenson, SteveR, SteveW-Tiiazllm, Andrew Stewart, Ash Stewart, Fiona Stewart, Hermione Stewart, Hugh Stewart, Jefferson Stewart, Jesse Stewart, John Stewart, Lee Stewart, Mark Stewart, Martin M Stewart, Nicholas John Stewart, Philip Stewart, Ranee Stewart, Raywin Stewart, W.K. Stewart, Thomas Stidham, Scott Stiffler, Henry Stiles, Hugh Stiles, William Stillwell, Suzanne & Richard Stirling, Eric Stirpe, Graham Stock, Benjamin Stocker, Paul Stockley, Peter Stoddart, Tim M. Stodden, Michael (Hoopy Frood) Stogner, Jakub Štogr, William Stokeley, Charlie Stoker, Tyson Stolte, Ady Stokes, Adam Stone, Clive Stone, Gwilym R Stone, Jeffrey Stone, Martin Stone, Paul Stone, Simon Stoneham, Teddy Stoner, Stoneshop (Mostly Harmless), Nicole Stoop, Arthur J. Stoppe, Peter Storch, Campbell Storey, Miles Storey, Nick Storey, Bill C Storts, Gail Stoten, Ryomi Stout-Holt, Clint Stovall, Nat Stow, Jim Stowe, Thomas Rainbow Stowe, Eric "Straav" Straavaldsen, Callum Strachan, Eric Strack, Robert Strack, Heather Stradling, Colin & Eleanor Strain, Bryan Straker, Alex Strassburg, Lauren Strauss-Jones, Dan Straw, Danielle Strawderman, Gerry Streberg, Walter Strijland, Gary Stringer, Hannah Stroh, Matthew Stroppel, Kathleen Stroud, Ace Stryker, Hamish Stuart, Phil Stuart, Tom Stuart, Peter Stubbe, John Stucker, Alex Stuckey, Nigel Stuckey, Andrew Styles, Subscribe to PewDiePie, Gareth Suddes, Michael Suissa, Rich Sulley, Lucy Sullivan, Martin Sullivan, Matthew Sullivan, Michael Patrick Sullivan, Todd Sullivan, Mark Sulston, Leonard Sultana (An Englishman In San Diego), Jeff Summers, Sharon Summers, Thomas Summers, Mei-Ting Sun, Max Sundeen, Stephen Sunderland, Bjørn Okkels Birk Sundgaard, David Sundin, Kip Sundquist, Peter Sundquist, Carolyn Sunners, John Surace, Chris Suslowicz, Adam Sussman, Graham Sutcliffe, Tim Suter, Anne Sutherland, Daniel Sutherland, James Sutherland, Joe Sutliff, Anthony Sutton, Pete Sutton, Toby Sutton-Long, Johan Svensson, Hans Swagemakers, Mark Swain, Jo Swaine, Chris Swan, Philip Swan, Elliott Swanson, Michael Swanson, Jan Swanton, Christopher Sweeney, Catherine Sweet, Damien Sweet, Nicholas Swift, William Swift, Matthew Swindells, Trent Swindells, Andrea Swinsco, I Dougal Sykora, Kaitlin Sylvester, Jason C Synodis, Thomas Syralist, Laszlo Szabo, Richard Szary, Glyn Szasz, Szabolcs Szepesi, Szabolcs Szilagyi, Matthew T, Salom T., T2K, B. Tabatabai, Claire Tagg, Ralph Tait, Harjit Takshak, Joseph Talbot, Keith Talbot, Philip XP Talbot, Tall Man with Glasses, Tommy Tallarico, Josh S. Talley, Seth Talley, Jonathan P Tallis, Gregory Talmo, A J Talsma-Williams, Christian Tamblyn, Xavier Tanaka, Harvey Tang, John Tankersley, Michele Tarantini, Valentina Tarantini, Marie Tarnowski, Troy Tarrant, John Tarrel, John Tarrow, S. Taushanoff, Andrew Tavares-Pitts and Chris Pitts, Anna Taylor, Bill Taylor, Bryan Taylor, Chris Taylor, Christopher Taylor, Connie Taylor, Dave Taylor, David Taylor, Deb Taylor, Georgette Taylor, Harry Taylor, James Taylor, Jane Taylor, Jeff Taylor, Nathan Taylor, Neil Taylor, Paul Taylor, Pete Taylor, Peter Taylor, Peterlea Taylor, Richard Taylor, Richard "arty" Taylor, Robert Taylor, Robert 'BeastlyBeast' Taylor, Russ Taylor, Sam William Taylor, Shereen Taylor, Simon J E Taylor, Stuart Taylor, Tim Taylor, William Taylor, Joe Taylor Jr., Tracy Teal, Ben Tedds, The Teemant Family, Kevin Tek | KickCast.Net, Alison Telfer, Abegale Templar, Mike Templeton, Molly Templeton, Will Templeton, Madeleine ten Haaf, Glenn Tenney, Brad Tennis, Fred Tepper, Aurora ter Heide, George Terezakis, Paolo A. Terlizzo, Terrible, Quin & Spencer Terry, Dan Tetsell, David Teubner, Helena Texier, Lee Thacker, Graham Thackery, Graham Thackery II, Graham Thackery III, Graham Thackery IV, Graham Thackery V, Sotirios Thanos, That Hoopy Zachery Bir, Jen Thatcher, The Bisbees of Hootenanny Hollow, The Gin Devil, The Great Pjohn, The Perkins Family, Peter Thejll, Theteam@42Abbeville.com, Jan Thie, Emma Thimbleby, Mike Thirlwell, Alan Thomas, Alun Thomas, Andy Thomas, Autumn Thomas, Chris & Michelle Thomas, Cormac Thomas, DYLAN THOMAS, Gareth Thomas, Hayley Thomas, Jess Thomas, Jordan (Pup Fidget) Thomas, Kev "Doris the Magic Sausage Roll" Thomas, Mike Thomas, Patrick J. Thomas, Rachel Thomas, Richard Thomas, Sheila Thomas, Sophy Thomas, Steve Thomas, Lee Thomas / londonfilmgeek, Sean M. Thomas, MD, Leivur Thomassen, Marina Thomopoulou, Andy Thompson, Dominic Thompson, John S J Thompson, Jon Thompson, Justin Thompson, Laura Thompson, Matt Thompson, Paul Anthony Thompson, William James Thompson, Ian Thompson-Corr, David Thomson, David G. Thomson, Ian Thomson, James "PCalc" Thomson, Marilyn Thomson, Sean Thomson, Sorcha Thomson, James Thorne, Frank Thornley, Jim Thornton, Henry Arthur Thorpe, Mike Threlfall, Douglas Throckmorton, Brand Thumim, Thomas Thumm, Mike Thurlow, Bronwyn Thurston, LaKara Ticeson, Jon Tickle, Phil Tidy, Christopher Tiffany, Helen Tiley, TimG, Frank Timmers, Scott Timmins, Monica Timms, Pekka Timonen, Brett Timperman, Timsk, Andreas Tingeltangel, TinklePit, Mark Tinkler, Armaan Tipirneni, Katrina Tipton, Mathew Tizard, To DJB with love. — DJV, To John, John N Tobias III, James Tobin, Kevin Tobin, Surrealism Today,

Stephen Todd, Arthur Tombs, Dafydd Tomos, Louise Tompkins, Alastair Toms, Caitlin Tong, Tony, Jackie Toombs, Lily Topchienkova, Katharina Topic, Stephen Topple, Jason Tor Adler, Leah Torly, Dave Tormey, Clifford Torng, Simon Toseland, Kev Toumaian, Henry Tovey, Andy Towler, Brad Town, Rob Townsend, Vincent 'K4' Townsend, Eric J.S. Traband, Anne-Marie Trace, James Trafford, Simon Trafford, Michael Trainor, Oz's Travels, Lynn Travis, Greg Trawinski, Mary Trax, Andreas Traxler, David Traynier, J Tree, Ross Tregaskis, Wade Tregaskis, Per Trelje, Ronald Tremblay, David Tremont, Karen Trethewey, Lindsay Trevarthen, Trey McKee & Associates, Peter Tribble, Christina Trick, Stephen Trigg, Karen Triggs, Stephen Trimingham, Michael Trinder, Stephanie Trinity Turner, Febo Troilo, Kevin Trojanowski, Jan Trompper, Michael Trosen, Matthew True, Mary Trussell, Carolyn Truxal, Justin Tsang, TSCLKD, Spero Tsindos, Vasyl Tsvirkunov, Robert C. Tuck, Alex Tucker, Colin D.H. Tucker, Benjamin Tudor Price, Adam Tuff, Jaap O. Tuinman, Peter Malcolm Tullett, Cheryl Tullis Sirois, Max Tundra, Andrew Turnbull, Austen Turner, Ben Turner, Jem Turner, Kieran Turner, Mike Turner, Nick Turner, Richard 'Oz' Turner, Rick Turner, Michael Turner Jones, Jari Turpeinen, Simon Turpin, Trevor Turpin, Jon Turton, Bill Tutt, Brad Tutt, Nomarque Twaine, Alex Twiston Davies, Michael and Vicky Twomey-Lee, Jack Tyler, Kilian Tyler, Ron Tyler, Carol Tyson Ward, Sven Uebelacker, Candace Uhlmeyer, Richard Ulmont Campbell, Coon Und Kai, Fiona Underhill, Greg Underwood, Percy Underwood, Tim Unerman, Will Ung, Hakan Unlu, Marin Untiedt, Ritika Upadhyay, Amandeep Kaur Uppal, Carey Upton, Clive Upton, Dr. Tim Urban, Richard Urbina, Lucia Uribe, Matthias Urlichs, Ben Urquhart, Wesley Urschel, Sarah Ursell, Tara Useller, Bonnie B. Usher, Cara Usher, Denise Uyehara, Hristo Uzunov, Vadjong, Alkesh Vaghmaria, Stef Valducci, Valentin, Claire Valentine, Karl Valentine, Rebecca Valentine, Christian Valentiner, Salvador García Valenzuela, Valerie, Matías Valero, Jill Valiant, Paul Vallis, Ramón Jeruël van Alteren, Sonja E van Amelsfort, Annette van Apeldoorn, Paul van Asseldonk, Danny van Bruggen, Vera van Dalen, David van Dantzig, Patrick Van de Casteele, Niels van de Ven, Jacko van der Meulen, Carl van der Smissen, Jaap van Diermen, Peter A. van Diest, Johan van Dissel, Michelle Van Ellis, Marjolein van Elteren, Wouter Van Eynde, Kia Van Farnhill, Dirk-Willem van Gulik, Bart van Halder, Ed van Hinte, M.H. Van Keuren, Tim van Laun, Cor van Leeuwen, Tristan van Leeuwen, Hans van Maanen, Peter van Marwijk, David "XLII" van Nederveen Meerkerk, Kyle Van Note, Gerard van Oel, Paul Van Opens, Ronald van Passel, Elizabeth Van Pelt, Robin van Sambeek, Jason Van Spronsen, Bruno Van Vaerenbergh, Ron Vanasdale II, Kevin Vance, Simon Vance, Adhemar Vandamme, Koen Vanduffel, Vanillicose, Timothy VanKleeck, Tyler VanLaningham, Harsha Vardhan, Mike Vardy, Tracey Varnava, Suzanna Vasquez, Christine Vassie, Evangelos Vassilatos, Andrew B. Vaughan, Craig Vaughton, VCR, Robin Veith, Nathanial Vella, Mr. Velocipede, Fabio Venni, Mark Vent, Vivek Venugopal, Tony & Susie Verbalis, Kris Verbeeck, Gerbert Verheij, Jarno Verhoeven, Bas Vermeulen, Stefaan "kuiken" Verscheure, Frances Versluys, Jan Vesely, Stephanie Viani, Kath Vickers, Quo Vide bv, Lars Absolut normales Viech Reißig, Corinna Vigier, Marie Vilain, Òscar Vilaplana, Jon Vile, Diego Villuendas Pellicero, Jesse Vincent, Rob Vincent, Robert Vincent, Marijke Karel Frieda Vinck & Stijn Pieter Alexander Vinck, Jeremy Vine, Florencia Viola, Matti Viren, Jakob Vith, Fabio Viziano, Aljoša Vizovišek, Vicky Vladic, Amy Vlismas, Vnend, Martin Vodrey, Angela Vogel-Orton, Matthias Vogt, Timo Vogt, The Void (TLMB), Stephanie Volk, Ruthie Vollweiler, Volsted, Anna-Christine Cath Nikolajsen von Karlshof, Kount von Kulmbacher, Armin von Werner, Jan Vosecký, The Vosper Mortimers, Alisa Voznaya, Martin Vuijk, Sanjay Vyas, Emanuel Vynck, Bruno W, Deana W, Jesse W, Simon W, Tom W, Ziad W, Stephen W H, Prof Paul W Miller, Vasco Wackrill, Daniel P Wade, Louise Romana Wade, Matthew Wade Smith, Philip Wadler, Kristjan Wager, John L. Waggott, Dominik 'monkeydom' Wagner, John Wagner, Michael Wagner, Wendy Wagner, Jon Wagnon, Benjamin Wainwright, Andrew Waite, Jocelyn Waite, waiwainl, Christopher Wakefield, Elly Wakeling, Jason Walberg, Christina Wald, Oscar Walden Rasin, Pierre Waldfried, Christopher Waldock, Rusty Waldrup, Gary Wales, Mark Wales, Chris 'Woodstock' Walker, Dave Walker, David Walker, Disco Stu Walker, Eliot Walker, Jade Walker, Mark Walker, Mick Walker, Nick Walker, Randy & Lisa Walker, Simon Walker, Sir Harold Walker, Steve Walker, Stephen Walkley, Mark Walkom, Alistair Wallace, Bryan Wallace, Jamie Wallace, William Wallace, Anthony Waller, Jim Waller, Jonathan Waller, Jonathan Wallington, Cameron Wallis, Mike Wallis, Rebecca Wallis, Ian J Walls, A Walmsley, Nick Walpole, Andrew Walsh, Clive Walsh, Simone Walsh, Stephen Walsh, Steve Walsh, Dr Matthew Walter, Gero Walter, Alexander Walters, Gareth Walters, Michael Walters, Jörg Walther, Alex Walton, Anthony Walton, Mark 'Aggrajag' Walton, Jim Wamsley, Dennis Wan, Helen Wand, Christopher Wang, Zeming Wang, Julian Wangemann, Anouk Waning, John Warble Blaster Beckemeier, Pamela Warburton, Daniel Ward, Gareth Ward, Graham Ward, Jeff Ward, Ken Ward, Lee Ward, Lucy Ward, Matthew Ward, Simon Ward, Timothy Ward, Patrick Ward-Perkins, Adam Wardell and Poppy (another non-wonder dog), Atlanta Wardell-Yerburgh, Alexander PT Warden, Helen Wardman, Simon Wares, Ed Warner, Ian Warner, Sam Warner, Andy Warren, Ellie Warren, Matt Warren, Phill Warren, Spencer Warren, Stephanie E. Washburn, Roy Wassink, Mo Watchman Storrar, Donald Waters, Ellen Waters, Steve Waterworth, John Wates, Alun Watkins, Fran Watkins, Russell & Jo Watkins, Ben Watson, Chris Watson, David Watson, Mark Watson, Paul Watson, Philip Watson, Shane Watson, Sylvia Watson, Tim Watson, Martin Watton, Colin Watts, Miles Watts, Philippa Watts, Simon G G Watts, Will Watts, The Watts Family, Andy Way, Todd Wayne Ramsey, Wayne the Sane, We Fix Space Junk, Tony Wearing, Adam Weatherford, James Weatherley, Jeremy Weathers, Andrew Weaver, Ben Weaver, Weaver, Dave Webb, Erin Webb, Lowri Webb, Nathan Webb, Peter Webb, Rick Webb, Stephen Webb, Orren Webber, Chris Weber, Hedda Weber, Markus R R Weber, Ronnie Weber, Ian Webster, Paul Webster, Dave & Stella Wedd, Anthony Wedick, Josh and Rachel Wedin, Barbara Weed, Amber Jo Weedon, Morgan Weeks, Jack Weeland, Mark Peter Wege, Alex Wehmeier, Adam Weiler, Andreas Weinberger, Matthias Weinberger, Yakov N. Weinberger, James Weiner, Brian Weisberg, Janine Weix, Andrew Welch, Brian Reginald Welch, Liz Weldrake, Ralf Eduard Welland, Edwin Welling, Wellis, Michael Anthony Wells, Phil Wells, Robert 'Weaselspoon' Wells, PJ Wellspring, Alexandra Welsby, Jeremy Welsh, Kimberly Welsh, Marcus Welsh, Sean Eric Welsh, Sjoerd Wenings, Dave Werber, Warner Werkhoven, Mike Werner, David Werran,

Stephen Wershing, R. Sean Wertens, Wertlingen, Grant Weryk, Ralph Wessels, Holger Weßling (Harvey), Glen West, Kevin West, Nigel West, Timoni West, Sean Elliott Westbrook, Bryan Westbrook (t4v), Westie, Judith Diane Weston, Kathy Weston, Richard Weston-Smith, Steph Wetch, Richard Wetzel, Jos Weyers, Jane Weyman, Andy Whale, Elaine Wharton, Angie Whatmore, Liz Wheatley, Nathan Wheatley, Al Wheeler, Ian Wheeler, Tarron Wheeler, Rachel Wheeley, Paul Whelan, Sean Whelan, Fiona Whitaker, Lena Whitaker, Richard Whitaker, Matt Whitby, Andy White, Barry White, Darren White, Graham White, Jeremy Paul White, John White, Martin White, Scott "Pip" White, Steve White, Teresa White, Vernon White, Jake Whitehead, Lee Whitehead, Mark Whitehead, Alan Whitehill, James Whitehouse, Jonathan Whiteland, David Whitelaw, Roger Whiteley, Kylie Whiterod-Robin, Chris Whiteside, Douglas Whiteside, Lee Whiteside, Paul Whiting, Jon Whitmore, Luke Whitmore, Rob Whitmore, Tony Whitmore, Luke Whittaker, Melanie Whittaker, Ruth Whittam, Stephen Whittam, Darren Whitworth, Lee Mark Whitworth, Jay Whyatt, Mark Whyte, Kenneth James Wiant, Jr., hayley wickens, Christopher Wickham, Dan Wickham, Manuel Wiebeck, Arjan Wiegman, Rick Wielens, Alia, Milo, Juliane and Fili Wiese, Carolin Wiese, Philip Wiesing, Werner Wiethege, Håvard Wigtil, Stefan Wiklund, Tom Wilbur, David Wilburn, Alex Wilcock and Richard Flowers, Simon Wilcox, Mike Wild, Schorsch Wild, Suss Wilén, Lynda Wiles, John Wilford, Mark Wilkes, Tim Wilkes, Roger, Anthony & Alfred Wilkey, Jamie Wilkins, Sharla Wilkins, Jamie Wilkinson, Laura Wilkinson, Samantha Wilkinson, Richard George Wilks, Martijn Willemse, Clare Williams, Cordelia Williams, Dave Williams, David Williams, David Norrie Williams, Deb Williams, Dennis P Williams, DL Williams, Emily Williams, Gareth Williams, Gavin Williams, Heidi Rees Williams, Ian Williams, Jason C. Williams, Jo/n Williams, John Williams, Lizzie Williams, Mark Williams, Martin Williams, Matthew Williams, Michael Eric Williams, Neil Williams, Robert Williams, Ross Williams, Si Williams, Simon Williams, Tony Williams, Andrew Williams (Archivist, Australian HHG Fan Club), Andy Williams Affleck, Catherine Williamson, Danny Williamson, Jason Williamson, Blake Willis, Daniel J. Willis, Jules Willis, Mark Willis, Nathan Willis, Katrin Willms, Gillo Willo, Leigh Willows, Mathew Wills, WillSoko, Anne Wilming, Laurens Wilming, Andreas Wilmsmeier, Alex Wilson, Amanda Wilson, Andrew Wilson, Andy Wilson, David Wilson, Dee Wilson, Derek Wilson, Gavin Wilson, Herbert Wilson, Ian Wilson, Kerry Wilson, Lisa Wilson, Mark Wilson, Michael Wilson, Paul Wilson, Rupert Wilson, Simon P. Wilson, Stephen Wilson, Steve "autom8on" Wilson, Susan Wilson, Thomas G! Wimsae, Matthew windle, Jeremy Windom, Dan Wineman, Mark Wing-Davey, John Winkelman, Kristina Winn, Susan Winn, Jeff Winningham, Christopher C. Winters, Tom Wintrell, Coll Wise Jr, Dave "not 42" Wisely, Nastassja Wiseman, Rich Wisneski, Tobias Wißmann, Simon Wistow, Aaron Witcher, Hylke Witjens, Faye Wix, wizofin, Wm Salt Hale, André Wognum, Brian James Wolden, Henning Wolf, Ian Wolf, Jhessail Wolf, Ryan Wolf, Wolf and Jojo, Michael Wolfe, J Wolfenden-Williams, Rainer Wolfsberger, Ben Wolfson, wolli, Stephen M. Wolterstorff, Elmien Wolvaardt, Stephen Wonfor, Keefe Wong, K Woo, Natalie Woo, Cara Wood, Charlotte Wood, Chris Wood, Daniel Wood, Danny Wood, Dean Wood, Gemma Wood, Heather Wood, Jon Wood, Lorenzo Wood, Marilen Wood, Mark Wood, Matthew Wood, Michael Wood, Peter Wood, Roger Wood, Ruth E Wood, Thomas Wood, Troy Ryan Wood, Lindy Woodburn, Hugh Woodhouse, Sarah Woodhouse, Christopher Woods, Frank Woods, Jonathan Woods, Rebecca Woods, Steve Woodward, woody@stormgate.co.uk, David Woof, Ben Wooliscroft, Mark Woollard, Sarah Woollett, Andrew Woolley, Denise E Woolley, Nick Woolley, Richard Woolley, Peg Woolsey, Martin Wooster, Naomi Wordsworth, John Worrall, Alec Worsfold, Stuart Worsley, Christopher Worth, Hayden Worth, Sally Wortley, wowbagger.com, Matthew Wray, Alan Wright, Anthony Wright, Blake Wright, Dan Wright, David Wright, Ian Wright, Jane Wright, Joseph Wright, Kevin Wright, Liz Wright, Morna Wright, Nigel Wright, Simon Wright, Tea Wright, Thomas R Wright, Wendy Wright, Jeffery Wright the sightless Scholar, Jonathan Wrigley, Robert B. Wrigley, Wtcher, Duncan Wu, William G Wu, Markus Wuttke, Tim Wuyts, www.bioget.com, Chris "Doc" Wyatt, Jim Wyatt, Matteson Wynn, Vin Wynne, Graham Wynne Jones, Debbie Wythe, House Xavier, Petyr Xyst, Max B. Yamaguchi, Takako Yamamura, Christie Yant, Beau Yarbrough, Rob Yarham, David Yarrow, Michael A Yasko SR, Ad Yates, Ian Yates, James Yates, Mark Yates, Trevor Ydreos, Steve Yelland, Brian Yesowitch, Yinch + Rebecca, Shui Ying Chang, Joan Yocum, Yordan Yordanov, Amy Young, Andrew Young, Chris Young, Christian Young, Forever Young, Heather Young, James Young, Jonathan Young, Nick Young, Peter Young, Rebecca Young, Roderick Young, Stephanie Young, Jenny Youngson, Mark C Yturralde, Wuyi Yu, Za Yuter, Z, and A Girl Called Ben, Noya Glick Zaadi, Enrico Zabeo, Darius Zahedy, Ann Zalokoski-Monroe, Marc Zampieri, Jan Zander, Zannalov & Kaynary, Mechelle Zarou, Gargleflurgle Zarxibrook, Milan Zavisic, Tamara Zavodska, Dara Zedaker, Audrey Zeichick, Julie Zeraschi, Paul J. Zerner, Carl-Mikael Zetterling, Zeyug, M Ziegenbein, Diana Ziegler, Gary Zielinski, Jennifer Zielinski, Sean Zieroth, Ophir Zilbiger, Martin Zimmer, Phill Zitt, Ziv, Gal Zohar, John K. Zopf, Jr., Agata Zukowska, Joshua Zupan, Jennifer Zwick, Matthew Zymet, ΓΕΡΑΣΙΜΟΣ

Caricature of Douglas Adams as Sir Lucius O'Trigger in a Cambridge production of Sheridan's play *The Rivals*, drawn by fellow cast member, and now celebrated comedian and writer, Griff Rhys Jones.